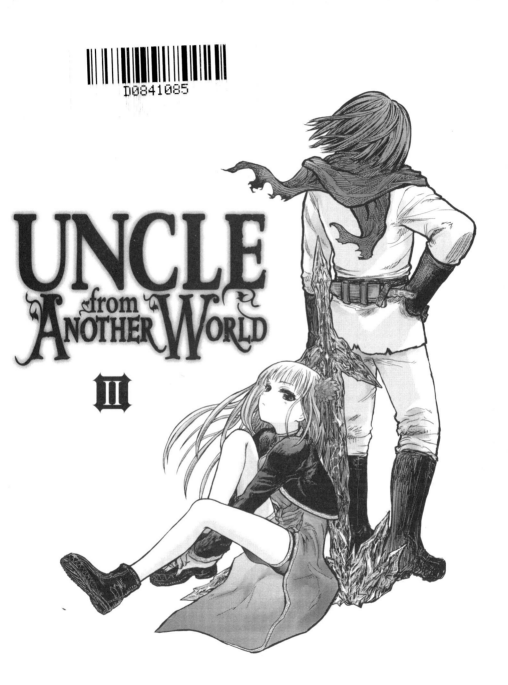

UNCLE from ANOTHER WORLD

II

Hotondoshindeiru
A Man Who Survived

CONTENTS

THE STORY SO FAR

Takafumi's uncle woke up from a seventeen-year coma, marking his return from the fantasy world of Granbahamal. In the fall of 2017, he struck up a roomshare arrangement with his nephew Takafumi and took up work as a YouTuber. Despite repeatedly falling for comment-trolling, he amassed two million views for his videos of supernatural feats performed with the arcane arts he brought home with him from the otherworld. In January 2018, after the two of them secured a stream of ad revenue, they were visited by Fujimiya—an old childhood friend of Takafumi with a crush on him—and they let her in on Uncle's secret...

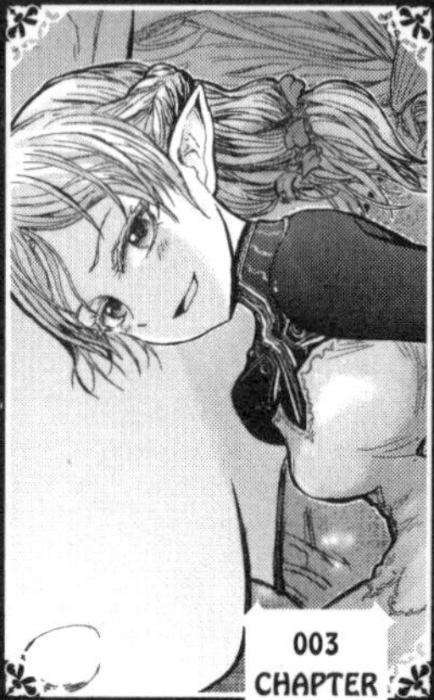

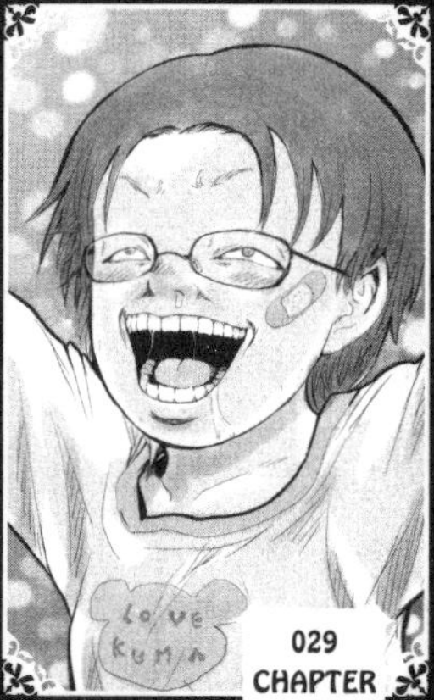
LoVe KUMA

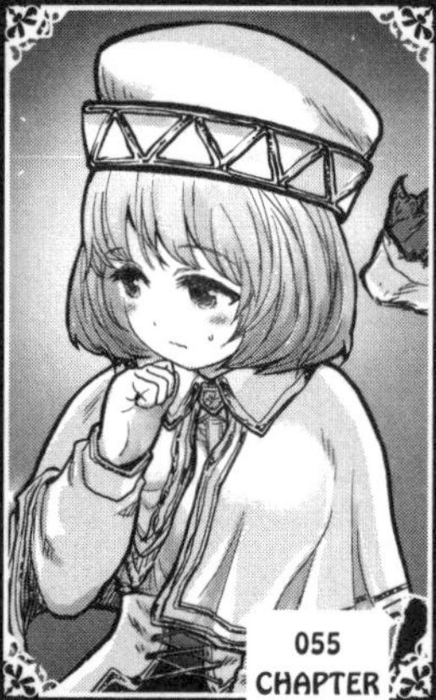

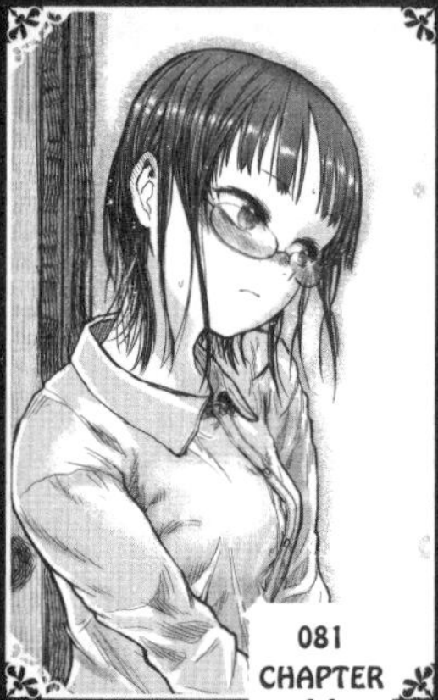

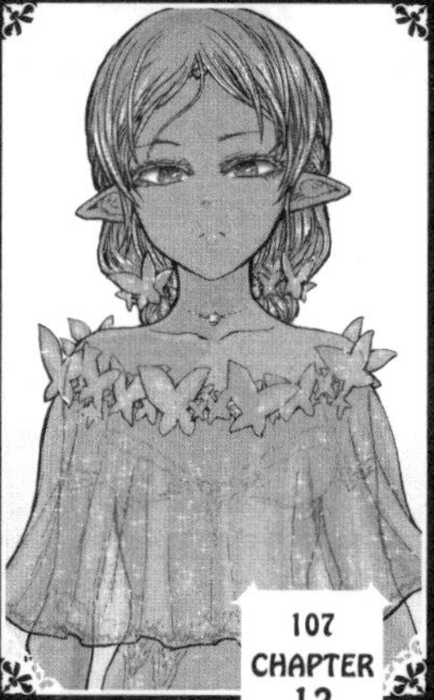

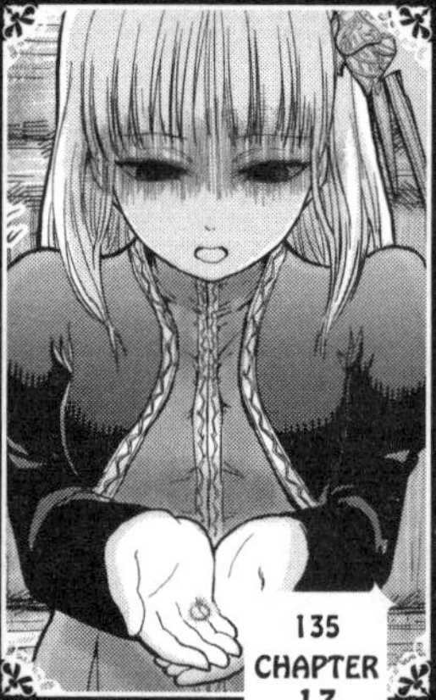

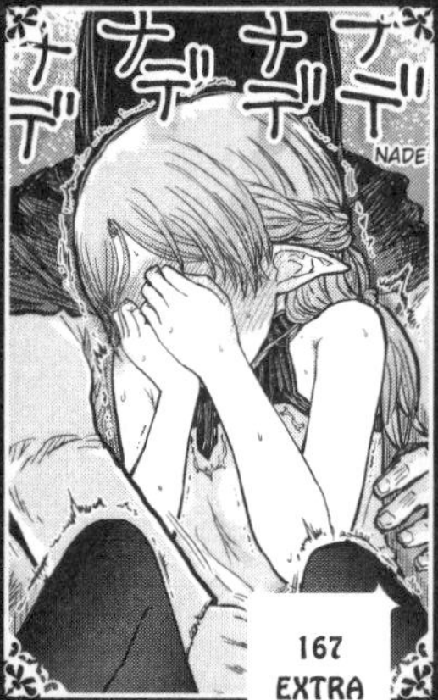
ナデ
ナデ
ナデ
NADE

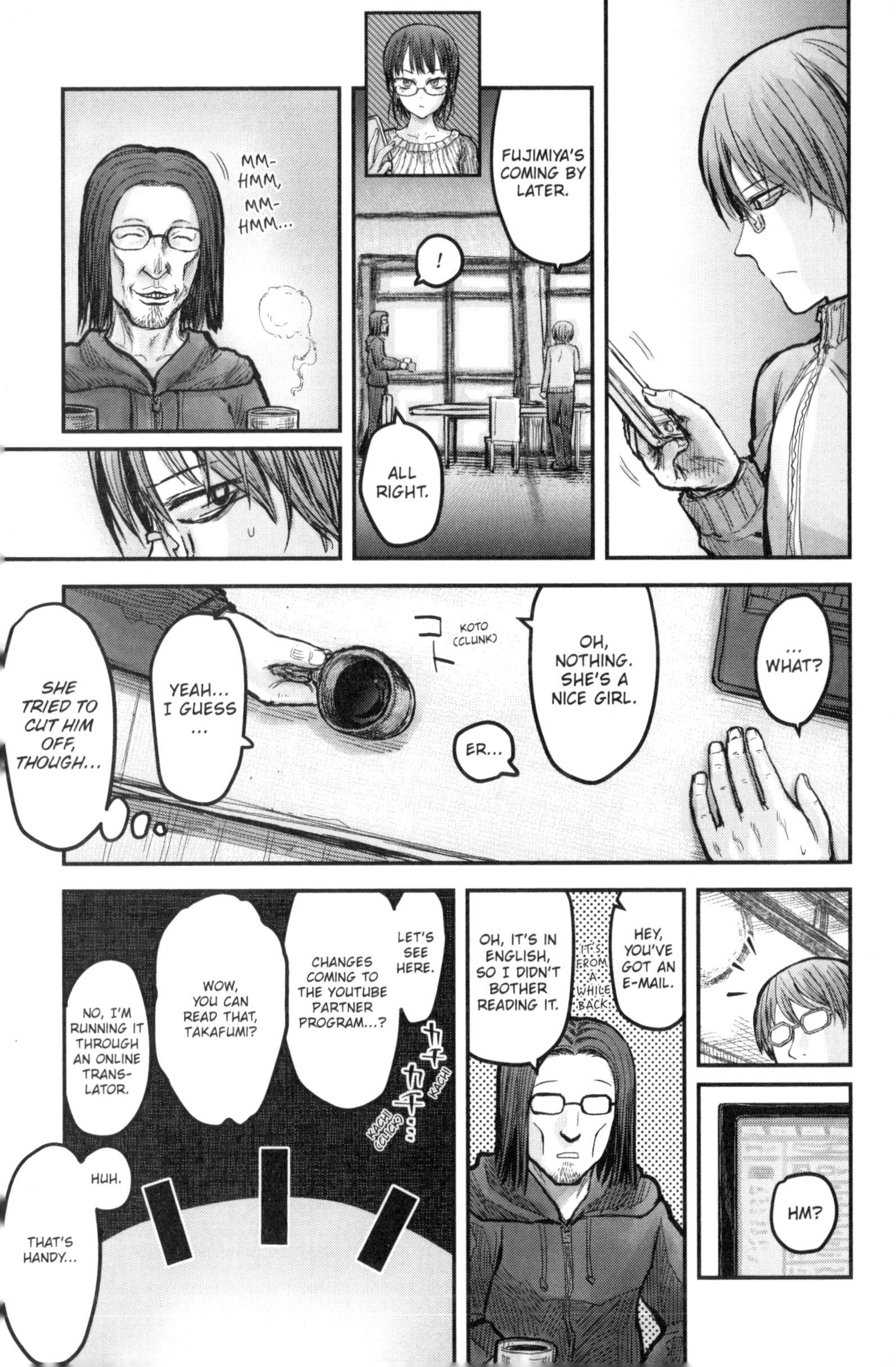
FUJIMIYA'S COMING BY LATER.
!
ALL RIGHT.
MM-HMM, MM-HMM...
...WHAT?
OH, NOTHING. SHE'S A NICE GIRL.
KOTO (CLUNK)
ER...
YEAH... I GUESS...
SHE TRIED TO CUT HIM OFF, THOUGH...
HM?
HEY, YOU'VE GOT AN E-MAIL.
IT'S FROM A WHILE BACK.
OH, IT'S IN ENGLISH, SO I DIDN'T BOTHER READING IT.
LET'S SEE HERE.
CHANGES COMING TO THE YOUTUBE PARTNER PROGRAM...?
KACHI KACHI (CLICK)
WOW, YOU CAN READ THAT, TAKAFUMI?
NO, I'M RUNNING IT THROUGH AN ONLINE TRANS-LATOR.
HUH.
THAT'S HANDY...

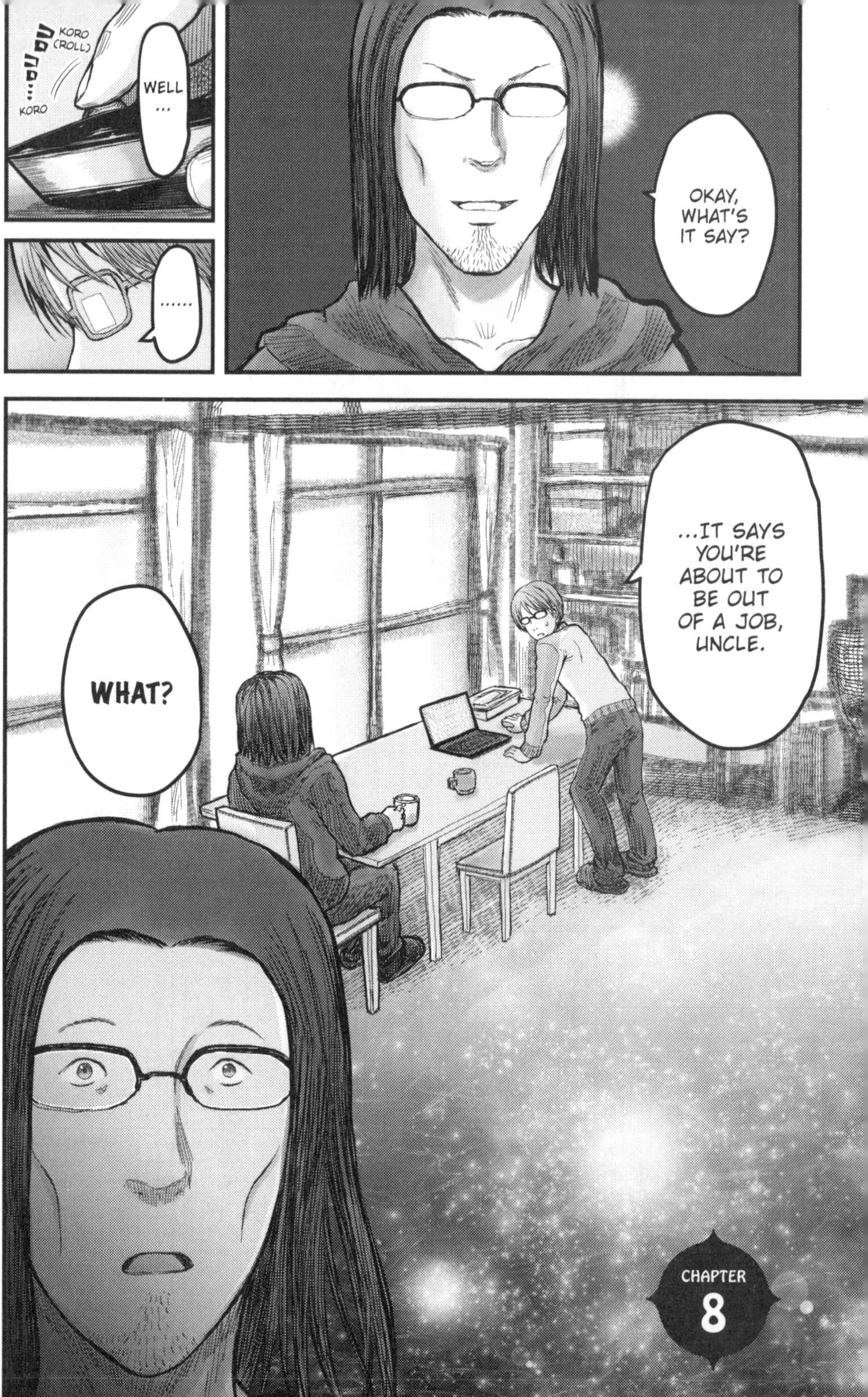
OKAY, WHAT'S IT SAY?
WELL ...
KORO (ROLL)
KORO
......
...IT SAYS YOU'RE ABOUT TO BE OUT OF A JOB, UNCLE.
WHAT?
CHAPTER 8

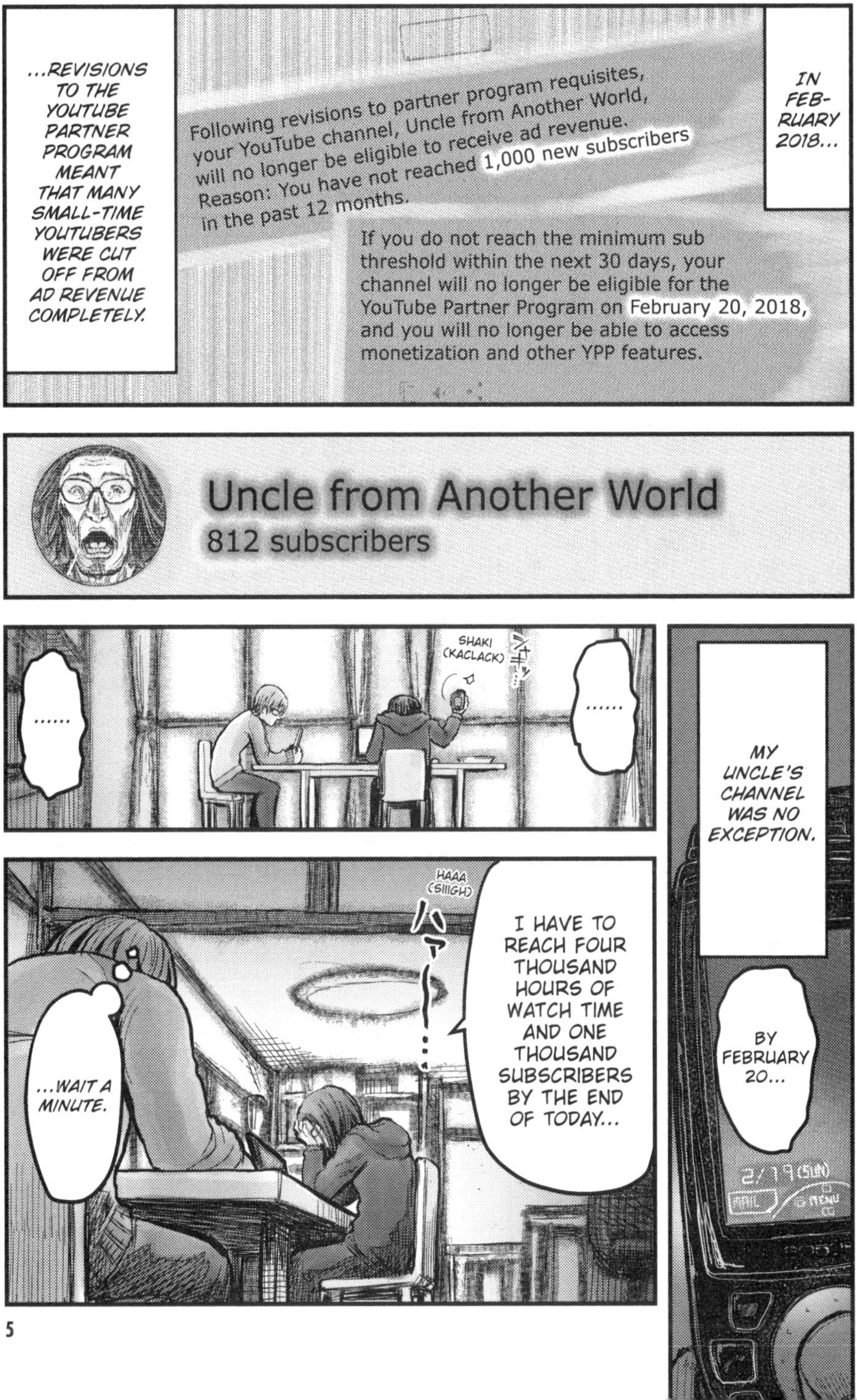
IN FEBRUARY 2018...
Following revisions to partner program requisites, your YouTube channel, Uncle from Another World, will no longer be eligible to receive ad revenue.
Reason: You have not reached 1,000 new subscribers in the past 12 months.
If you do not reach the minimum sub threshold within the next 30 days, your channel will no longer be eligible for the YouTube Partner Program on February 20, 2018, and you will no longer be able to access monetization and other YPP features.
...REVISIONS TO THE YOUTUBE PARTNER PROGRAM MEANT THAT MANY SMALL-TIME YOUTUBERS WERE CUT OFF FROM AD REVENUE COMPLETELY.
Uncle from Another World
812 subscribers
MY UNCLE'S CHANNEL WAS NO EXCEPTION.
BY FEBRUARY 20...
2/19 (SUN)
......
SHAKI (KACLACK)
......
HAAA (SIIIGH)
I HAVE TO REACH FOUR THOUSAND HOURS OF WATCH TIME AND ONE THOUSAND SUBSCRIBERS BY THE END OF TODAY...
...WAIT A MINUTE.

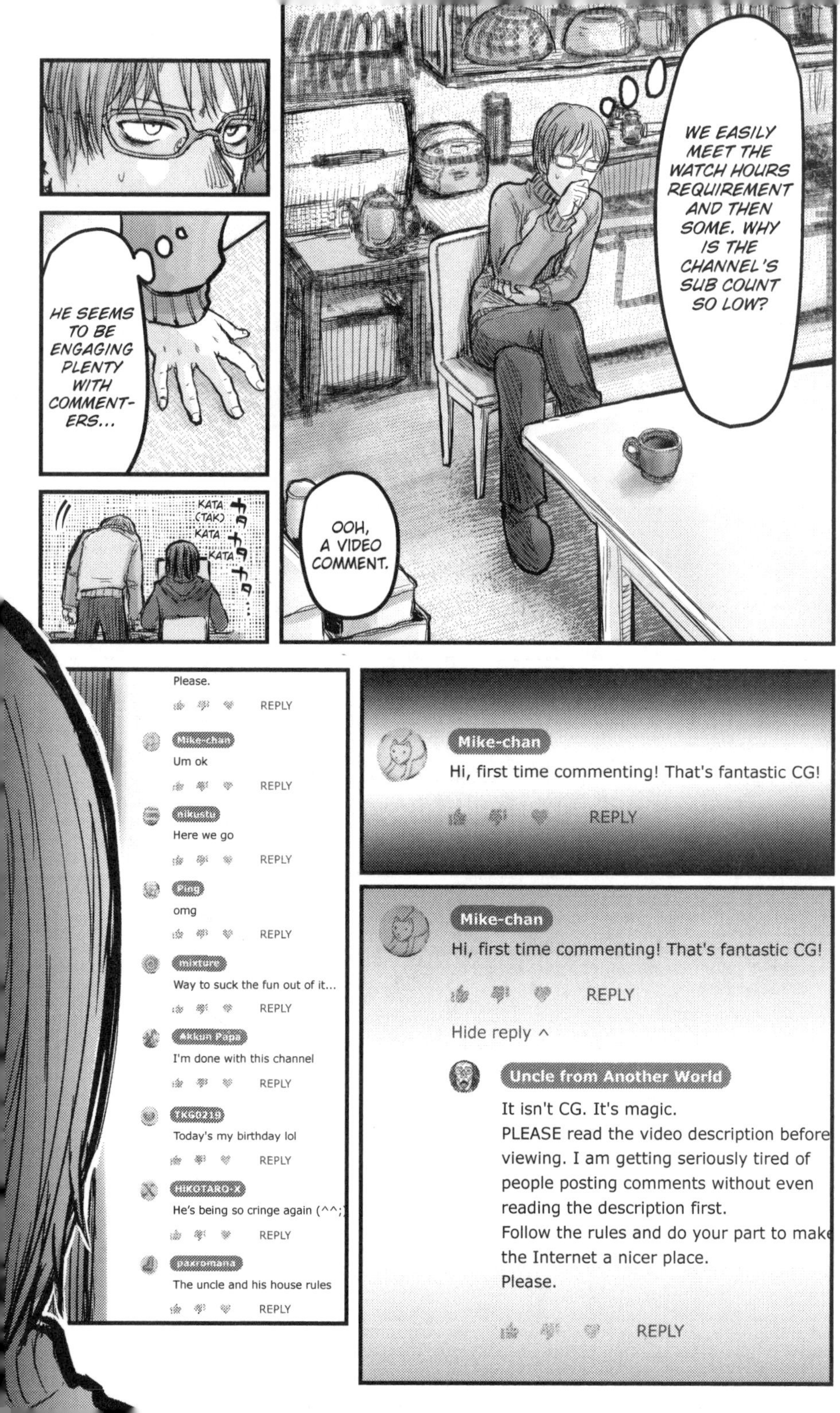
WE EASILY MEET THE WATCH HOURS REQUIREMENT AND THEN SOME. WHY IS THE CHANNEL'S SUB COUNT SO LOW?
OOH, A VIDEO COMMENT.
HE SEEMS TO BE ENGAGING PLENTY WITH COMMENTERS...
KATA (TAK) KATA KATA
Mike-chan
Hi, first time commenting! That's fantastic CG!
REPLY
Mike-chan
Hi, first time commenting! That's fantastic CG!
REPLY
Hide reply ^
Uncle from Another World
It isn't CG. It's magic.
PLEASE read the video description before viewing. I am getting seriously tired of people posting comments without even reading the description first.
Follow the rules and do your part to make the Internet a nicer place.
Please.
REPLY
Please.
REPLY
Mike-chan
Um ok
REPLY
nikustu
Here we go
REPLY
Ping
omg
REPLY
mixture
Way to suck the fun out of it...
REPLY
Akkun Papa
I'm done with this channel
REPLY
TKG0219
Today's my birthday lol
REPLY
HIKOTARO-X
He's being so cringe again (^^;
REPLY
paxromana
The uncle and his house rules
REPLY

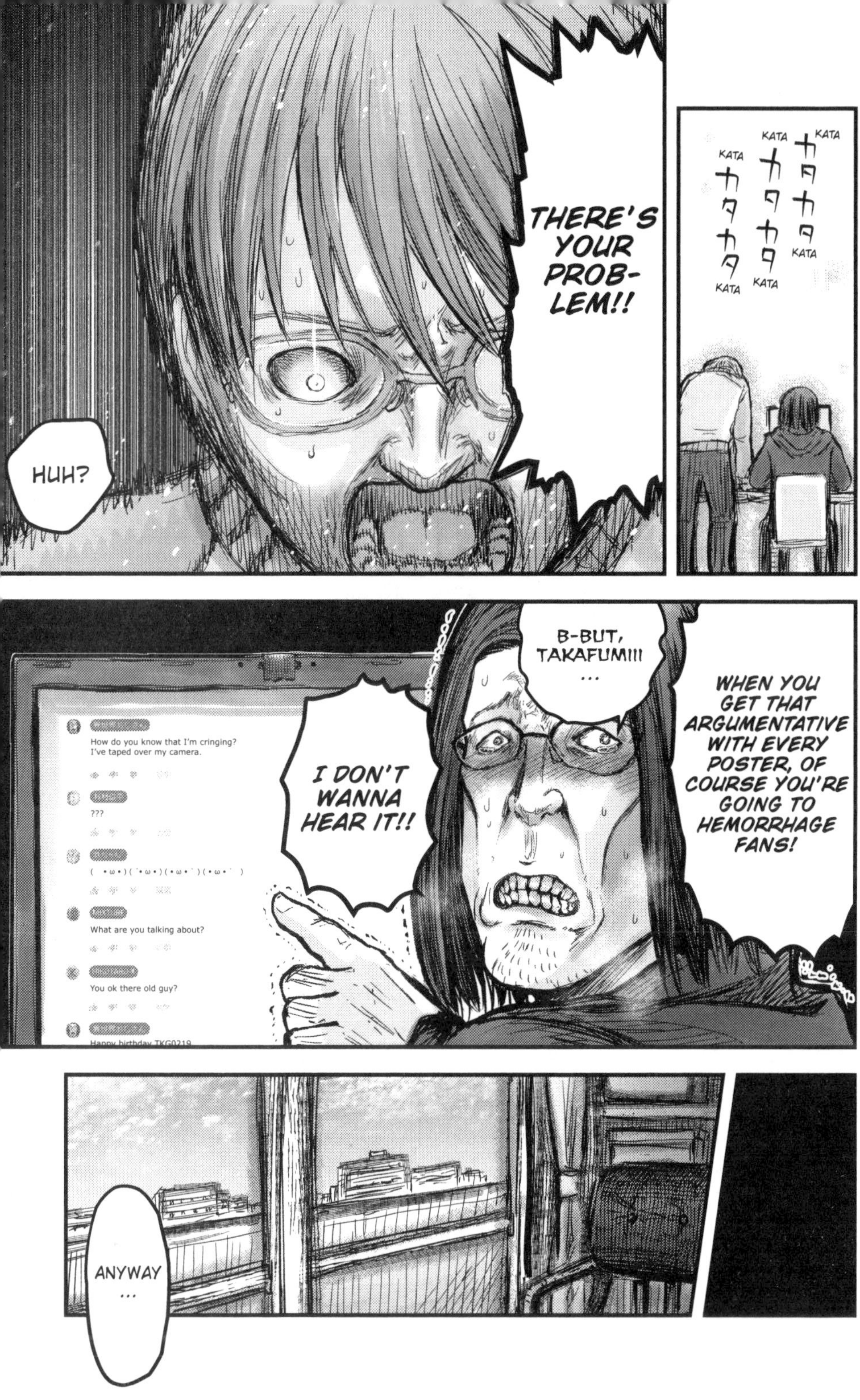

カタカタ
KATA KATA
カタカタ
KATA KATA
カタカタ
KATA KATA
THERE'S YOUR PROB-LEM!!
HUH?
WHEN YOU GET THAT ARGUMENTATIVE WITH EVERY POSTER, OF COURSE YOU'RE GOING TO HEMORRHAGE FANS!
B-BUT, TAKAFUMI!!! ...
I DON'T WANNA HEAR IT!!
How do you know that I'm cringing? I've taped over my camera.
???
What are you talking about?
You ok there old guy?
Happy birthday TKG0219
ANYWAY ...

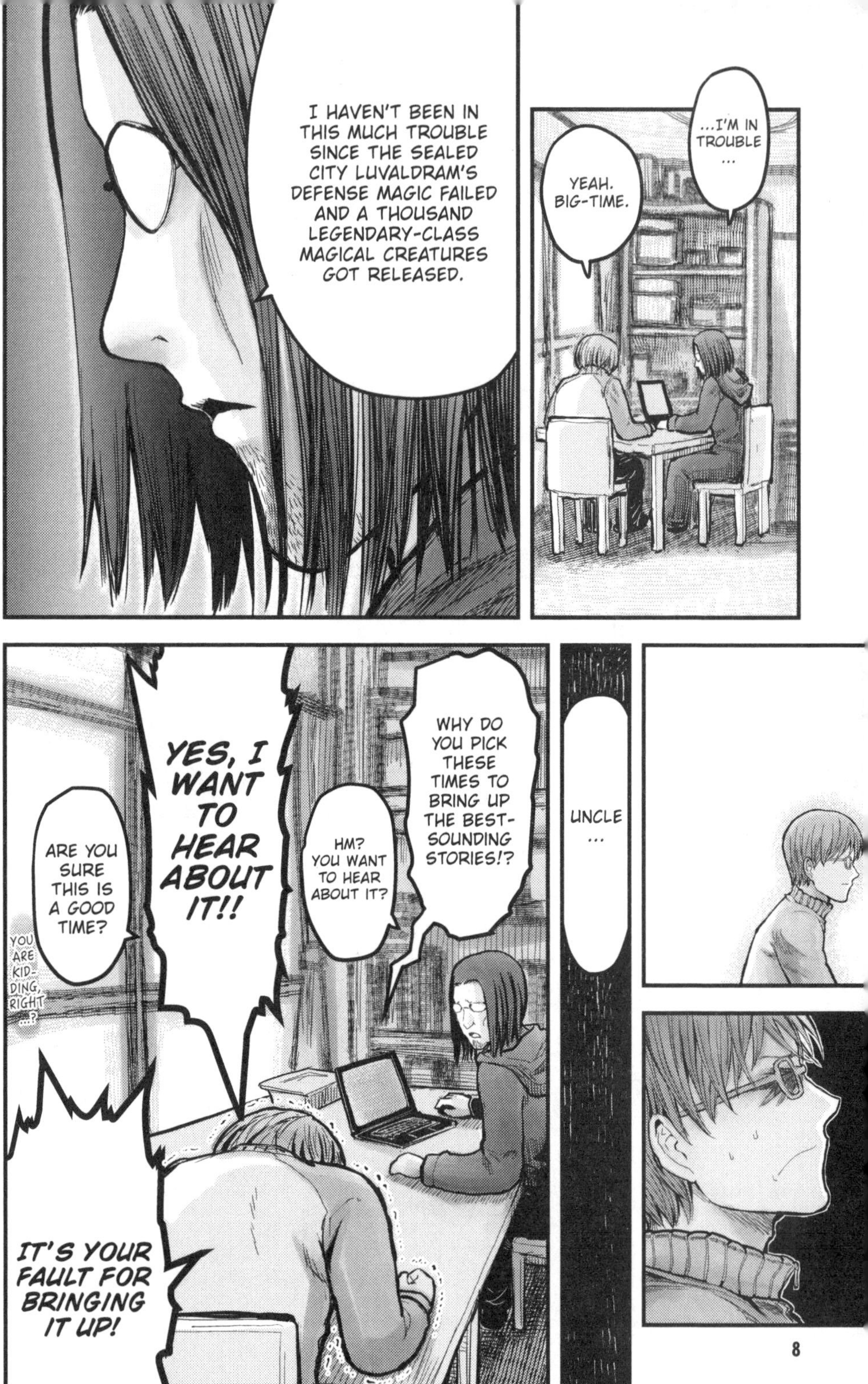
...I'M IN TROUBLE ...
YEAH. BIG-TIME.
I HAVEN'T BEEN IN THIS MUCH TROUBLE SINCE THE SEALED CITY LUVALDRAM'S DEFENSE MAGIC FAILED AND A THOUSAND LEGENDARY-CLASS MAGICAL CREATURES GOT RELEASED.
UNCLE ...
WHY DO YOU PICK THESE TIMES TO BRING UP THE BEST-SOUNDING STORIES!?
HM? YOU WANT TO HEAR ABOUT IT?
YES, I WANT TO HEAR ABOUT IT!!
ARE YOU SURE THIS IS A GOOD TIME?
YOU ARE KID-DING, RIGHT ...?
IT'S YOUR FAULT FOR BRINGING IT UP!

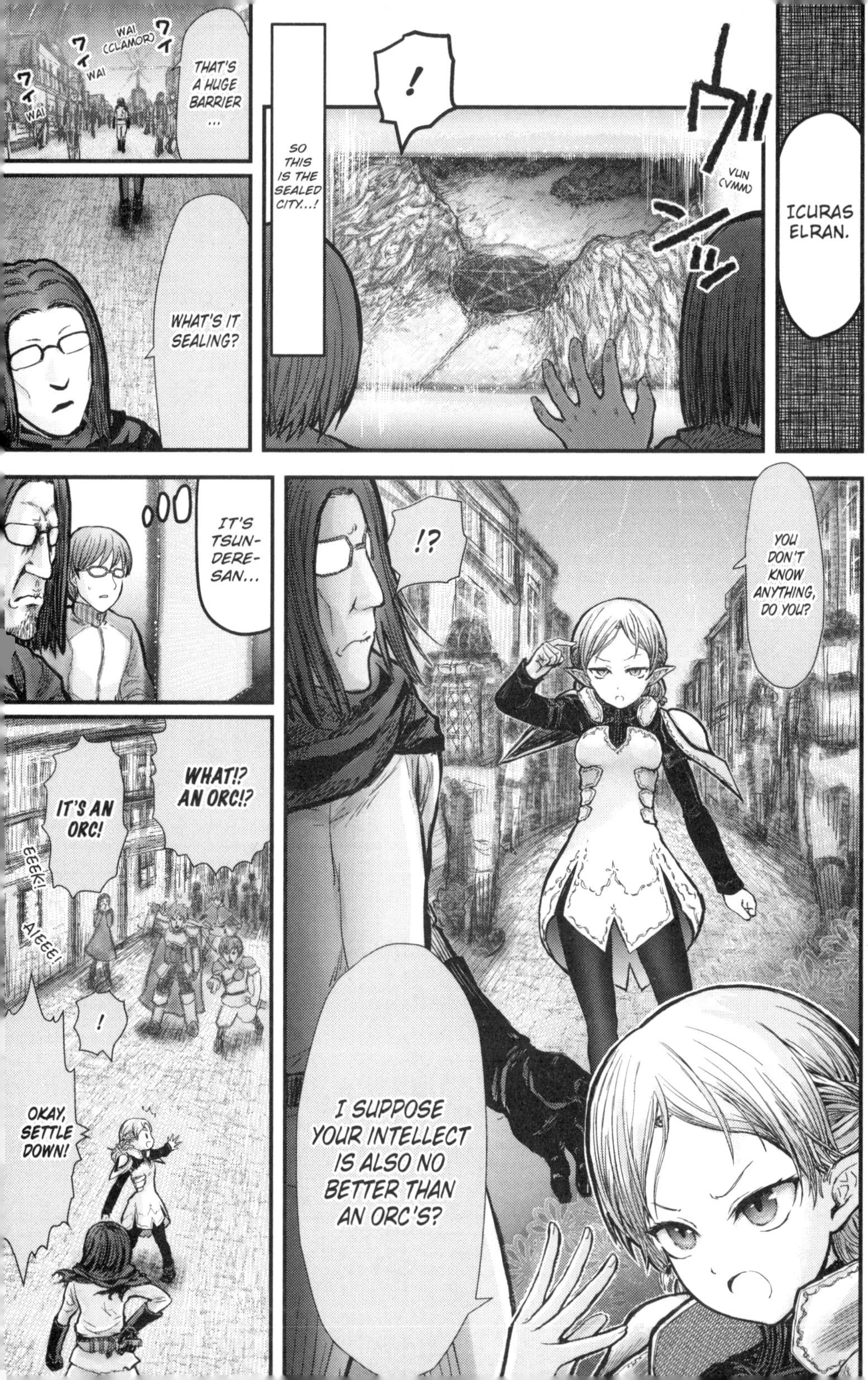
ICURAS ELRAN.
!
VUN (VMM)
SO THIS IS THE SEALED CITY...!
WAI (CLAMOR)
WAI
WAI
THAT'S A HUGE BARRIER...
WHAT'S IT SEALING?
YOU DON'T KNOW ANYTHING, DO YOU?
!?
I SUPPOSE YOUR INTELLECT IS ALSO NO BETTER THAN AN ORC'S?
IT'S TSUNDERE-SAN...
WHAT!? AN ORC!?
IT'S AN ORC!
EEEK!
AIEEE!
!
OKAY, SETTLE DOWN!

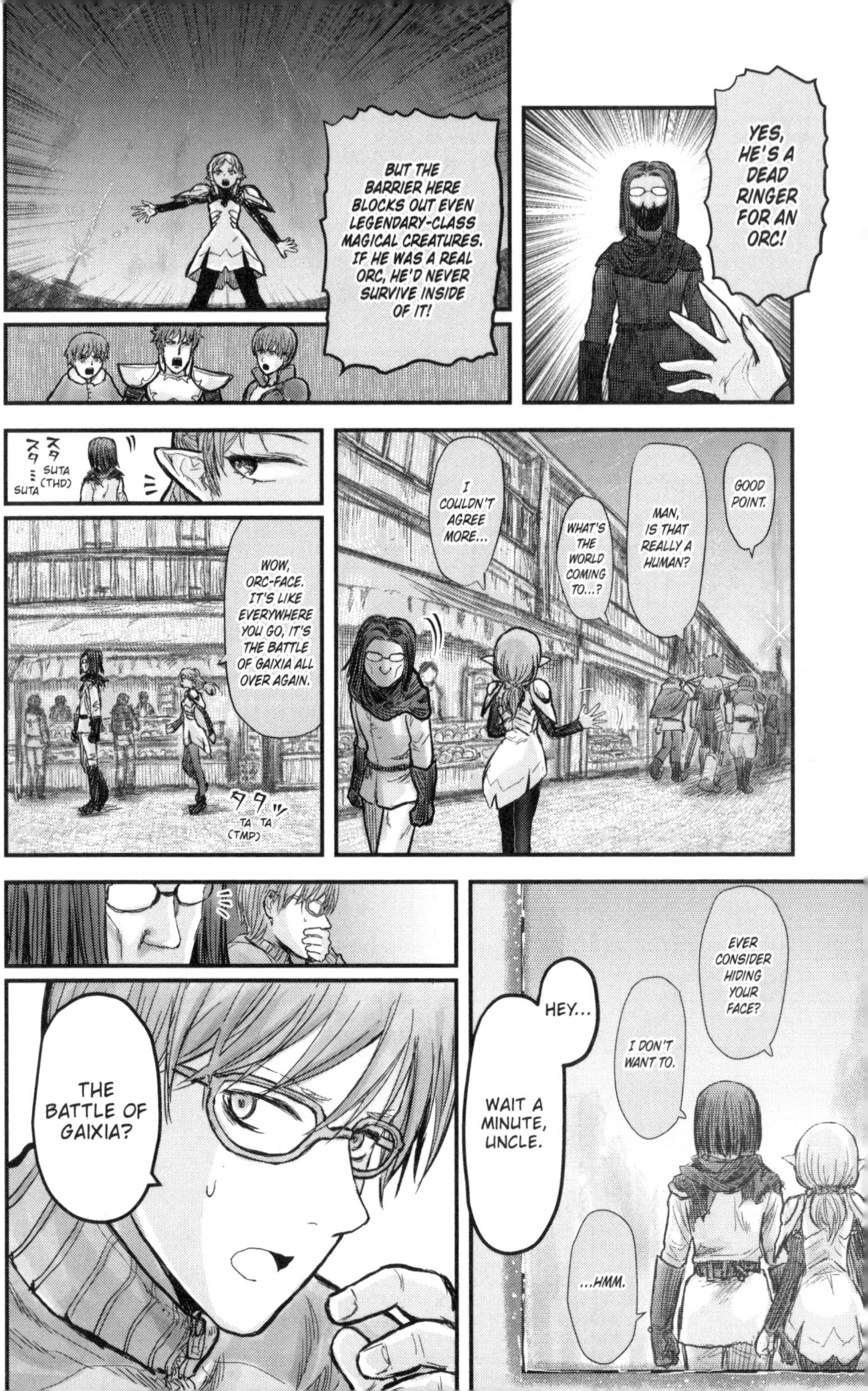
YES, HE'S A DEAD RINGER FOR AN ORC!
BUT THE BARRIER HERE BLOCKS OUT EVEN LEGENDARY-CLASS MAGICAL CREATURES. IF HE WAS A REAL ORC, HE'D NEVER SURVIVE INSIDE OF IT!
GOOD POINT.
MAN, IS THAT REALLY A HUMAN?
WHAT'S THE WORLD COMING TO...?
I COULDN'T AGREE MORE...
SUTA SUTA (THD)
WOW, ORC-FACE. IT'S LIKE EVERYWHERE YOU GO, IT'S THE BATTLE OF GAIXIA ALL OVER AGAIN.
TA TA (TMP)
EVER CONSIDER HIDING YOUR FACE?
I DON'T WANT TO.
HEY...
WAIT A MINUTE, UNCLE.
...HMM.
THE BATTLE OF GAIXIA?

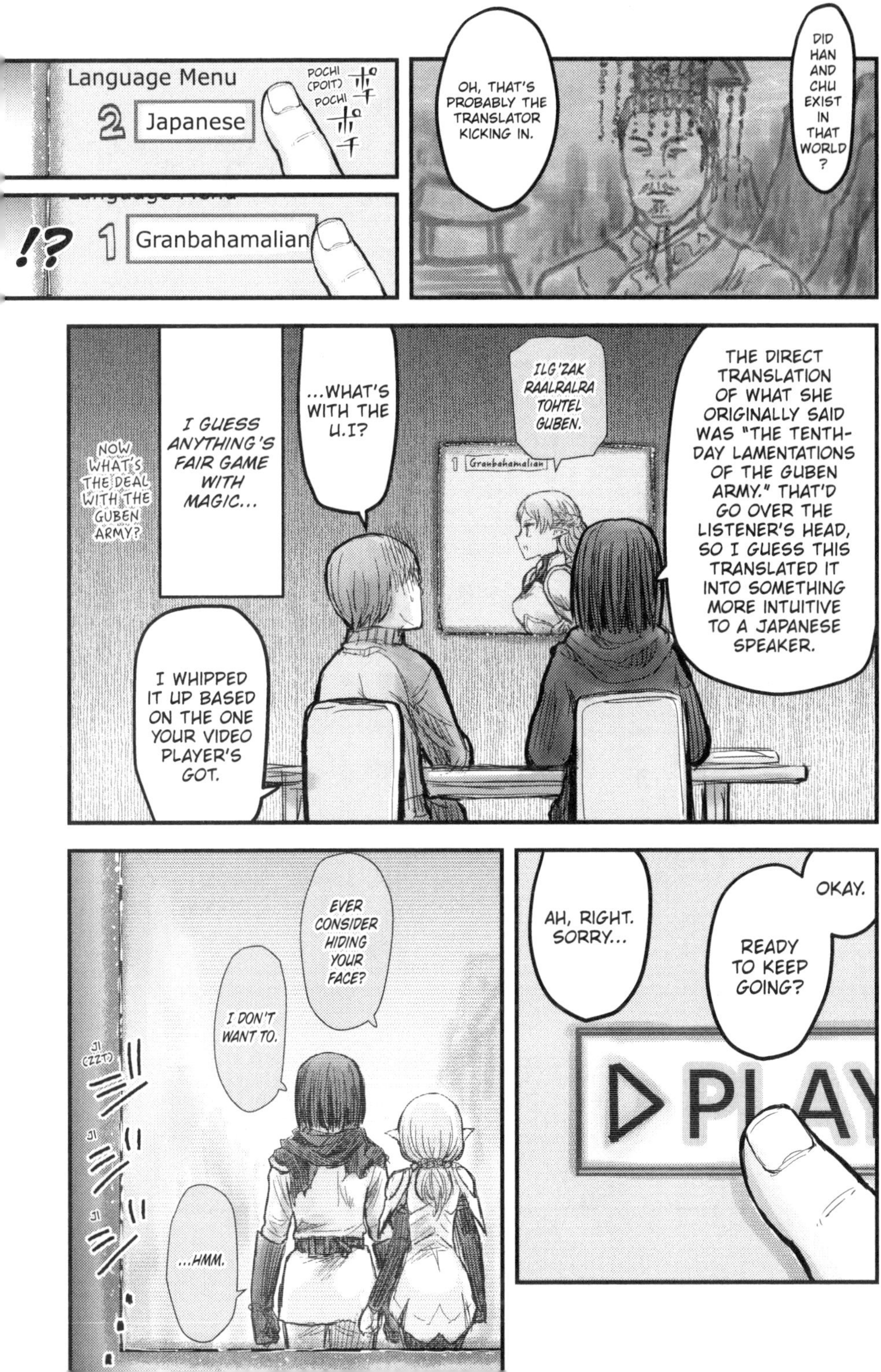
DID HAN AND CHU EXIST IN THAT WORLD?
OH, THAT'S PROBABLY THE TRANSLATOR KICKING IN.
Language Menu
2 Japanese
POCHI (POIT)
POCHI
1 Granbahamalian
!?
THE DIRECT TRANSLATION OF WHAT SHE ORIGINALLY SAID WAS "THE TENTH-DAY LAMENTATIONS OF THE GUBEN ARMY." THAT'D GO OVER THE LISTENER'S HEAD, SO I GUESS THIS TRANSLATED IT INTO SOMETHING MORE INTUITIVE TO A JAPANESE SPEAKER.
ILG'ZAK RAALRALRA TOHTEL GUBEN.
1 Granbahamalian
...WHAT'S WITH THE U.I?
I GUESS ANYTHING'S FAIR GAME WITH MAGIC...
NOW WHAT'S THE DEAL WITH THE GUBEN ARMY?
I WHIPPED IT UP BASED ON THE ONE YOUR VIDEO PLAYER'S GOT.
OKAY.
READY TO KEEP GOING?
AH, RIGHT. SORRY...
PLAY
EVER CONSIDER HIDING YOUR FACE?
I DON'T WANT TO.
JI (ZZZT)
JI
JI
...HMM.

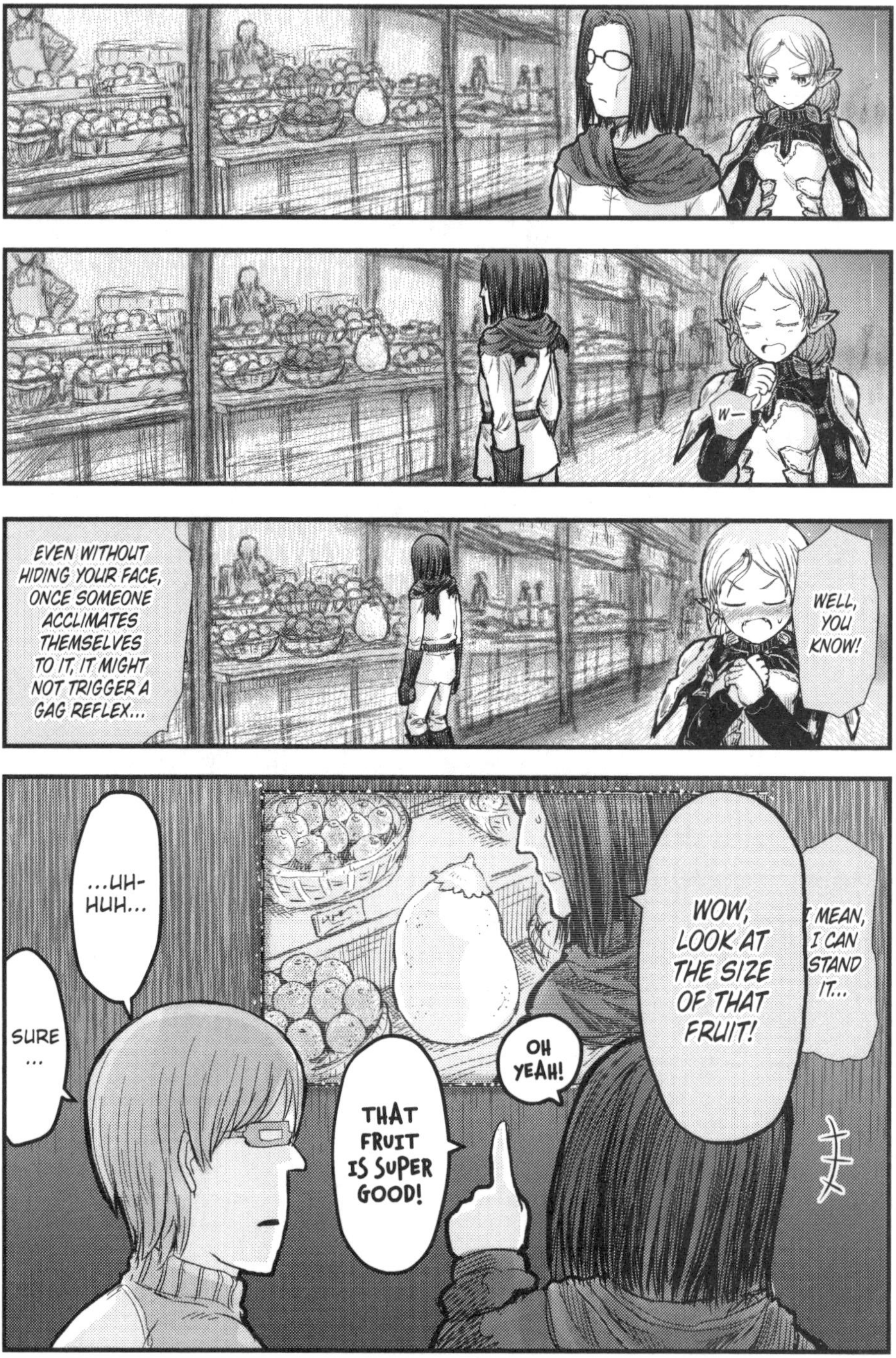
W—
WELL, YOU KNOW!
EVEN WITHOUT HIDING YOUR FACE, ONCE SOMEONE ACCLIMATES THEMSELVES TO IT, IT MIGHT NOT TRIGGER A GAG REFLEX...
I MEAN, I CAN STAND IT...
WOW, LOOK AT THE SIZE OF THAT FRUIT!
OH YEAH!
THAT FRUIT IS SUPER GOOD!
...UH-HUH...
SURE ...

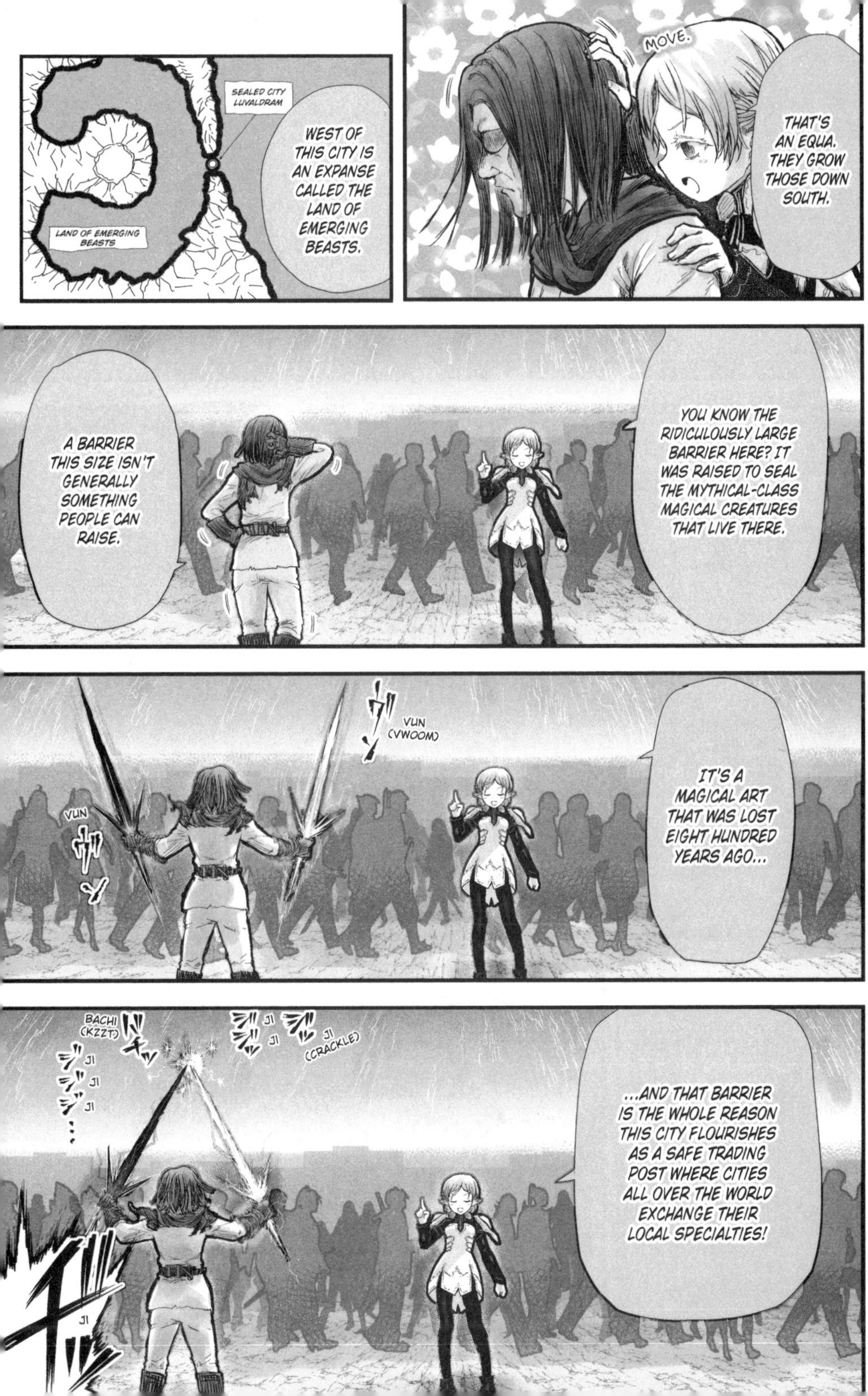
THAT'S AN EQUA. THEY GROW THOSE DOWN SOUTH.
MOVE.
WEST OF THIS CITY IS AN EXPANSE CALLED THE LAND OF EMERGING BEASTS.
SEALED CITY LUVALDRAM
LAND OF EMERGING BEASTS
YOU KNOW THE RIDICULOUSLY LARGE BARRIER HERE? IT WAS RAISED TO SEAL THE MYTHICAL-CLASS MAGICAL CREATURES THAT LIVE THERE.
A BARRIER THIS SIZE ISN'T GENERALLY SOMETHING PEOPLE CAN RAISE.
IT'S A MAGICAL ART THAT WAS LOST EIGHT HUNDRED YEARS AGO...
VUN (VWOOM)
VUN
...AND THAT BARRIER IS THE WHOLE REASON THIS CITY FLOURISHES AS A SAFE TRADING POST WHERE CITIES ALL OVER THE WORLD EXCHANGE THEIR LOCAL SPECIALTIES!
JI JI JI (CRACKLE)
BACHI (KZZT)
JI JI JI
JI

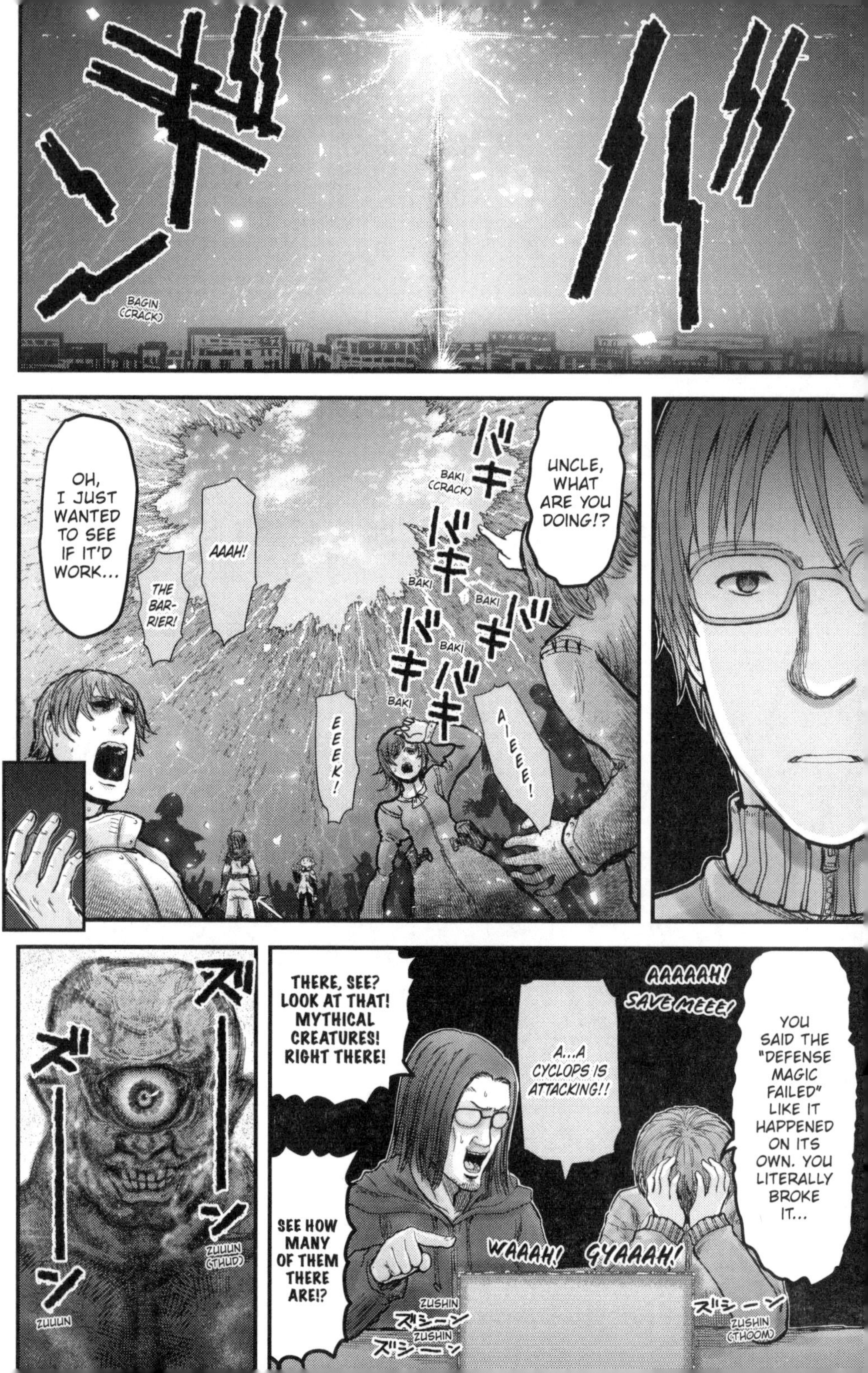
BAGIN (CRACK)
UNCLE, WHAT ARE YOU DOING!?
BAKI (CRACK)
BAKI
BAKI
BAKI
BAKI
AIEEE!
EEEK!
AAAH!
THE BARRIER!
OH, I JUST WANTED TO SEE IF IT'D WORK…
AAAAAH! SAVE MEEE!
YOU SAID THE "DEFENSE MAGIC FAILED" LIKE IT HAPPENED ON ITS OWN. YOU LITERALLY BROKE IT…
A…A CYCLOPS IS ATTACKING!!
THERE, SEE? LOOK AT THAT! MYTHICAL CREATURES! RIGHT THERE!
GYAAAH!
WAAAH!
SEE HOW MANY OF THEM THERE ARE!?
ズシーン
ZUSHIN (THOOM)
ズシーン
ZUSHIN
ズシーン
ZUSHIN
ZUUUN (THUD)
ZUUUN

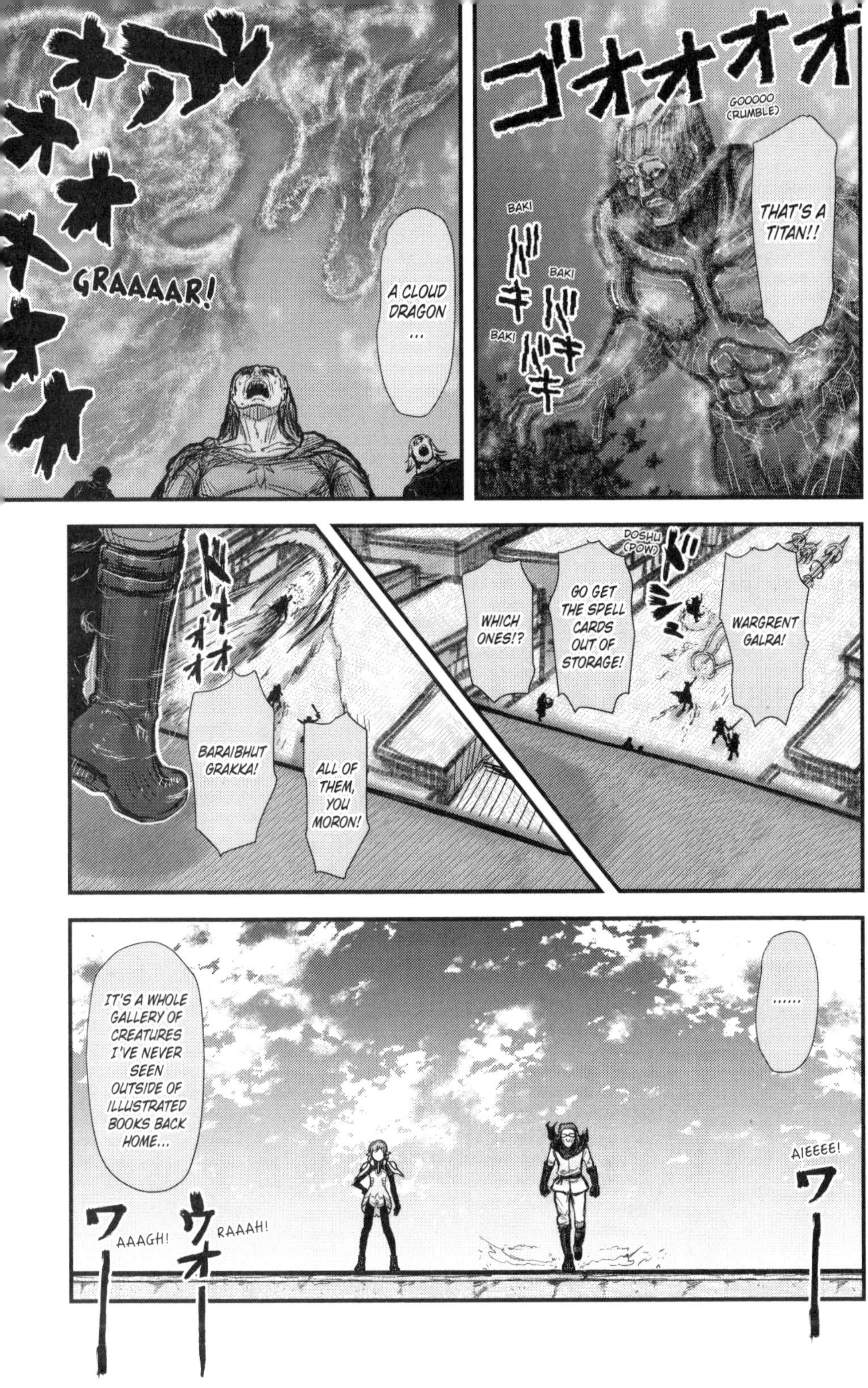
ゴオオオオ
GOOOOO (RUMBLE)
THAT'S A TITAN!!
BAKI
BAKI
BAKI
A CLOUD DRAGON ...
GRAAAAR!
DOSHU (POW)
WARGRENT GALRA!
GO GET THE SPELL CARDS OUT OF STORAGE!
WHICH ONES!?
BARAIBHUT GRAKKA!
ALL OF THEM, YOU MORON!
......
AIEEEE!
IT'S A WHOLE GALLERY OF CREATURES I'VE NEVER SEEN OUTSIDE OF ILLUSTRATED BOOKS BACK HOME...
RAAAH!
AAAGH!

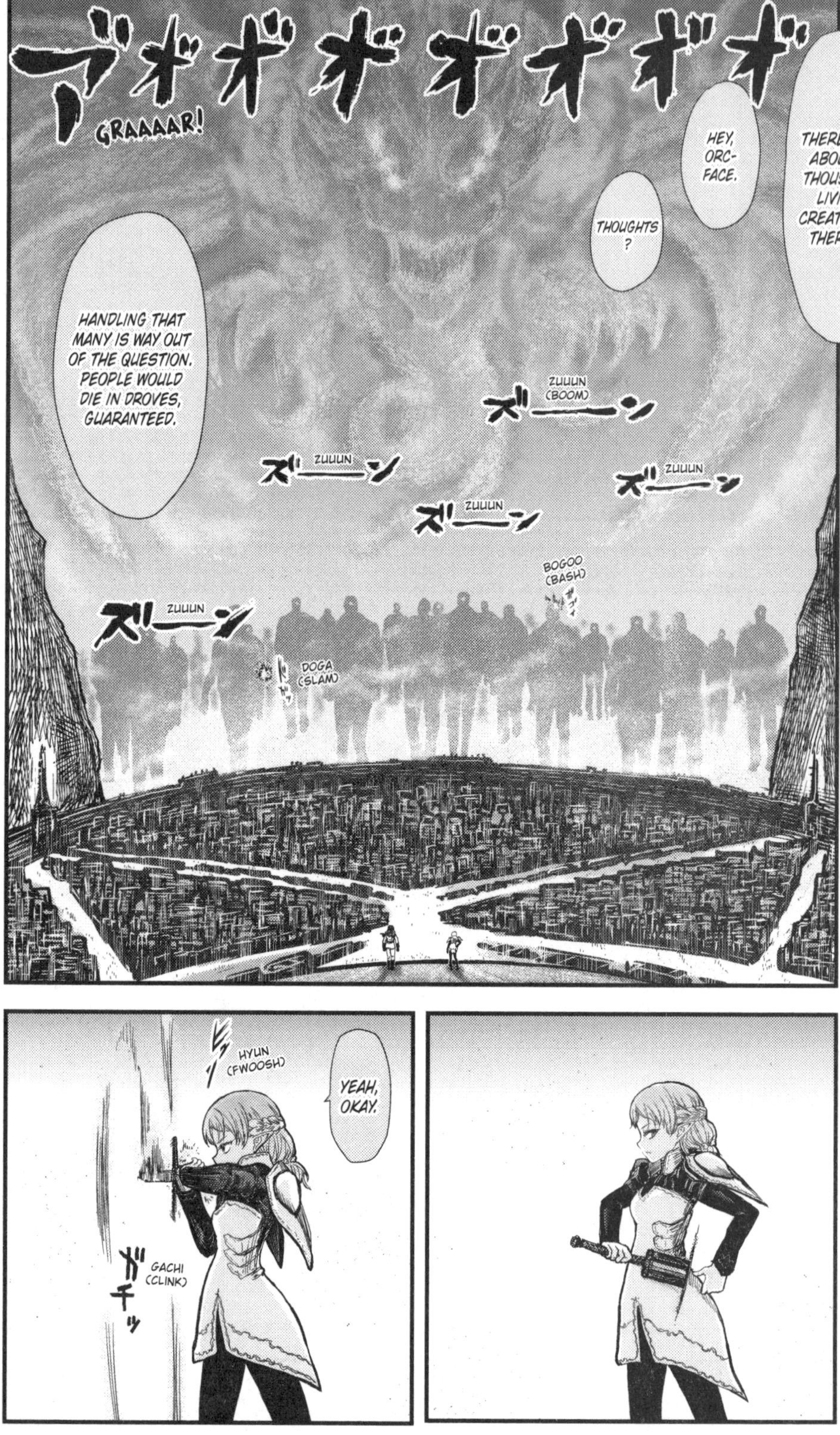

GRAAAAR!
THERE ARE ABOUT A THOUSAND LIVING CREATURES THERE...
HEY, ORC-FACE.
THOUGHTS?
HANDLING THAT MANY IS WAY OUT OF THE QUESTION. PEOPLE WOULD DIE IN DROVES, GUARANTEED.
ZUUUN (BOOM)
ZUUUN
ZUUUN
ZUUUN
BOGOO (BASH)
ZUUUN
DOGA (SLAM)
HYUN (FWOOSH)
YEAH, OKAY.
GACHI (CLINK)

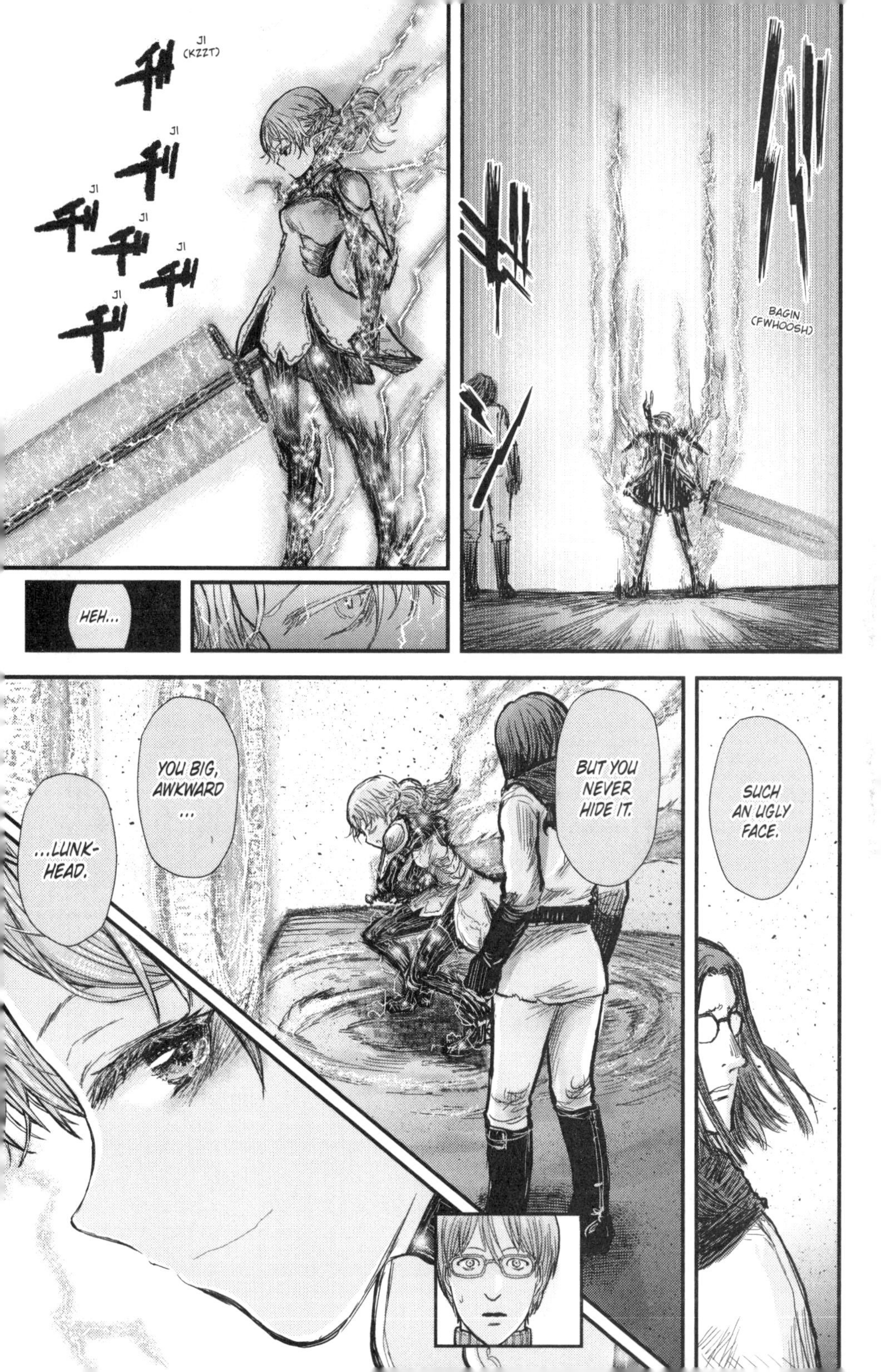
BAGIN
(FWHOOSH)
JI
(KZZT)
JI
JI
JI
JI
JI
HEH...
SUCH AN UGLY FACE.
BUT YOU NEVER HIDE IT.
YOU BIG, AWKWARD ...
...LUNK-HEAD.

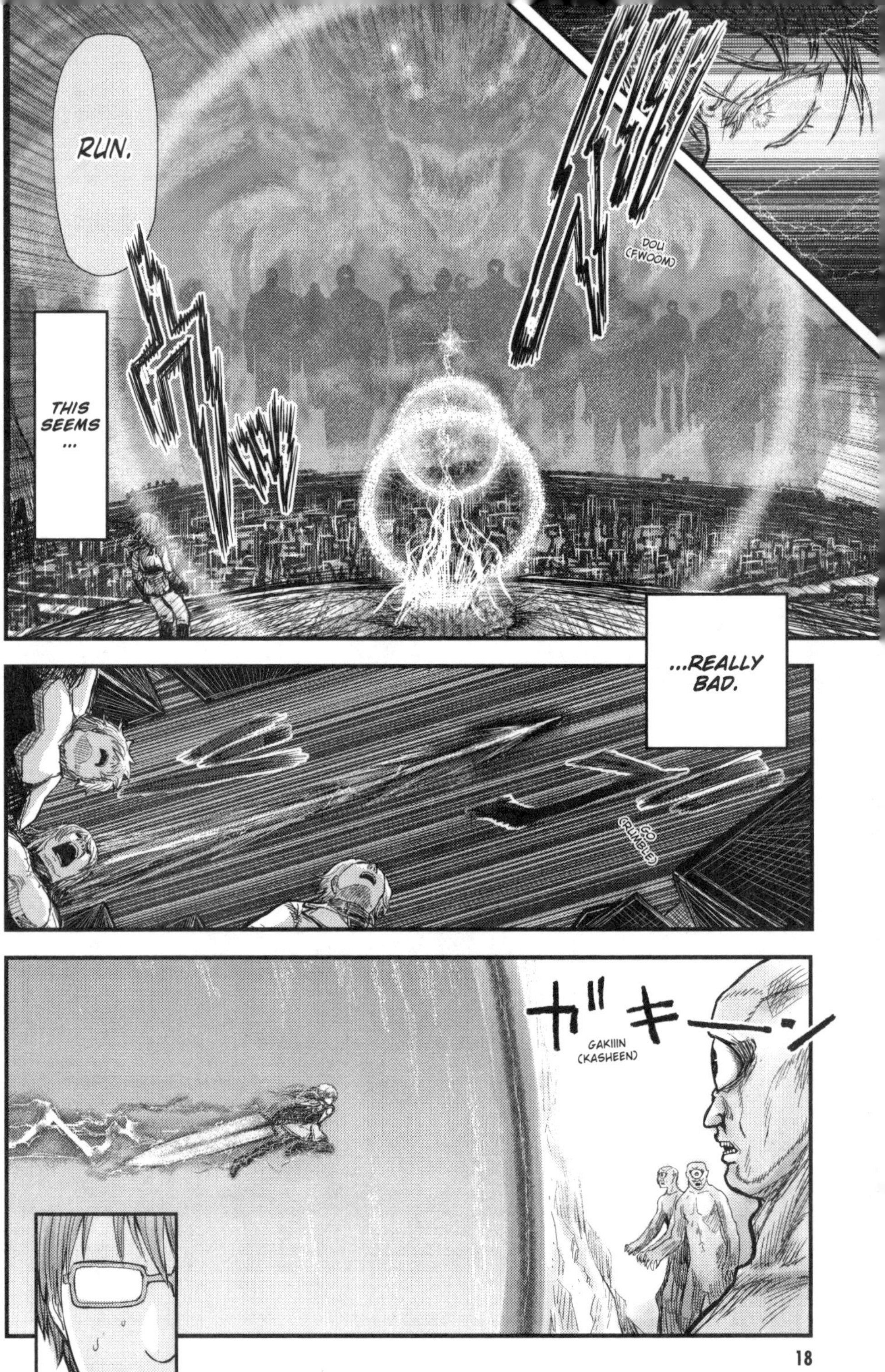
DOU (FWOOM)
RUN.
THIS SEEMS ...
...REALLY BAD.
GO (RUMBLE)
ガキーン
GAKIIIN (KASHEEN)

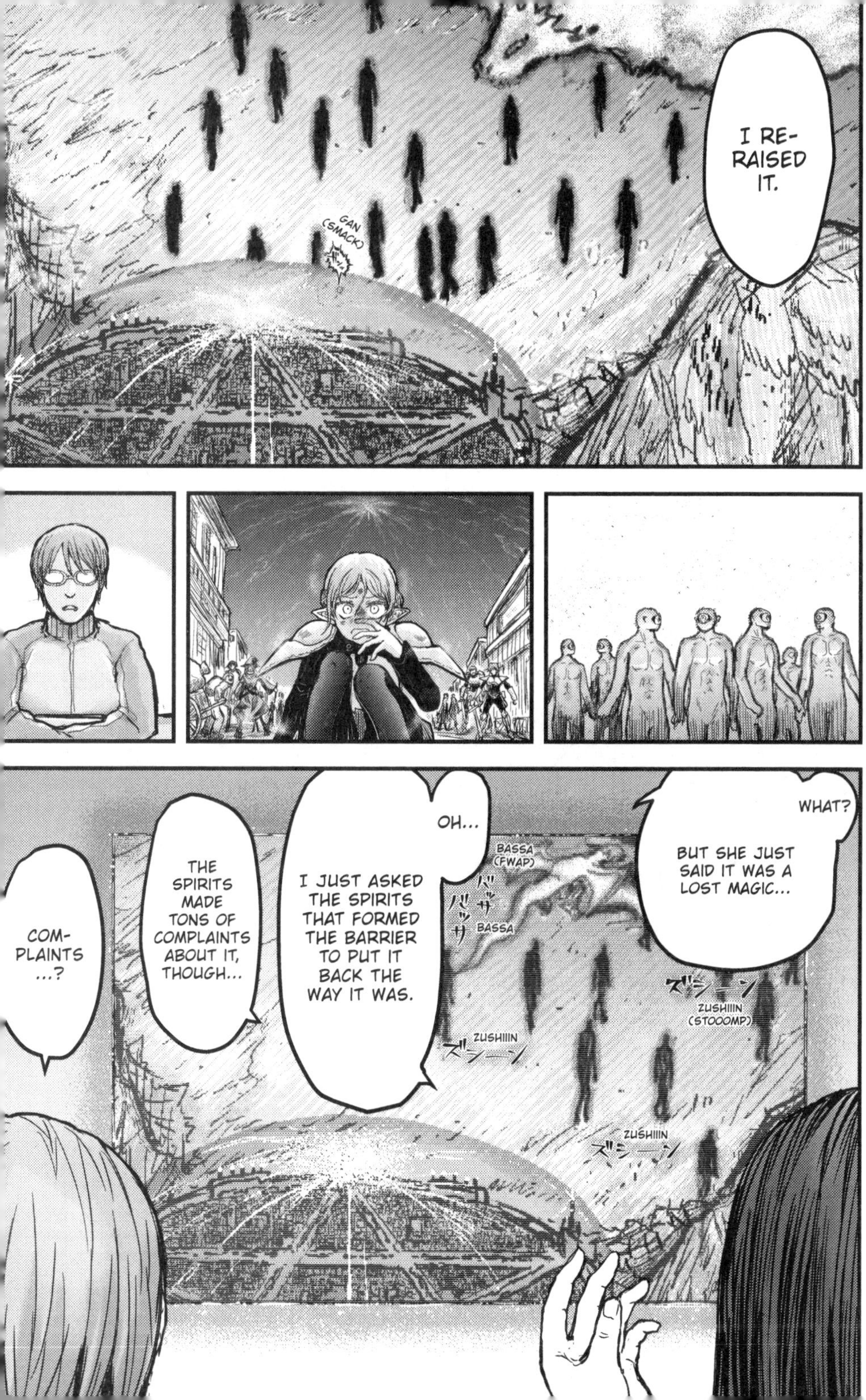
I RE-RAISED IT.
GAN (SMACK)
WHAT?
BUT SHE JUST SAID IT WAS A LOST MAGIC...
BASSA (FWAP)
BASSA
ZUSHIIN (STOOOMP)
OH...
I JUST ASKED THE SPIRITS THAT FORMED THE BARRIER TO PUT IT BACK THE WAY IT WAS.
ZUSHIIN
ZUSHIIN
THE SPIRITS MADE TONS OF COMPLAINTS ABOUT IT, THOUGH...
COM-PLAINTS ...?

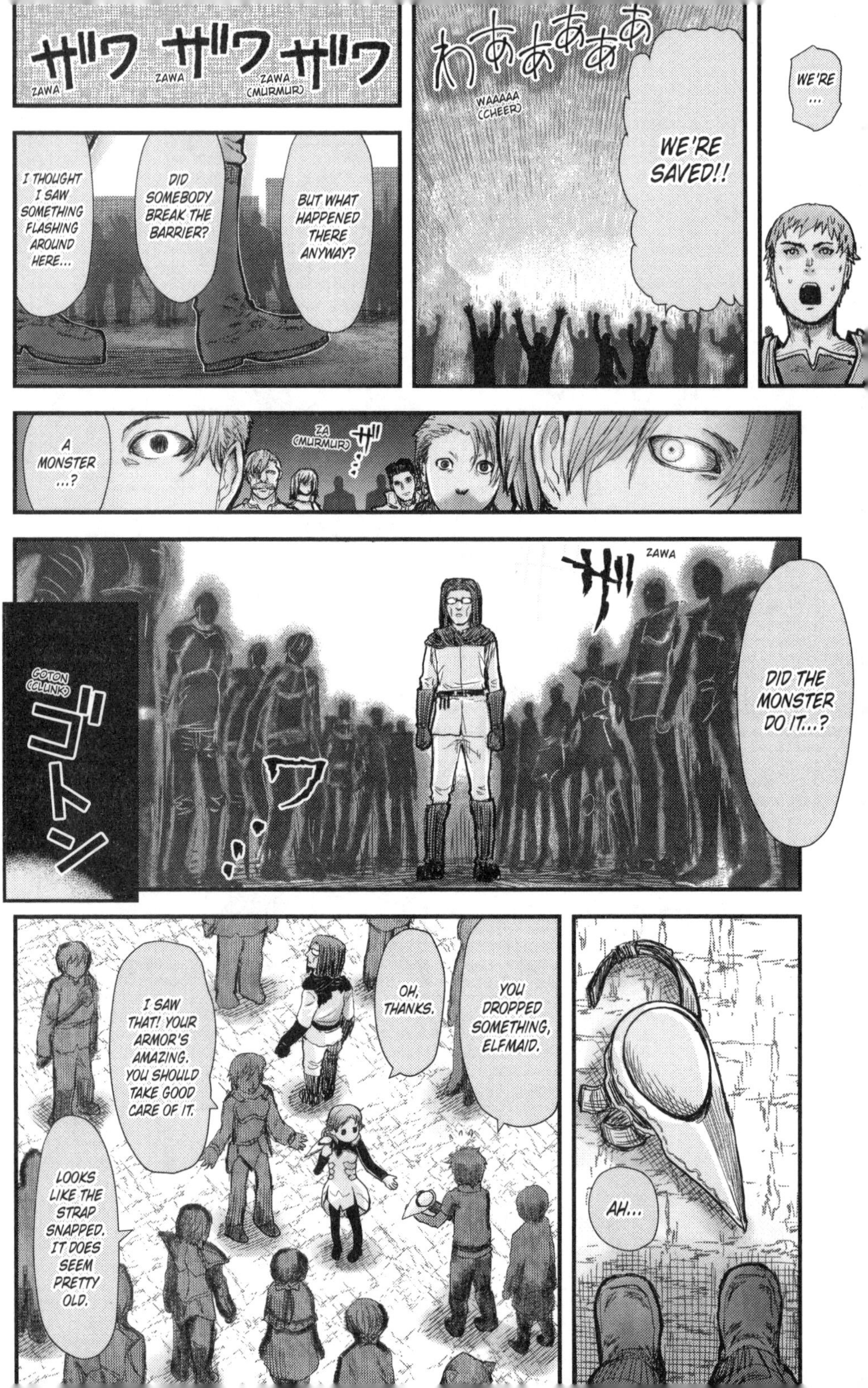
WE'RE ...
わあああああ
WAAAAA (CHEER)
WE'RE SAVED!!
ザワ ザワ ザワ
ZAWA
ZAWA
ZAWA (MURMUR)
BUT WHAT HAPPENED THERE ANYWAY?
DID SOMEBODY BREAK THE BARRIER?
I THOUGHT I SAW SOMETHING FLASHING AROUND HERE...
ザ...
ZA (MURMUR)
A MONSTER ...?
ザワ
ZAWA
DID THE MONSTER DO IT...?
ゴトン
GOTON (CLUNK)
AH...
YOU DROPPED SOMETHING, ELFMAID.
OH, THANKS.
I SAW THAT! YOUR ARMOR'S AMAZING. YOU SHOULD TAKE GOOD CARE OF IT.
LOOKS LIKE THE STRAP SNAPPED. IT DOES SEEM PRETTY OLD.

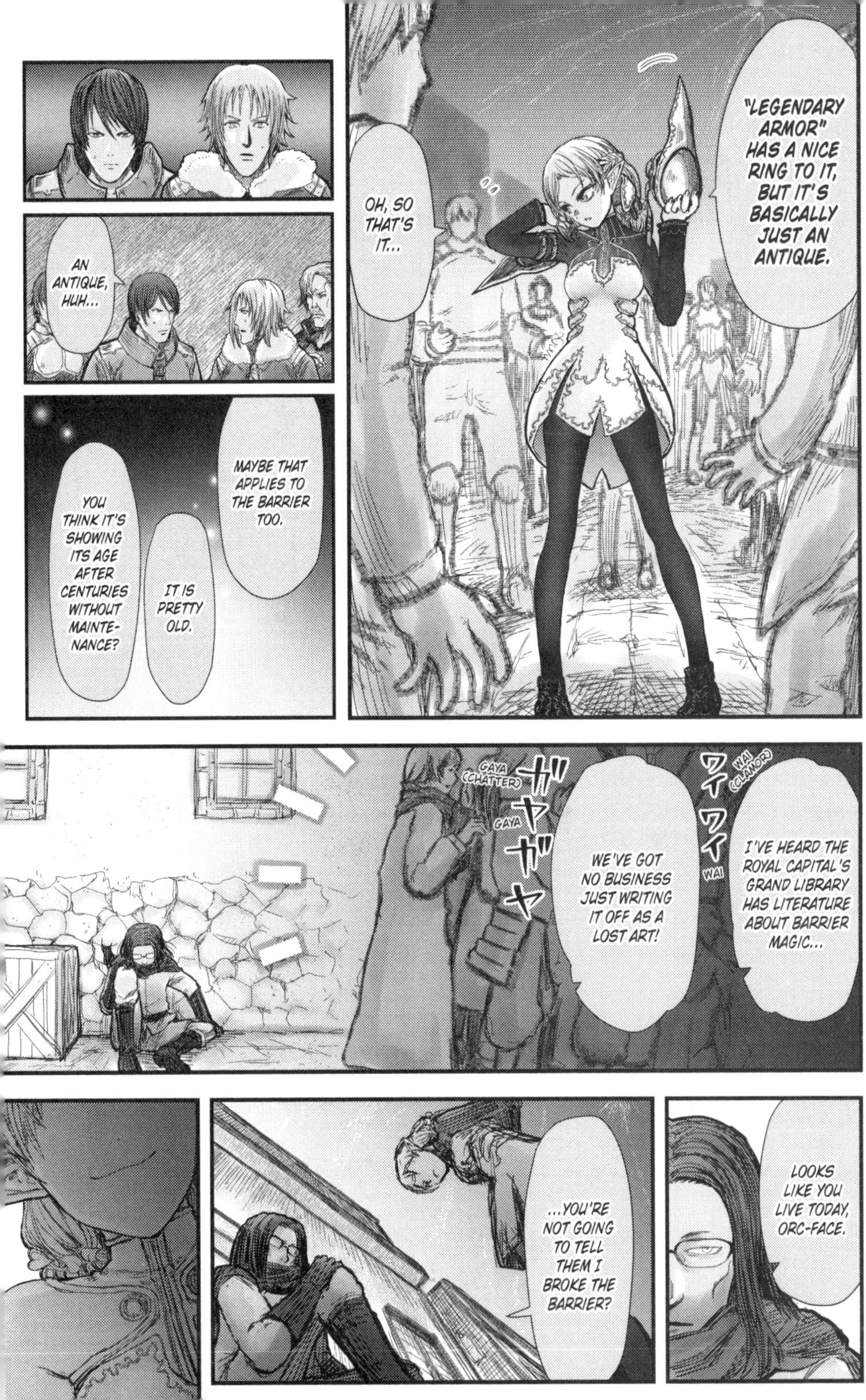
"LEGENDARY ARMOR" HAS A NICE RING TO IT, BUT IT'S BASICALLY JUST AN ANTIQUE.
OH, SO THAT'S IT...
AN ANTIQUE, HUH...
MAYBE THAT APPLIES TO THE BARRIER TOO.
IT IS PRETTY OLD.
YOU THINK IT'S SHOWING ITS AGE AFTER CENTURIES WITHOUT MAINTE-NANCE?
ワイワイ
WAI (CLAMOR)
WAI
I'VE HEARD THE ROYAL CAPITAL'S GRAND LIBRARY HAS LITERATURE ABOUT BARRIER MAGIC...
ガヤガヤ
GAYA (CHATTER)
GAYA
WE'VE GOT NO BUSINESS JUST WRITING IT OFF AS A LOST ART!
LOOKS LIKE YOU LIVE TODAY, ORC-FACE.
...YOU'RE NOT GOING TO TELL THEM I BROKE THE BARRIER?

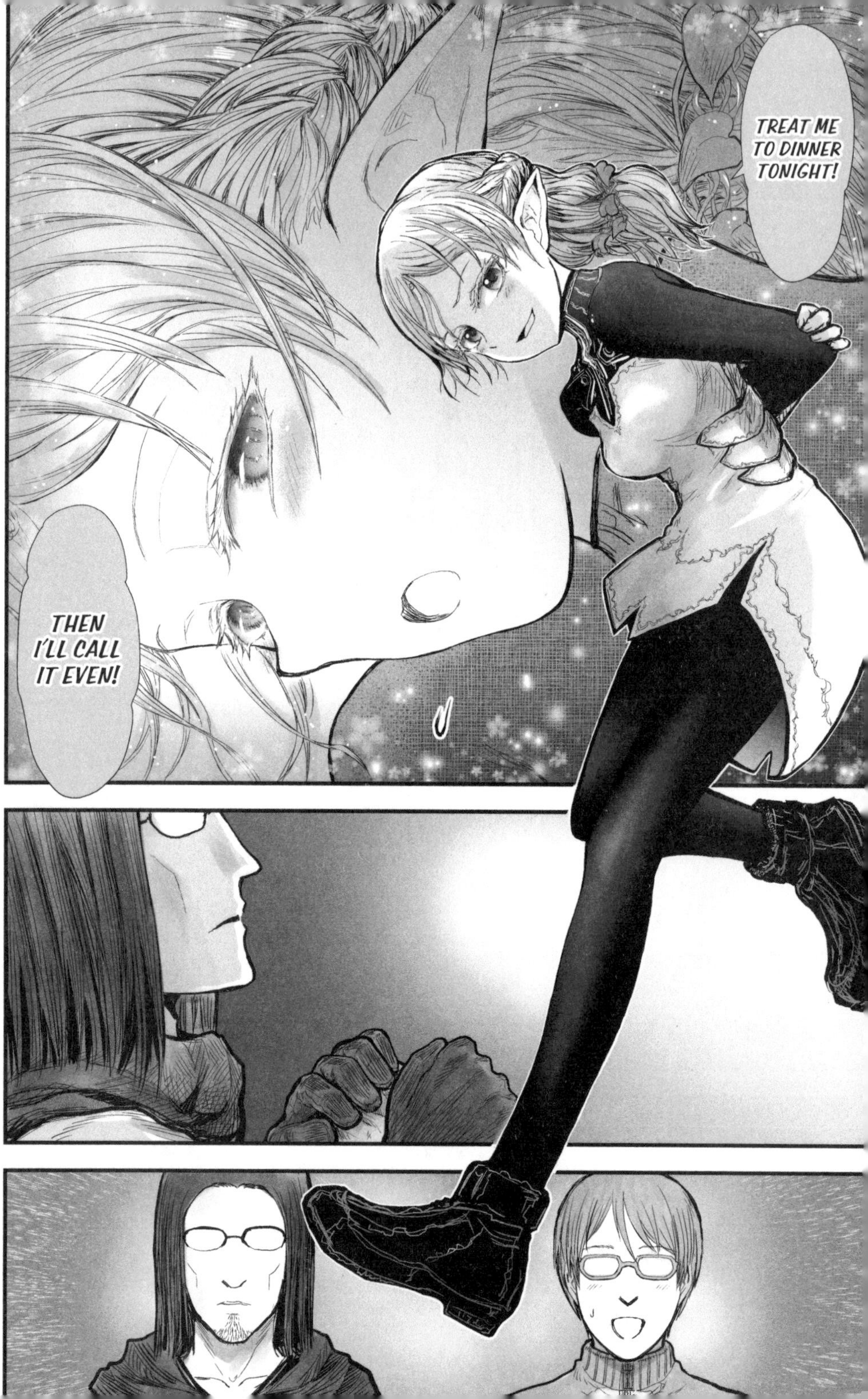
TREAT ME TO DINNER TONIGHT!
THEN I'LL CALL IT EVEN!

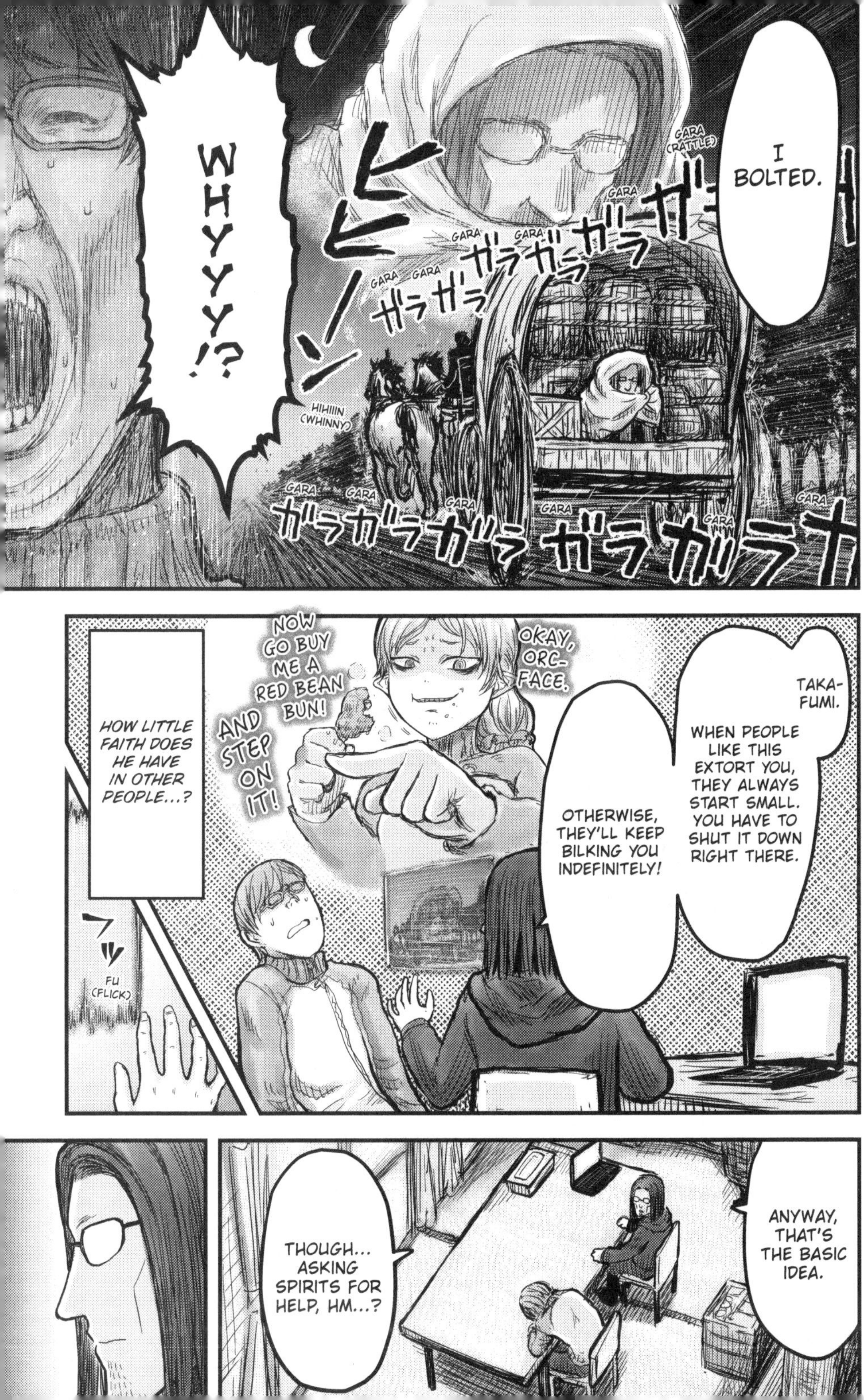
I BOLTED.
GARA (RATTLE)
GARA
ガラ
GARA GARA GARA GARA
ガラガラガラガラ
HIHIIIN (WHINNY)
WHYYYY!?
GARA GARA GARA GARA GARA GARA
ガラガラガラガラガラ
TAKA-FUMI.
WHEN PEOPLE LIKE THIS EXTORT YOU, THEY ALWAYS START SMALL. YOU HAVE TO SHUT IT DOWN RIGHT THERE.
OTHERWISE, THEY'LL KEEP BILKING YOU INDEFINITELY!
OKAY, ORC-FACE.
NOW GO BUY ME A RED BEAN BUN!
AND STEP ON IT!
HOW LITTLE FAITH DOES HE HAVE IN OTHER PEOPLE...?
FU (FLICK)
ANYWAY, THAT'S THE BASIC IDEA.
THOUGH... ASKING SPIRITS FOR HELP, HM...?

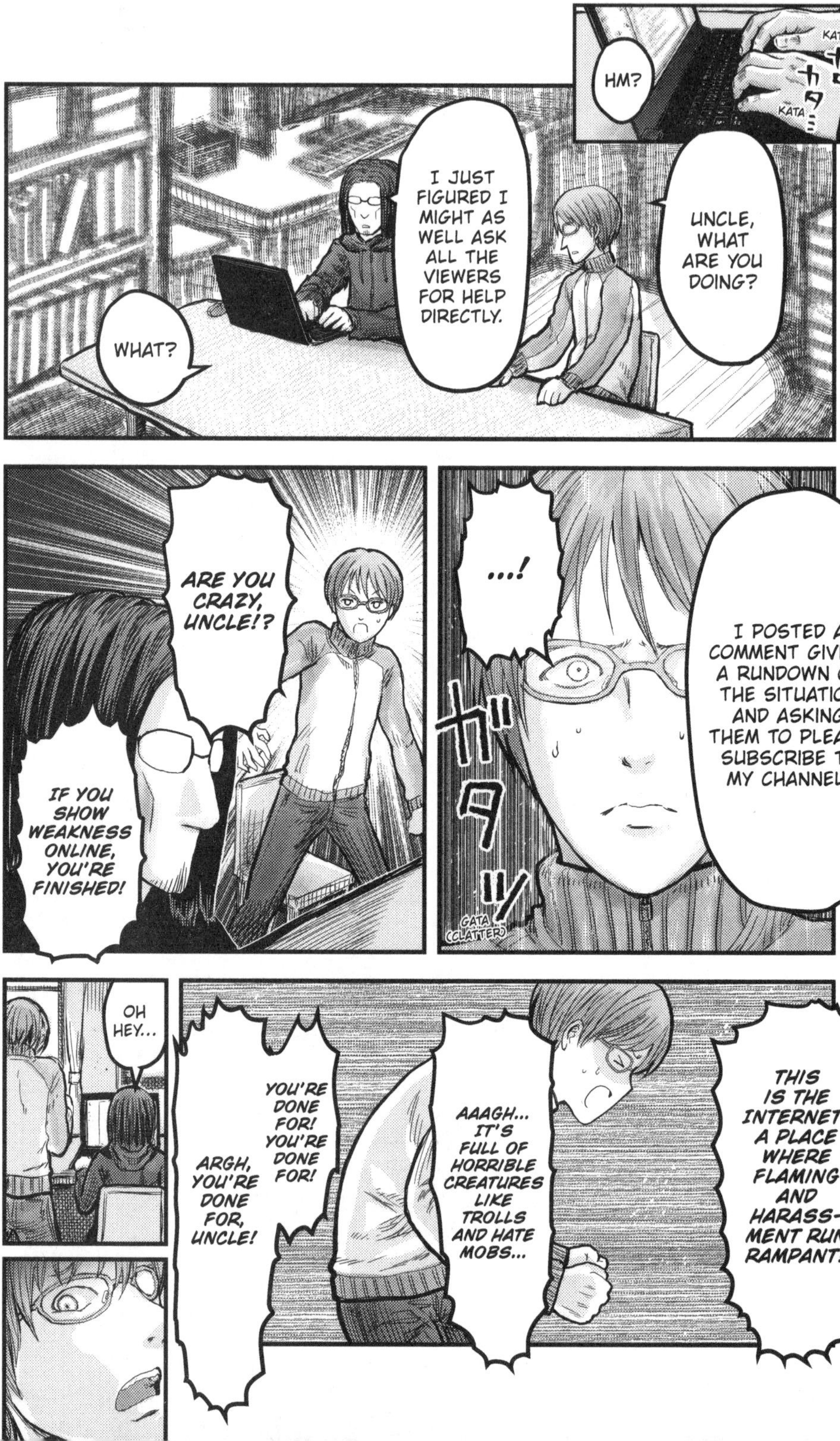
KATA
KATA (TAK)
KATA
HM?
UNCLE, WHAT ARE YOU DOING?
I JUST FIGURED I MIGHT AS WELL ASK ALL THE VIEWERS FOR HELP DIRECTLY.
WHAT?
I POSTED A COMMENT GIVING A RUNDOWN OF THE SITUATION AND ASKING THEM TO PLEASE SUBSCRIBE TO MY CHANNEL.
...!
GATA (CLATTER)
ARE YOU CRAZY, UNCLE!?
IF YOU SHOW WEAKNESS ONLINE, YOU'RE FINISHED!
THIS IS THE INTERNET! A PLACE WHERE FLAMING AND HARASS-MENT RUN RAMPANT!
AAAGH... IT'S FULL OF HORRIBLE CREATURES LIKE TROLLS AND HATE MOBS...
YOU'RE DONE FOR! YOU'RE DONE FOR!
ARGH, YOU'RE DONE FOR, UNCLE!
OH HEY...

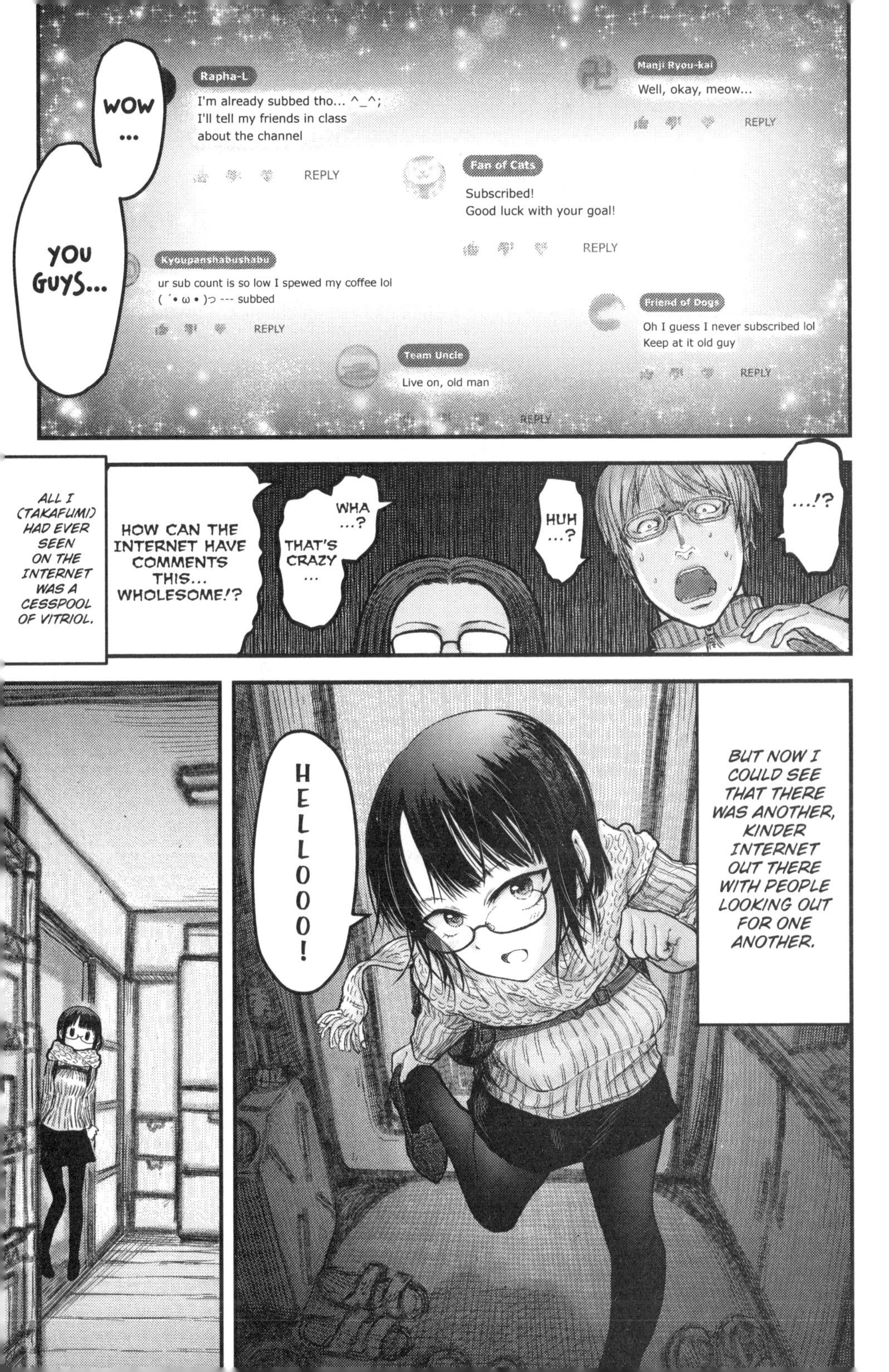
Manji Ryou-kai
Well, okay, meow...
REPLY
Rapha-L
I'm already subbed tho... ^_^; I'll tell my friends in class about the channel
REPLY
Fan of Cats
Subscribed! Good luck with your goal!
REPLY
Kyoupanshabushabu
ur sub count is so low I spewed my coffee lol (´• ω •)つ --- subbed
REPLY
Friend of Dogs
Oh I guess I never subscribed lol Keep at it old guy
REPLY
Team Uncle
Live on, old man
REPLY
WOW ...
YOU GUYS...
...!?
HUH ...?
WHA ...?
THAT'S CRAZY ...
HOW CAN THE INTERNET HAVE COMMENTS THIS... WHOLESOME!?
ALL I (TAKAFUMI) HAD EVER SEEN ON THE INTERNET WAS A CESSPOOL OF VITRIOL.
BUT NOW I COULD SEE THAT THERE WAS ANOTHER, KINDER INTERNET OUT THERE WITH PEOPLE LOOKING OUT FOR ONE ANOTHER.
HELLOOOO!

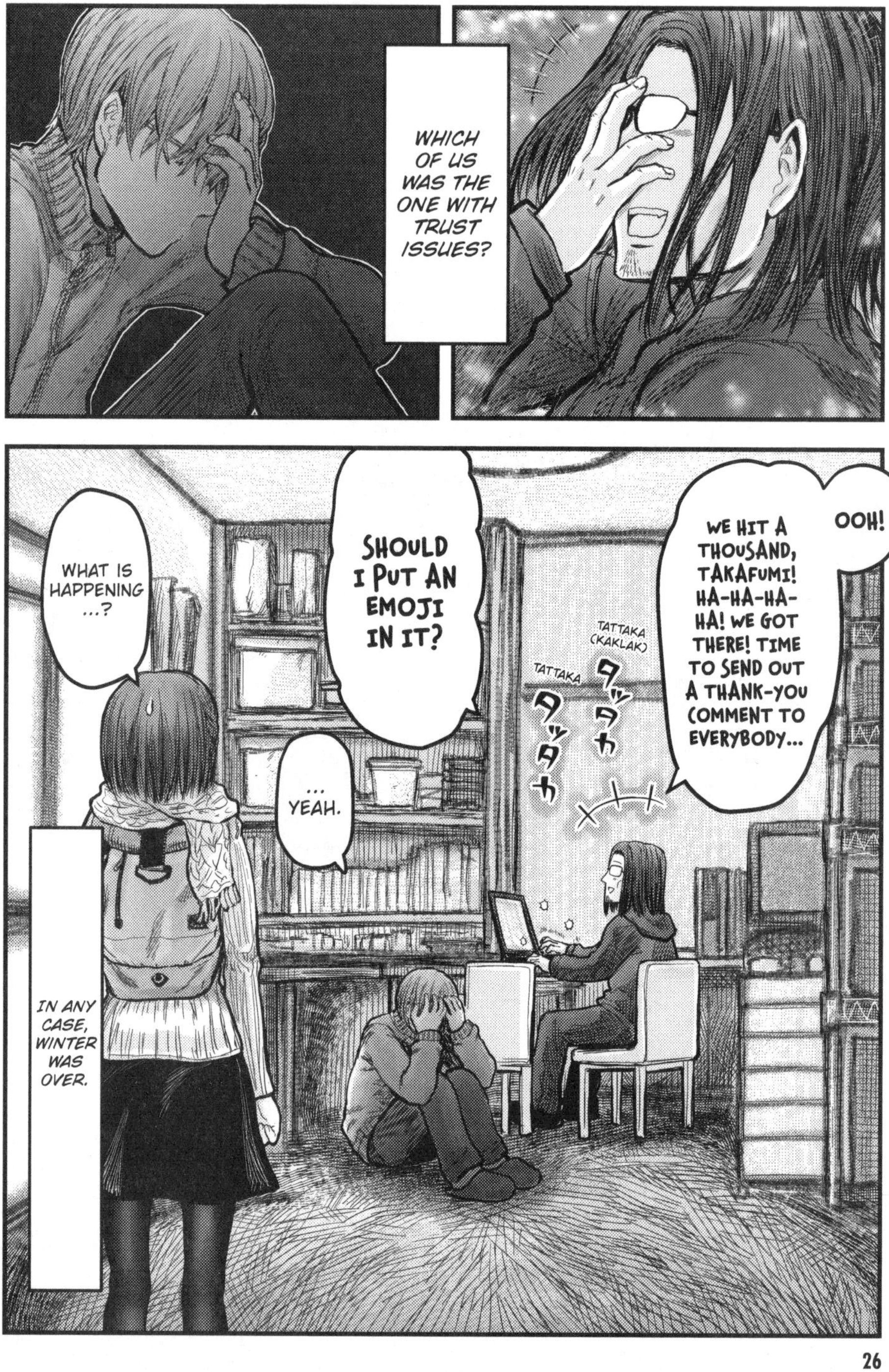
WHICH OF US WAS THE ONE WITH TRUST ISSUES?
OOH!
WE HIT A THOUSAND, TAKAFUMI! HA-HA-HA-HA! WE GOT THERE! TIME TO SEND OUT A THANK-YOU COMMENT TO EVERYBODY...
TATTAKA (KAKLAK)
タッタカ
TATTAKA
タッタカ
SHOULD I PUT AN EMOJI IN IT?
... YEAH.
WHAT IS HAPPENING ...?
IN ANY CASE, WINTER WAS OVER.

Battle of Gaixia

The Battle of Gaixia was an incident chronicled in the *Records of the Grand Historian*, a ancient text covering the history of China. In the battle, Xiang Yu of Chu was surrounded on all sides by Han forces, then heard songs from Chu being sung and lamented that Chu had already fallen to the Han. In Japanese, this is the origin of the phrase *shimen soka* ("hearing Chu songs from all four sides") and means "surrounded by enemies."

Source: Daijirin *dictionary*

TIPS

UNCLE from ANOTHER WORLD

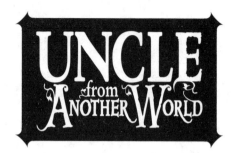

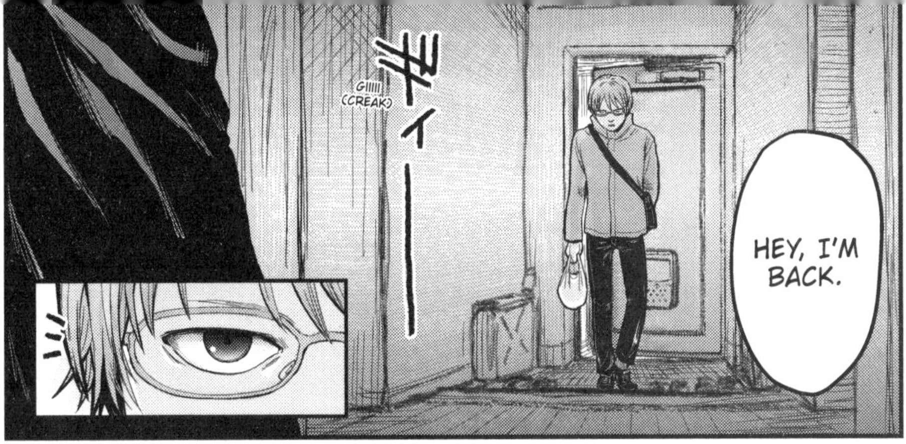
GIIII (CREAK)
HEY, I'M BACK.

MARCH 2018

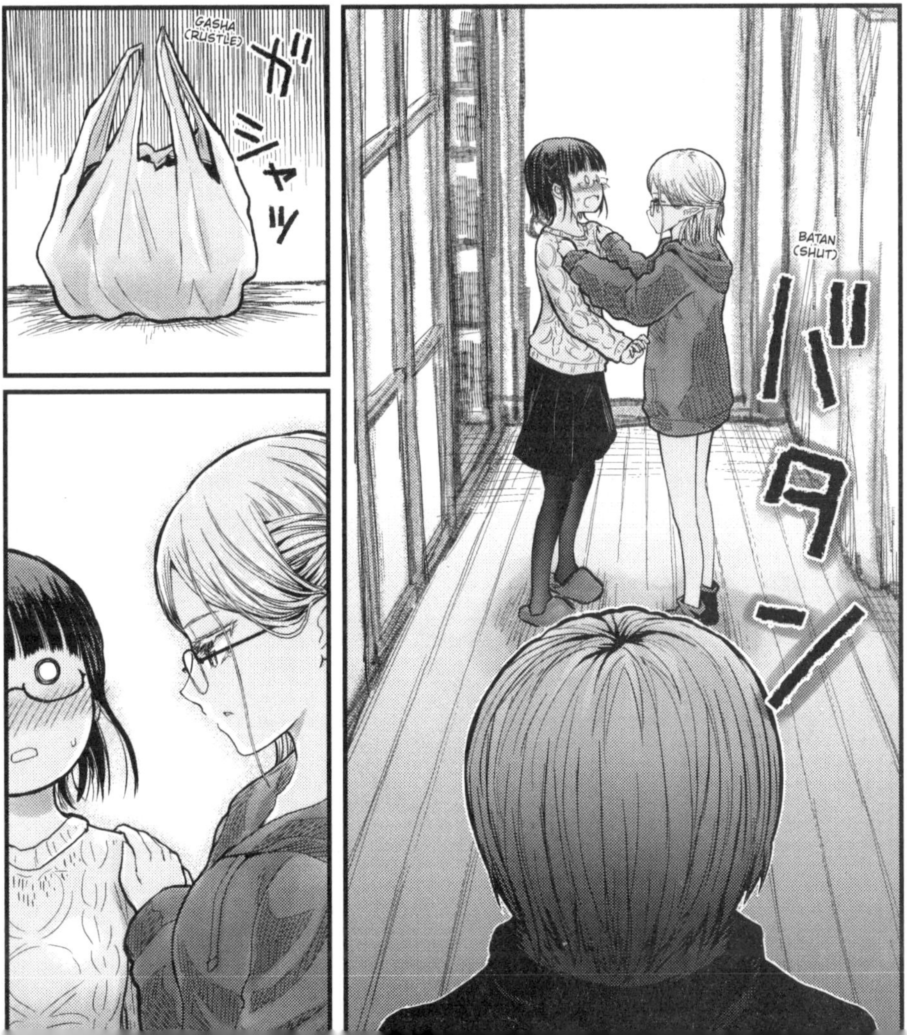
BATAN (SHUT)
GASHA (RUSTLE)

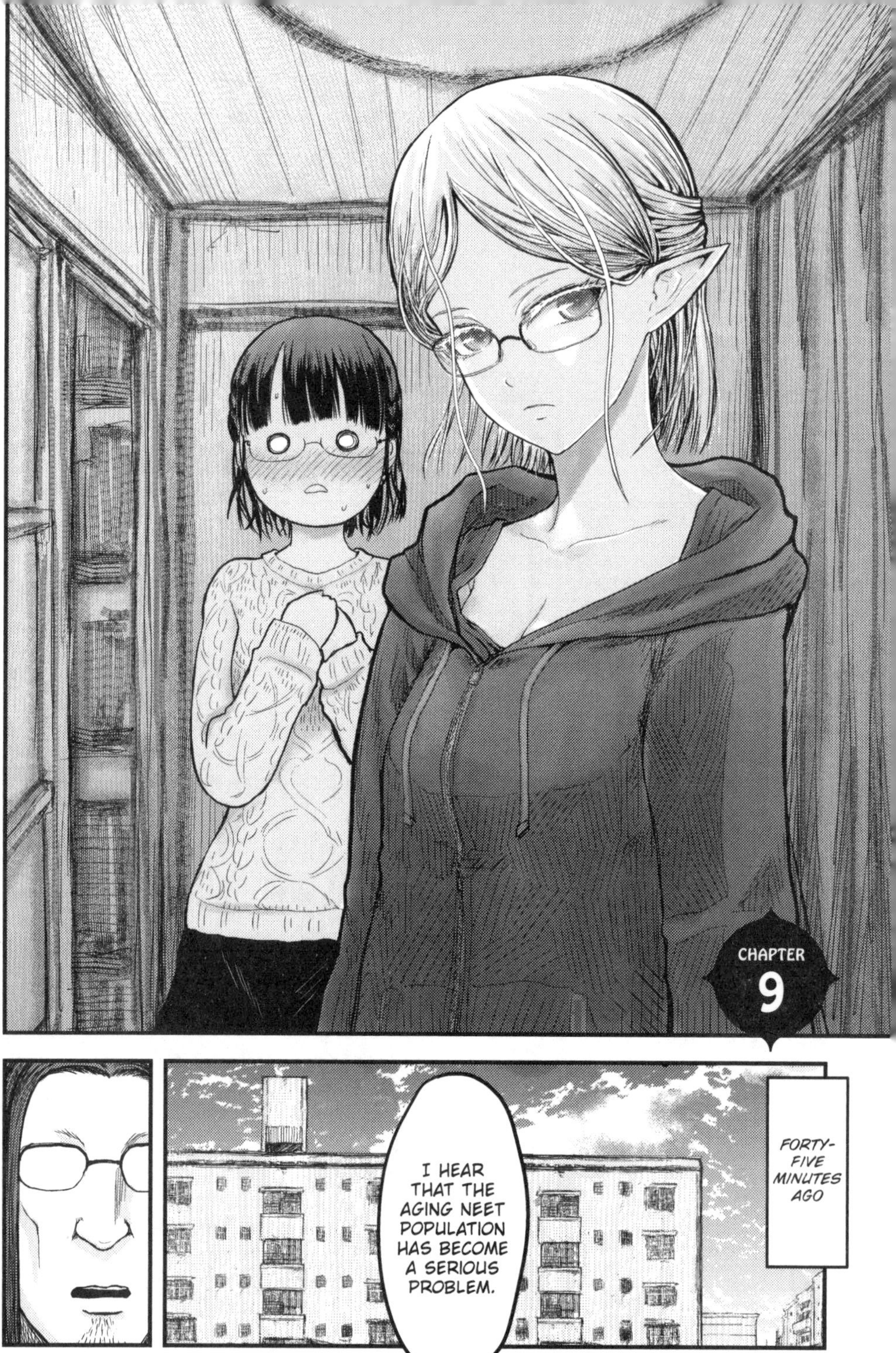
CHAPTER
9
FORTY-FIVE MINUTES AGO
I HEAR THAT THE AGING NEET POPULATION HAS BECOME A SERIOUS PROBLEM.

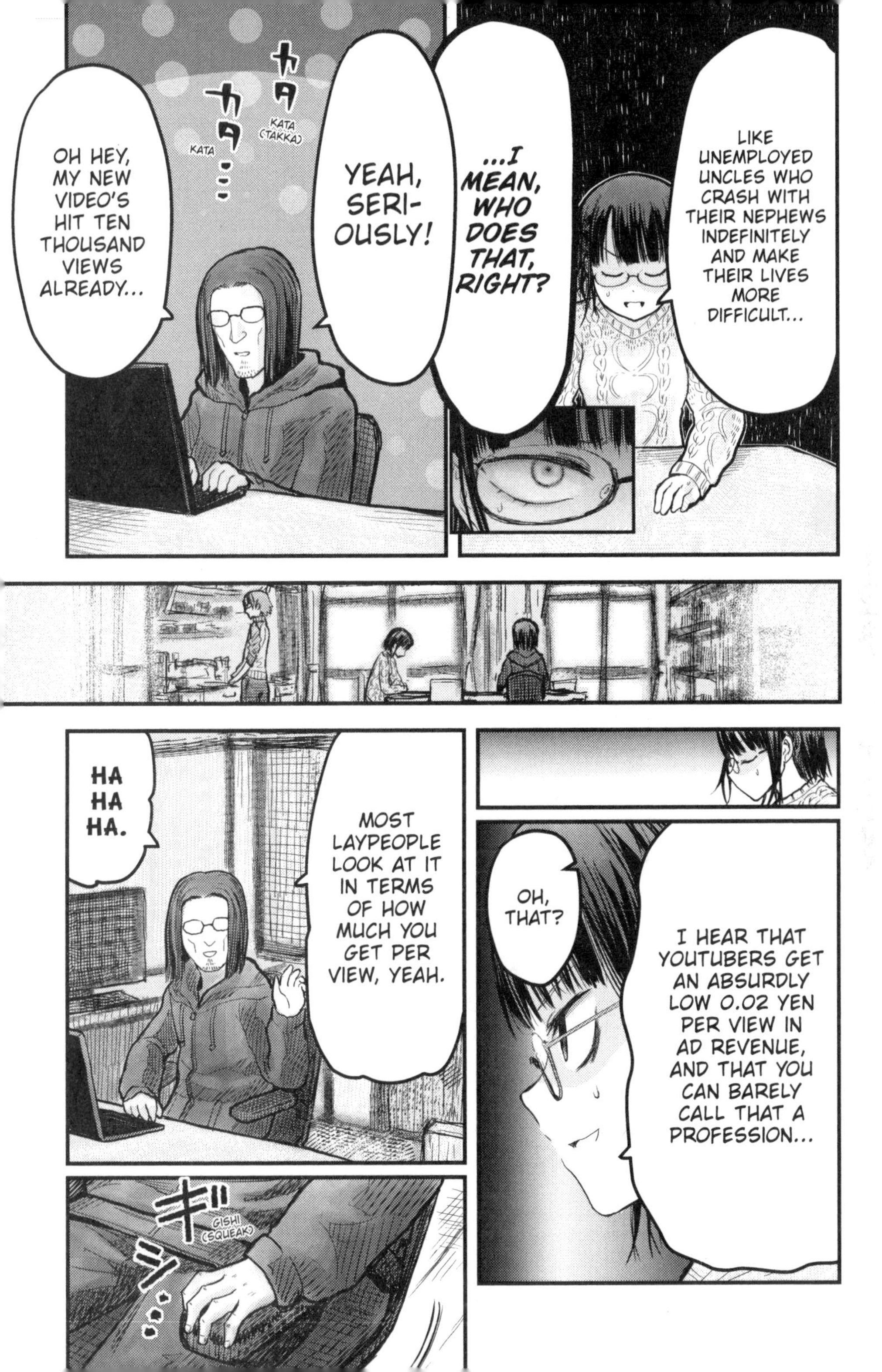
LIKE UNEMPLOYED UNCLES WHO CRASH WITH THEIR NEPHEWS INDEFINITELY AND MAKE THEIR LIVES MORE DIFFICULT...
...I MEAN, WHO DOES THAT, RIGHT?
YEAH, SERI-OUSLY!
KATA (TAKKA)
KATA
OH HEY, MY NEW VIDEO'S HIT TEN THOUSAND VIEWS ALREADY...
I HEAR THAT YOUTUBERS GET AN ABSURDLY LOW 0.02 YEN PER VIEW IN AD REVENUE, AND THAT YOU CAN BARELY CALL THAT A PROFESSION...
OH, THAT?
MOST LAYPEOPLE LOOK AT IT IN TERMS OF HOW MUCH YOU GET PER VIEW, YEAH.
HA HA HA.
GISHI (SQUEAK)

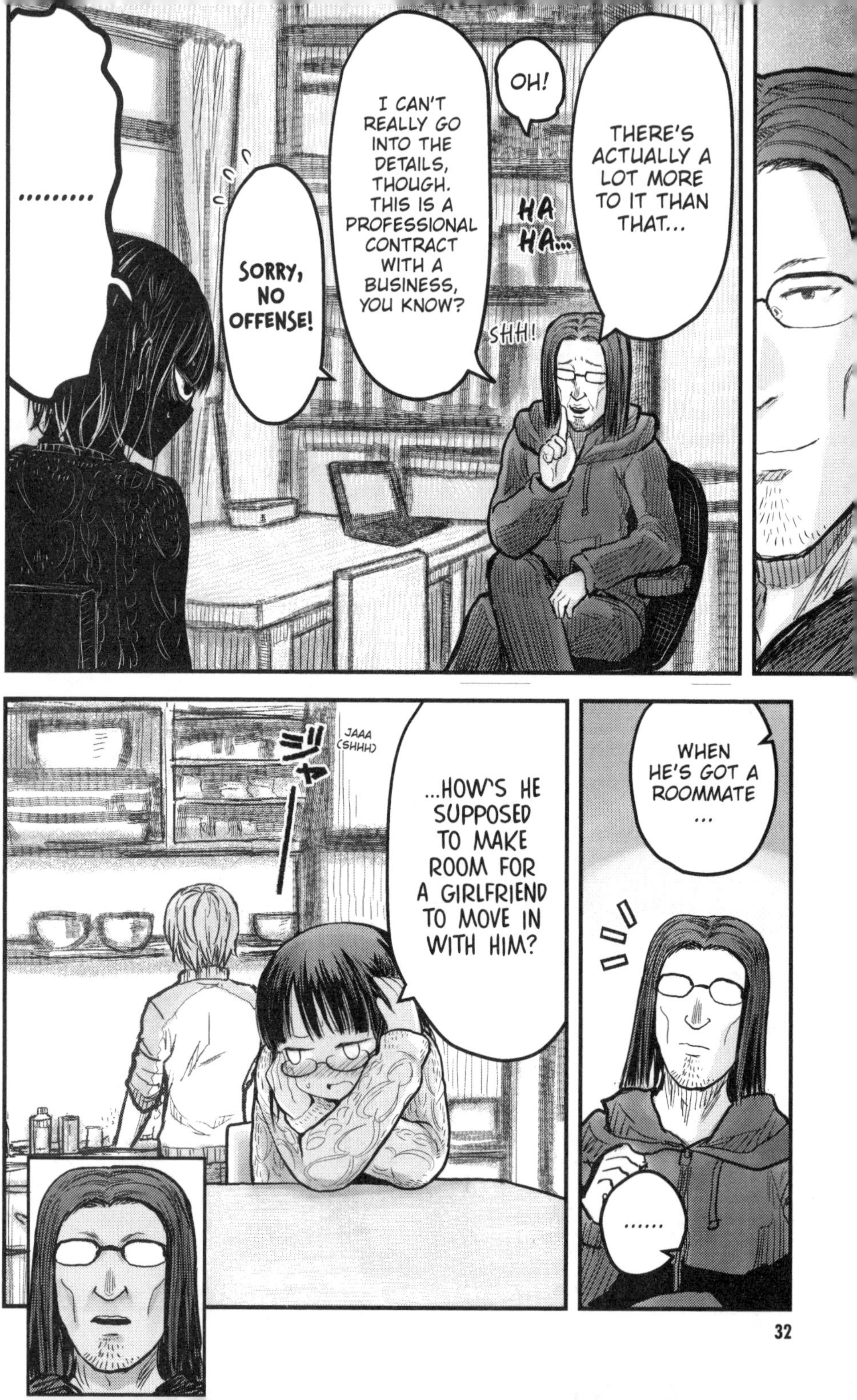
THERE'S ACTUALLY A LOT MORE TO IT THAN THAT...
OH!
HA HA...
I CAN'T REALLY GO INTO THE DETAILS, THOUGH. THIS IS A PROFESSIONAL CONTRACT WITH A BUSINESS, YOU KNOW?
SHH!
SORRY, NO OFFENSE!
....
WHEN HE'S GOT A ROOMMATE...
......
...HOW'S HE SUPPOSED TO MAKE ROOM FOR A GIRLFRIEND TO MOVE IN WITH HIM?
JAAA (SHHH)
ジャー

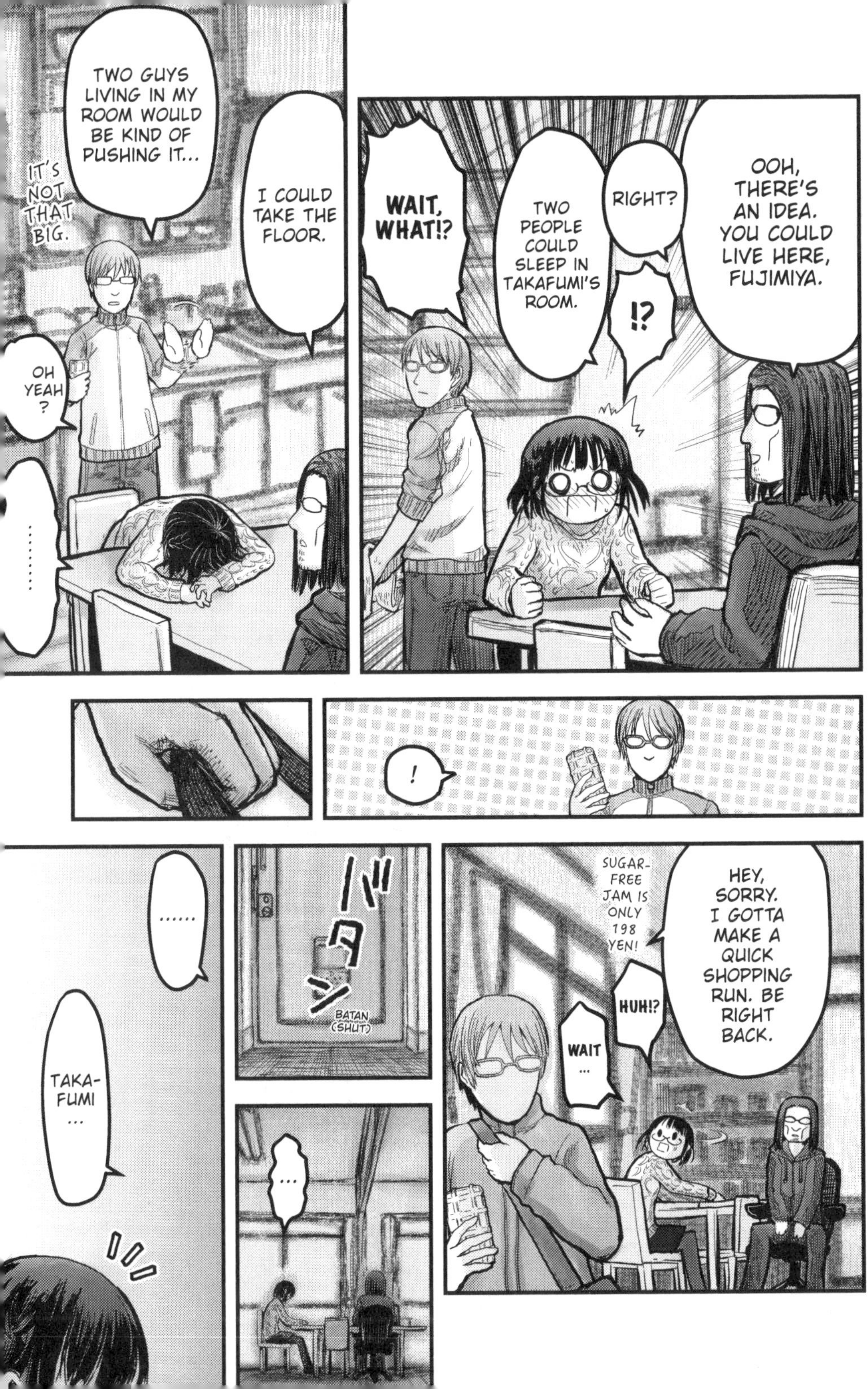
OOH, THERE'S AN IDEA. YOU COULD LIVE HERE, FUJIMIYA.
RIGHT?
!?
TWO PEOPLE COULD SLEEP IN TAKAFUMI'S ROOM.
WAIT, WHAT!?
TWO GUYS LIVING IN MY ROOM WOULD BE KIND OF PUSHING IT...
I COULD TAKE THE FLOOR.
IT'S NOT THAT BIG.
OH YEAH?
......
!
SUGAR-FREE JAM IS ONLY 198 YEN!
HEY, SORRY. I GOTTA MAKE A QUICK SHOPPING RUN. BE RIGHT BACK.
HUH!?
WAIT...
バタン
BATAN (SHUT)
...
......
TAKAFUMI...

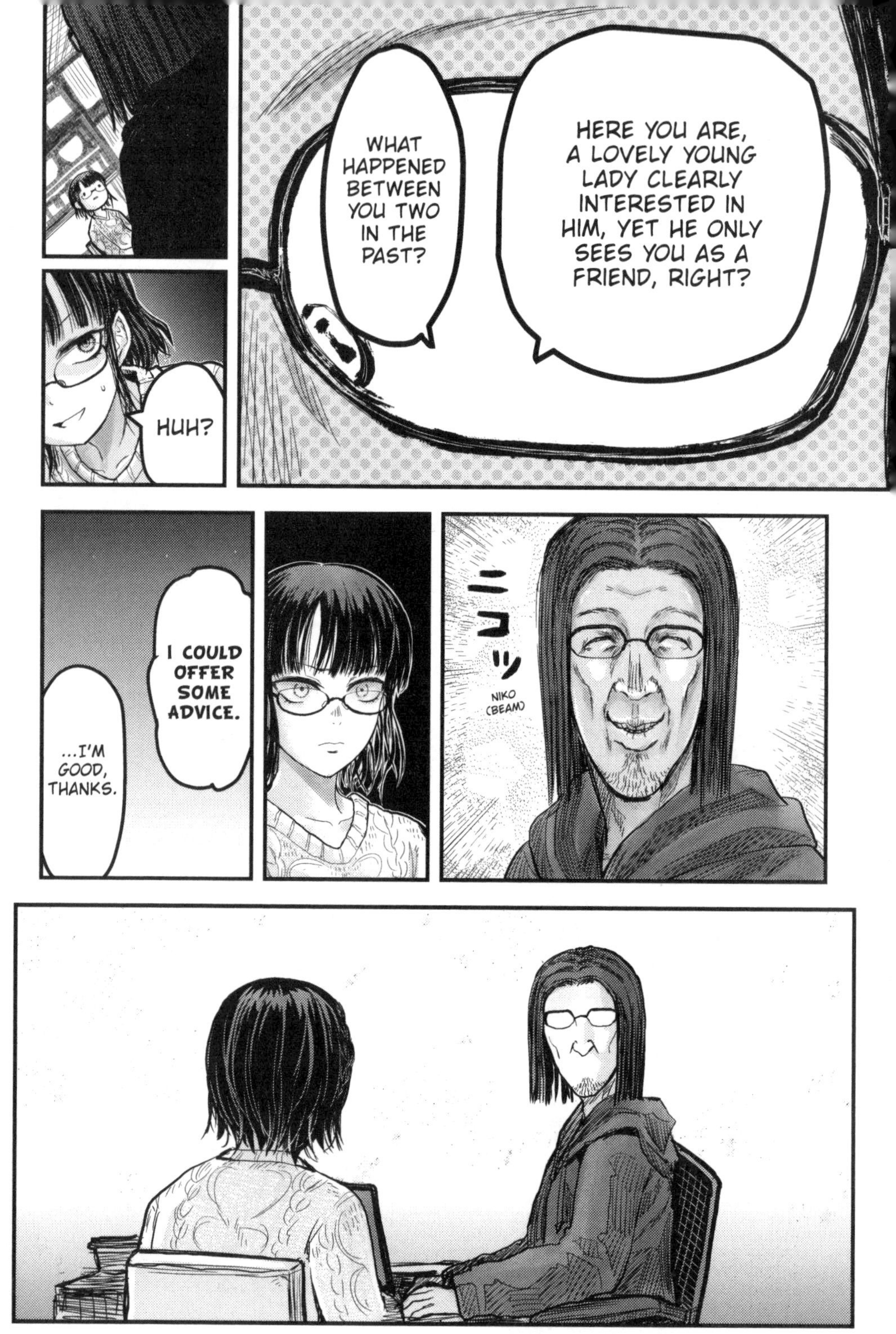
HERE YOU ARE, A LOVELY YOUNG LADY CLEARLY INTERESTED IN HIM, YET HE ONLY SEES YOU AS A FRIEND, RIGHT?
WHAT HAPPENED BETWEEN YOU TWO IN THE PAST?
HUH?
ニコッ
NIKO (BEAM)
I COULD OFFER SOME ADVICE.
...I'M GOOD, THANKS.

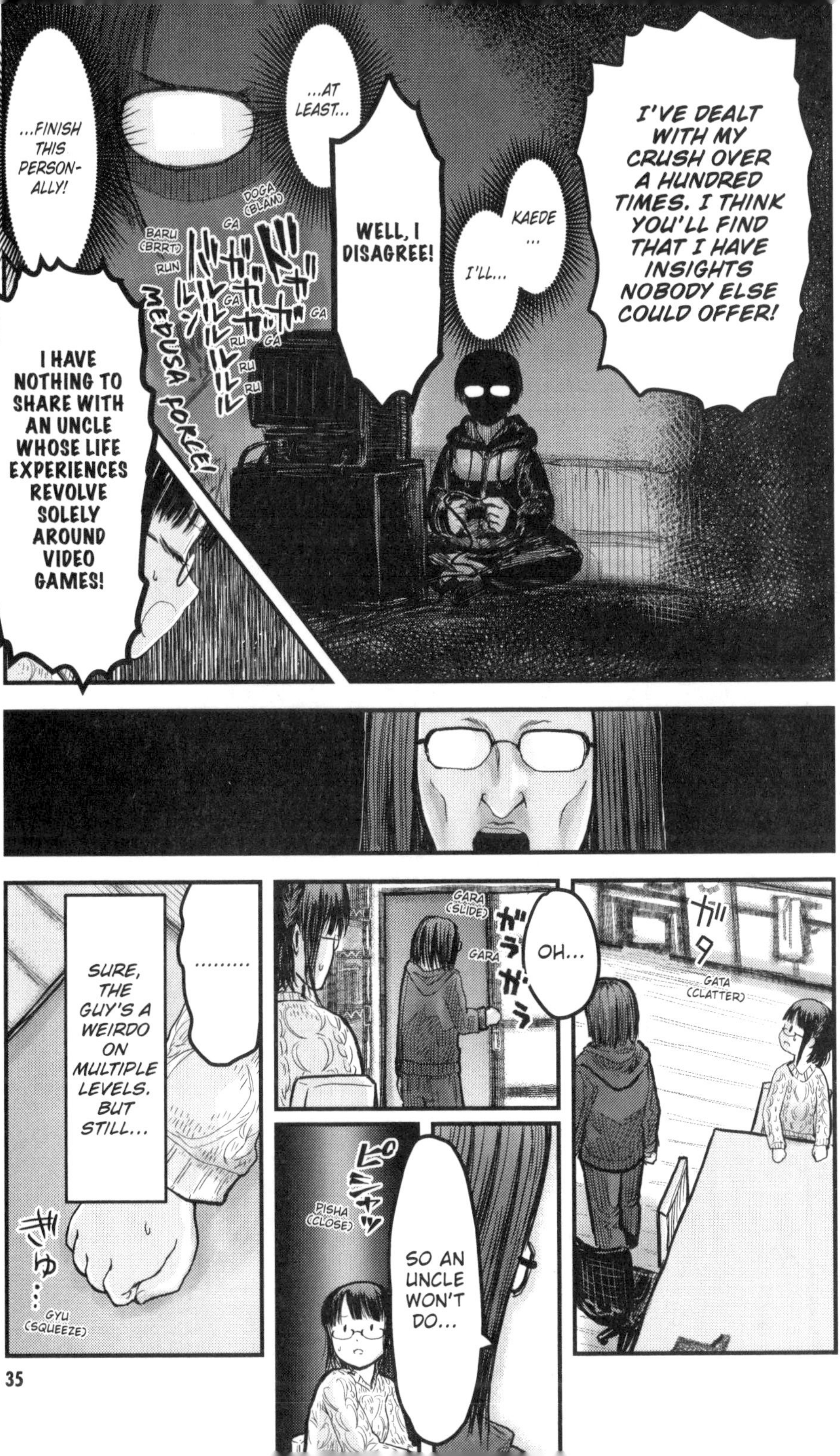
I'VE DEALT WITH MY CRUSH OVER A HUNDRED TIMES. I THINK YOU'LL FIND THAT I HAVE INSIGHTS NOBODY ELSE COULD OFFER!
KAEDE...
I'LL...
...AT LEAST...
WELL, I DISAGREE!
...FINISH THIS PERSON-ALLY!
DOGA (BLAM)
GA
GA
GA
GA
BARU (BRRT)
RUN
RU
RU
RU
MEDUSA FORCE!
I HAVE NOTHING TO SHARE WITH AN UNCLE WHOSE LIFE EXPERIENCES REVOLVE SOLELY AROUND VIDEO GAMES!
GATA (CLATTER)
OH...
GARA (SLIDE)
GARA
PISHA (CLOSE)
SO AN UNCLE WON'T DO...
....
SURE, THE GUY'S A WEIRDO ON MULTIPLE LEVELS. BUT STILL...
GYU (SQUEEZE)

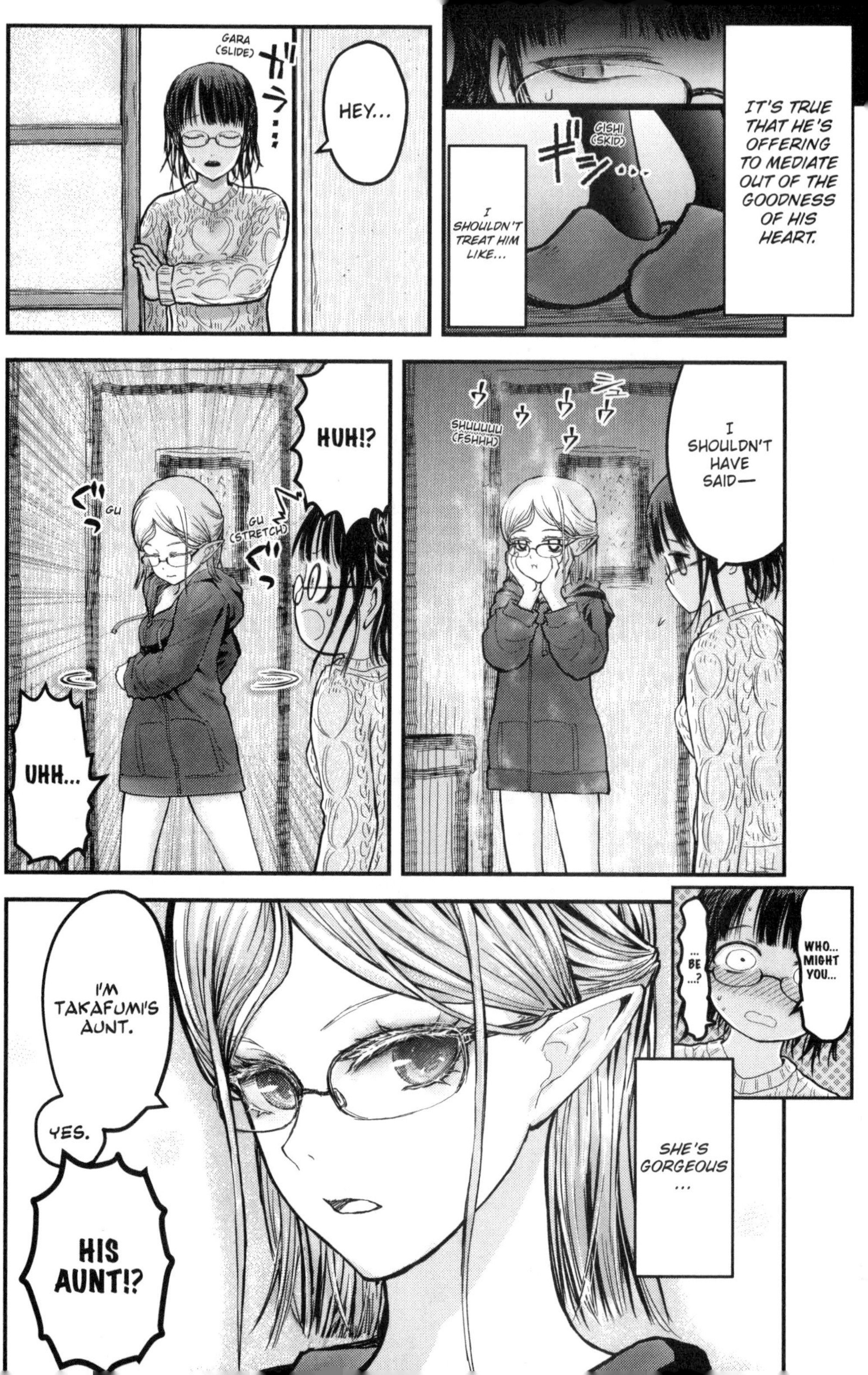

IT'S TRUE THAT HE'S OFFERING TO MEDIATE OUT OF THE GOODNESS OF HIS HEART.
GISHI (SKID)
I SHOULDN'T TREAT HIM LIKE...
GARA (SLIDE)
HEY...
I SHOULDN'T HAVE SAID—
SHUUUUU (FSHHH)
HUH!?
GU (STRETCH)
GU
UHH...
WHO... MIGHT YOU...
... BE ...?
SHE'S GORGEOUS...
I'M TAKAFUMI'S AUNT.
YES.
HIS AUNT!?

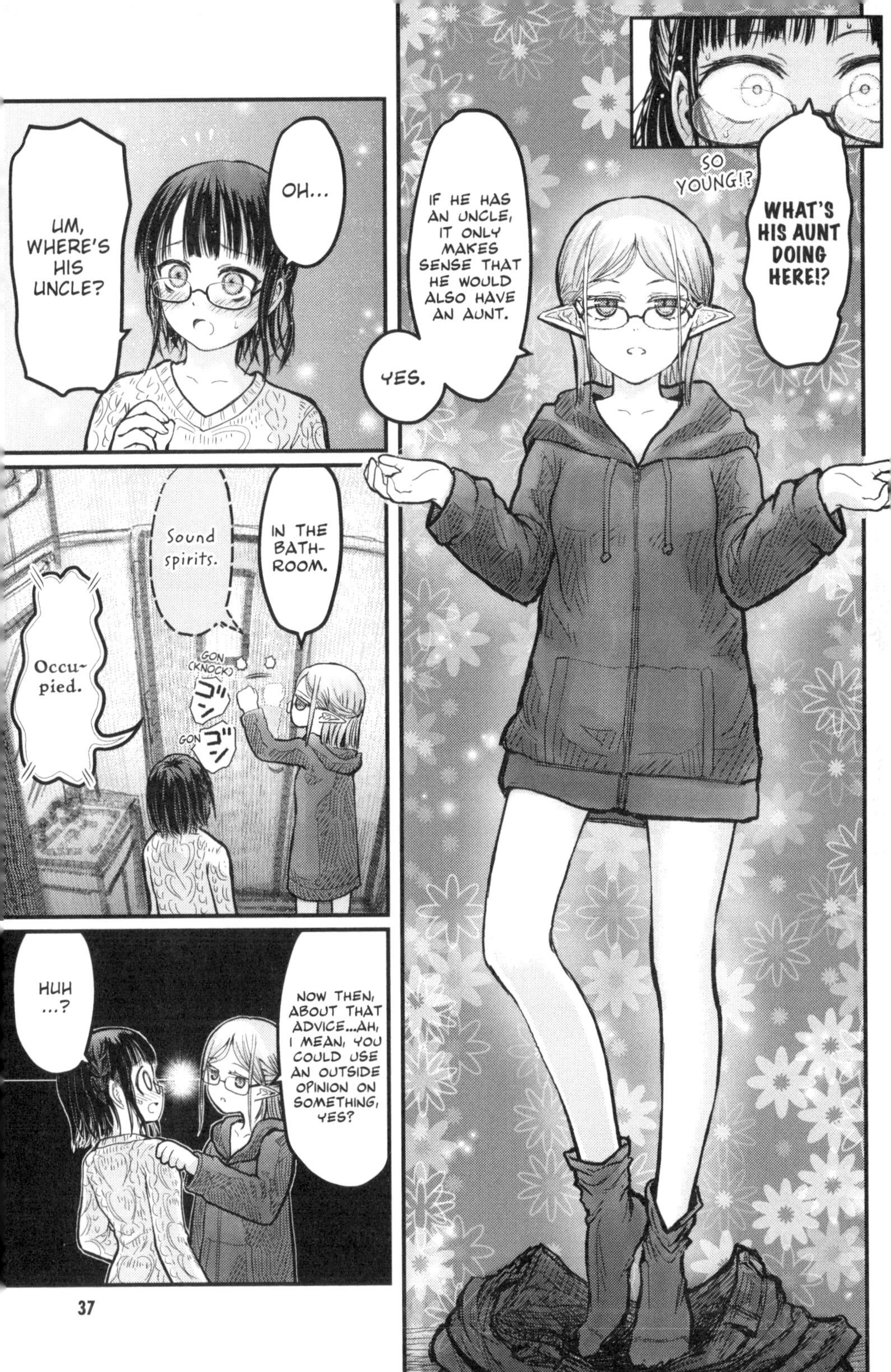
WHAT'S HIS AUNT DOING HERE!?
SO YOUNG!?
IF HE HAS AN UNCLE, IT ONLY MAKES SENSE THAT HE WOULD ALSO HAVE AN AUNT.
YES.
OH...
UM, WHERE'S HIS UNCLE?
IN THE BATHROOM.
Sound spirits.
GON (KNOCK)
ゴン
GON
ゴン
Occupied.
NOW THEN, ABOUT THAT ADVICE...AH, I MEAN, YOU COULD USE AN OUTSIDE OPINION ON SOMETHING, YES?
HUH ...?

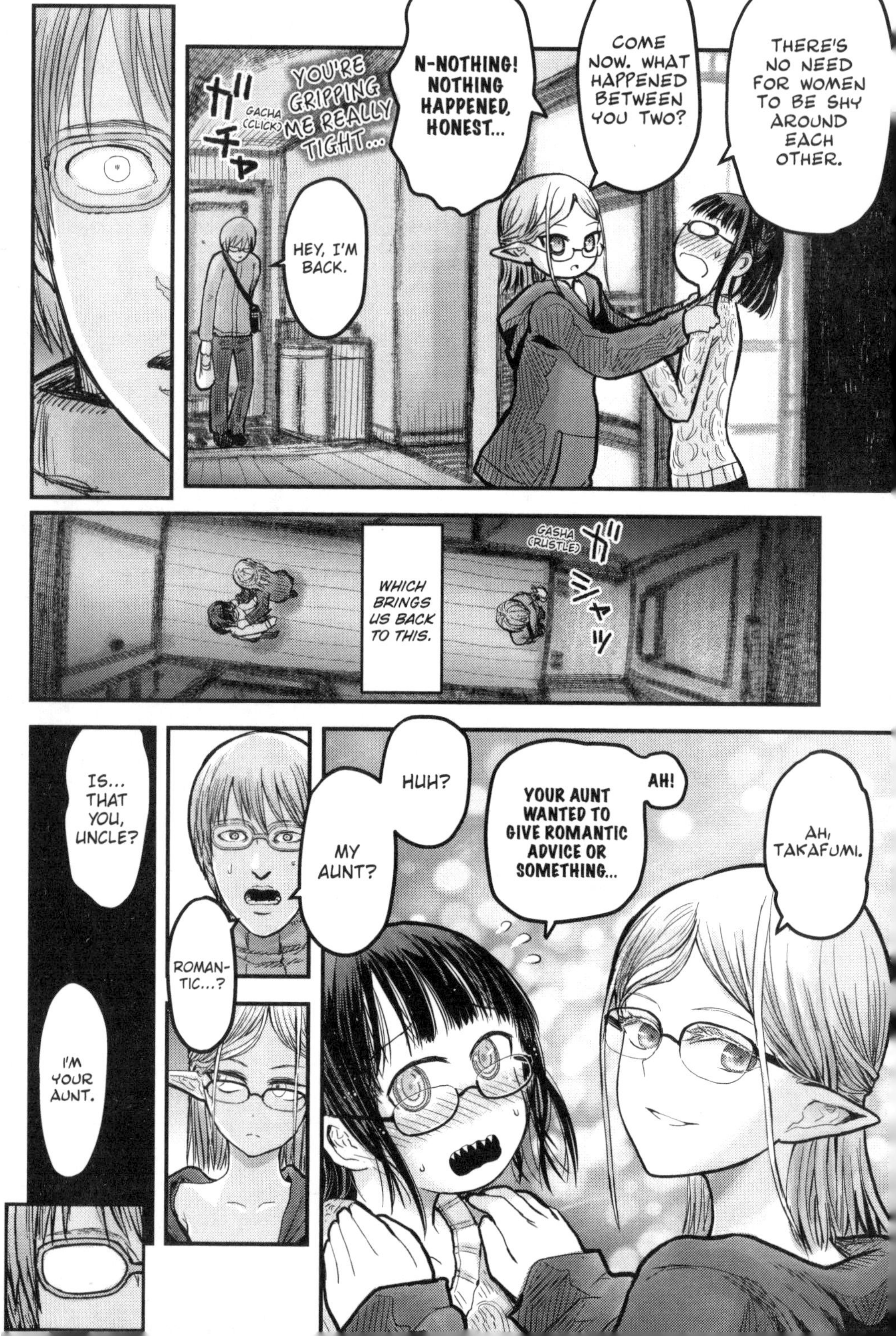
THERE'S NO NEED FOR WOMEN TO BE SHY AROUND EACH OTHER.
COME NOW. WHAT HAPPENED BETWEEN YOU TWO?
N-NOTHING! NOTHING HAPPENED, HONEST...
YOU'RE GRIPPING ME REALLY TIGHT...
ガチャ
GACHA (CLICK)
HEY, I'M BACK.
ガシャッ
GASHA (RUSTLE)
WHICH BRINGS US BACK TO THIS.
AH, TAKAFUMI.
AH!
YOUR AUNT WANTED TO GIVE ROMANTIC ADVICE OR SOMETHING...
HUH?
MY AUNT?
ROMAN-TIC...?
IS... THAT YOU, UNCLE?
I'M YOUR AUNT.

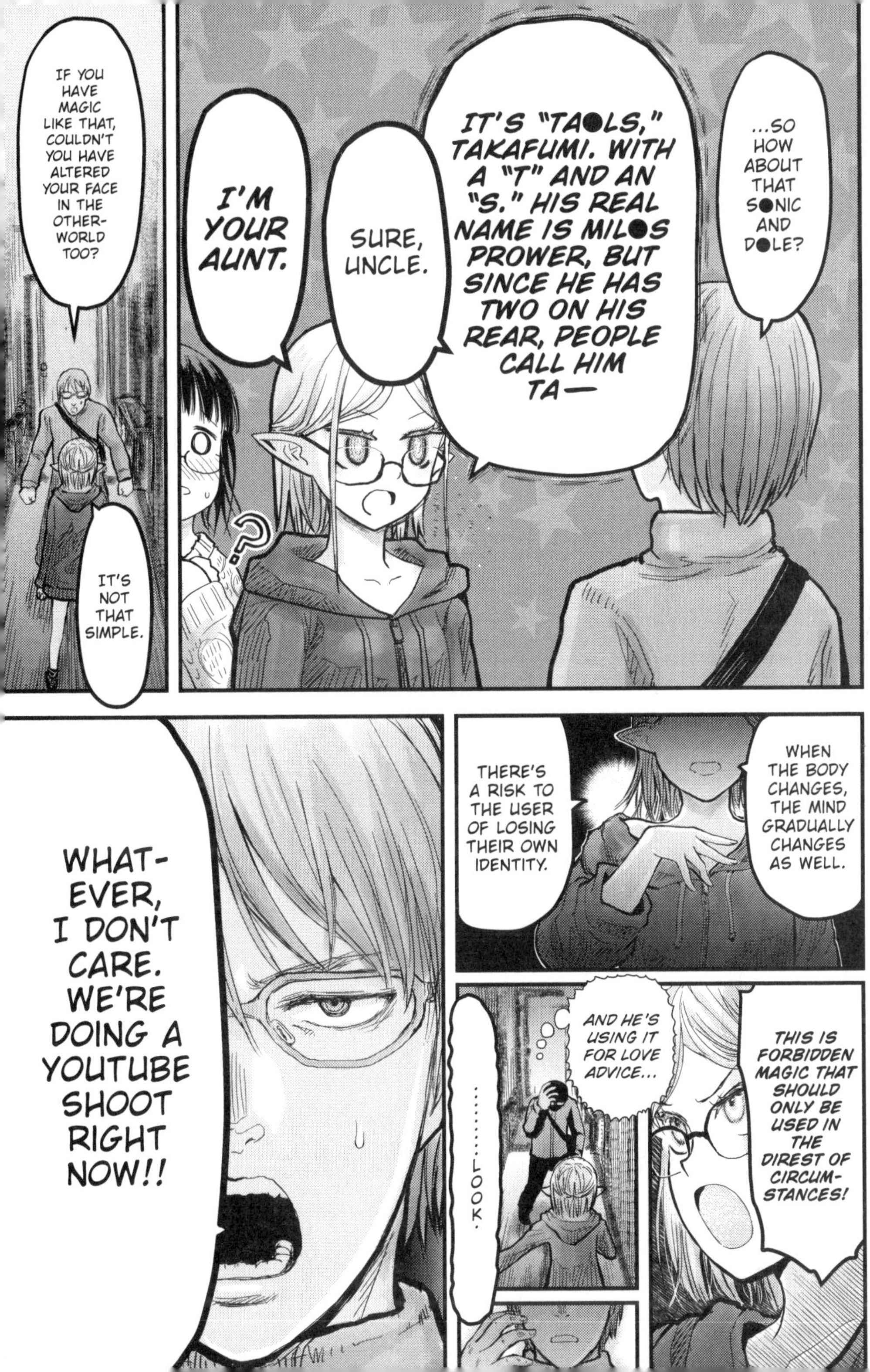
...SO HOW ABOUT THAT S●NIC AND D●LE?
IT'S "TA●LS," TAKAFUMI. WITH A "T" AND AN "S." HIS REAL NAME IS MIL●S PROWER, BUT SINCE HE HAS TWO ON HIS REAR, PEOPLE CALL HIM TA—
SURE, UNCLE.
I'M YOUR AUNT.
IF YOU HAVE MAGIC LIKE THAT, COULDN'T YOU HAVE ALTERED YOUR FACE IN THE OTHER-WORLD TOO?
IT'S NOT THAT SIMPLE.
WHEN THE BODY CHANGES, THE MIND GRADUALLY CHANGES AS WELL.
THERE'S A RISK TO THE USER OF LOSING THEIR OWN IDENTITY.
THIS IS FORBIDDEN MAGIC THAT SHOULD ONLY BE USED IN THE DIREST OF CIRCUM-STANCES!
AND HE'S USING IT FOR LOVE ADVICE...
......LOOK.
WHAT-EVER, I DON'T CARE. WE'RE DOING A YOUTUBE SHOOT RIGHT NOW!!

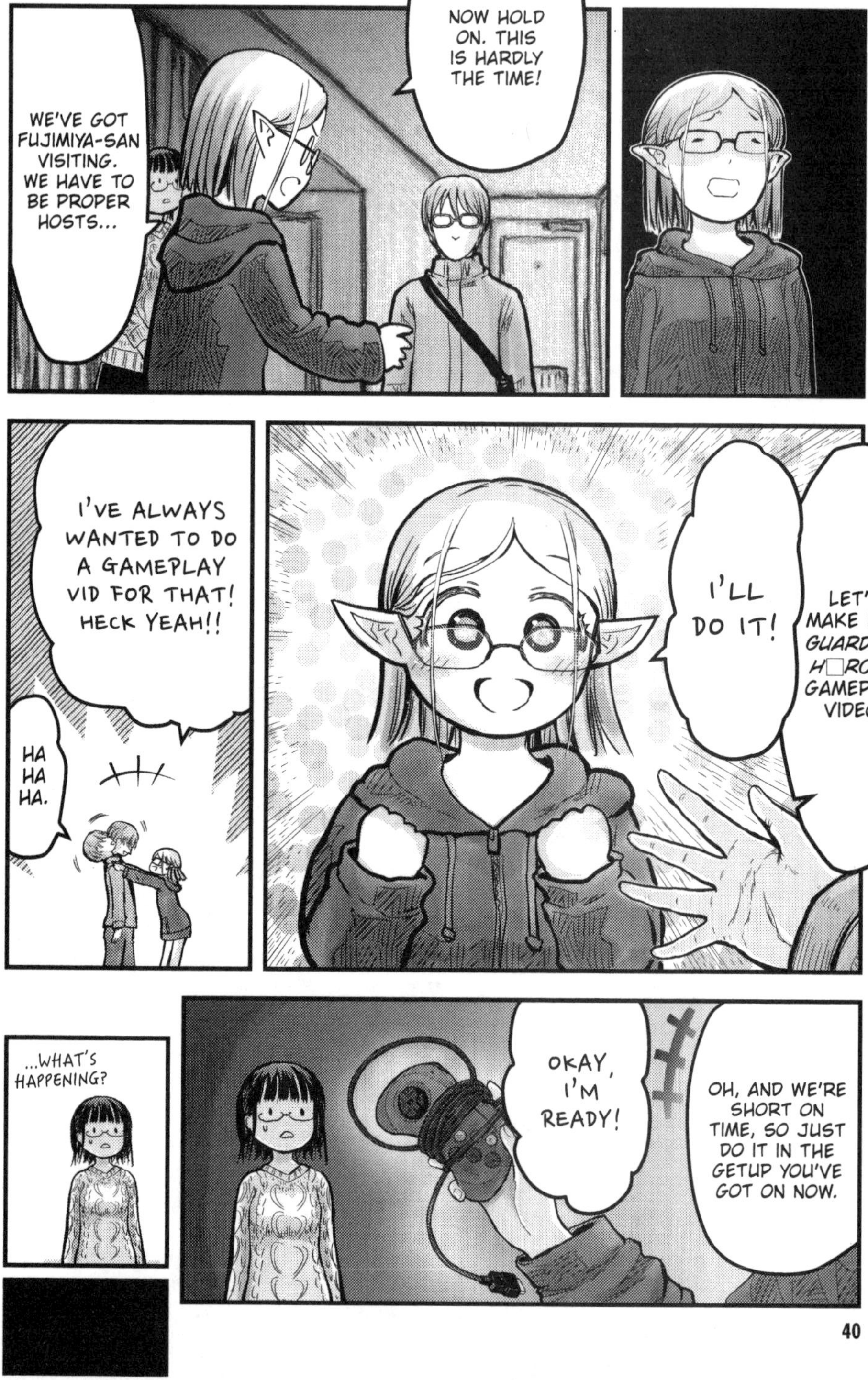
NOW HOLD ON. THIS IS HARDLY THE TIME!
WE'VE GOT FUJIMIYA-SAN VISITING. WE HAVE TO BE PROPER HOSTS...
LET'S MAKE IT A *GUARDIAN H□ROES* GAMEPLAY VIDEO.
I'LL DO IT!
I'VE ALWAYS WANTED TO DO A GAMEPLAY VID FOR THAT! HECK YEAH!!
HA HA HA.
OH, AND WE'RE SHORT ON TIME, SO JUST DO IT IN THE GETUP YOU'VE GOT ON NOW.
OKAY, I'M READY!
...WHAT'S HAPPENING?

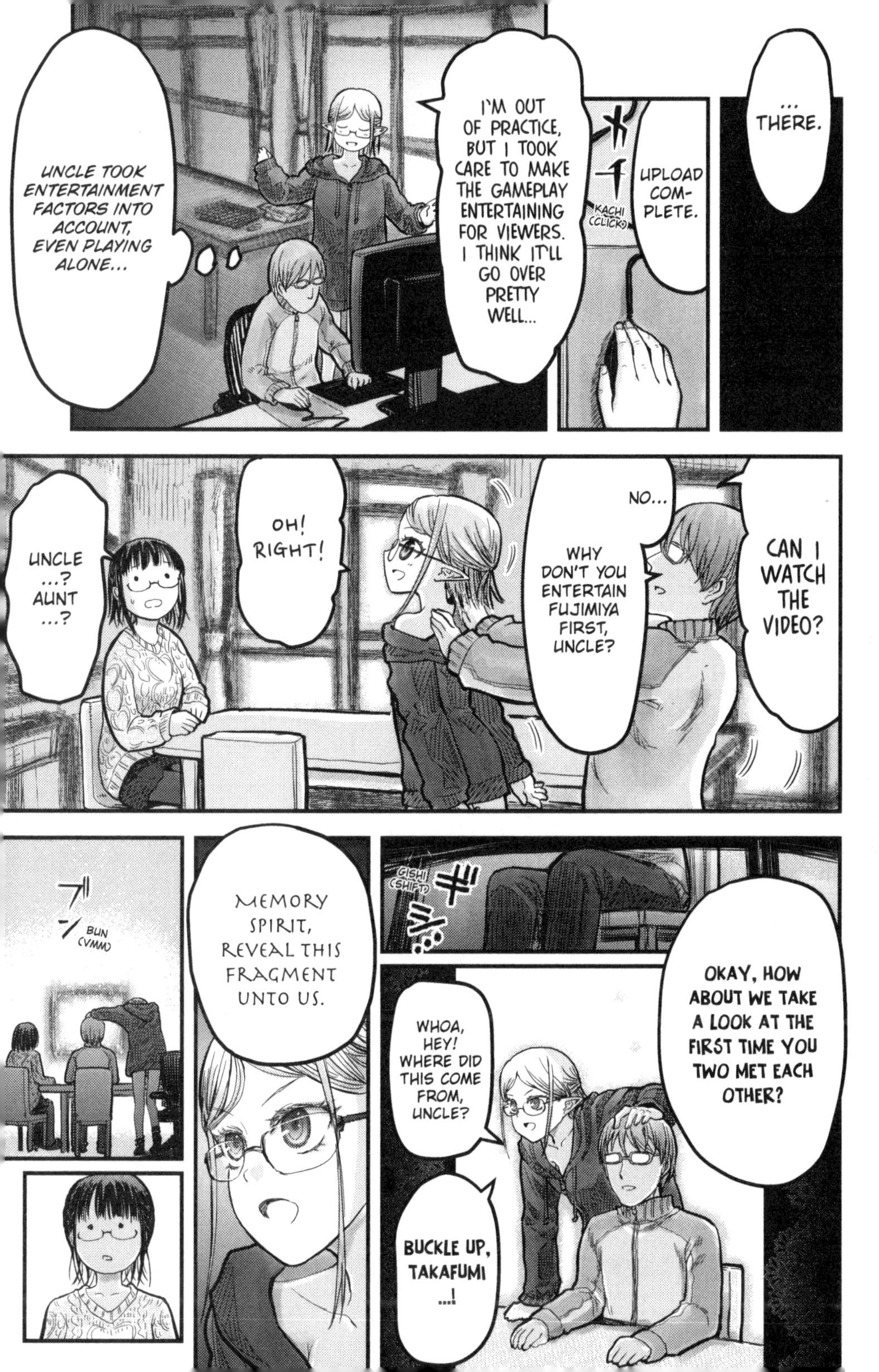
... THERE.
UPLOAD COM-PLETE.
KACHI (CLICK)
I'M OUT OF PRACTICE, BUT I TOOK CARE TO MAKE THE GAMEPLAY ENTERTAINING FOR VIEWERS. I THINK IT'LL GO OVER PRETTY WELL...
UNCLE TOOK ENTERTAINMENT FACTORS INTO ACCOUNT, EVEN PLAYING ALONE...
CAN I WATCH THE VIDEO?
NO...
WHY DON'T YOU ENTERTAIN FUJIMIYA FIRST, UNCLE?
OH! RIGHT!
UNCLE ...? AUNT ...?
GISHI (SHIFT)
OKAY, HOW ABOUT WE TAKE A LOOK AT THE FIRST TIME YOU TWO MET EACH OTHER?
WHOA, HEY! WHERE DID THIS COME FROM, UNCLE?
BUCKLE UP, TAKAFUMI ...!
MEMORY SPIRIT, REVEAL THIS FRAGMENT UNTO US.
BUN (VMM)

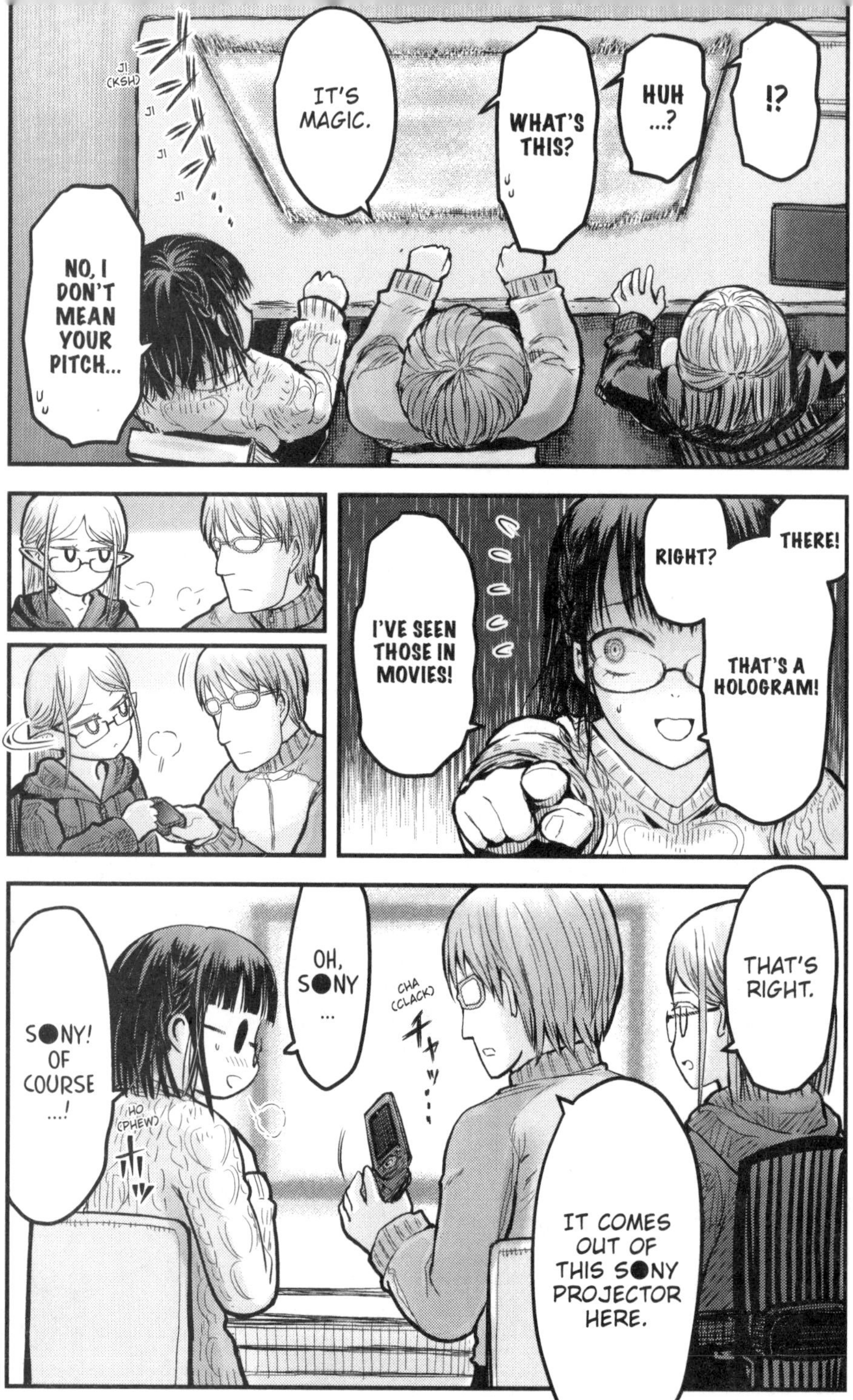
!?
HUH ...?
WHAT'S THIS?
IT'S MAGIC.
JI (KSH) JI JI JI
NO, I DON'T MEAN YOUR PITCH...
THERE!
RIGHT?
THAT'S A HOLOGRAM!
I'VE SEEN THOSE IN MOVIES!
THAT'S RIGHT.
IT COMES OUT OF THIS S●NY PROJECTOR HERE.
CHA (CLACK)
OH, S●NY ...
HO (PHEW)
S●NY! OF COURSE ...!

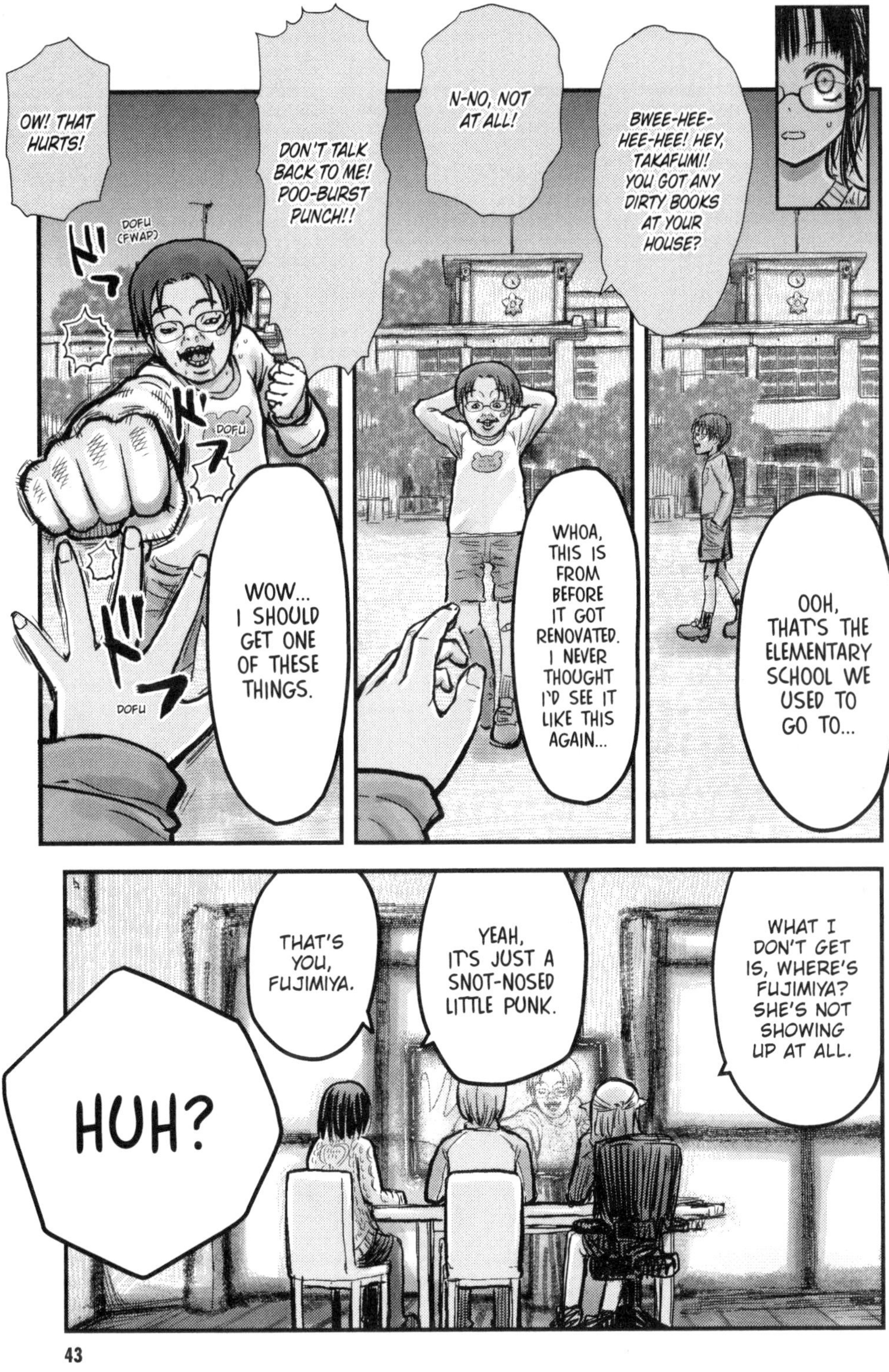
BWEE-HEE-HEE-HEE! HEY, TAKAFUMI! YOU GOT ANY DIRTY BOOKS AT YOUR HOUSE?
OOH, THAT'S THE ELEMENTARY SCHOOL WE USED TO GO TO...
N-NO, NOT AT ALL!
WHOA, THIS IS FROM BEFORE IT GOT RENOVATED. I NEVER THOUGHT I'D SEE IT LIKE THIS AGAIN...
DON'T TALK BACK TO ME! POO-BURST PUNCH!!
OW! THAT HURTS!
DOFU (FWAP)
DOFU
DOFU
WOW... I SHOULD GET ONE OF THESE THINGS.
WHAT I DON'T GET IS, WHERE'S FUJIMIYA? SHE'S NOT SHOWING UP AT ALL.
YEAH, IT'S JUST A SNOT-NOSED LITTLE PUNK.
THAT'S YOU, FUJIMIYA.
HUH?

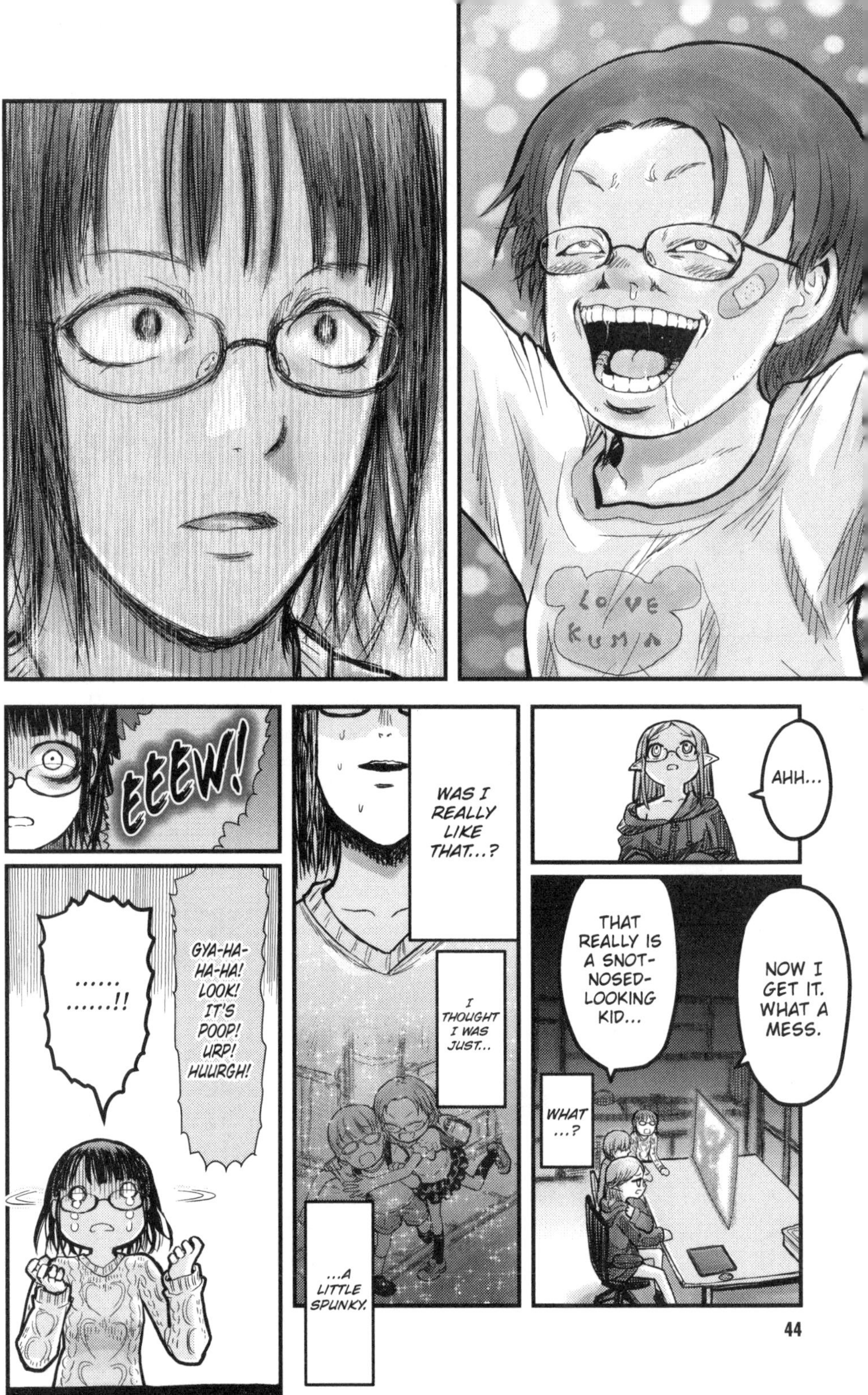
LOVE KUMA
AHH...
NOW I GET IT. WHAT A MESS.
THAT REALLY IS A SNOT-NOSED-LOOKING KID...
WHAT ...?
WAS I REALLY LIKE THAT...?
I THOUGHT I WAS JUST...
...A LITTLE SPUNKY.
EEEW!
GYA-HA-HA-HA! LOOK! IT'S POOP! URP! HUURGH!
....!!

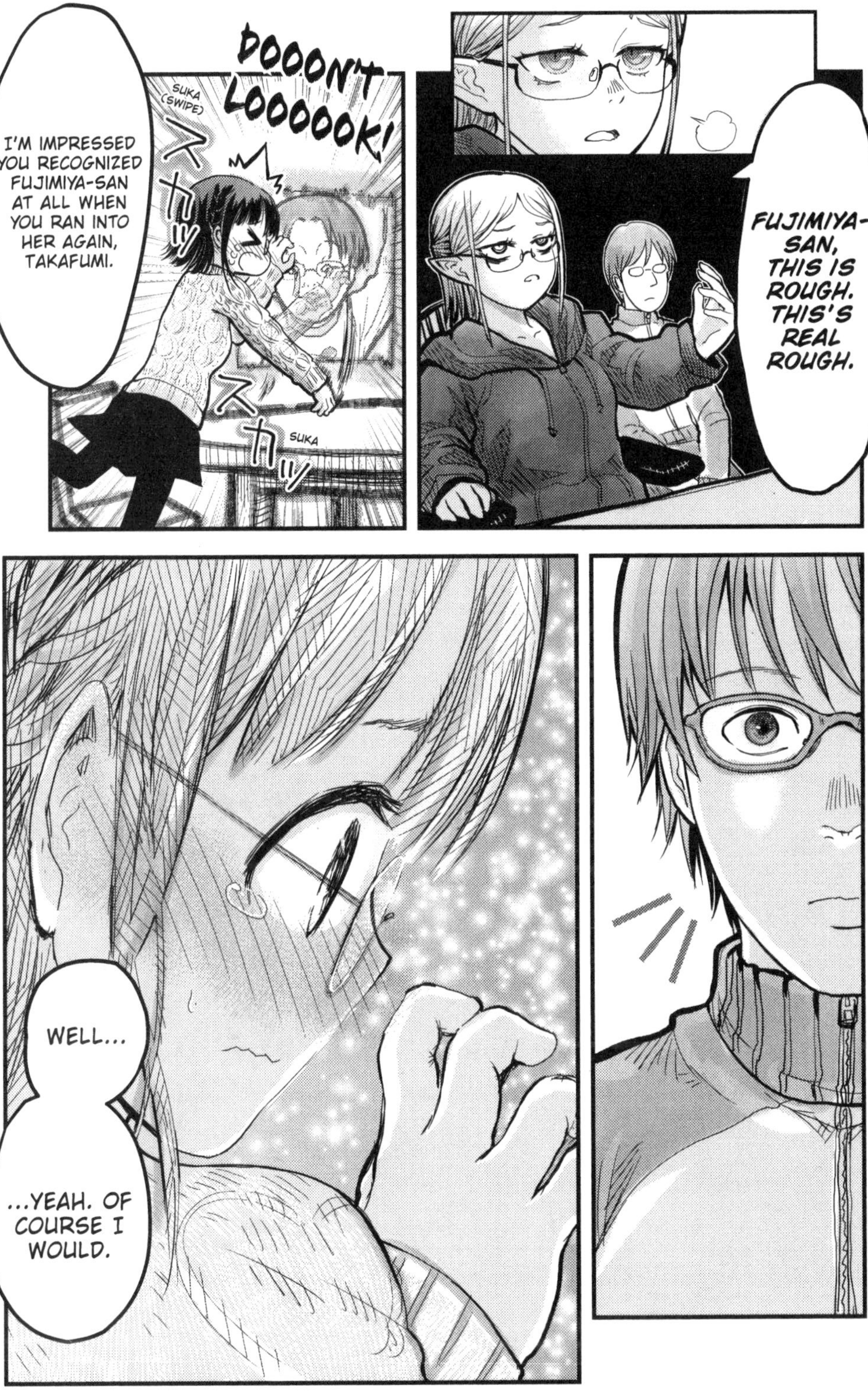
FUJIMIYA-SAN, THIS IS ROUGH. THIS'S REAL ROUGH.
DOOON'T LOOOOOOK!
SUKA (SWIPE)
I'M IMPRESSED YOU RECOGNIZED FUJIMIYA-SAN AT ALL WHEN YOU RAN INTO HER AGAIN, TAKAFUMI.
SUKA
WELL...
...YEAH. OF COURSE I WOULD.

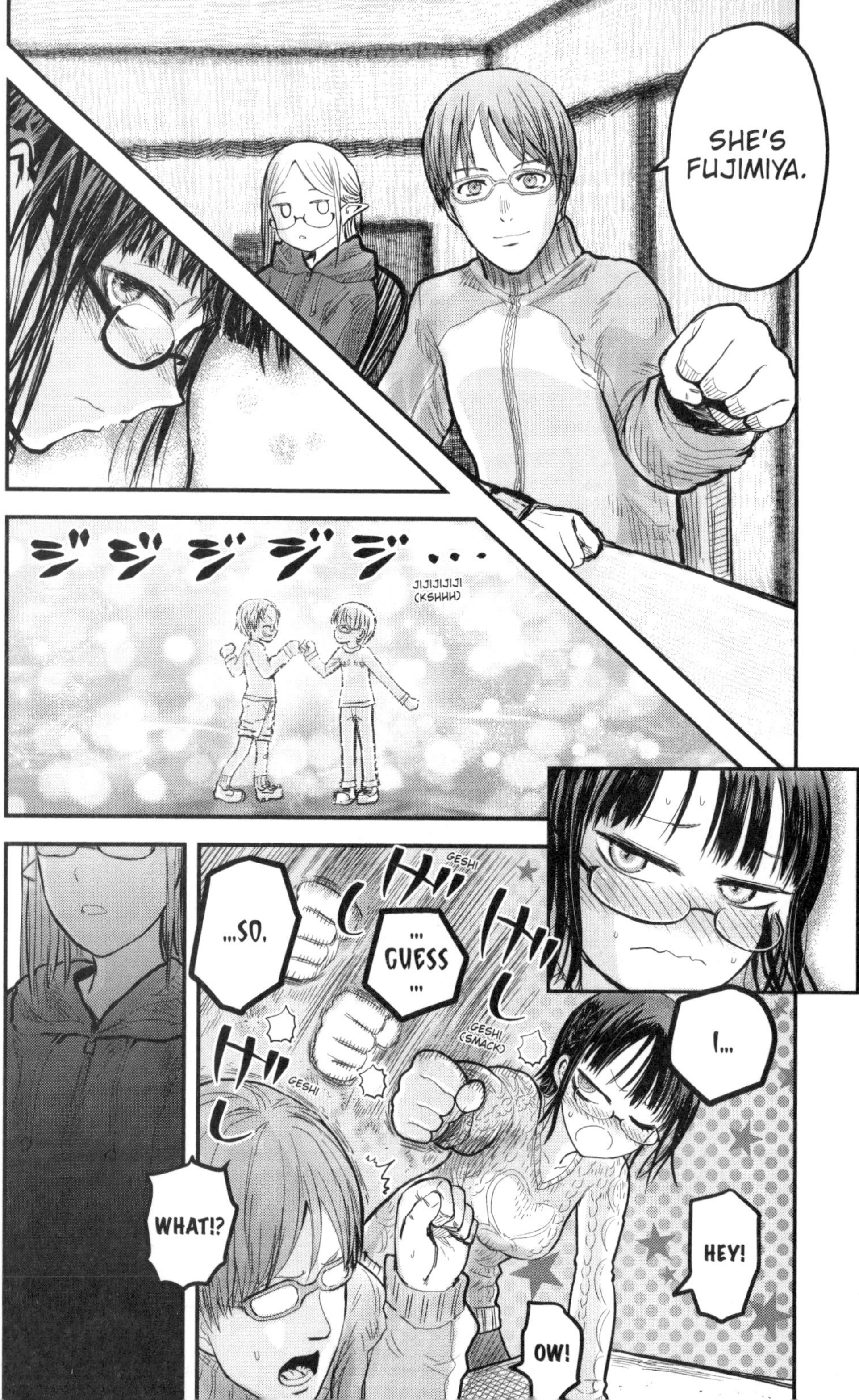

SHE'S FUJIMIYA.
ジジジジジ...
JIJIJIJIJI (KSHHH)
I...
...GUESS...
...SO.
ゲシ
GESHI
げし
GESHI (SMACK)
ゲシ
GESHI
HEY!
OW!
WHAT!?

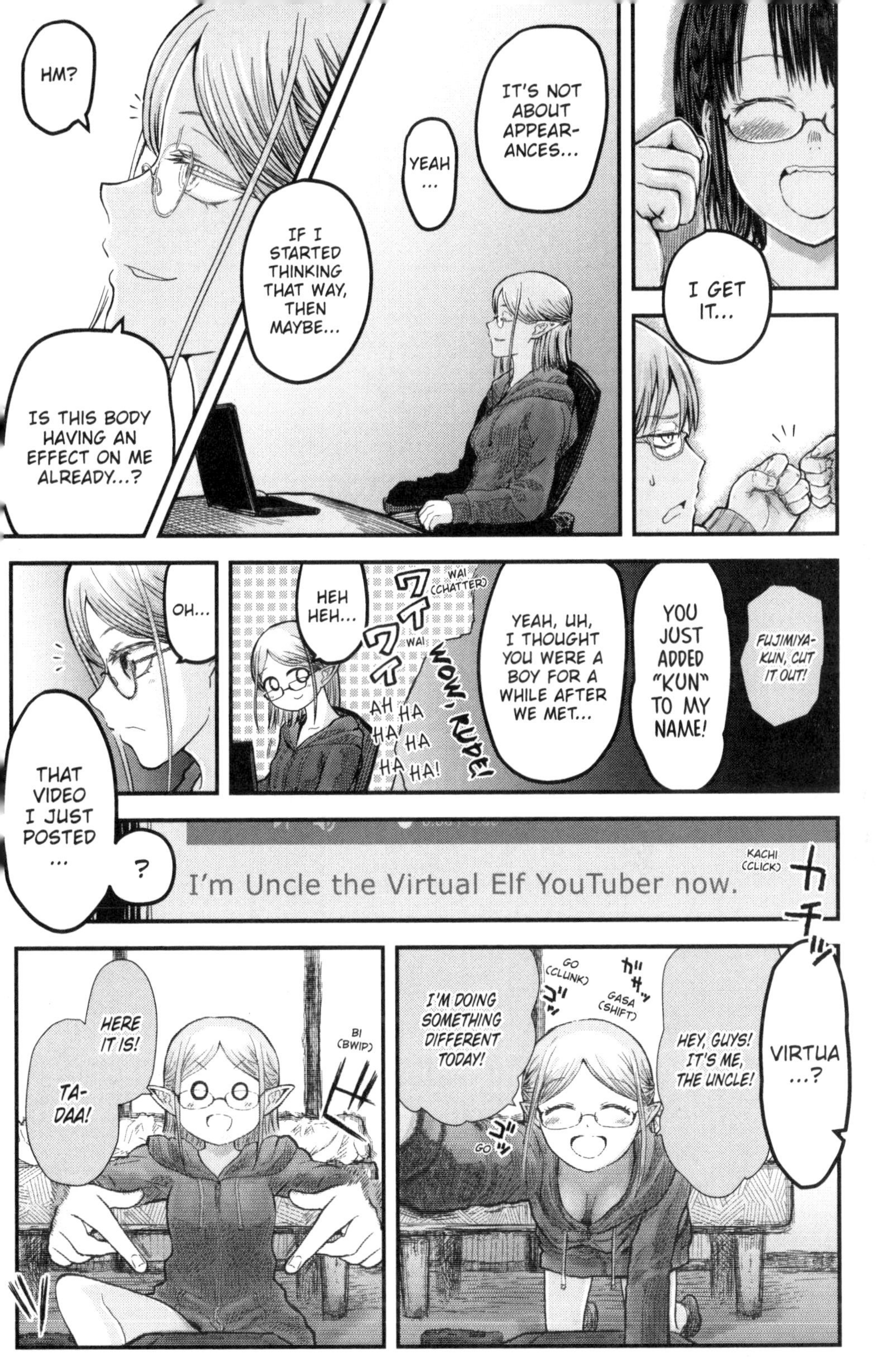
I GET IT...
IT'S NOT ABOUT APPEARANCES...
YEAH...
IF I STARTED THINKING THAT WAY, THEN MAYBE...
HM?
IS THIS BODY HAVING AN EFFECT ON ME ALREADY...?
FUJIMIYA-KUN, CUT IT OUT!
YOU JUST ADDED "KUN" TO MY NAME!
YEAH, UH, I THOUGHT YOU WERE A BOY FOR A WHILE AFTER WE MET...
WAI (CHATTER)
WAI
WOW, RUDE!
HEH HEH...
AH HA HA! HA HA HA HA!
OH...
THAT VIDEO I JUST POSTED...
?
KACHI (CLICK)
I'm Uncle the Virtual Elf YouTuber now.
VIRTUA...?
HEY, GUYS! IT'S ME, THE UNCLE!
GASA (SHIFT)
GO (CLUNK)
I'M DOING SOMETHING DIFFERENT TODAY!
GO
BI (BWIP)
HERE IT IS!
TA-DAA!

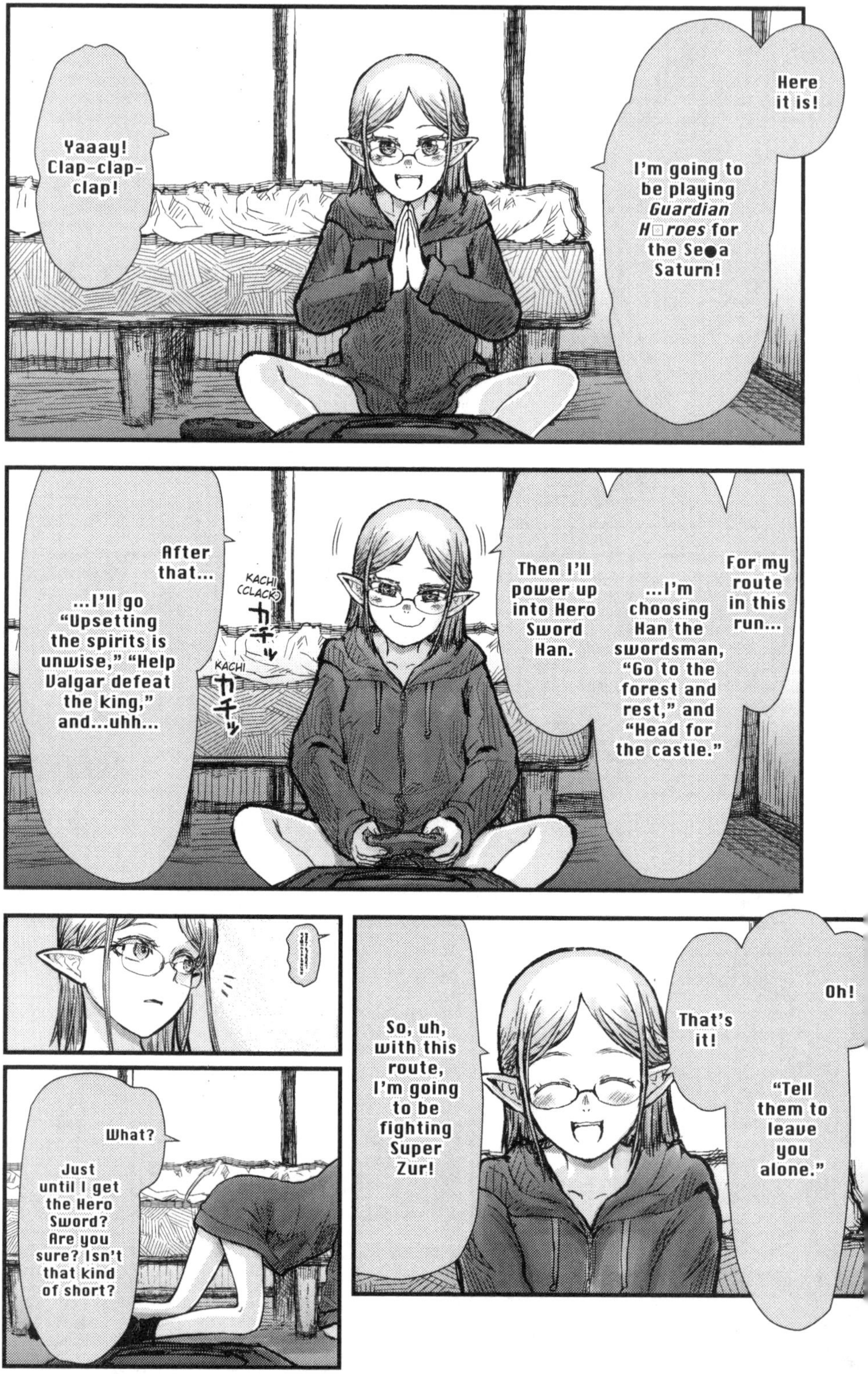
Here it is!
I'm going to be playing *Guardian H☐roes* for the Se●a Saturn!
Yaaay! Clap-clap-clap!
For my route in this run...
...I'm choosing Han the swordsman, "Go to the forest and rest," and "Head for the castle."
Then I'll power up into Hero Sword Han.
KACHI (CLACK)
カチッ
KACHI
カチッ
After that...
...I'll go "Upsetting the spirits is unwise," "Help Valgar defeat the king," and...uhh...
Oh!
That's it!
"Tell them to leave you alone."
So, uh, with this route, I'm going to be fighting Super Zur!
What?
Just until I get the Hero Sword? Are you sure? Isn't that kind of short?

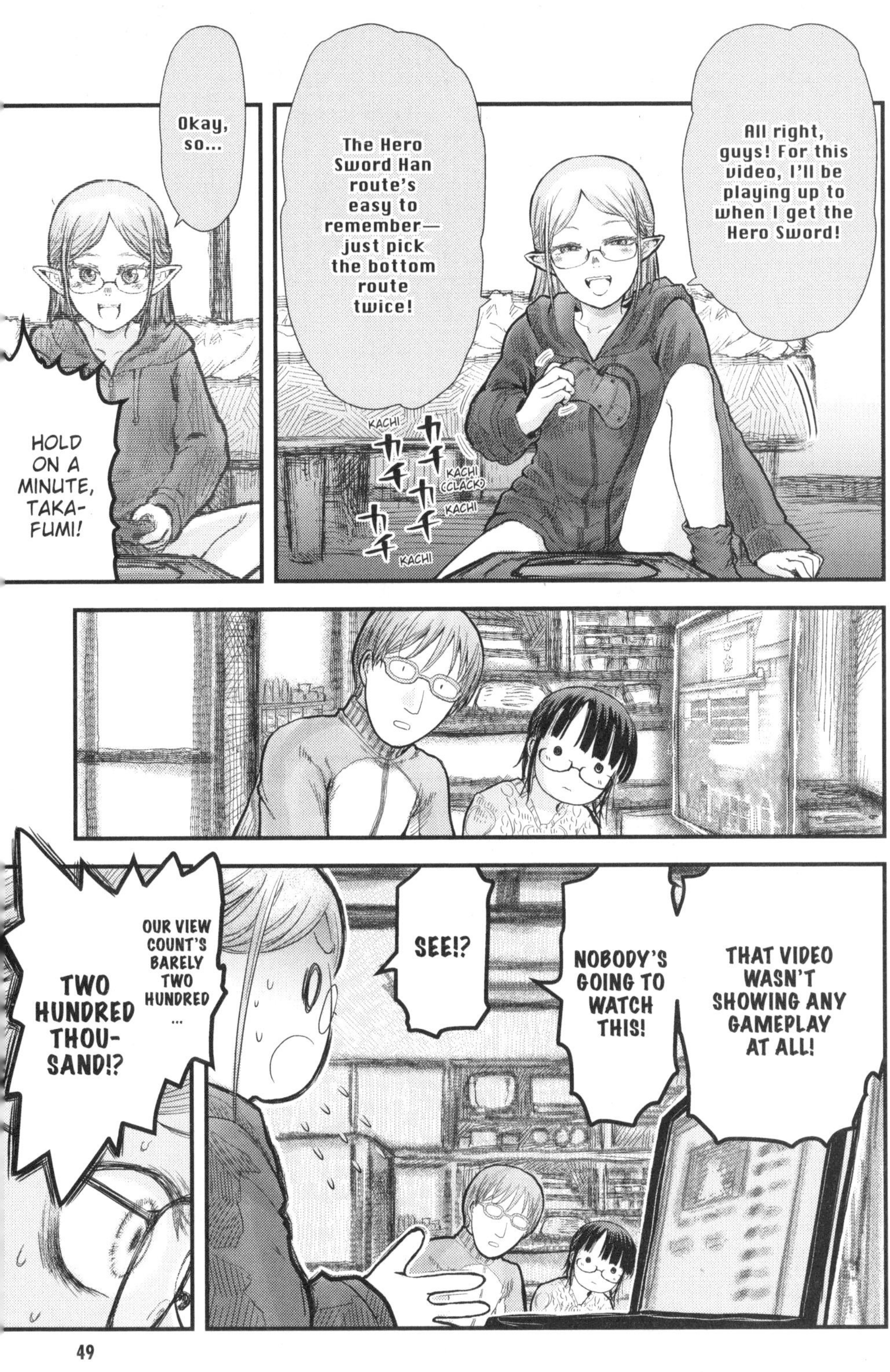
All right, guys! For this video, I'll be playing up to when I get the Hero Sword!
The Hero Sword Han route's easy to remember—just pick the bottom route twice!
カチ KACHI
カチ KACHI (CLACK)
カチ KACHI
カチ KACHI
カチ
Okay, so...
HOLD ON A MINUTE, TAKA-FUMI!
THAT VIDEO WASN'T SHOWING ANY GAMEPLAY AT ALL!
NOBODY'S GOING TO WATCH THIS!
SEE!?
OUR VIEW COUNT'S BARELY TWO HUNDRED ...
TWO HUNDRED THOU-SAND!?

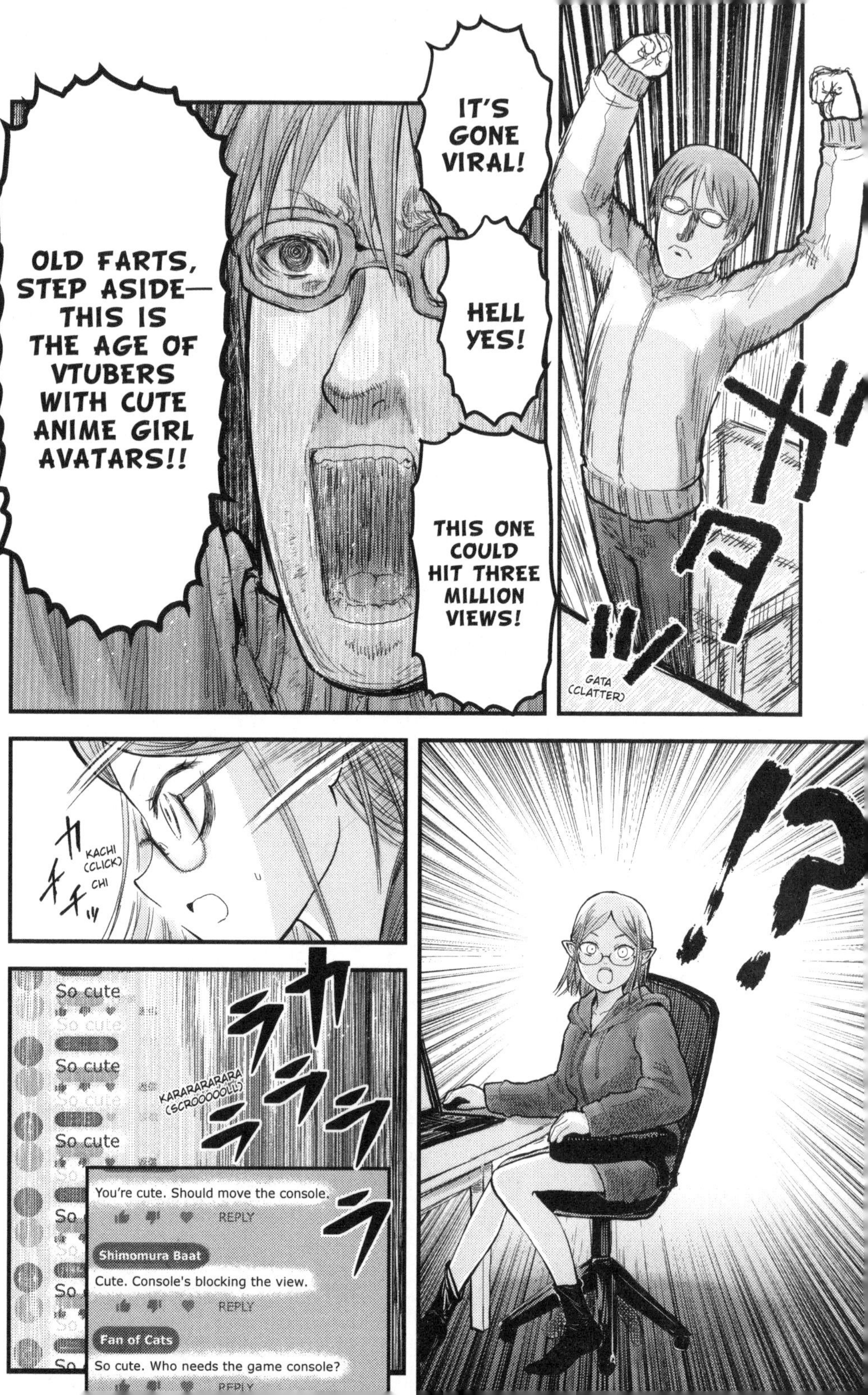
GATA (CLATTER)
IT'S GONE VIRAL!
HELL YES!
THIS ONE COULD HIT THREE MILLION VIEWS!
OLD FARTS, STEP ASIDE—THIS IS THE AGE OF VTUBERS WITH CUTE ANIME GIRL AVATARS!!
!?
KACHI (CLICK) CHI
KARARARARARA (SCROOOOOLL)
So cute
So cute
So cute
You're cute. Should move the console.
REPLY
Shimomura Baat
Cute. Console's blocking the view.
REPLY
Fan of Cats
So cute. Who needs the game console?
REPLY

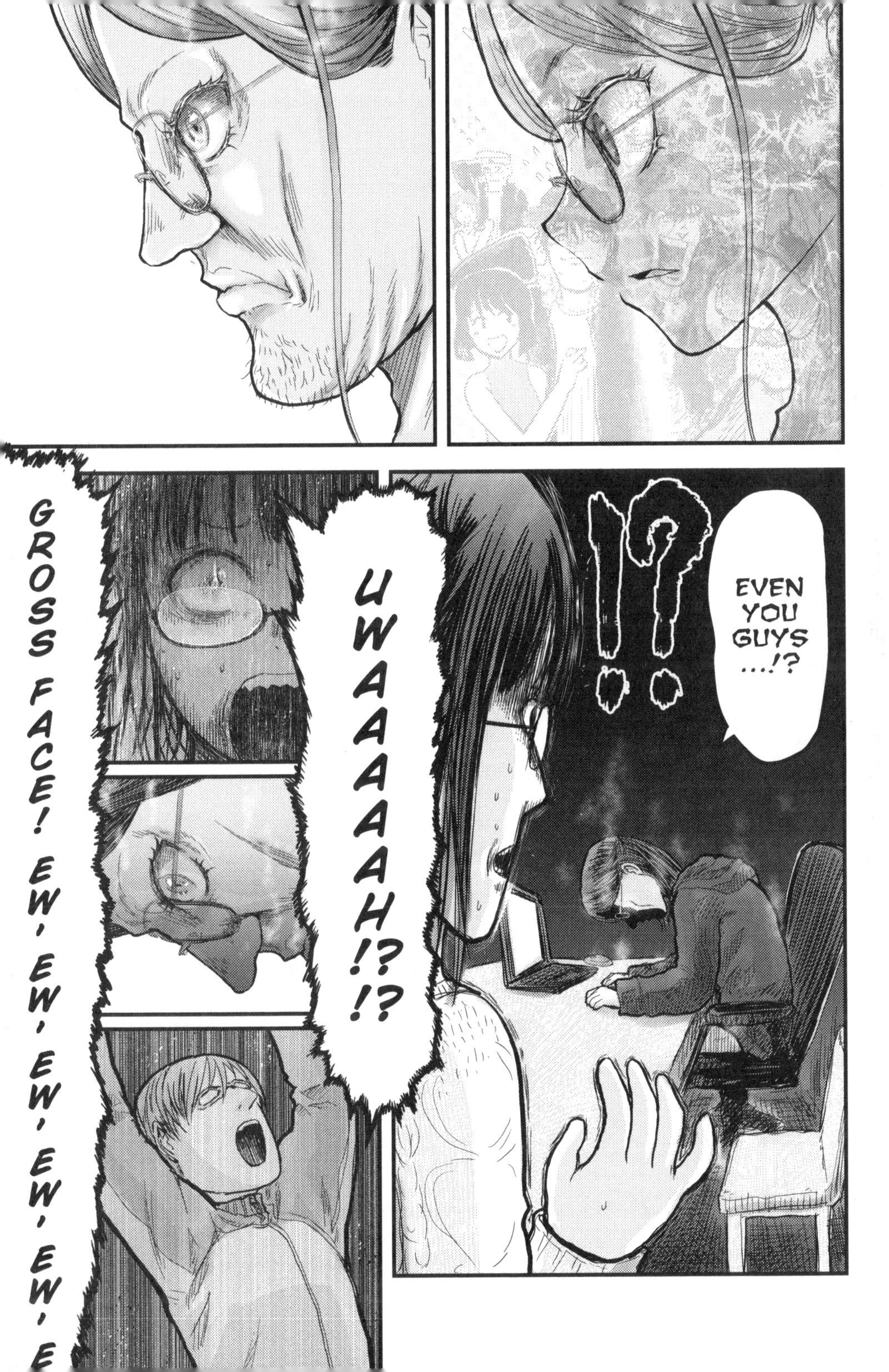
!?
EVEN YOU GUYS ...!?
UWAAAAAAH!?!?
GROSS FACE! EW, EW, EW, EW, EW, E

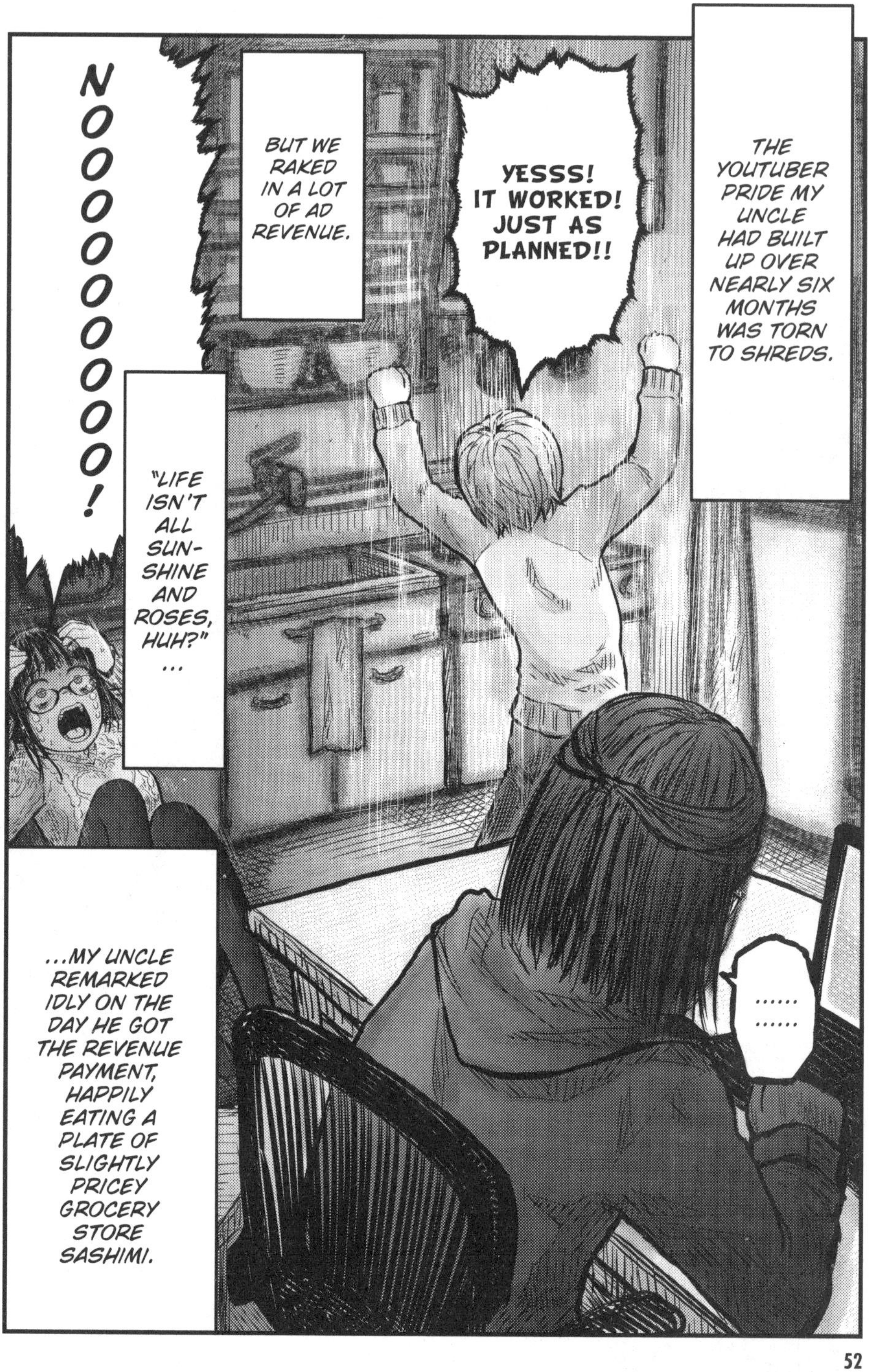
THE YOUTUBER PRIDE MY UNCLE HAD BUILT UP OVER NEARLY SIX MONTHS WAS TORN TO SHREDS.
YESSS! IT WORKED! JUST AS PLANNED!!
BUT WE RAKED IN A LOT OF AD REVENUE.
NOOOOOOOOOOOOO!
"LIFE ISN'T ALL SUN-SHINE AND ROSES, HUH?" ...
...MY UNCLE REMARKED IDLY ON THE DAY HE GOT THE REVENUE PAYMENT, HAPPILY EATING A PLATE OF SLIGHTLY PRICEY GROCERY STORE SASHIMI.
....

Virtual YouTuber

A form of YouTuber.
Typically does video streaming with a 2D or 3D CG avatar.
They're also referred to as VTubers.

TIPS

UNCLE from ANOTHER WORLD

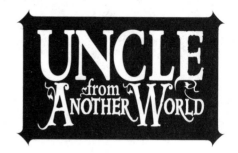

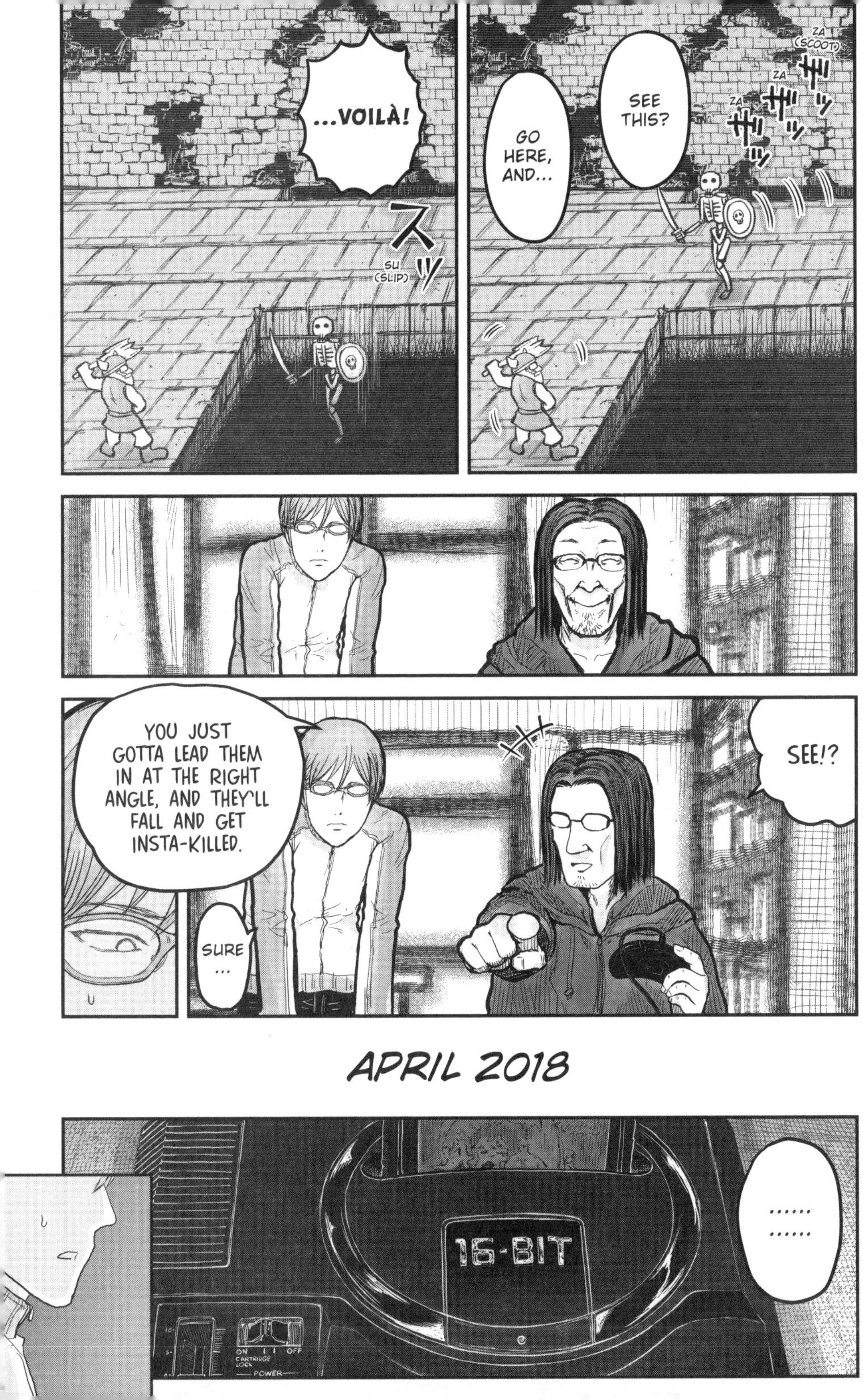
SEE THIS?
GO HERE, AND...
ZA (SCOOT)
ZA
ZA
...VOILÀ!
SU (SLIP)
SEE!?
YOU JUST GOTTA LEAD THEM IN AT THE RIGHT ANGLE, AND THEY'LL FALL AND GET INSTA-KILLED.
SURE...
APRIL 2018
....
16-BIT
ON OFF CARTRIDGE LOCK
POWER

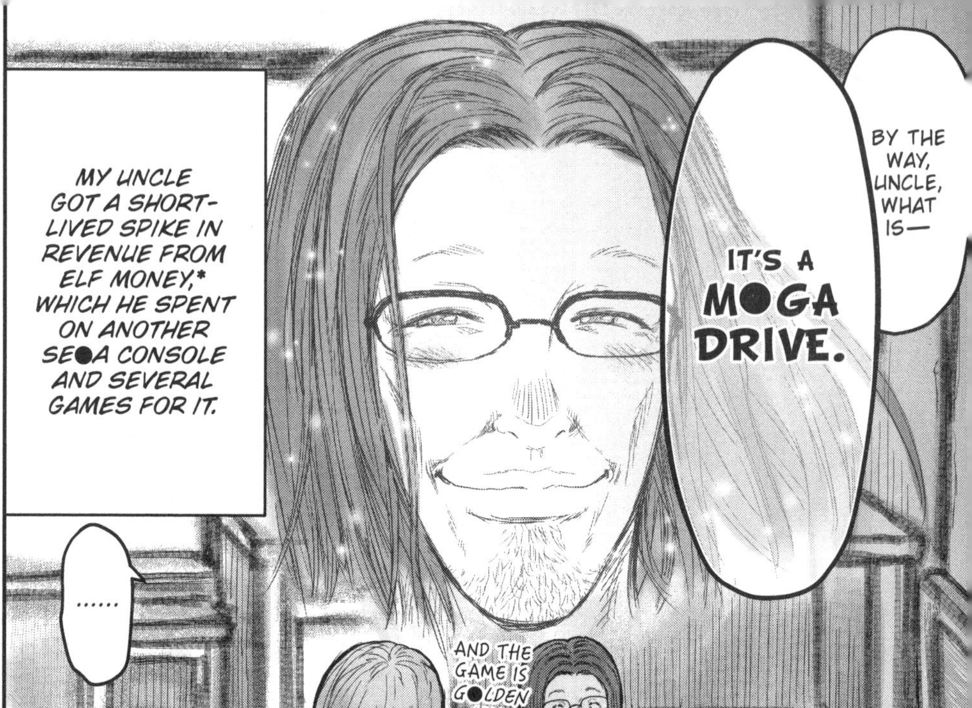
BY THE WAY, UNCLE, WHAT IS—
IT'S A MOGA DRIVE.
MY UNCLE GOT A SHORT-LIVED SPIKE IN REVENUE FROM ELF MONEY,* WHICH HE SPENT ON ANOTHER SE●A CONSOLE AND SEVERAL GAMES FOR IT.
......
AND THE GAME IS G●LDEN AXE!
HE HAD THIS TWINKLE IN HIS EYE THAT MADE IT HARD FOR ME TO SAY NO.

*SEE CHAPTER 9

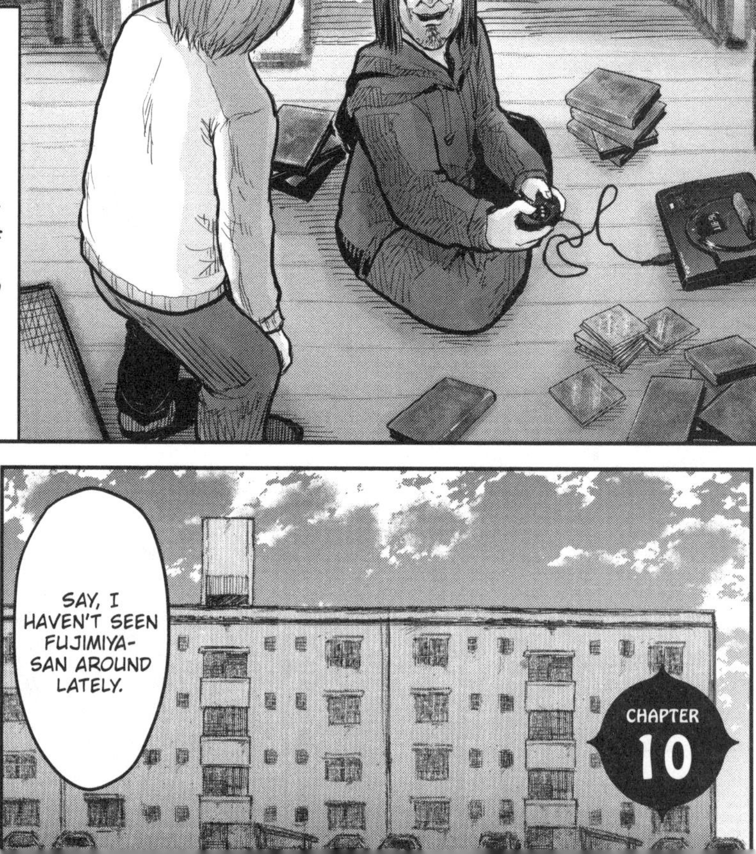
SAY, I HAVEN'T SEEN FUJIMIYA-SAN AROUND LATELY.
CHAPTER 10

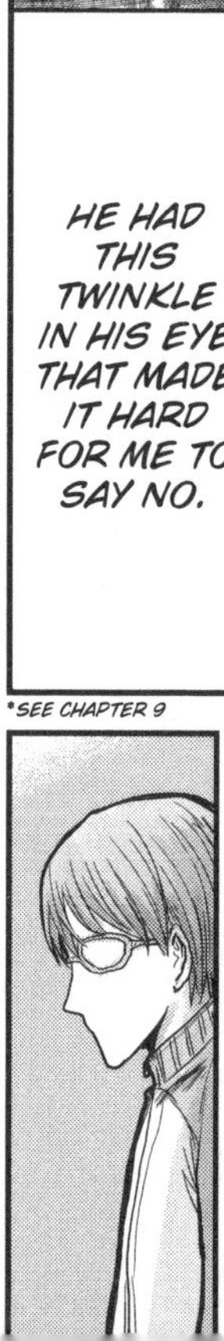

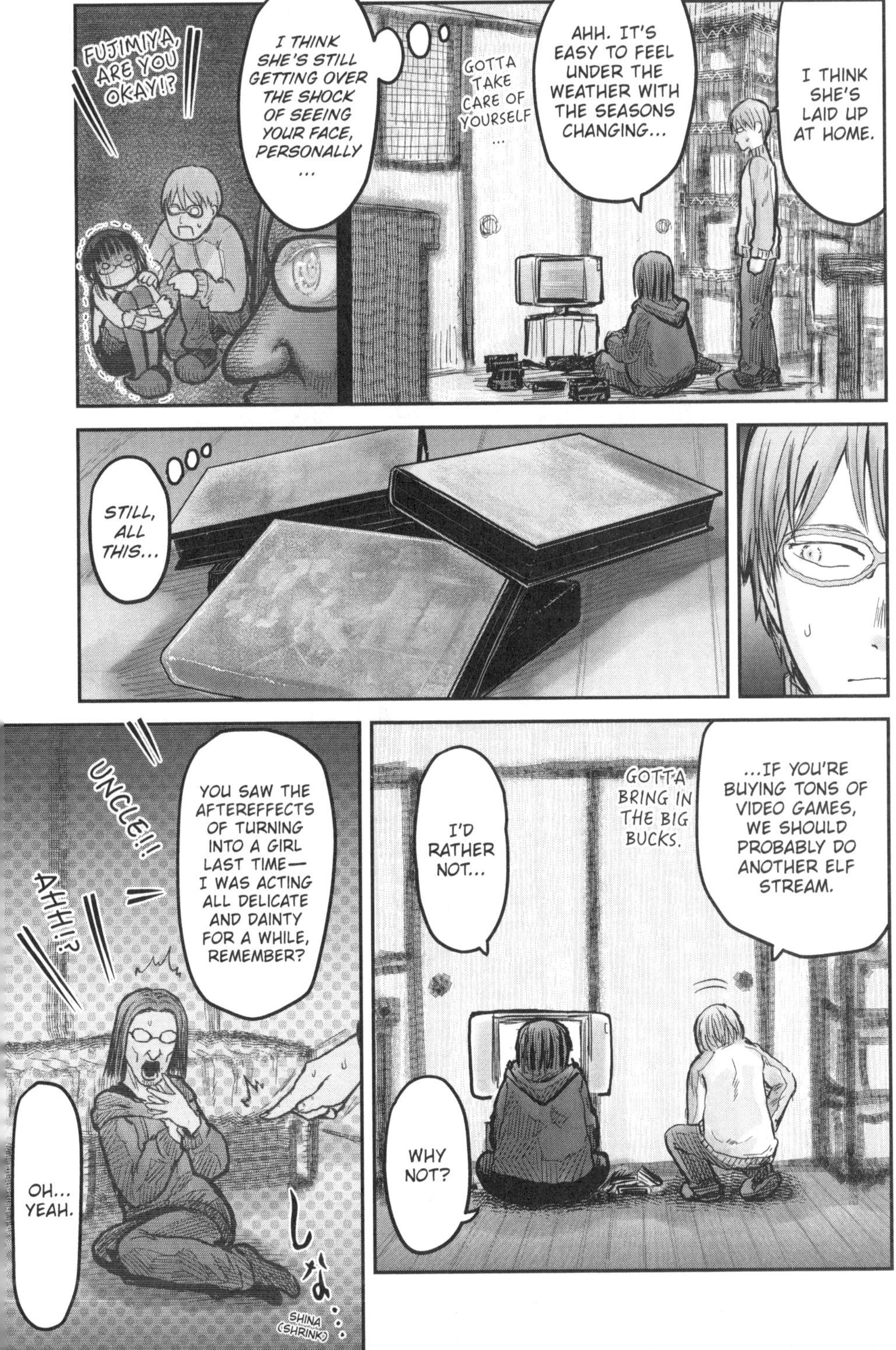
I THINK SHE'S LAID UP AT HOME.
AHH. IT'S EASY TO FEEL UNDER THE WEATHER WITH THE SEASONS CHANGING...
GOTTA TAKE CARE OF YOURSELF...
I THINK SHE'S STILL GETTING OVER THE SHOCK OF SEEING YOUR FACE, PERSONALLY...
FUJIMIYA, ARE YOU OKAY!?
STILL, ALL THIS...
...IF YOU'RE BUYING TONS OF VIDEO GAMES, WE SHOULD PROBABLY DO ANOTHER ELF STREAM.
GOTTA BRING IN THE BIG BUCKS.
I'D RATHER NOT...
WHY NOT?
YOU SAW THE AFTEREFFECTS OF TURNING INTO A GIRL LAST TIME— I WAS ACTING ALL DELICATE AND DAINTY FOR A WHILE, REMEMBER?
UNCLE!!!
AHH!?
OH... YEAH.
しな...
SHINA (SHRINK)

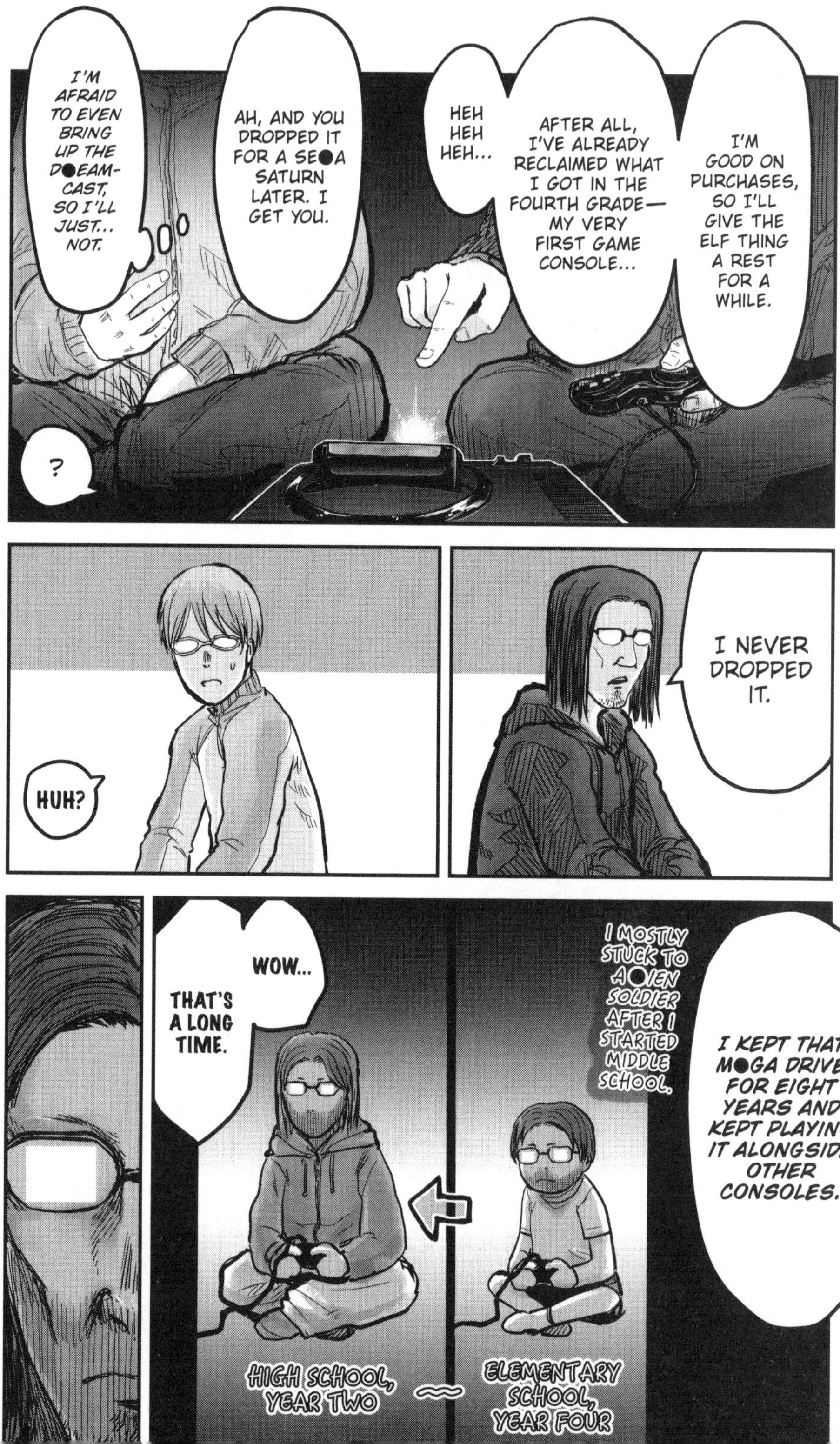
I'M GOOD ON PURCHASES, SO I'LL GIVE THE ELF THING A REST FOR A WHILE.
AFTER ALL, I'VE ALREADY RECLAIMED WHAT I GOT IN THE FOURTH GRADE—MY VERY FIRST GAME CONSOLE...
HEH HEH HEH...
AH, AND YOU DROPPED IT FOR A SE●A SATURN LATER. I GET YOU.
I'M AFRAID TO EVEN BRING UP THE D●EAM-CAST, SO I'LL JUST... NOT.
?
I NEVER DROPPED IT.
HUH?
I KEPT THAT M●GA DRIVE FOR EIGHT YEARS AND KEPT PLAYING IT ALONGSIDE OTHER CONSOLES.
I MOSTLY STUCK TO A○IEN SOLDIER AFTER I STARTED MIDDLE SCHOOL.
ELEMENTARY SCHOOL, YEAR FOUR
HIGH SCHOOL, YEAR TWO
WOW...
THAT'S A LONG TIME.

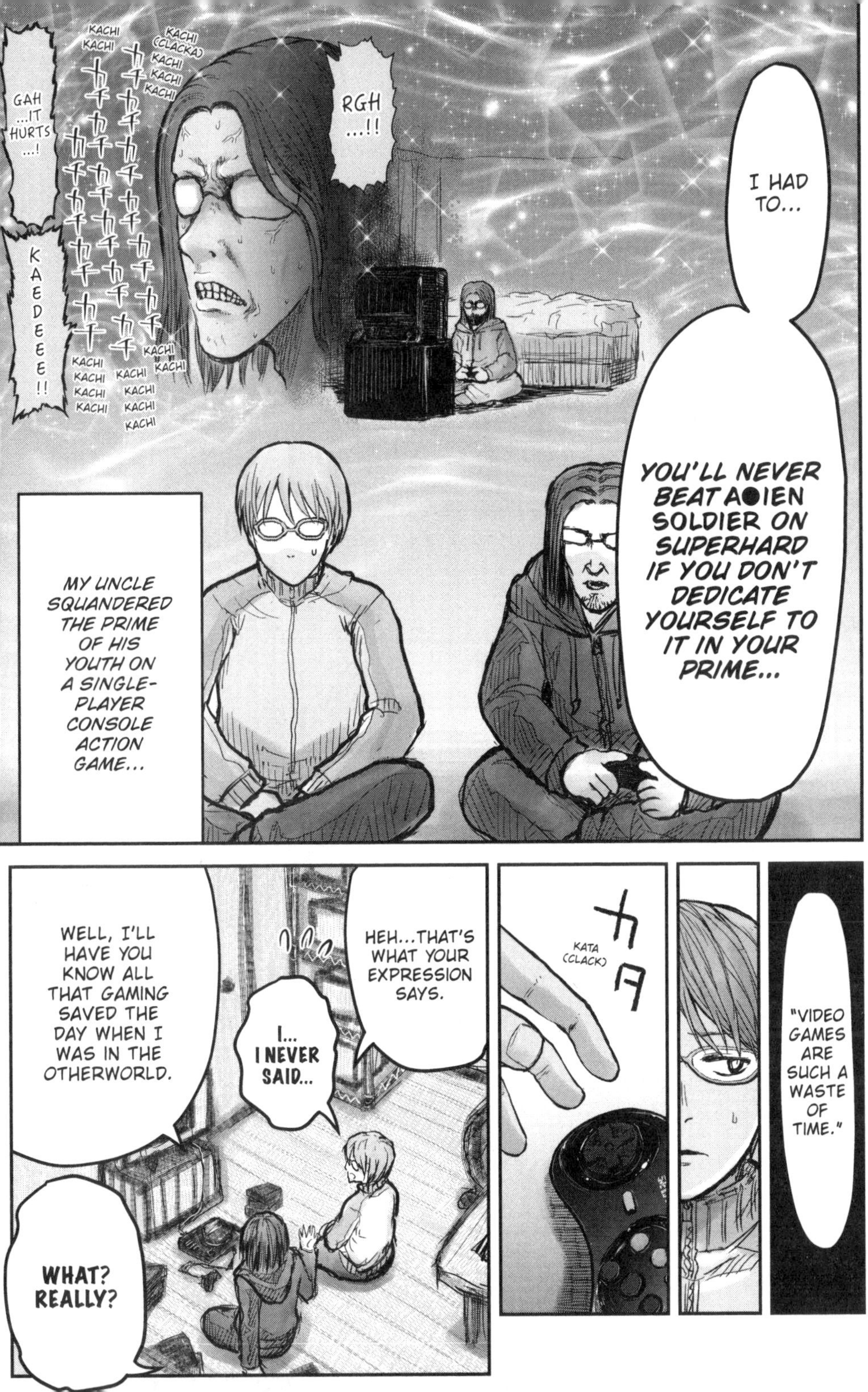
I HAD TO...
RGH ...!!
KACHI (CLACKA) KACHI KACHI KACHI
KACHI KACHI
GAH ...IT HURTS ...!
KAEDEEE!!
KACHI KACHI
KACHI KACHI KACHI KACHI
KACHI KACHI KACHI KACHI
YOU'LL NEVER BEAT A●IEN SOLDIER ON SUPERHARD IF YOU DON'T DEDICATE YOURSELF TO IT IN YOUR PRIME...
MY UNCLE SQUANDERED THE PRIME OF HIS YOUTH ON A SINGLE-PLAYER CONSOLE ACTION GAME...
"VIDEO GAMES ARE SUCH A WASTE OF TIME."
KATA (CLACK)
HEH...THAT'S WHAT YOUR EXPRESSION SAYS.
I... I NEVER SAID...
WELL, I'LL HAVE YOU KNOW ALL THAT GAMING SAVED THE DAY WHEN I WAS IN THE OTHERWORLD.
WHAT? REALLY?

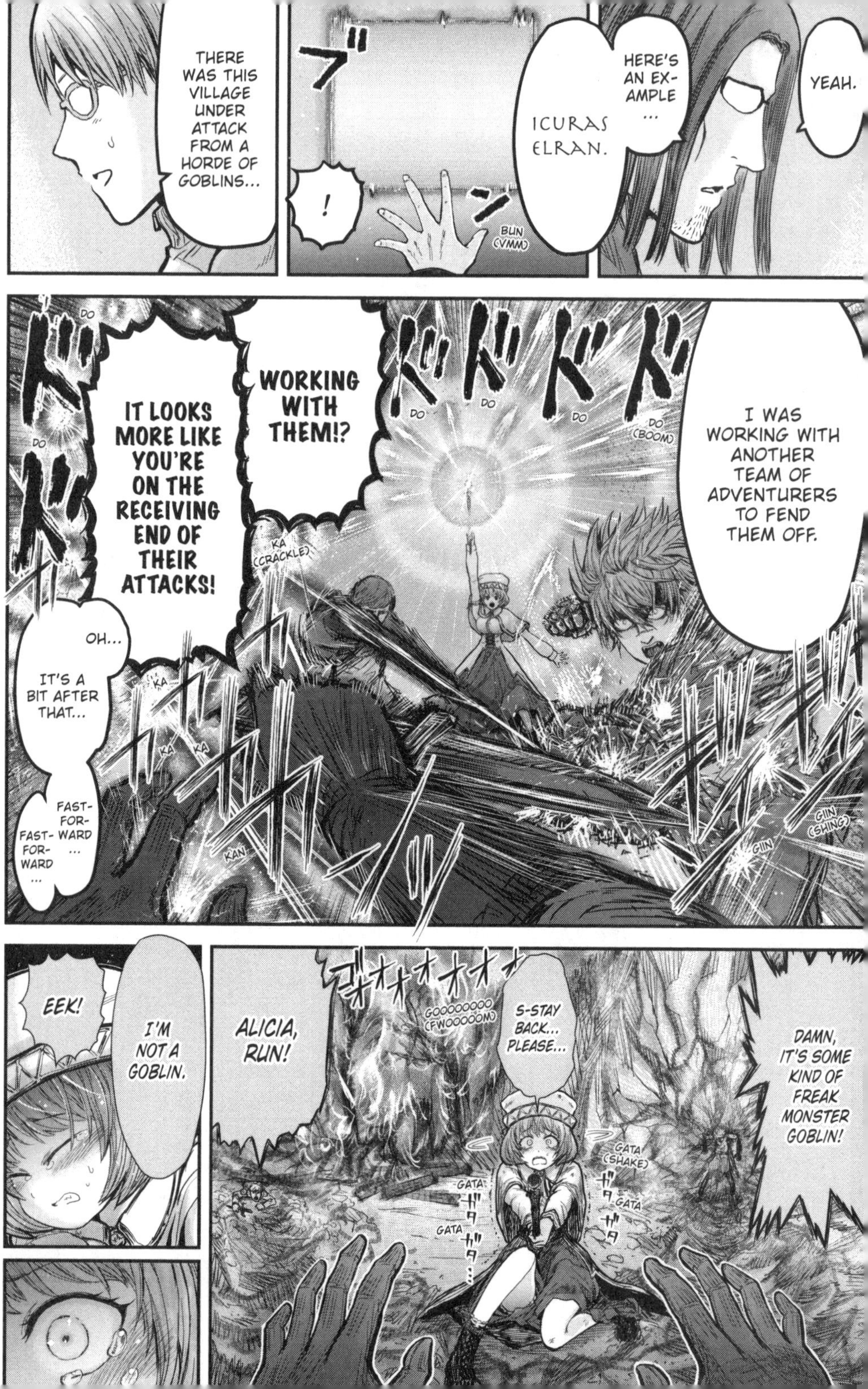
YEAH.
HERE'S AN EX-AMPLE...
ICURAS ELRAN.
BUN (VMM)
!
THERE WAS THIS VILLAGE UNDER ATTACK FROM A HORDE OF GOBLINS...
I WAS WORKING WITH ANOTHER TEAM OF ADVENTURERS TO FEND THEM OFF.
DO DO DO DO DO (BOOM)
WORKING WITH THEM!?
IT LOOKS MORE LIKE YOU'RE ON THE RECEIVING END OF THEIR ATTACKS!
DO DO
KA (CRACKLE)
GIIN (SHING)
GIIN
KA KA KA
KAN
OH...
IT'S A BIT AFTER THAT...
FAST-FORWARD...
FAST-FORWARD...
DAMN, IT'S SOME KIND OF FREAK MONSTER GOBLIN!
S-STAY BACK... PLEASE...
GOOOOOOOO (FWOOOOOM)
ALICIA, RUN!
GATA (SHAKE)
GATA GATA GATA
I'M NOT A GOBLIN.
EEK!

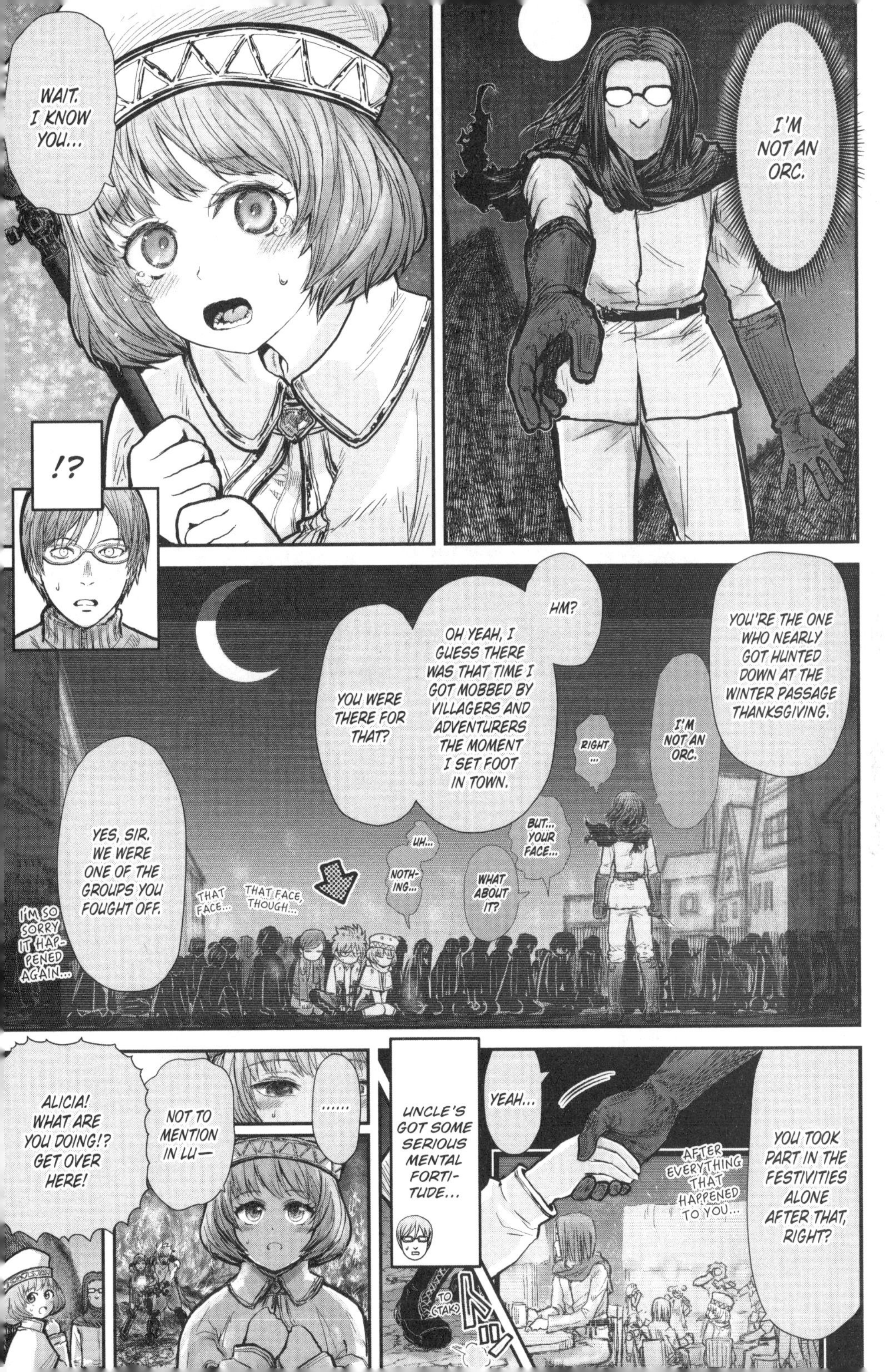
I'M NOT AN ORC.
WAIT. I KNOW YOU...
!?
YOU'RE THE ONE WHO NEARLY GOT HUNTED DOWN AT THE WINTER PASSAGE THANKSGIVING.
I'M NOT AN ORC.
RIGHT...
HM?
OH YEAH, I GUESS THERE WAS THAT TIME I GOT MOBBED BY VILLAGERS AND ADVENTURERS THE MOMENT I SET FOOT IN TOWN.
YOU WERE THERE FOR THAT?
BUT... YOUR FACE...
WHAT ABOUT IT?
UH...
NOTHING...
THAT FACE, THOUGH...
THAT FACE...
YES, SIR. WE WERE ONE OF THE GROUPS YOU FOUGHT OFF.
I'M SO SORRY IT HAPPENED AGAIN...
YOU TOOK PART IN THE FESTIVITIES ALONE AFTER THAT, RIGHT?
YEAH...
AFTER EVERYTHING THAT HAPPENED TO YOU...
UNCLE'S GOT SOME SERIOUS MENTAL FORTITUDE...
TO STAKO
......
NOT TO MENTION IN LU—
ALICIA! WHAT ARE YOU DOING!? GET OVER HERE!

SWORDS-MAN	HOLY MAGE	MARTIAL ARTIST
EDGAR	**ALICIA**	**RAIGA**

TH-THAT'S NOT TRUE AT ALL! ....I THINK.

EVEN IF HE ISN'T AN ORC, HE'S A CREATURE THAT'S BORDERLINE MONSTER.

YES...

THAT DUDE'S CLEARLY GONNA SIDE WITH THE GOBLINS!

SILLY ALICIA!

WHAT? WORK TOGETH-ER?

HISO HISO HISO HISO HISO HISO (PSST)

YEAH, SURE. I'M IN.

THE PAY WILL BE— ...HUH?

WOULD YOU BE WILLING TO HELP US!?

THE VILLAGE OF DOLD IS UP AHEAD. WE ACCEPTED A REQUEST TO DEFEND THEM FROM A HORDE OF GOBLINS, BUT WE'RE NOT SURE WE HAVE THE FIREPOWER TO HANDLE THEM ALL.

....

UM, EXCUSE ME!

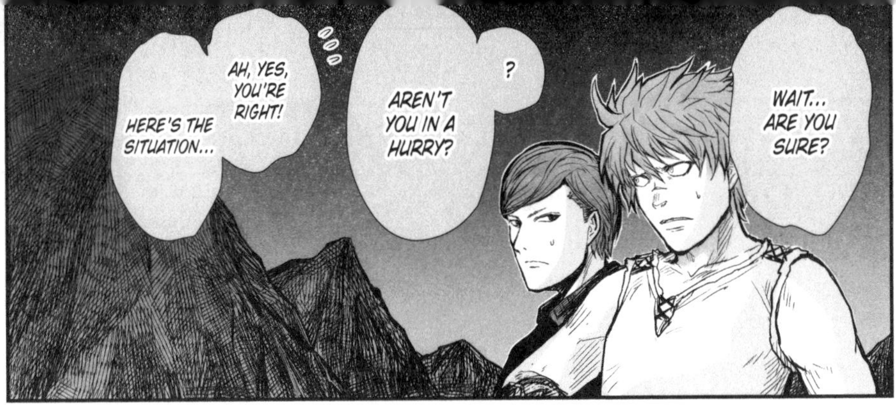
WAIT... ARE YOU SURE?
?
AREN'T YOU IN A HURRY?
AH, YES, YOU'RE RIGHT!
HERE'S THE SITUATION...

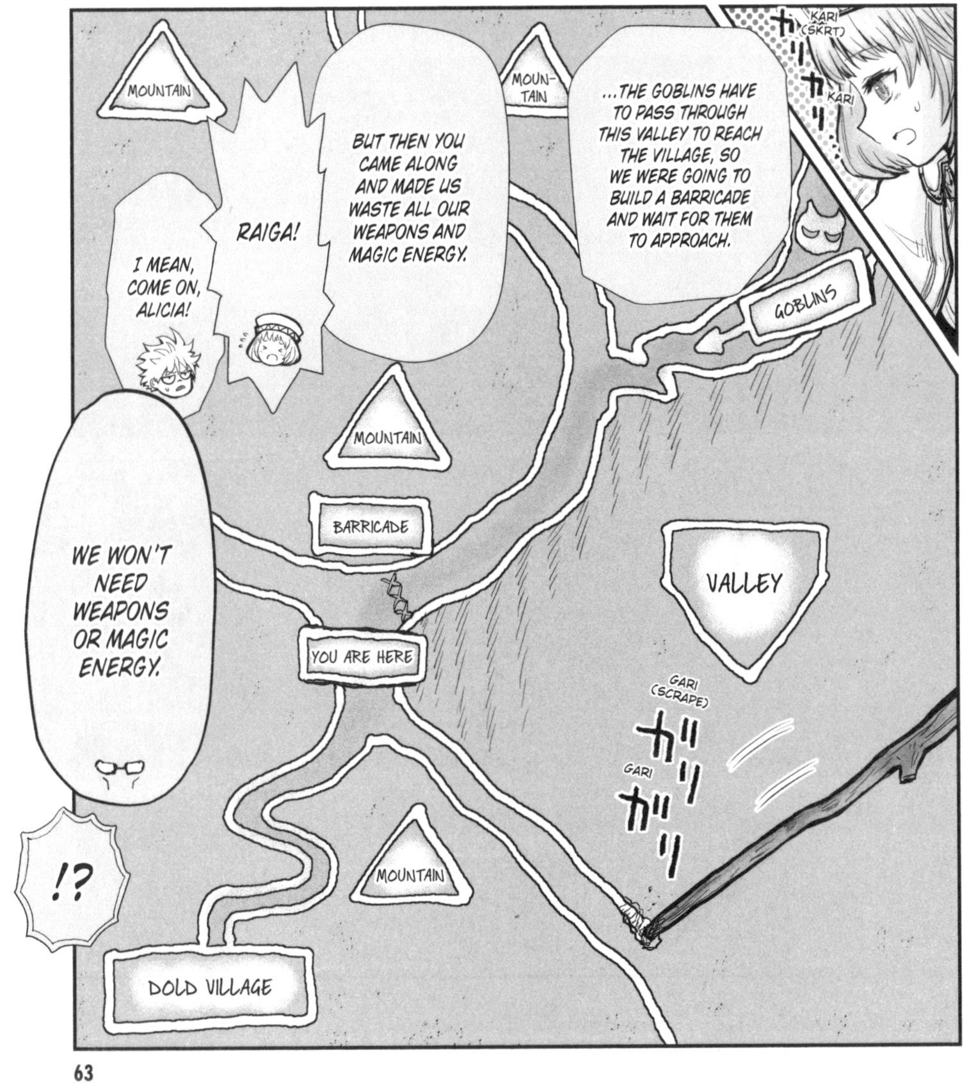
カリ KARI (SKRT)
カリ KARI
...THE GOBLINS HAVE TO PASS THROUGH THIS VALLEY TO REACH THE VILLAGE, SO WE WERE GOING TO BUILD A BARRICADE AND WAIT FOR THEM TO APPROACH.
MOUNTAIN
BUT THEN YOU CAME ALONG AND MADE US WASTE ALL OUR WEAPONS AND MAGIC ENERGY.
RAIGA!
MOUNTAIN
I MEAN, COME ON, ALICIA!
GOBLINS
MOUNTAIN
BARRICADE
VALLEY
WE WON'T NEED WEAPONS OR MAGIC ENERGY.
YOU ARE HERE
ガリ GARI (SCRAPE)
ガリ GARI
!?
MOUNTAIN
DOLD VILLAGE

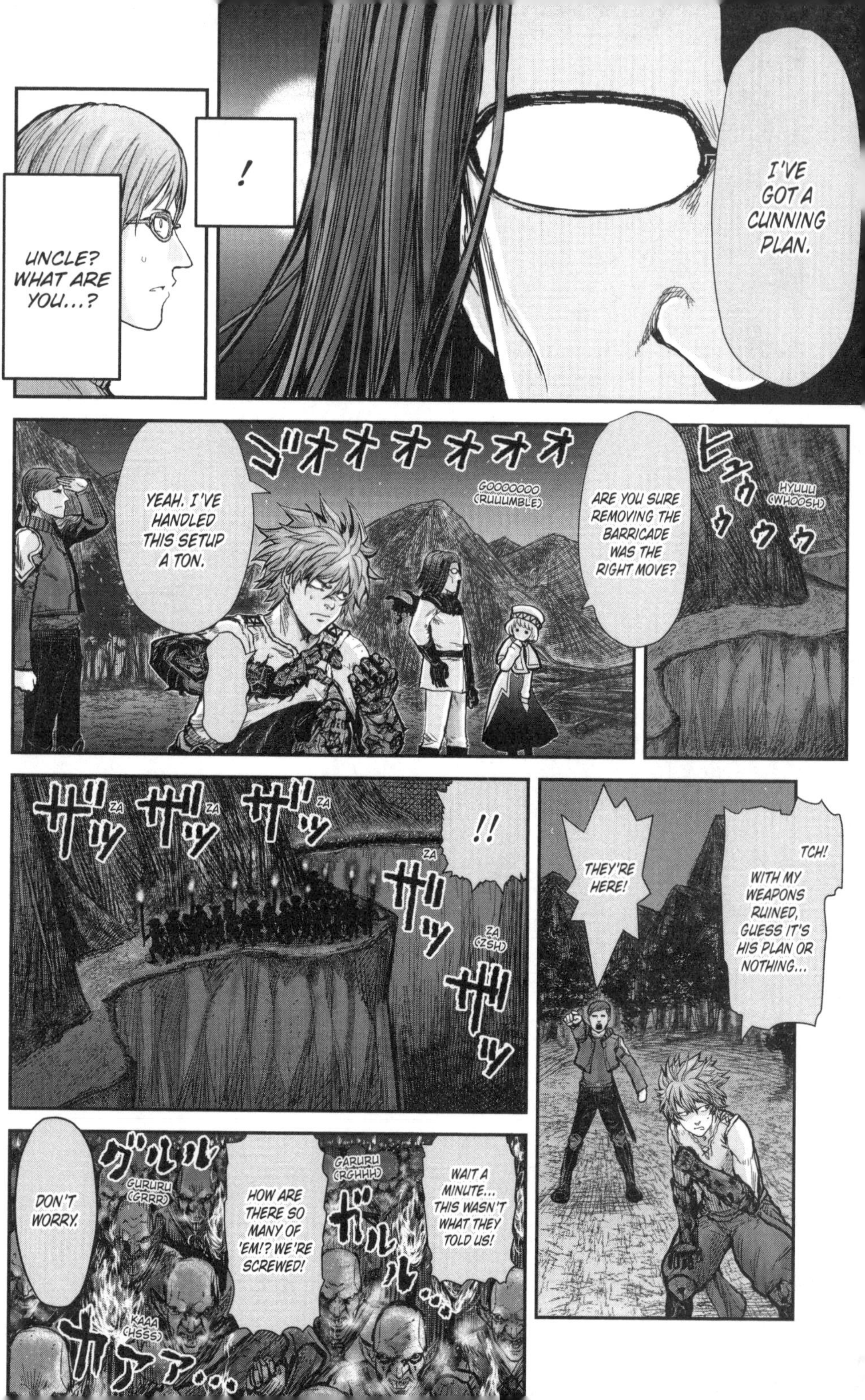

I'VE GOT A CUNNING PLAN.
!
UNCLE? WHAT ARE YOU...?
HYUUU (WHOOSH)
ARE YOU SURE REMOVING THE BARRICADE WAS THE RIGHT MOVE?
GOOOOOOO (RUUUMBLE)
YEAH. I'VE HANDLED THIS SETUP A TON.
TCH! WITH MY WEAPONS RUINED, GUESS IT'S HIS PLAN OR NOTHING...
THEY'RE HERE!
!!
ZA
ZA
ZA
ZA
ZA (ZSH)
WAIT A MINUTE... THIS WASN'T WHAT THEY TOLD US!
GARURU (RGHHH)
HOW ARE THERE SO MANY OF 'EM!? WE'RE SCREWED!
GURURU (GRRR)
KAAA (HSSS)
DON'T WORRY.

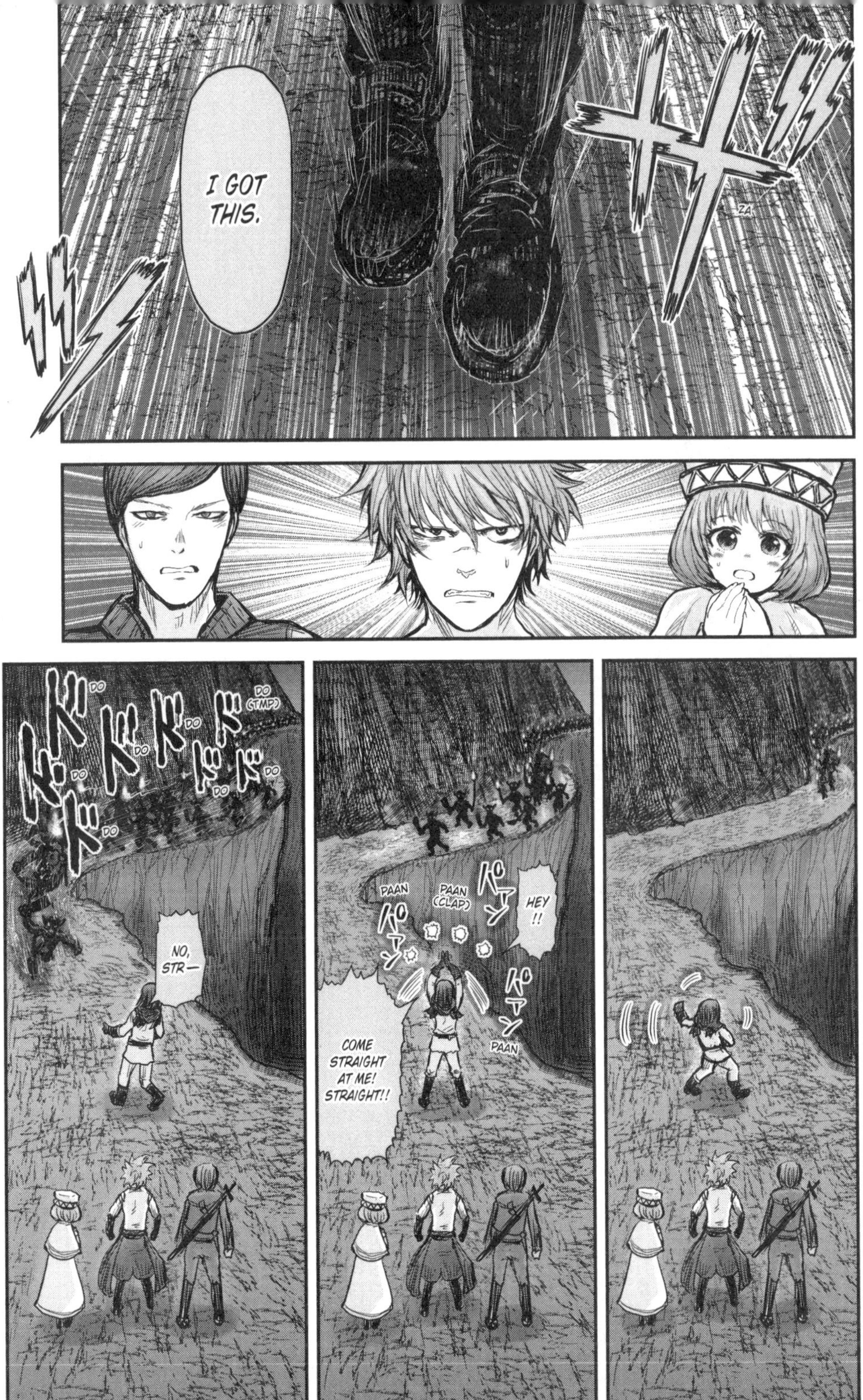
I GOT THIS.
ZA
PAAN
PAAN (CLAP)
HEY!!
PAAN
COME STRAIGHT AT ME! STRAIGHT!!
DO DO DO DO DO (TMP)
DO DO DO
NO, STR—

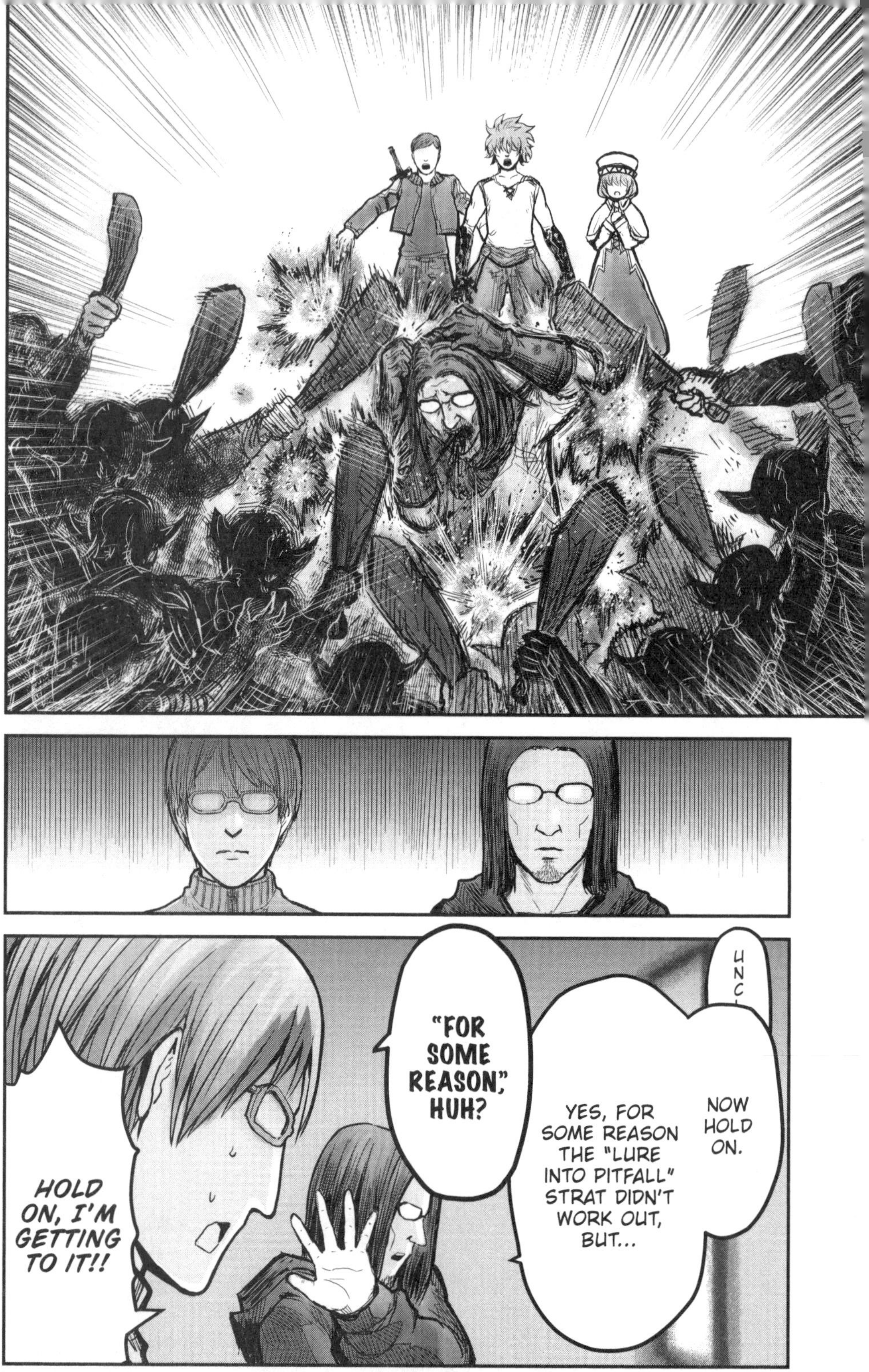
UNC
YES, FOR SOME REASON THE "LURE INTO PITFALL" STRAT DIDN'T WORK OUT, BUT...
NOW HOLD ON.
"FOR SOME REASON," HUH?
HOLD ON, I'M GETTING TO IT!!

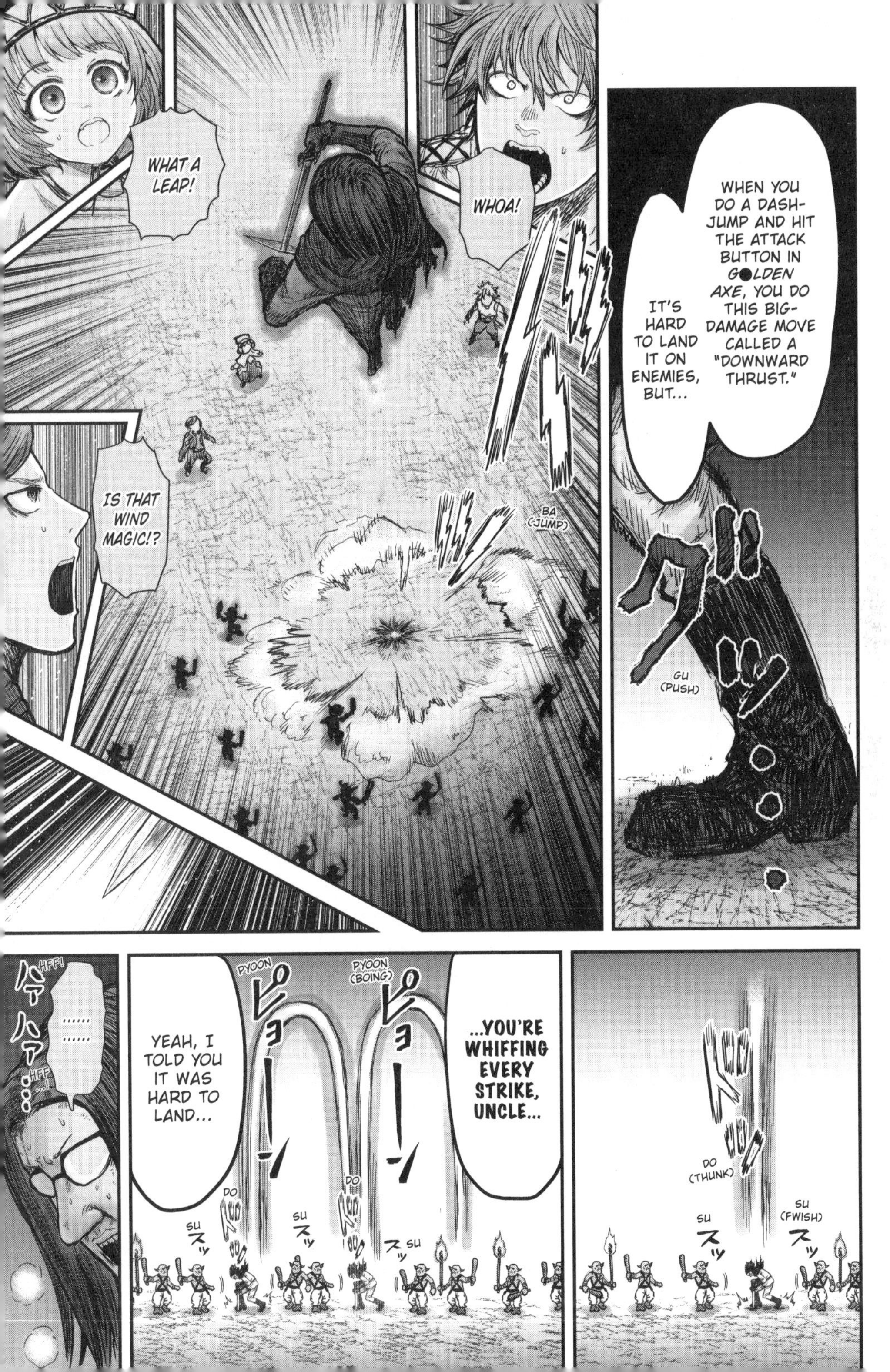
WHEN YOU DO A DASH-JUMP AND HIT THE ATTACK BUTTON IN GOLDEN AXE, YOU DO THIS BIG-DAMAGE MOVE CALLED A "DOWNWARD THRUST."
IT'S HARD TO LAND IT ON ENEMIES, BUT...
GU (PUSH)
WHOA!
WHAT A LEAP!
BA (JUMP)
IS THAT WIND MAGIC!?
DO (THUNK)
SU (FWISH)
SU
...YOU'RE WHIFFING EVERY STRIKE, UNCLE...
PYOON (BOING)
PYOON
SU
DO
DO
SU
SU
YEAH, I TOLD YOU IT WAS HARD TO LAND...
HFF!
......
......
HFF

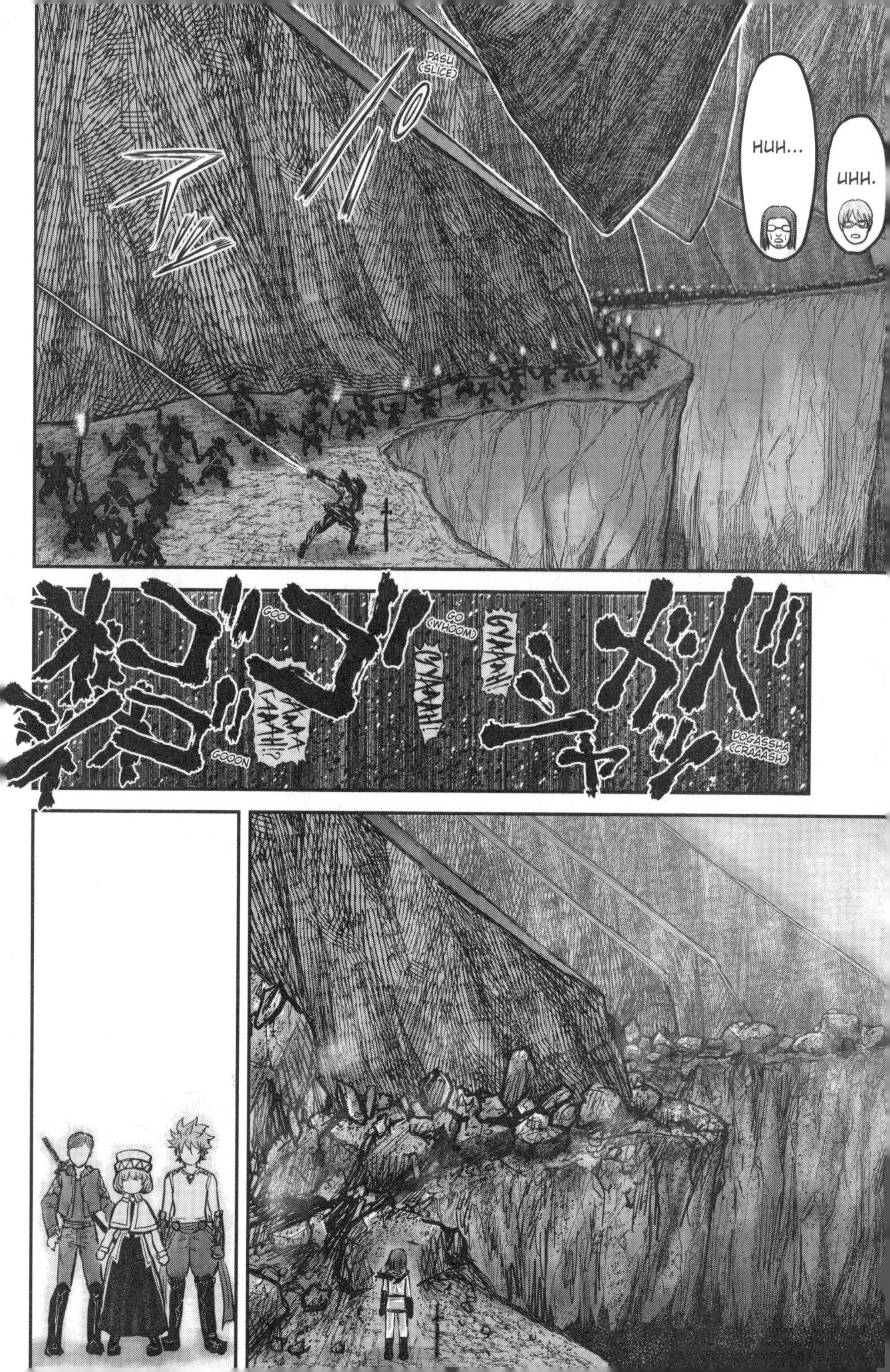
HUH...
UHH.
PASU (SLICE)
DOGASSHA (CRAAASH)
GYAAAAH
GYAAAAH
GO (WHOOM)
GOO
AAAA GAAAAH!?
GOOON

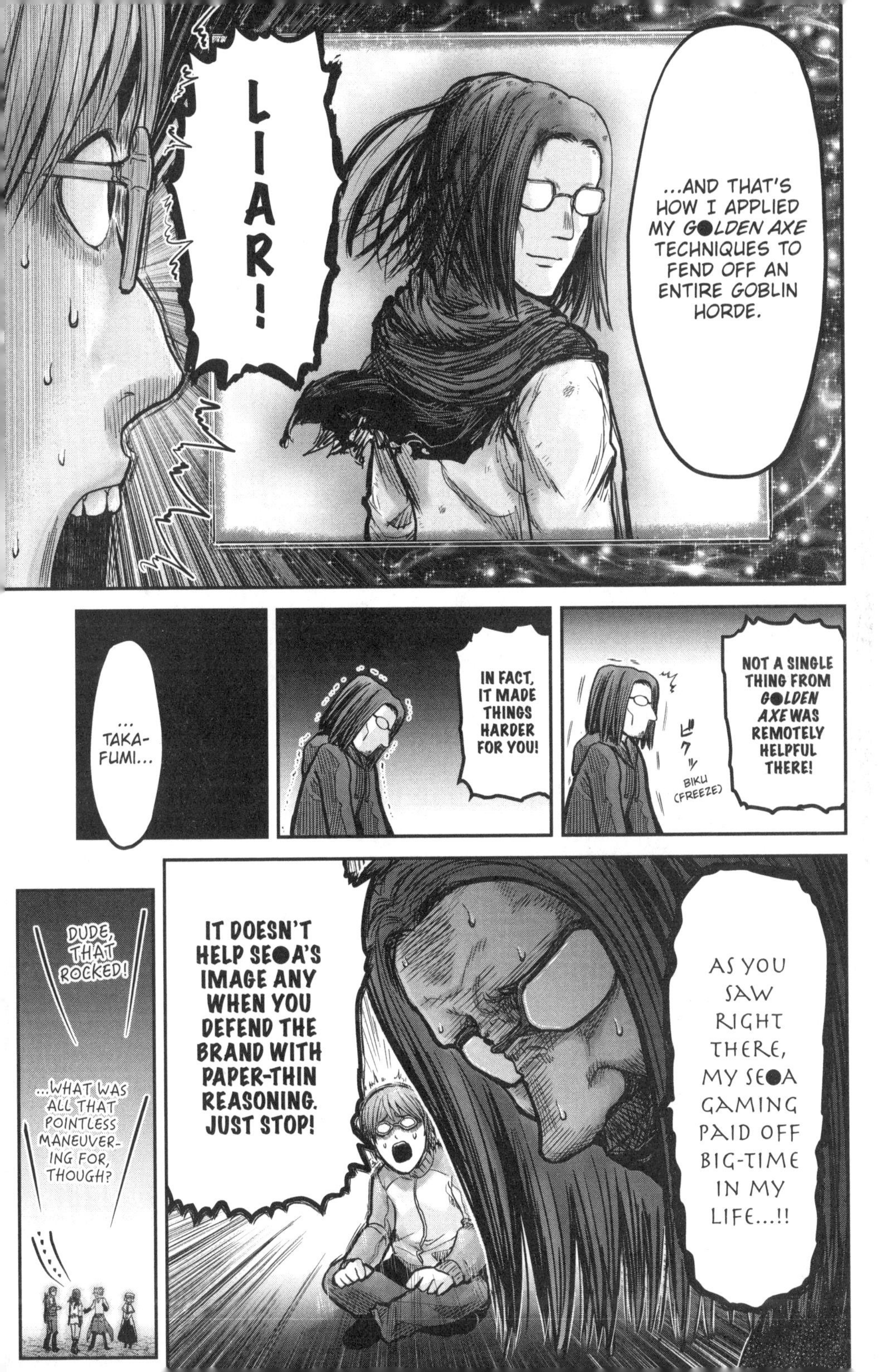
...AND THAT'S HOW I APPLIED MY G●LDEN AXE TECHNIQUES TO FEND OFF AN ENTIRE GOBLIN HORDE.
LIAR!
NOT A SINGLE THING FROM G●LDEN AXE WAS REMOTELY HELPFUL THERE!
ビクッ
BIKU (FREEZE)
IN FACT, IT MADE THINGS HARDER FOR YOU!
... TAKA-FUMI...
AS YOU SAW RIGHT THERE, MY SE●A GAMING PAID OFF BIG-TIME IN MY LIFE...!!
IT DOESN'T HELP SE●A'S IMAGE ANY WHEN YOU DEFEND THE BRAND WITH PAPER-THIN REASONING. JUST STOP!
DUDE, THAT ROCKED!
...WHAT WAS ALL THAT POINTLESS MANEUVER-ING FOR, THOUGH?

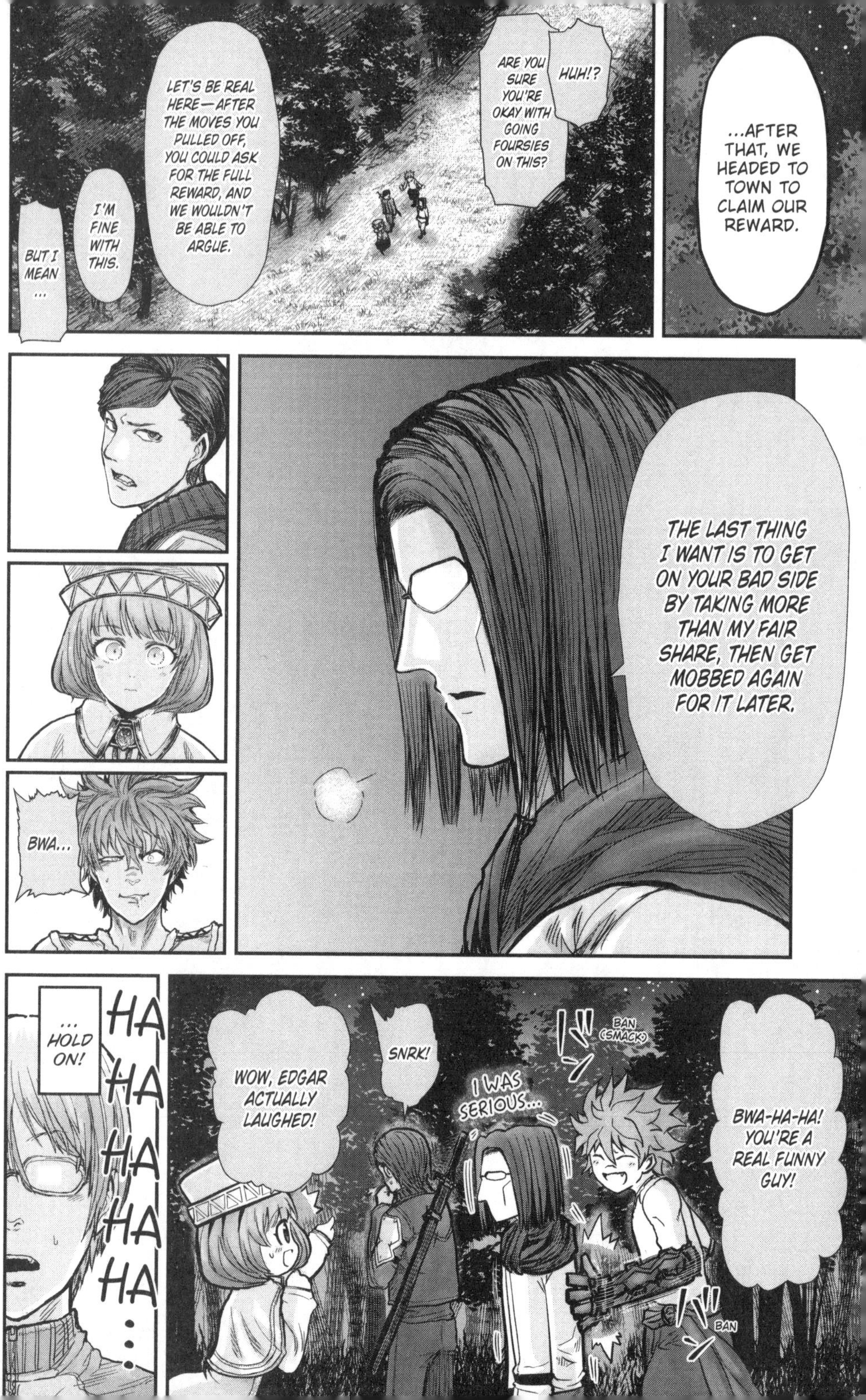
...AFTER THAT, WE HEADED TO TOWN TO CLAIM OUR REWARD.
HUH!?
ARE YOU SURE YOU'RE OKAY WITH GOING FOURSIES ON THIS?
LET'S BE REAL HERE—AFTER THE MOVES YOU PULLED OFF, YOU COULD ASK FOR THE FULL REWARD, AND WE WOULDN'T BE ABLE TO ARGUE.
I'M FINE WITH THIS.
BUT I MEAN...
THE LAST THING I WANT IS TO GET ON YOUR BAD SIDE BY TAKING MORE THAN MY FAIR SHARE, THEN GET MOBBED AGAIN FOR IT LATER.
BWA...
BWA-HA-HA! YOU'RE A REAL FUNNY GUY!
BAN (SMACK)
I WAS SERIOUS...
SNRK!
WOW, EDGAR ACTUALLY LAUGHED!
BAN
HA HA HA HA HA HA...
...HOLD ON!

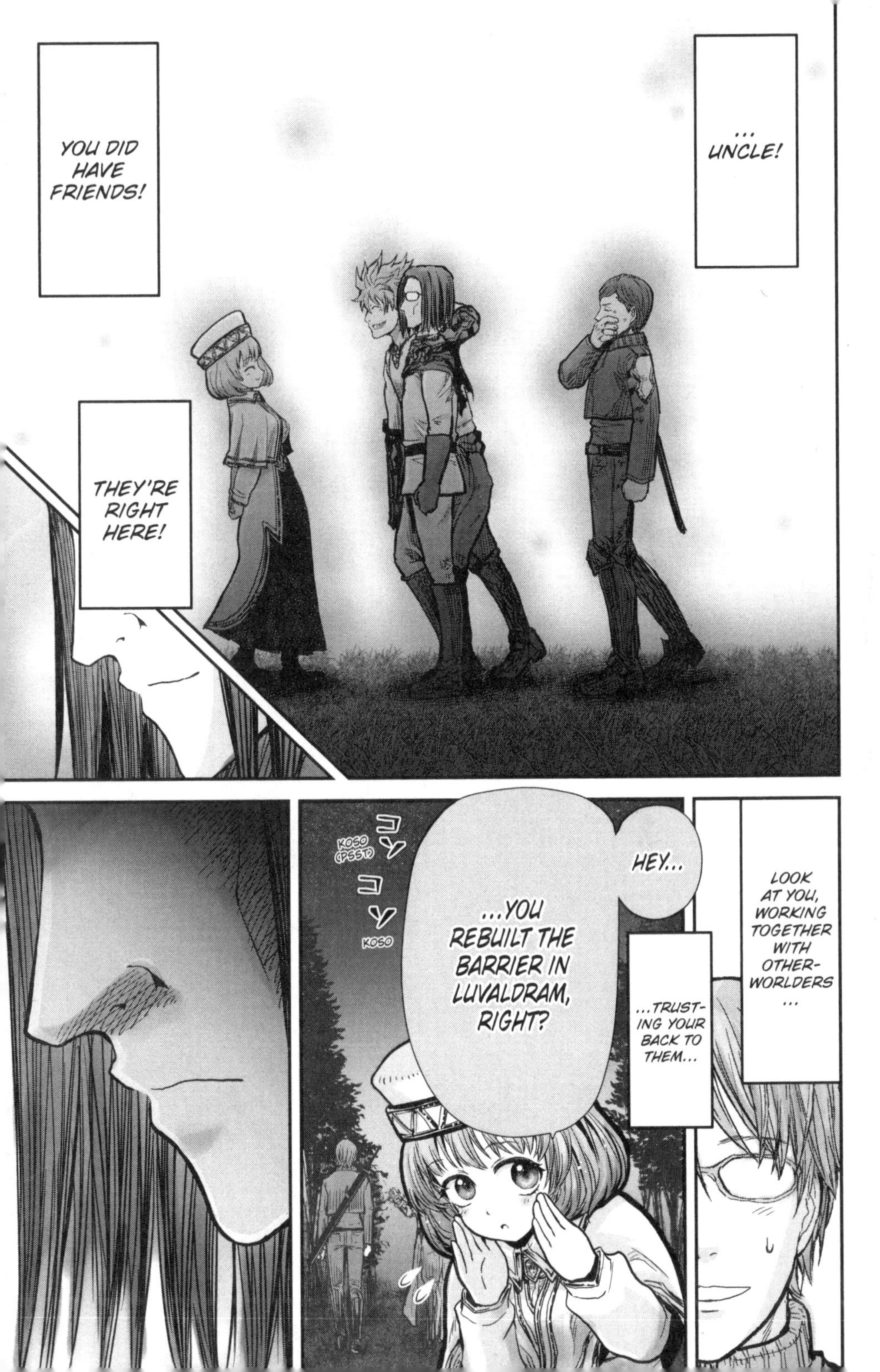
...UNCLE!
YOU DID HAVE FRIENDS!
THEY'RE RIGHT HERE!
LOOK AT YOU, WORKING TOGETHER WITH OTHER-WORLDERS...
...TRUSTING YOUR BACK TO THEM...
KOSO (PSST)
KOSO
HEY...
...YOU REBUILT THE BARRIER IN LUVALDRAM, RIGHT?

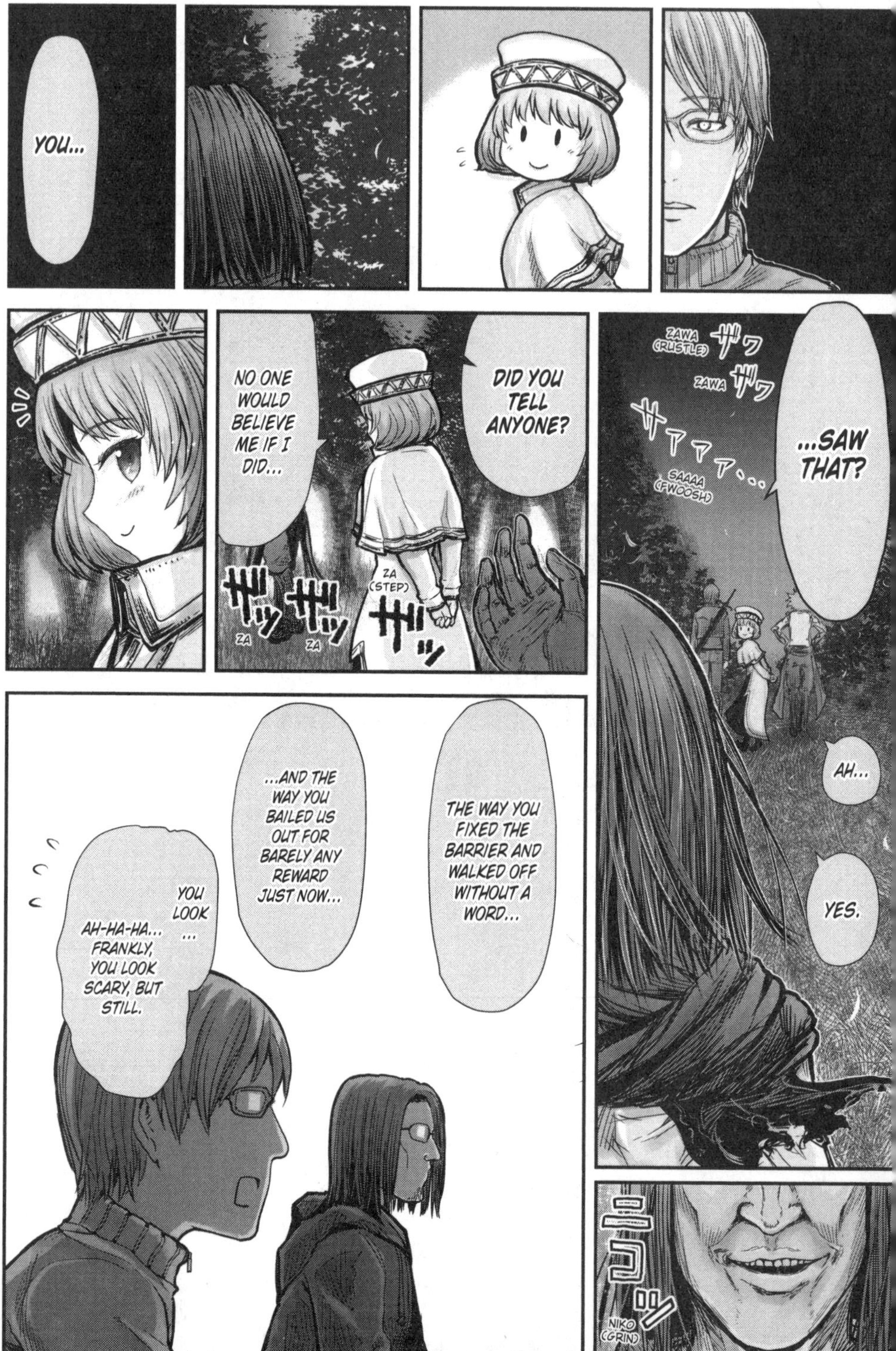

YOU...
...SAW THAT?
ZAWA (RUSTLE) ザワ
ZAWA ザワ
サァァァ...
SAAAA (FWOOSH)
AH...
YES.
DID YOU TELL ANYONE?
NO ONE WOULD BELIEVE ME IF I DID...
ZA (STEP)
ZA
ZA
THE WAY YOU FIXED THE BARRIER AND WALKED OFF WITHOUT A WORD...
...AND THE WAY YOU BAILED US OUT FOR BARELY ANY REWARD JUST NOW...
YOU LOOK ...
AH-HA-HA... FRANKLY, YOU LOOK SCARY, BUT STILL.
NIKO (GRIN)

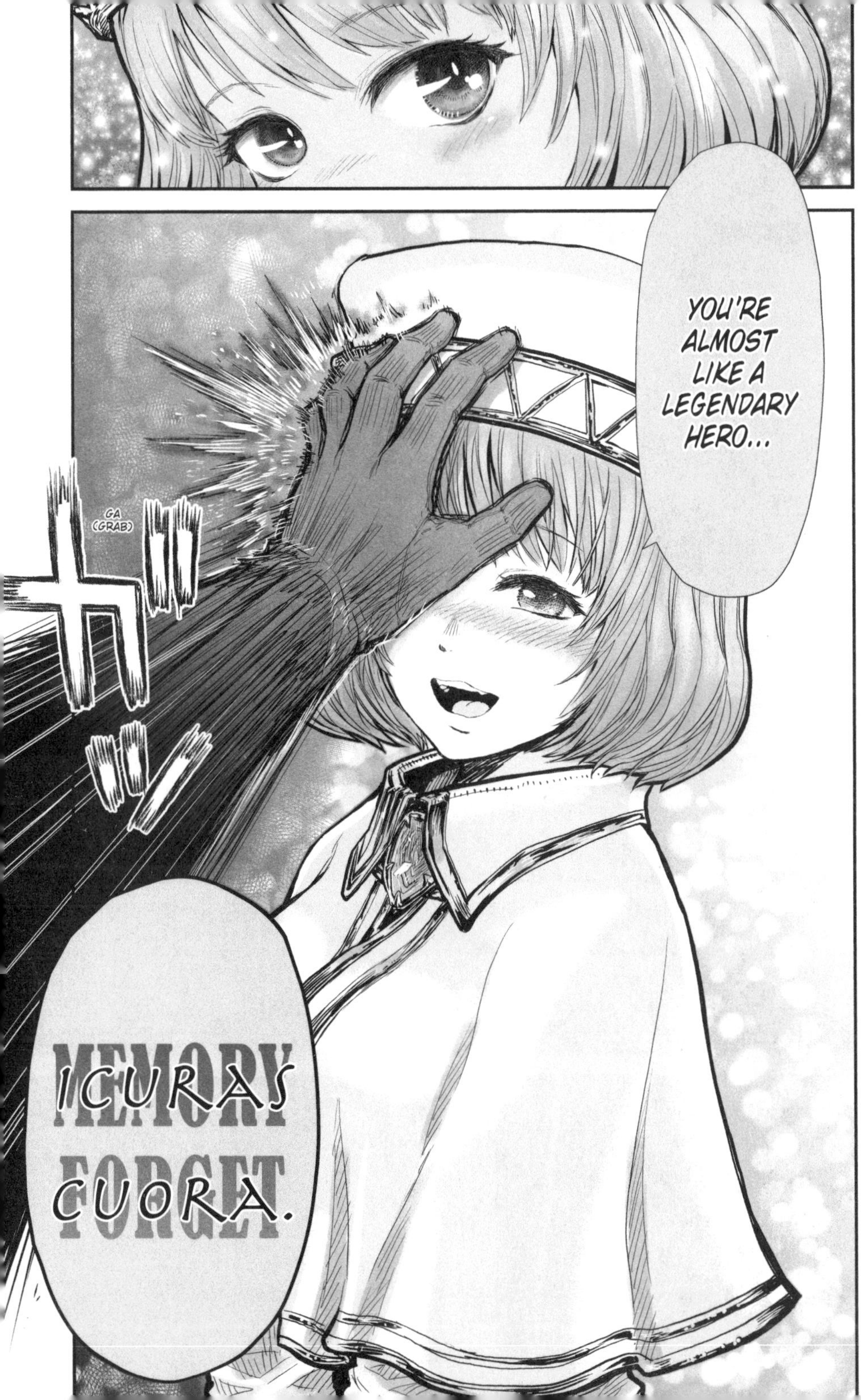
YOU'RE ALMOST LIKE A LEGENDARY HERO...
GA (GRAB)
MEMORY FORGET
ICURAS CUORA.

UGK!

HIIN
(FWEEN)

WHY...!?

GA
(GRAB)

GA
(GRAB)

WHA
—!?

...YOU
...

I
TRUSTED
...

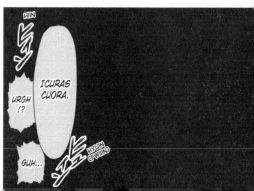

HIIN

URGH
!?

ICURAS
CUORA.

GUH...

HYUIN
(FWIIN)

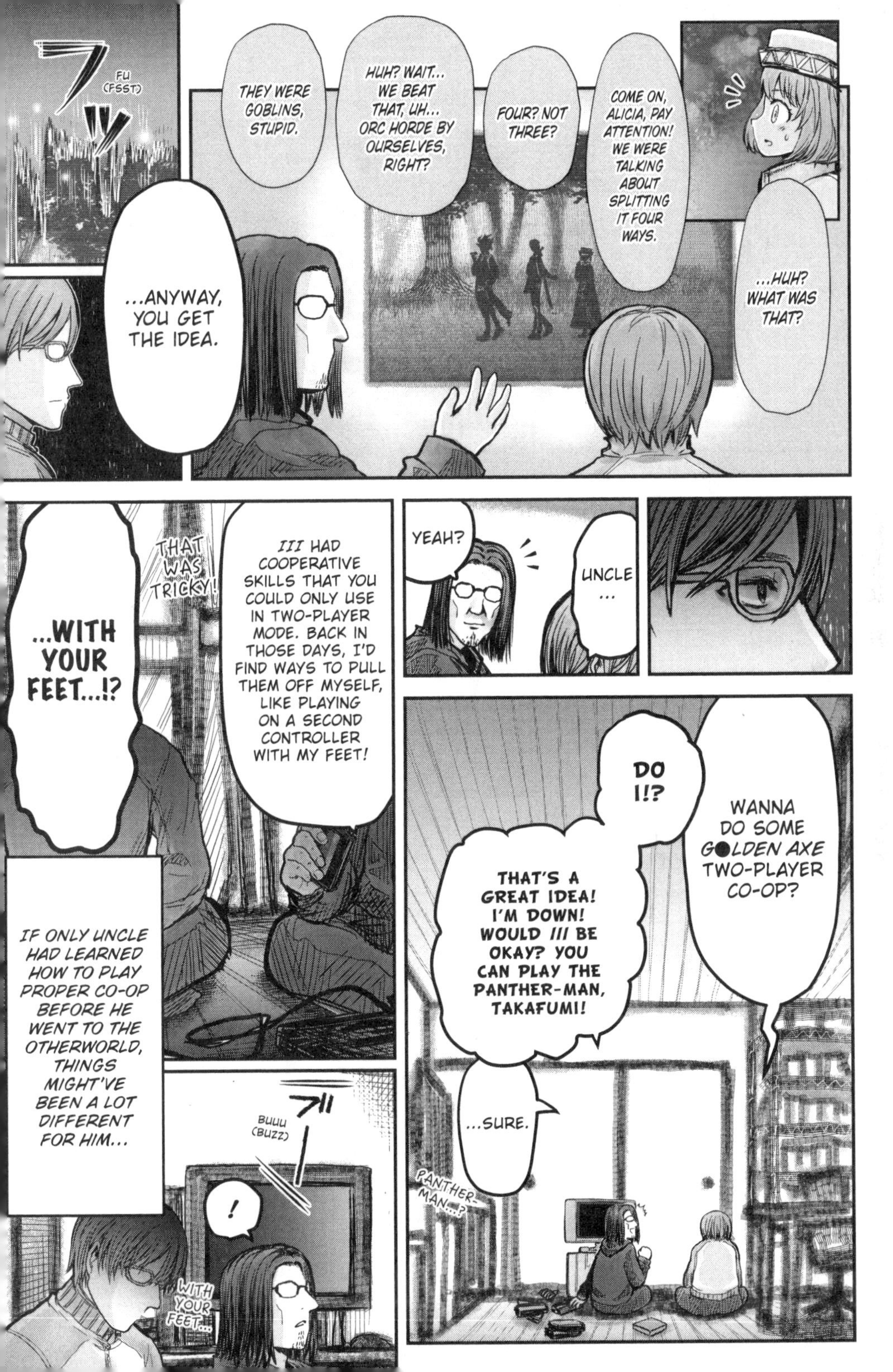
COME ON, ALICIA, PAY ATTENTION! WE WERE TALKING ABOUT SPLITTING IT FOUR WAYS.
...HUH? WHAT WAS THAT?
FOUR? NOT THREE?
HUH? WAIT... WE BEAT THAT, UH... ORC HORDE BY OURSELVES, RIGHT?
THEY WERE GOBLINS, STUPID.
...ANYWAY, YOU GET THE IDEA.
FU (FSST)
UNCLE...
YEAH?
III HAD COOPERATIVE SKILLS THAT YOU COULD ONLY USE IN TWO-PLAYER MODE. BACK IN THOSE DAYS, I'D FIND WAYS TO PULL THEM OFF MYSELF, LIKE PLAYING ON A SECOND CONTROLLER WITH MY FEET!
THAT WAS TRICKY!
...WITH YOUR FEET...!?
WANNA DO SOME GOLDEN AXE TWO-PLAYER CO-OP?
DO I!?
THAT'S A GREAT IDEA! I'M DOWN! WOULD III BE OKAY? YOU CAN PLAY THE PANTHER-MAN, TAKAFUMI!
...SURE.
PANTHER-MAN...?
IF ONLY UNCLE HAD LEARNED HOW TO PLAY PROPER CO-OP BEFORE HE WENT TO THE OTHERWORLD, THINGS MIGHT'VE BEEN A LOT DIFFERENT FOR HIM...
BUUU (BUZZ)
!
WITH YOUR FEET...

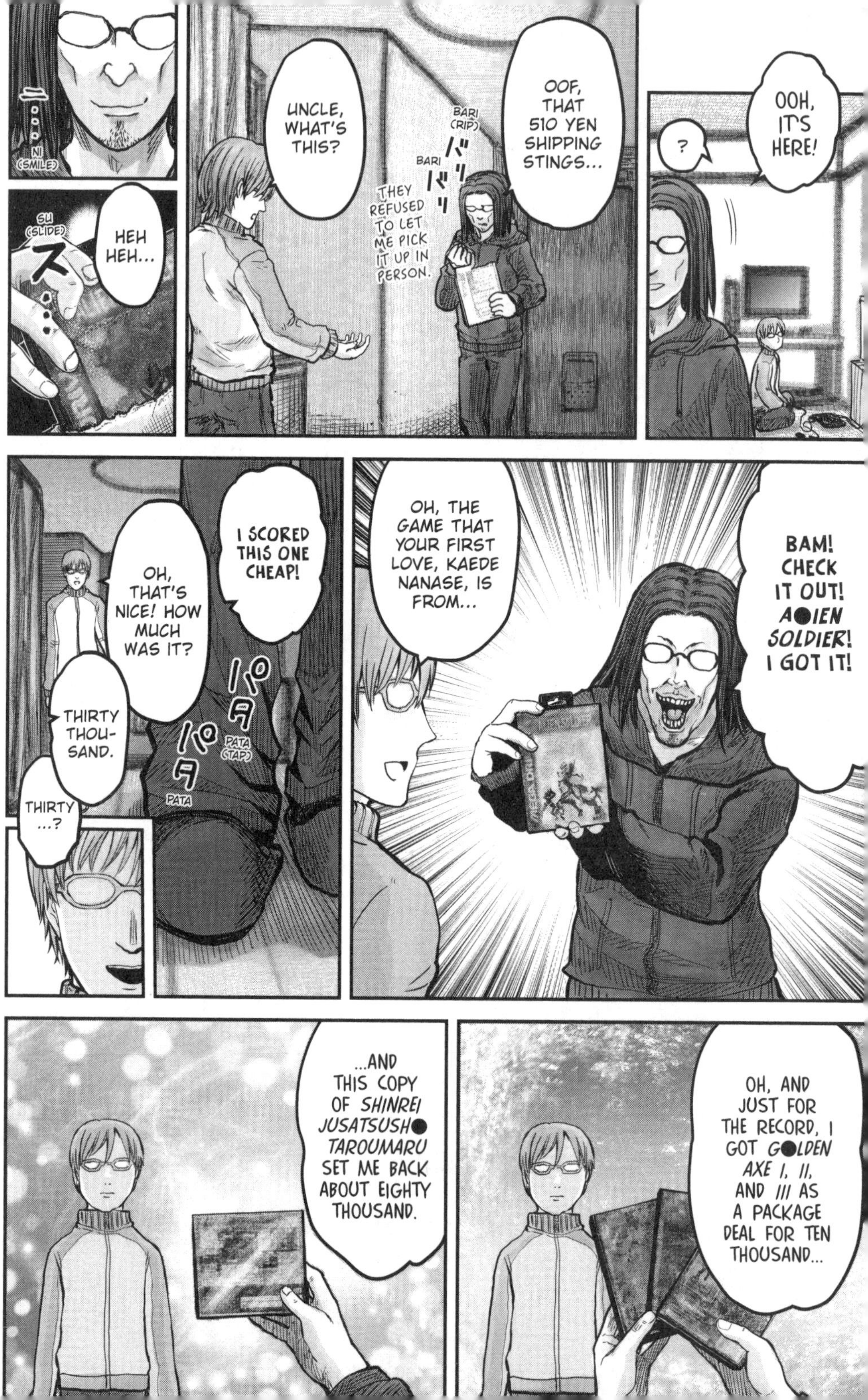
OOH, IT'S HERE!
?
OOF, THAT 510 YEN SHIPPING STINGS...
BARI (RIP)
BARI
THEY REFUSED TO LET ME PICK IT UP IN PERSON.
UNCLE, WHAT'S THIS?
NI (SMILE)
SU (SLIDE)
HEH HEH...
BAM! CHECK IT OUT! *A●IEN SOLDIER*! I GOT IT!
OH, THE GAME THAT YOUR FIRST LOVE, KAEDE NANASE, IS FROM...
I SCORED THIS ONE CHEAP!
OH, THAT'S NICE! HOW MUCH WAS IT?
PATA (TAP)
PATA
THIRTY THOUSAND.
THIRTY ...?
OH, AND JUST FOR THE RECORD, I GOT *G●LDEN AXE I, II,* AND *III* AS A PACKAGE DEAL FOR TEN THOUSAND...
...AND THIS COPY OF *SHINREI JUSATSUSH● TAROUMARU* SET ME BACK ABOUT EIGHTY THOUSAND.

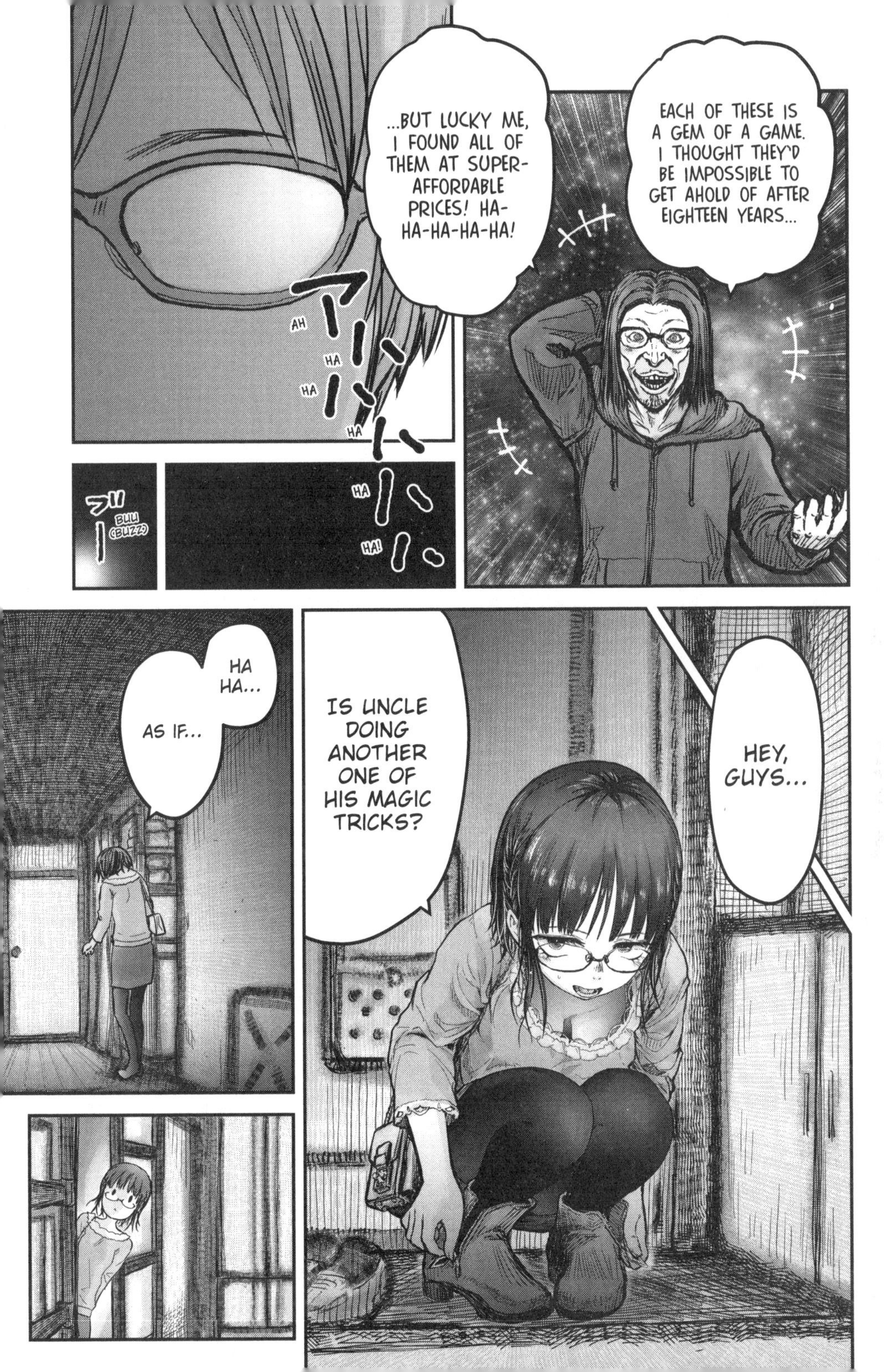

EACH OF THESE IS A GEM OF A GAME. I THOUGHT THEY'D BE IMPOSSIBLE TO GET AHOLD OF AFTER EIGHTEEN YEARS...
...BUT LUCKY ME, I FOUND ALL OF THEM AT SUPER-AFFORDABLE PRICES! HA-HA-HA-HA-HA!
AH
HA
HA
HA
HA
HA!
BUU (BUZZ)
HEY, GUYS...
IS UNCLE DOING ANOTHER ONE OF HIS MAGIC TRICKS?
HA HA...
AS IF...

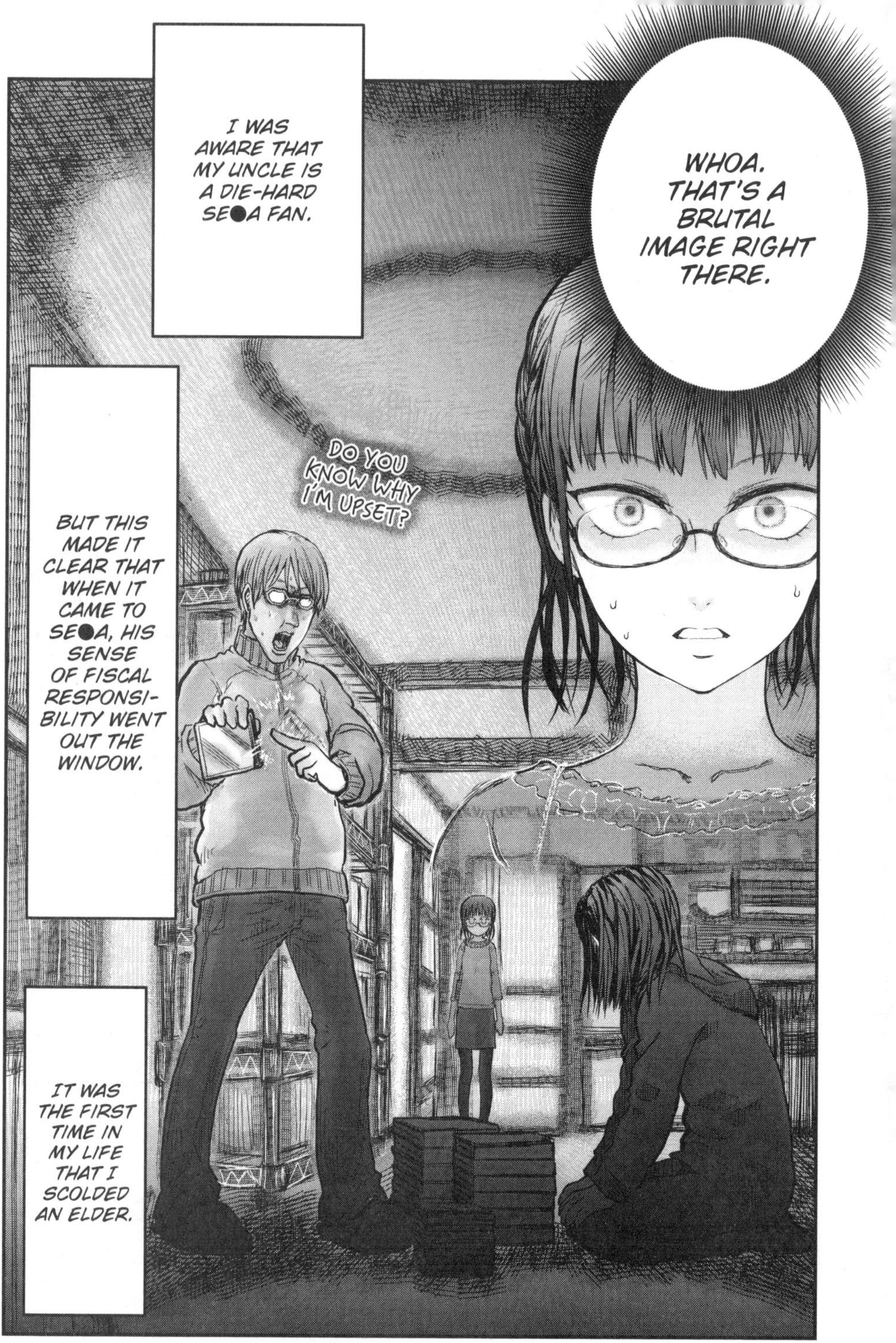
WHOA. THAT'S A BRUTAL IMAGE RIGHT THERE.
I WAS AWARE THAT MY UNCLE IS A DIE-HARD SE●A FAN.
DO YOU KNOW WHY I'M UPSET?
BUT THIS MADE IT CLEAR THAT WHEN IT CAME TO SE●A, HIS SENSE OF FISCAL RESPONSI-BILITY WENT OUT THE WINDOW.
IT WAS THE FIRST TIME IN MY LIFE THAT I SCOLDED AN ELDER.

Original MSRP

A●ien Soldier: ¥6,800
G●lden Axe: ¥6,000
G●lden Axe II: ¥6,000
G●lden Axe III: ¥6,800
Shinrei Jusatsush● Taroumaru: ¥5,800

TIPS

UNCLE from ANOTHER WORLD

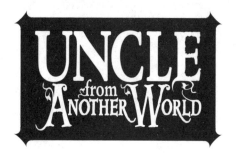

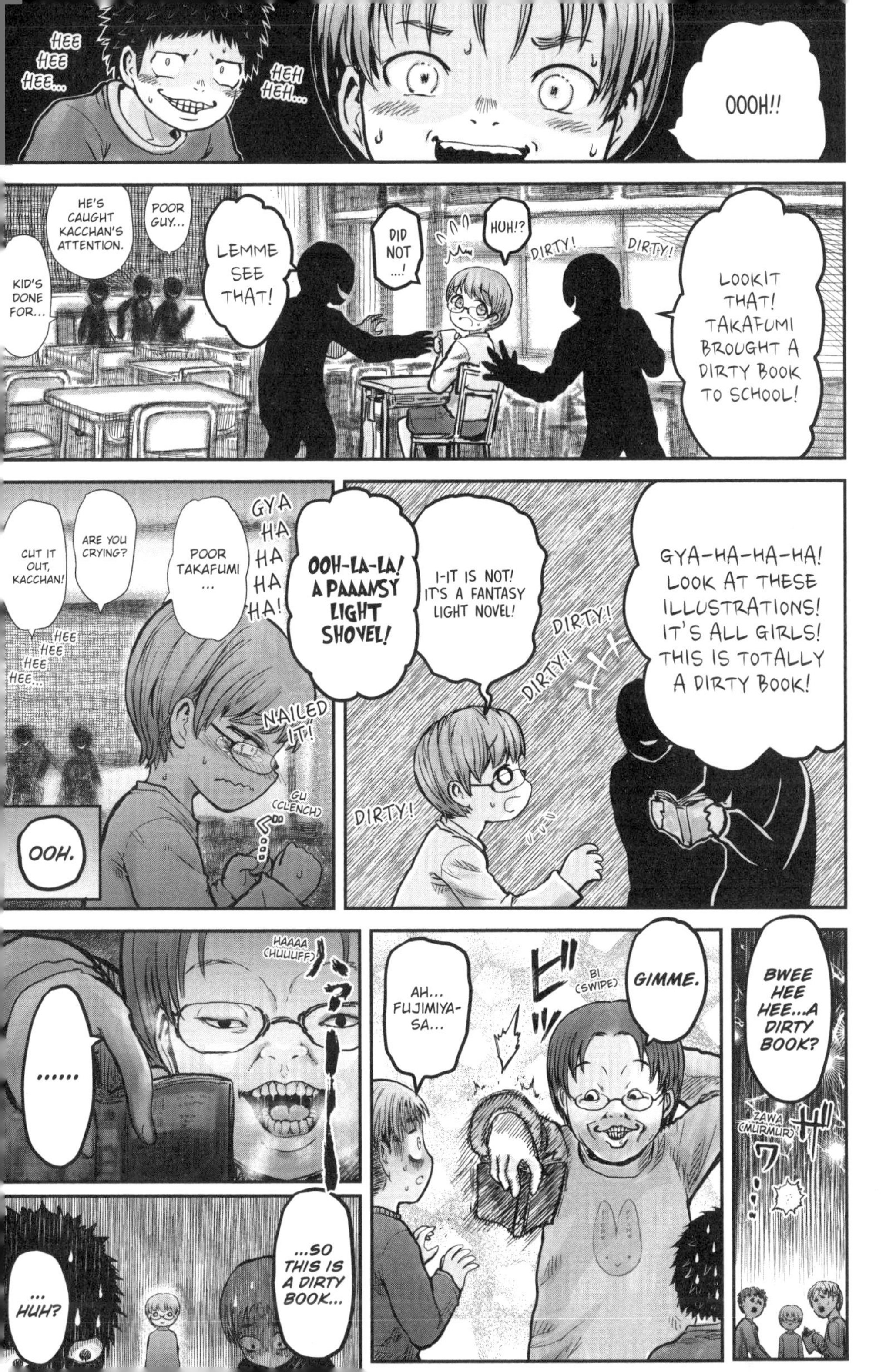
OOOH!!
HEE HEE HEE...
HEH HEH...
LOOKIT THAT! TAKAFUMI BROUGHT A DIRTY BOOK TO SCHOOL!
DIRTY!
DIRTY!
HUH!?
DID NOT ...!
LEMME SEE THAT!
POOR GUY...
HE'S CAUGHT KACCHAN'S ATTENTION.
KID'S DONE FOR...
GYA-HA-HA-HA! LOOK AT THESE ILLUSTRATIONS! IT'S ALL GIRLS! THIS IS TOTALLY A DIRTY BOOK!
DIRTY!
DIRTY!
I-IT IS NOT! IT'S A FANTASY LIGHT NOVEL!
OOH-LA-LA! A PAAANSY LIGHT SHOVEL!
DIRTY!
GYA HA HA HA HA!
POOR TAKAFUMI ...
ARE YOU CRYING?
CUT IT OUT, KACCHAN!
HEE HEE HEE HEE...
NAILED IT!
GU (CLENCH)
OOH.
BWEE HEE HEE...A DIRTY BOOK?
ZAWA (MURMUR)
GIMME.
BI (SWIPE)
AH... FUJIMIYA-SA...
HAAAA (HUUUFF)
......
...SO THIS IS A DIRTY BOOK...
... HUH?

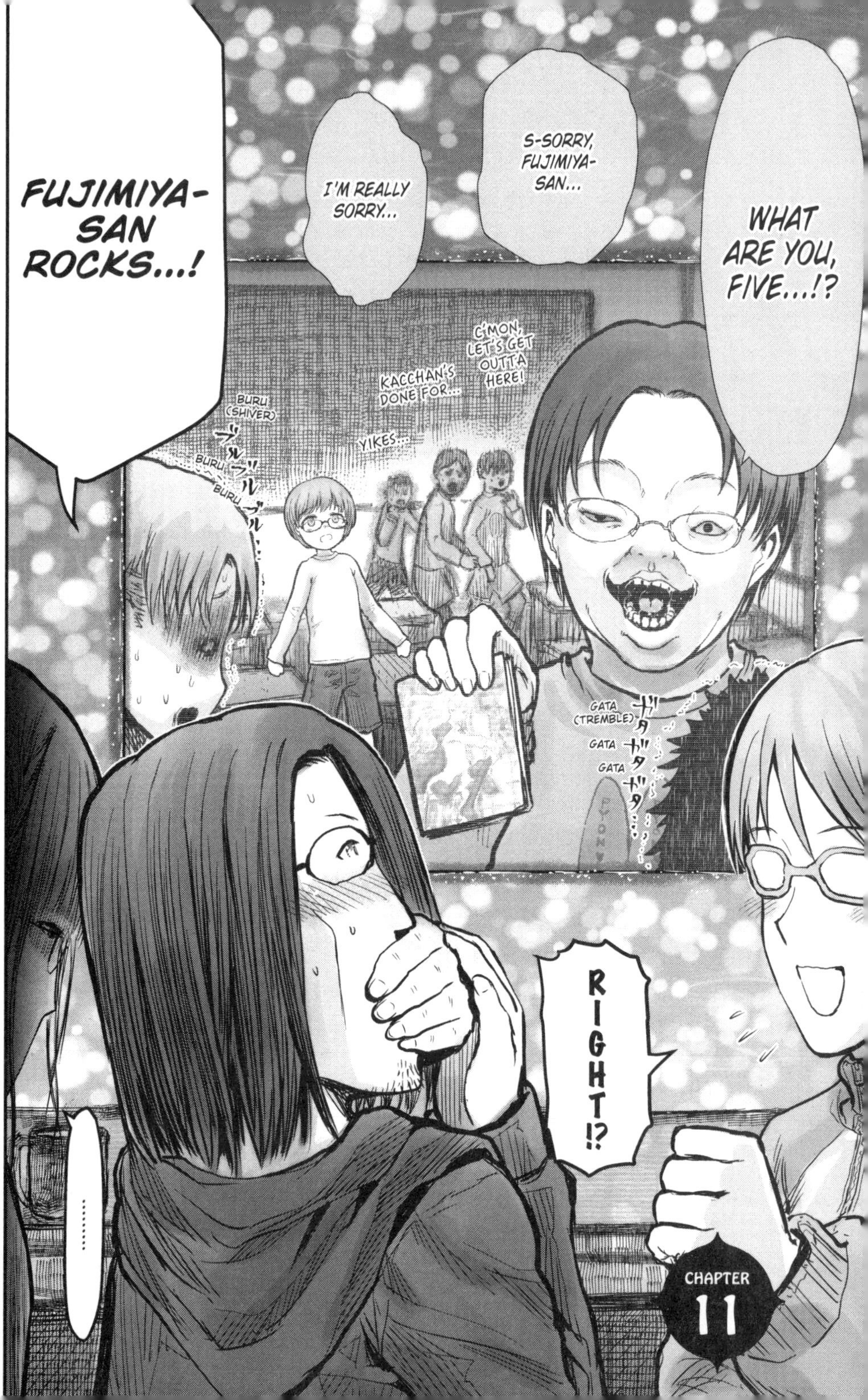
WHAT ARE YOU, FIVE...!?
S-SORRY, FUJIMIYA-SAN...
I'M REALLY SORRY...
FUJIMIYA-SAN ROCKS...!
C'MON, LET'S GET OUTTA HERE!
KACCHAN'S DONE FOR...
YIKES...
GATA (TREMBLE) GATA GATA
BURU (SHIVER) BURU BURU
RIGHT!?
......
CHAPTER 11

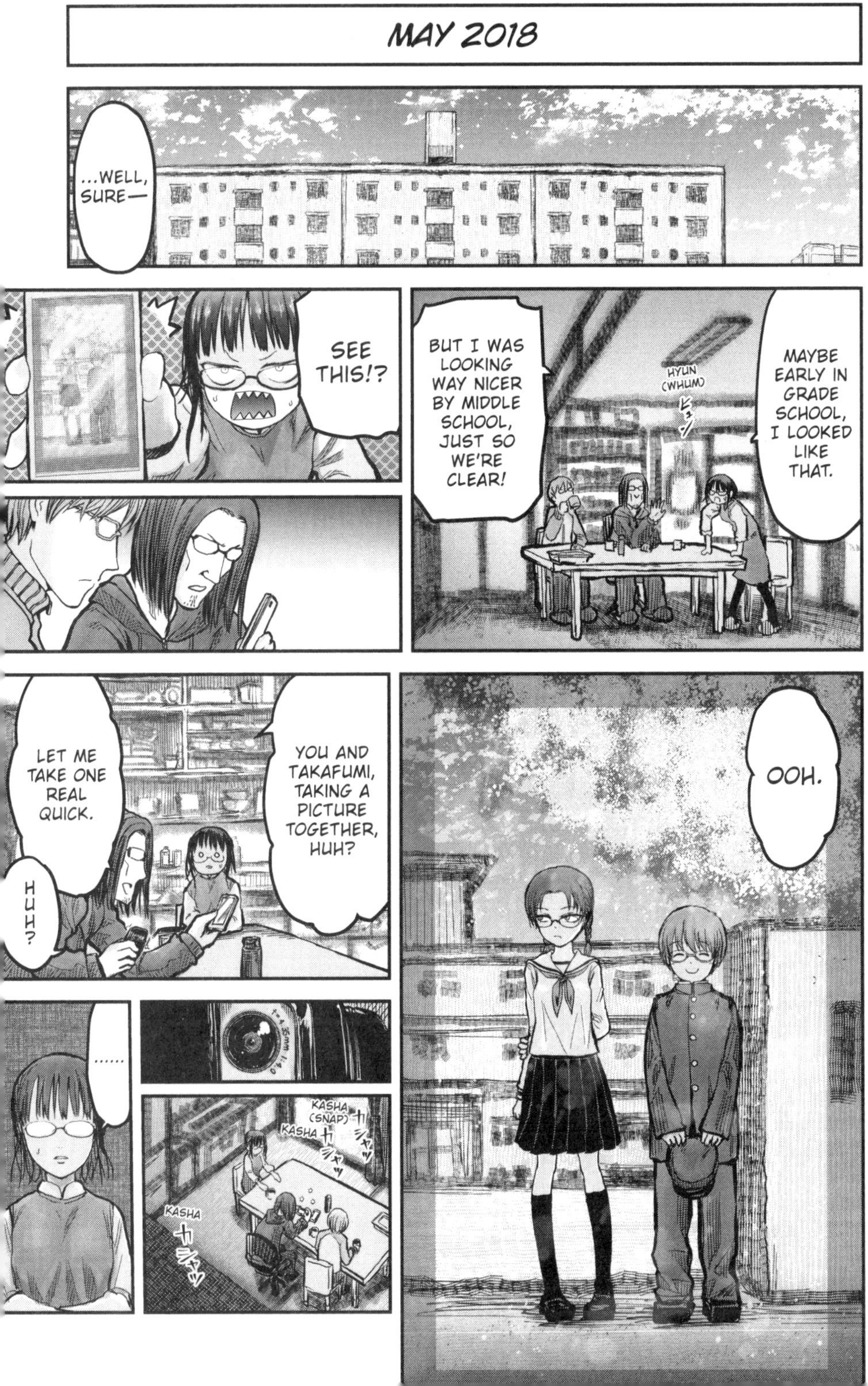
MAY 2018
...WELL, SURE—
MAYBE EARLY IN GRADE SCHOOL, I LOOKED LIKE THAT.
HYUN (WHUM)
BUT I WAS LOOKING WAY NICER BY MIDDLE SCHOOL, JUST SO WE'RE CLEAR!
SEE THIS!?
OOH.
YOU AND TAKAFUMI, TAKING A PICTURE TOGETHER, HUH?
LET ME TAKE ONE REAL QUICK.
HUH?
KASHA (SNAP)
KASHA
KASHA
......

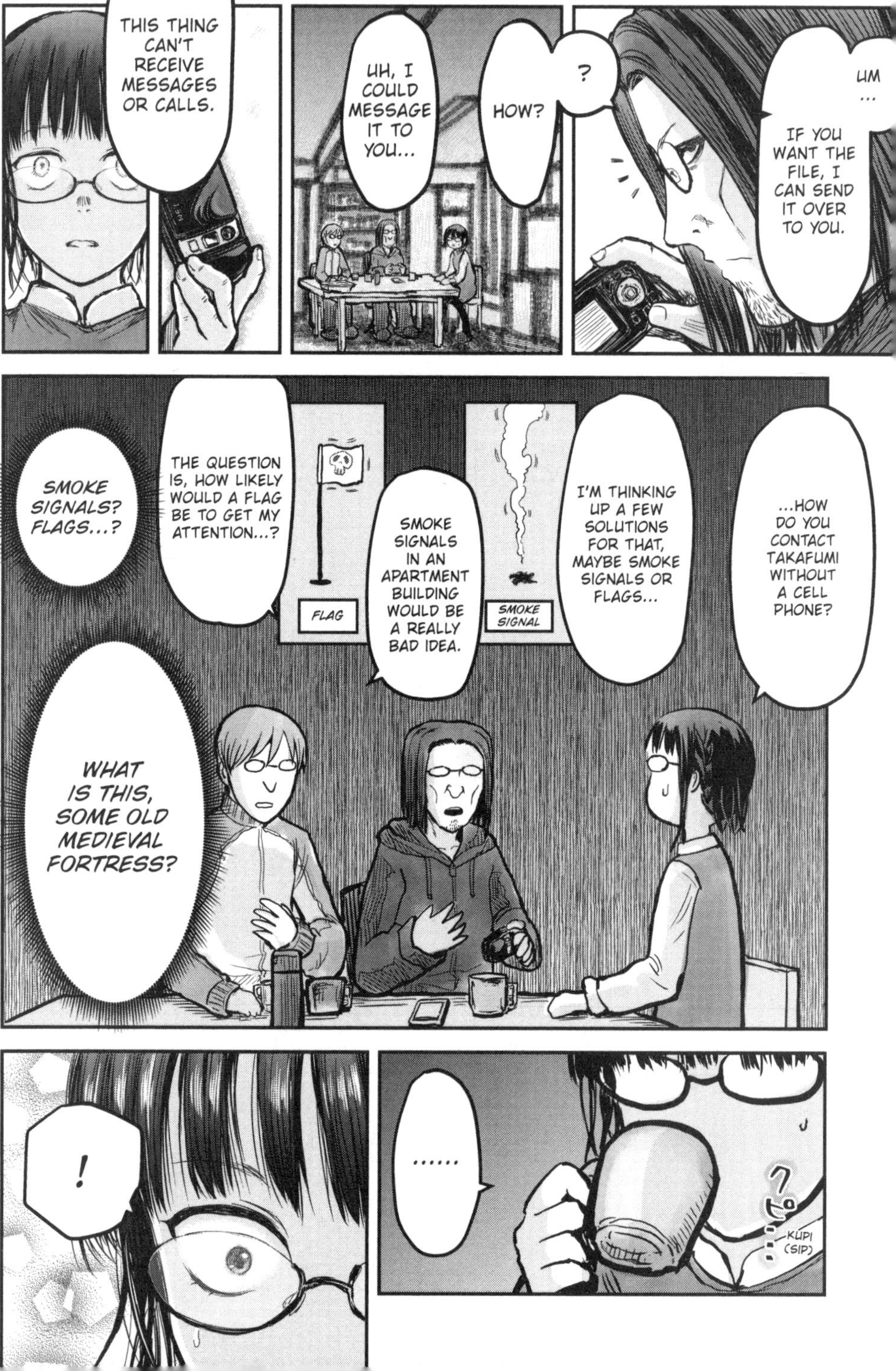
UM ...
IF YOU WANT THE FILE, I CAN SEND IT OVER TO YOU.
?
HOW?
UH, I COULD MESSAGE IT TO YOU...
THIS THING CAN'T RECEIVE MESSAGES OR CALLS.
...HOW DO YOU CONTACT TAKAFUMI WITHOUT A CELL PHONE?
I'M THINKING UP A FEW SOLUTIONS FOR THAT, MAYBE SMOKE SIGNALS OR FLAGS...
SMOKE SIGNAL
SMOKE SIGNALS IN AN APARTMENT BUILDING WOULD BE A REALLY BAD IDEA.
FLAG
THE QUESTION IS, HOW LIKELY WOULD A FLAG BE TO GET MY ATTENTION...?
SMOKE SIGNALS? FLAGS...?
WHAT IS THIS, SOME OLD MEDIEVAL FORTRESS?
KUPI (SIP)
......
!

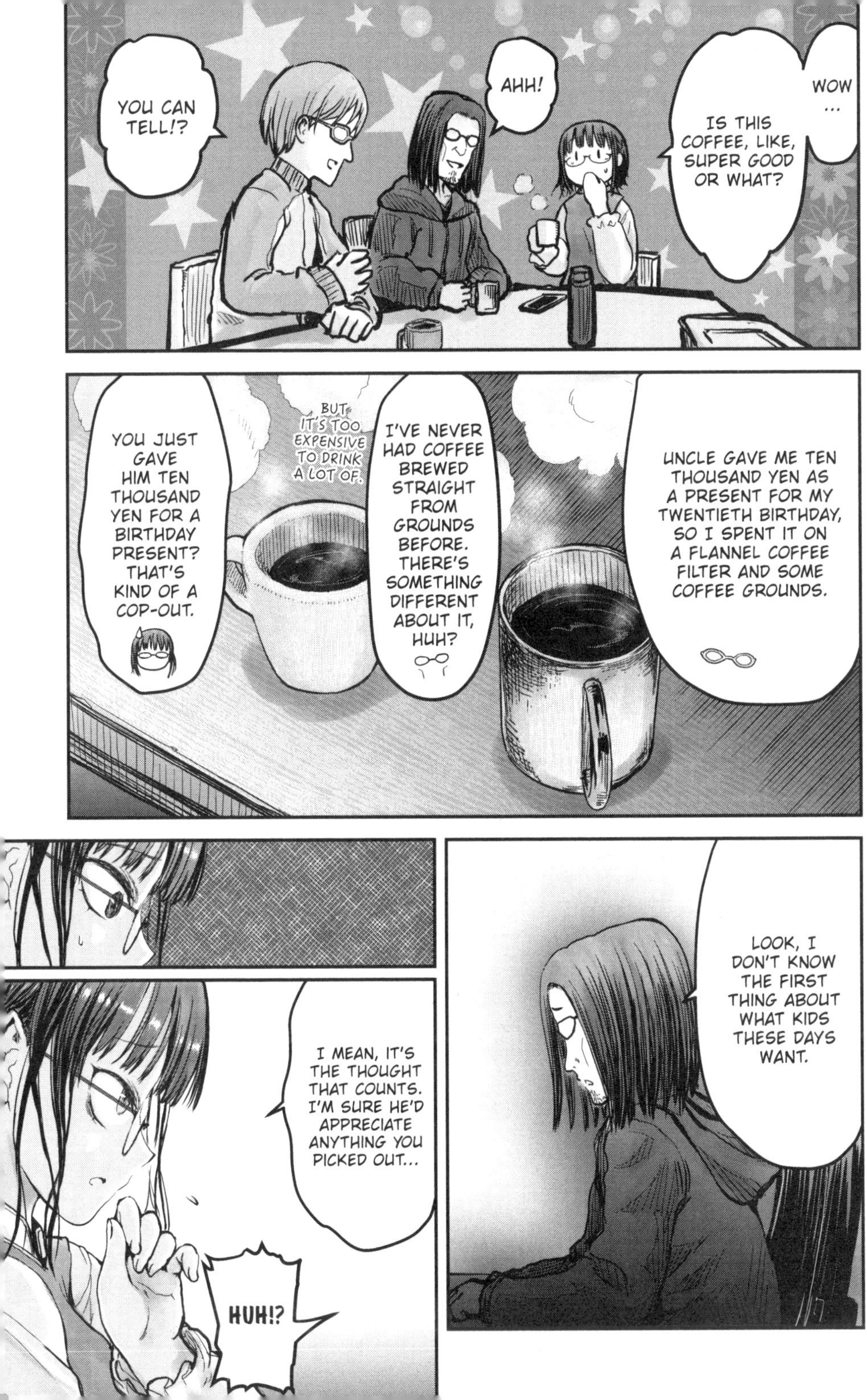
WOW ...
IS THIS COFFEE, LIKE, SUPER GOOD OR WHAT?
AHH!
YOU CAN TELL!?
UNCLE GAVE ME TEN THOUSAND YEN AS A PRESENT FOR MY TWENTIETH BIRTHDAY, SO I SPENT IT ON A FLANNEL COFFEE FILTER AND SOME COFFEE GROUNDS.
I'VE NEVER HAD COFFEE BREWED STRAIGHT FROM GROUNDS BEFORE. THERE'S SOMETHING DIFFERENT ABOUT IT, HUH?
BUT IT'S TOO EXPENSIVE TO DRINK A LOT OF.
YOU JUST GAVE HIM TEN THOUSAND YEN FOR A BIRTHDAY PRESENT? THAT'S KIND OF A COP-OUT.
LOOK, I DON'T KNOW THE FIRST THING ABOUT WHAT KIDS THESE DAYS WANT.
I MEAN, IT'S THE THOUGHT THAT COUNTS. I'M SURE HE'D APPRECIATE ANYTHING YOU PICKED OUT...
HUH!?

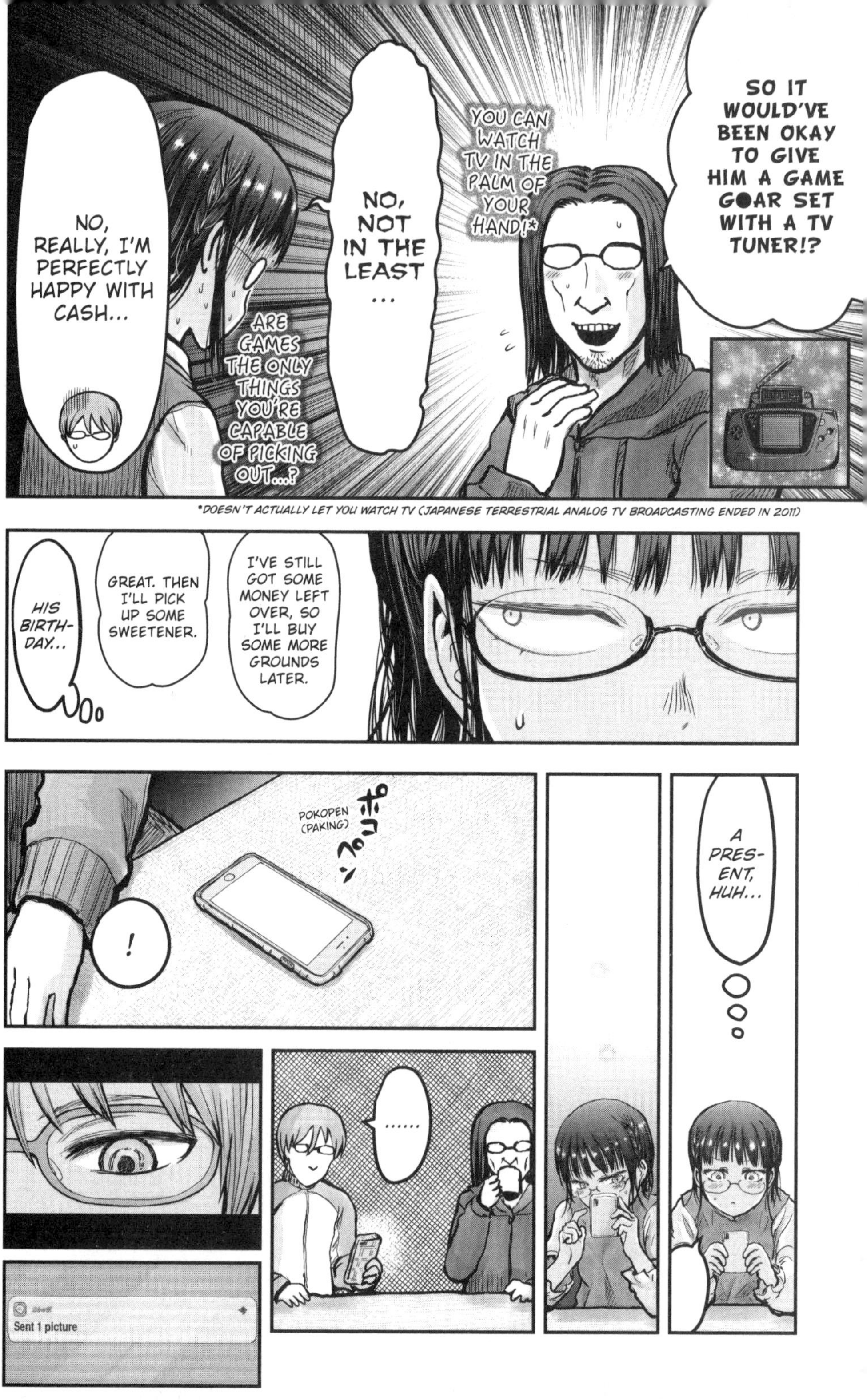
SO IT WOULD'VE BEEN OKAY TO GIVE HIM A GAME G●AR SET WITH A TV TUNER!?
YOU CAN WATCH TV IN THE PALM OF YOUR HAND!*
NO, NOT IN THE LEAST...
ARE GAMES THE ONLY THINGS YOU'RE CAPABLE OF PICKING OUT...?
NO, REALLY, I'M PERFECTLY HAPPY WITH CASH...
*DOESN'T ACTUALLY LET YOU WATCH TV (JAPANESE TERRESTRIAL ANALOG TV BROADCASTING ENDED IN 2011)
I'VE STILL GOT SOME MONEY LEFT OVER, SO I'LL BUY SOME MORE GROUNDS LATER.
GREAT. THEN I'LL PICK UP SOME SWEETENER.
HIS BIRTH-DAY...
A PRES-ENT, HUH...
POKOPEN (PAKING)
!
......
Sent 1 picture

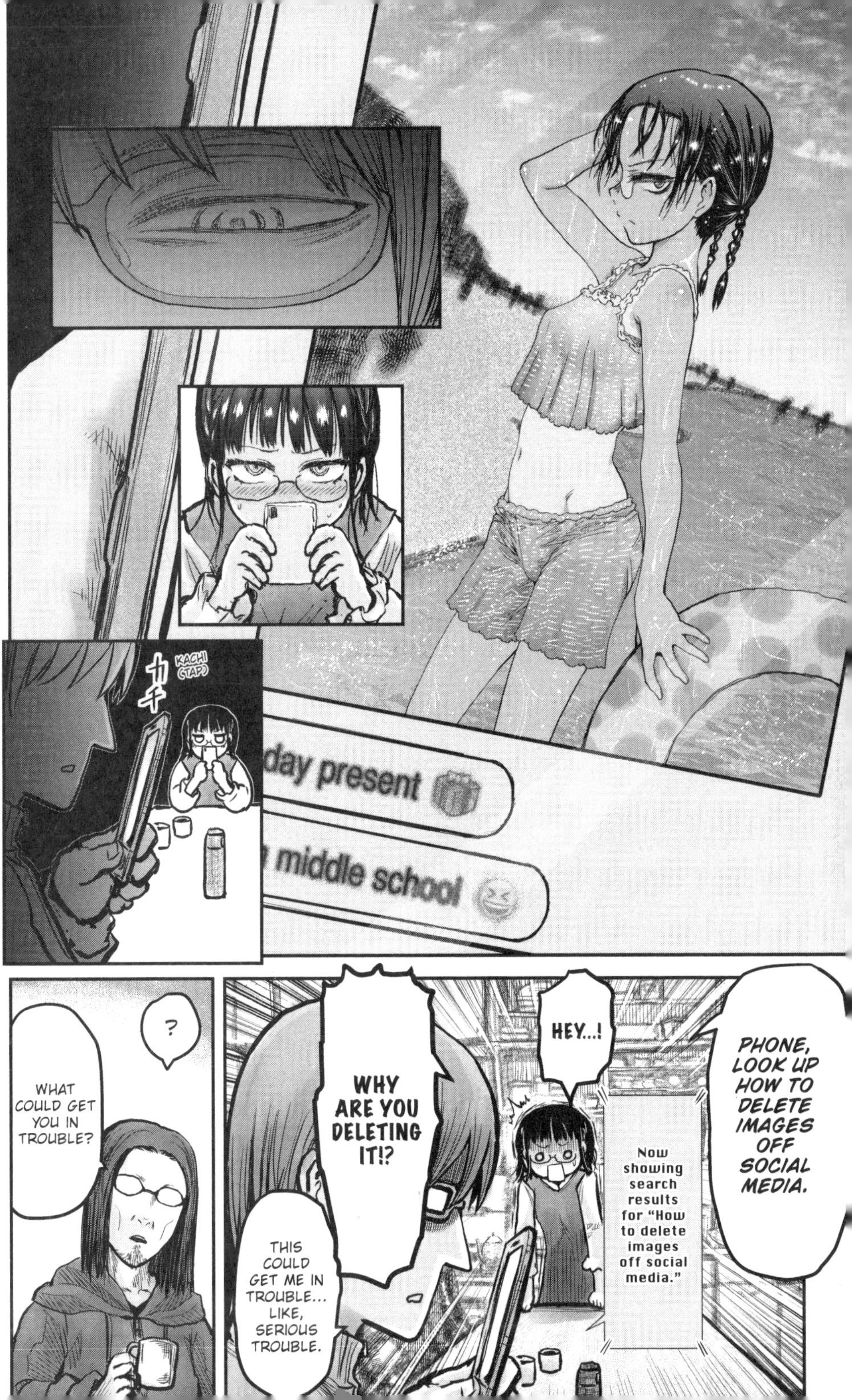
day present
middle school
カチ
KACHI (TAP)
PHONE, LOOK UP HOW TO DELETE IMAGES OFF SOCIAL MEDIA.
Now showing search results for "How to delete images off social media."
HEY...!
WHY ARE YOU DELETING IT!?
THIS COULD GET ME IN TROUBLE... LIKE, SERIOUS TROUBLE.
?
WHAT COULD GET YOU IN TROUBLE?

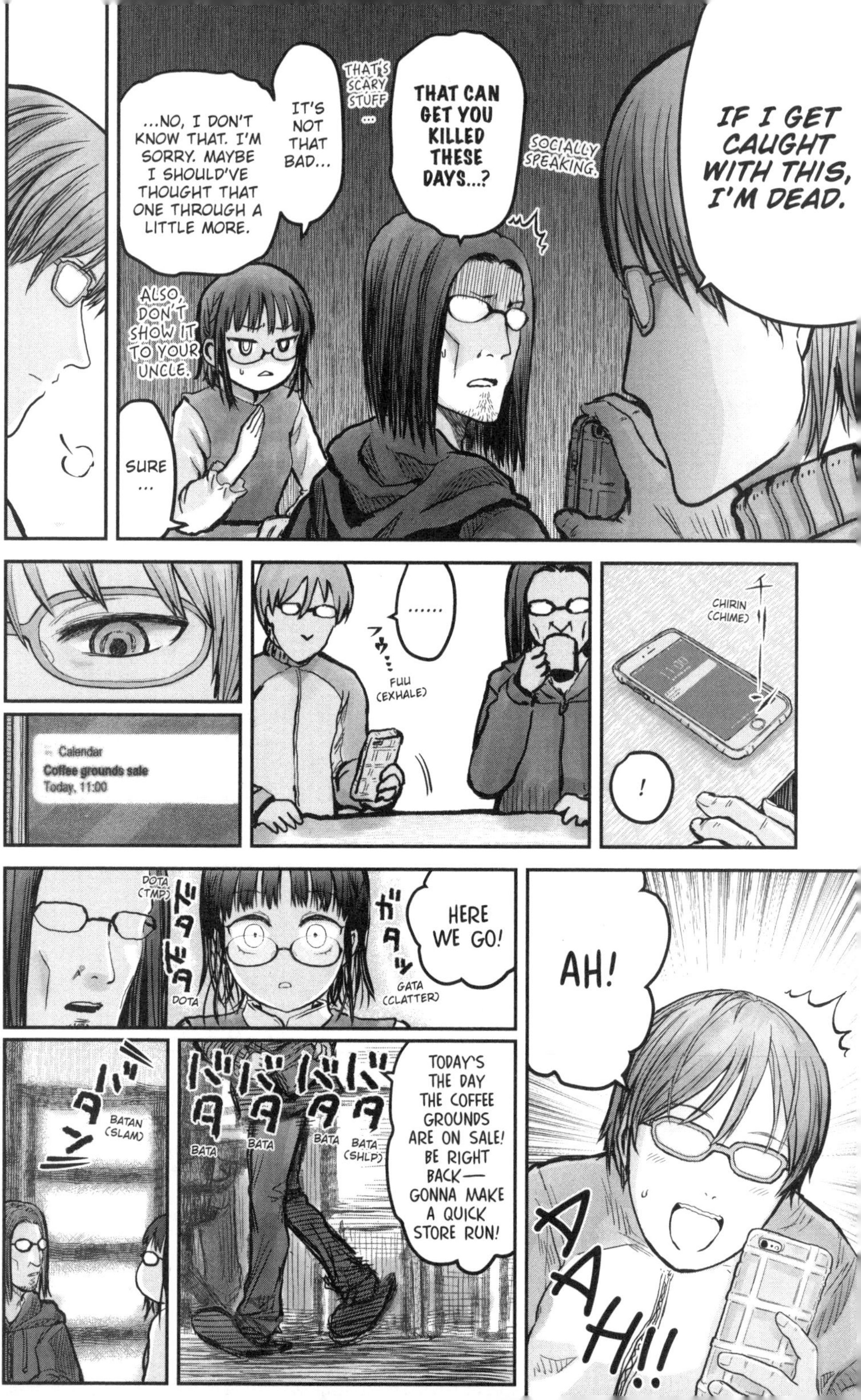
IF I GET CAUGHT WITH THIS, I'M DEAD.
SOCIALLY SPEAKING.
THAT CAN GET YOU KILLED THESE DAYS...?
THAT'S SCARY STUFF...
IT'S NOT THAT BAD...
...NO, I DON'T KNOW THAT. I'M SORRY. MAYBE I SHOULD'VE THOUGHT THAT ONE THROUGH A LITTLE MORE.
ALSO, DON'T SHOW IT TO YOUR UNCLE.
SURE...
CHIRIN (CHIME)
!
......
FUU (EXHALE)
Calendar
Coffee grounds sale
Today, 11:00
AH!
AAH!!
GATA (CLATTER)
HERE WE GO!
DOTA (TMP)
DOTA
TODAY'S THE DAY THE COFFEE GROUNDS ARE ON SALE! BE RIGHT BACK— GONNA MAKE A QUICK STORE RUN!
BATA (SHLP)
BATA
BATA
BATA
BATAN (SLAM)

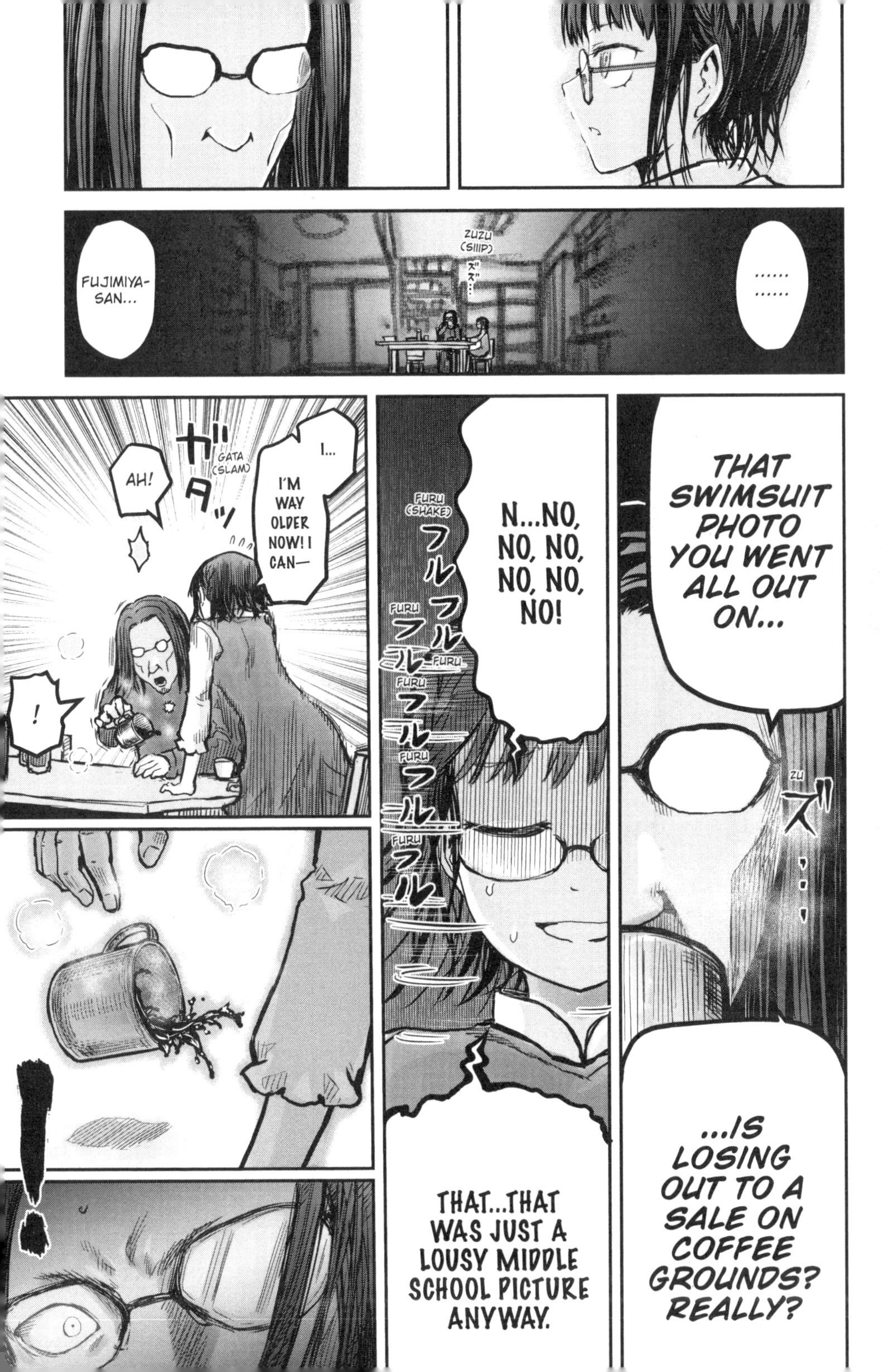
......
......
ZUZU (SIIIP)
ズズ…
FUJIMIYA-SAN...
THAT SWIMSUIT PHOTO YOU WENT ALL OUT ON...
ZU
ズ…
...IS LOSING OUT TO A SALE ON COFFEE GROUNDS? REALLY?
FURU (SHAKE) FURU FURU FURU FURU FURU
フルフルフルフルフルフル
N...NO, NO, NO, NO, NO, NO!
THAT...THAT WAS JUST A LOUSY MIDDLE SCHOOL PICTURE ANYWAY.
I...
I'M WAY OLDER NOW! I CAN—
GATA (SLAM)
ガタッ
AH!
!
!

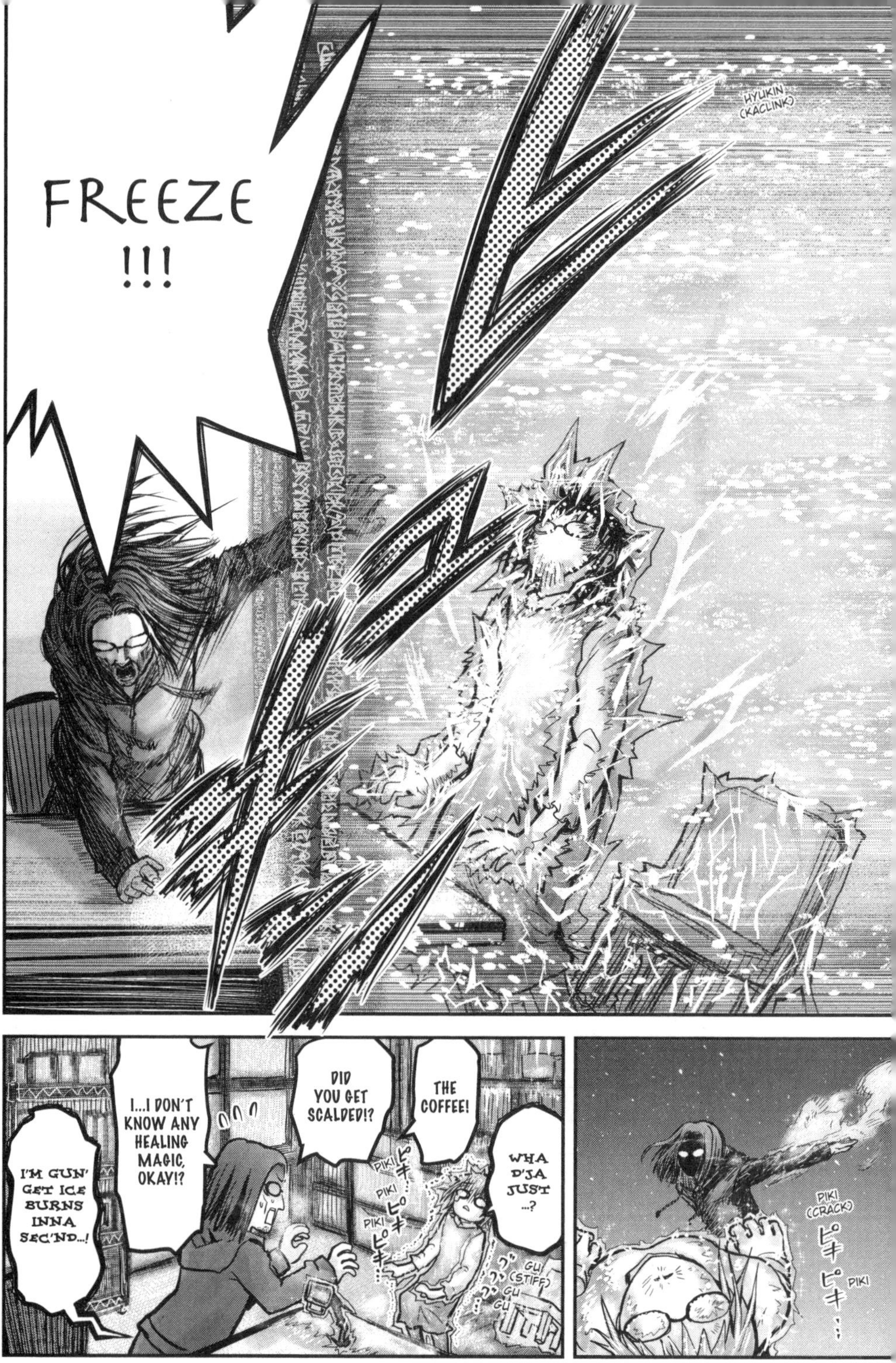
HYUKIN (KACLINK)
FREEZE !!!
PIKI (CRACK)
ピキ ピキ
PIKI
WHA D'JA JUST ...?
THE COFFEE!
DID YOU GET SCALDED!?
PIKI ピキ
PIKI ピキ
PIKI ピキ
GU (STIFF)
GU
GU
I...I DON'T KNOW ANY HEALING MAGIC, OKAY!?
I'M GUN' GET ICE BURNS INNA SEC'ND...!

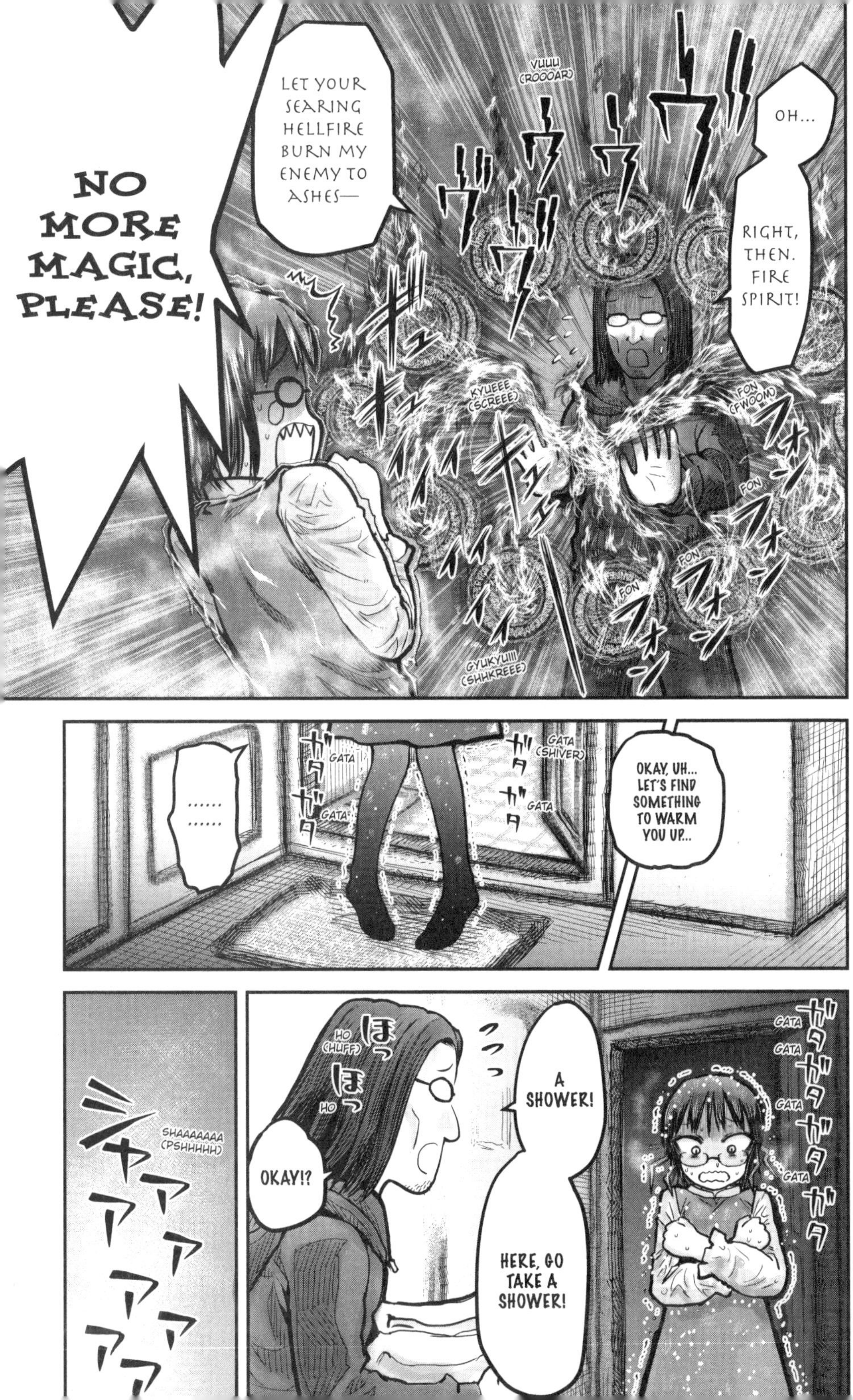
OH...
RIGHT, THEN. FIRE SPIRIT!
VUUU (ROOOAR)
LET YOUR SEARING HELLFIRE BURN MY ENEMY TO ASHES—
NO MORE MAGIC, PLEASE!
FON (FWOOM)
FON
FON
FON
KYUEEE (SCREEE)
GYUKYUIII (SHHKREEE)
OKAY, UH... LET'S FIND SOMETHING TO WARM YOU UP...
GATA (SHIVER)
GATA
GATA
GATA
......
......
GATA
GATA
GATA
GATA
A SHOWER!
HERE, GO TAKE A SHOWER!
HO (HUFF)
HO
OKAY!?
SHAAAAAAA (PSHHHHH)

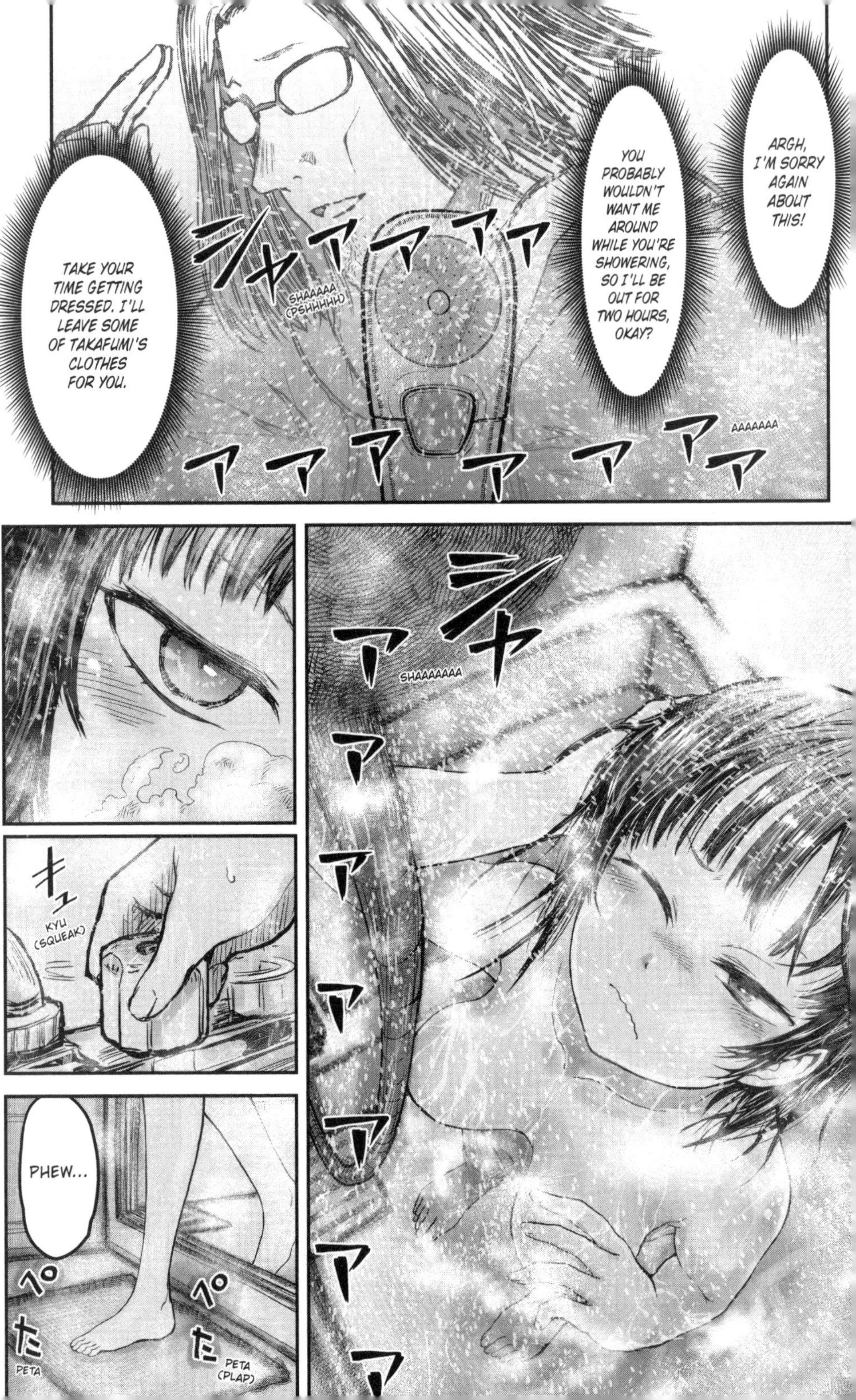
ARGH, I'M SORRY AGAIN ABOUT THIS!
YOU PROBABLY WOULDN'T WANT ME AROUND WHILE YOU'RE SHOWERING, SO I'LL BE OUT FOR TWO HOURS, OKAY?
シャアアア
SHAAAAA (PSHHHHHH)
TAKE YOUR TIME GETTING DRESSED. I'LL LEAVE SOME OF TAKAFUMI'S CLOTHES FOR YOU.
アアアアアア
AAAAAAA
シャアアアアアア
SHAAAAAAA
キュ
KYU (SQUEAK)
PHEW...
ペた
PETA
ペた
PETA (PLAP)

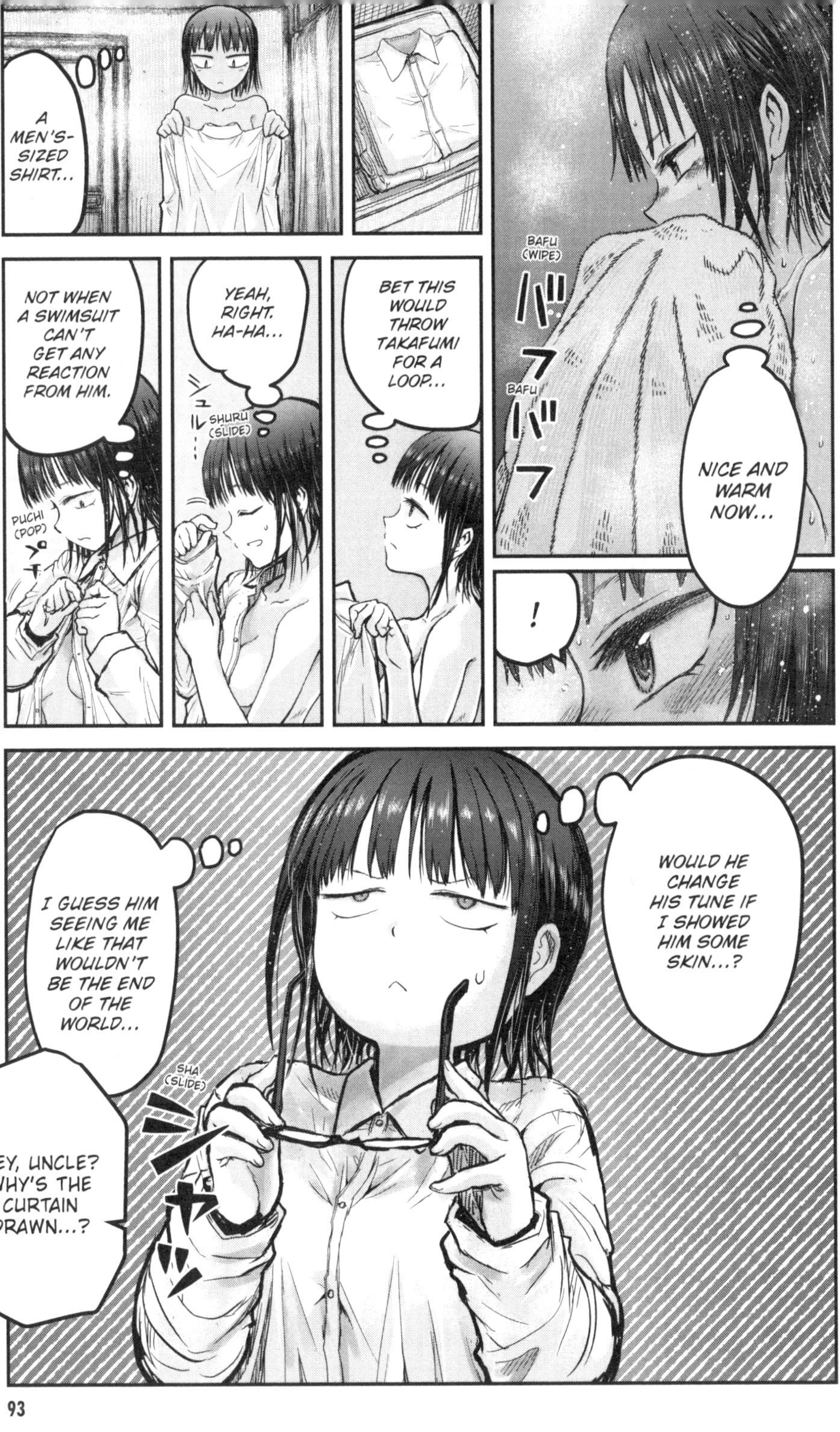
BAFU (WIPE)
BAFU
NICE AND WARM NOW...
!
A MEN'S-SIZED SHIRT...
BET THIS WOULD THROW TAKAFUMI FOR A LOOP...
YEAH, RIGHT. HA-HA...
SHURU (SLIDE)
NOT WHEN A SWIMSUIT CAN'T GET ANY REACTION FROM HIM.
PUCHI (POP)
WOULD HE CHANGE HIS TUNE IF I SHOWED HIM SOME SKIN...?
I GUESS HIM SEEING ME LIKE THAT WOULDN'T BE THE END OF THE WORLD...
SHA (SLIDE)
HEY, UNCLE? WHY'S THE CURTAIN DRAWN...?

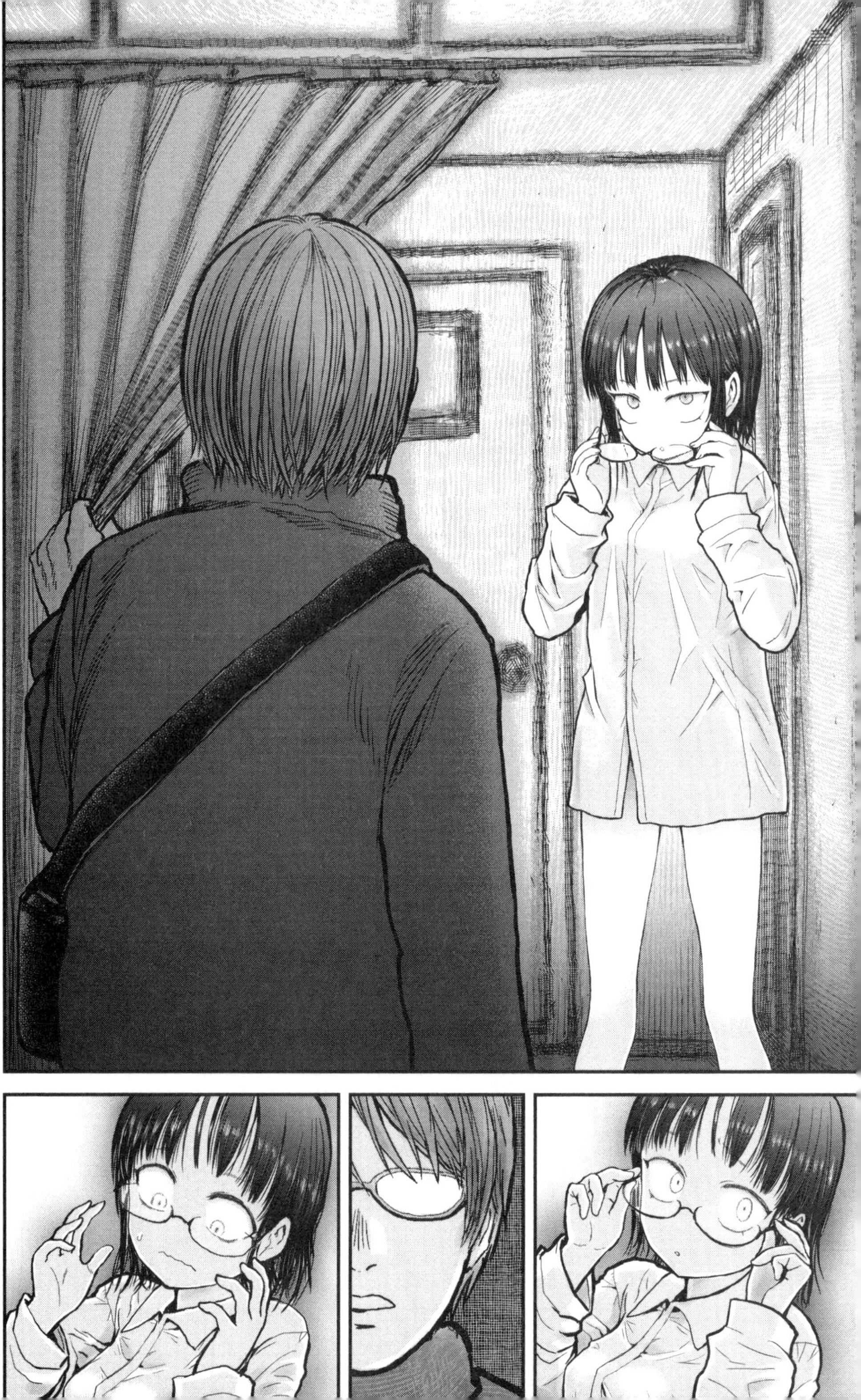

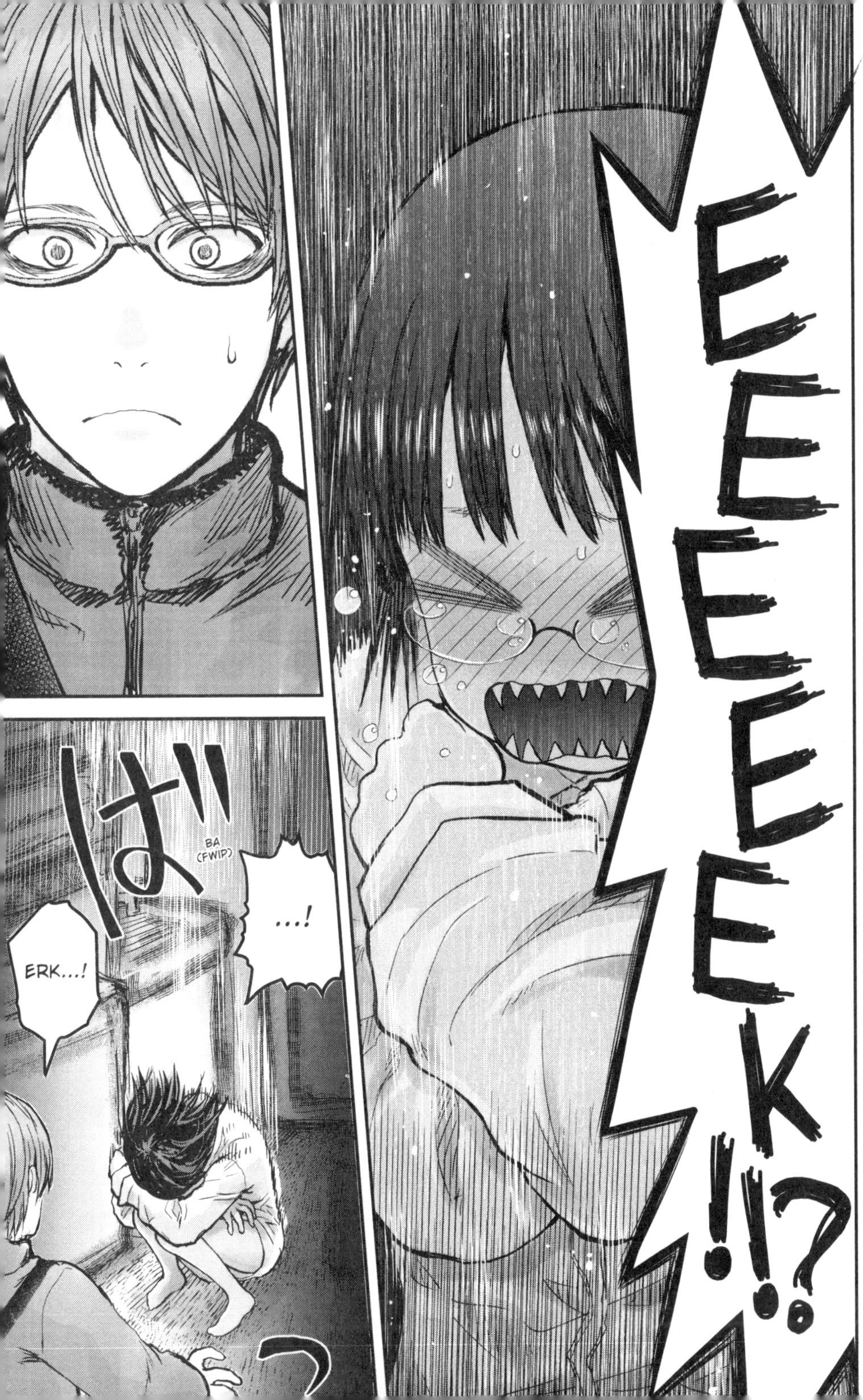
EEEEEK!!?
BA
(FWIP)
...!
ERK...!

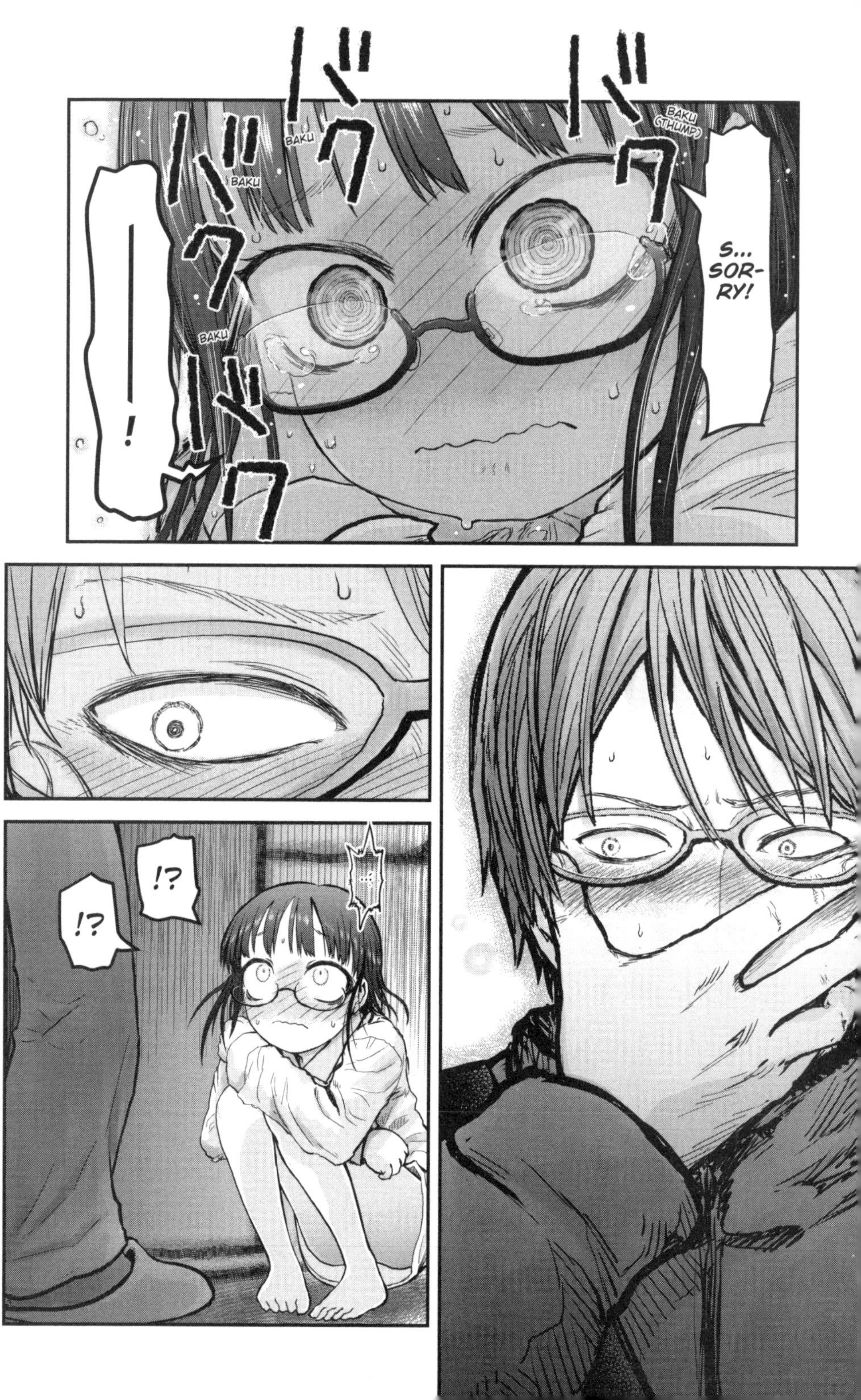
BAKU (THUMP)
S... SORRY!
BAKU
BAKU
BAKU
—!
...!
!?
!?

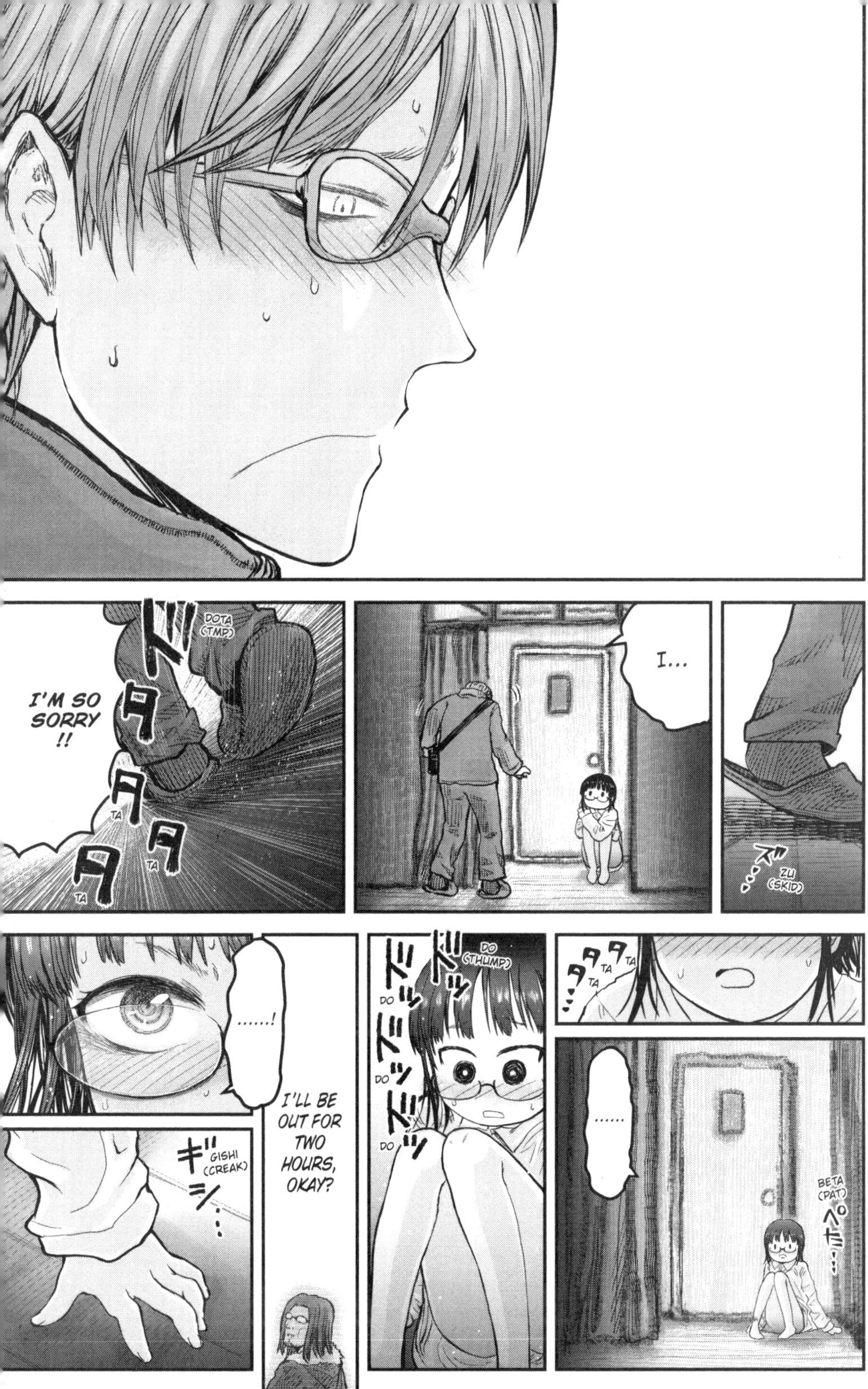
ZU (SKID)
I...
DOTA (TMP)
I'M SO SORRY !!
TA
TA
TA
TA TA TA
......
BETA (PAT)
DO (THUMP)
DO
DO
DO
I'LL BE OUT FOR TWO HOURS, OKAY?
......!
GISHI (CREAK)

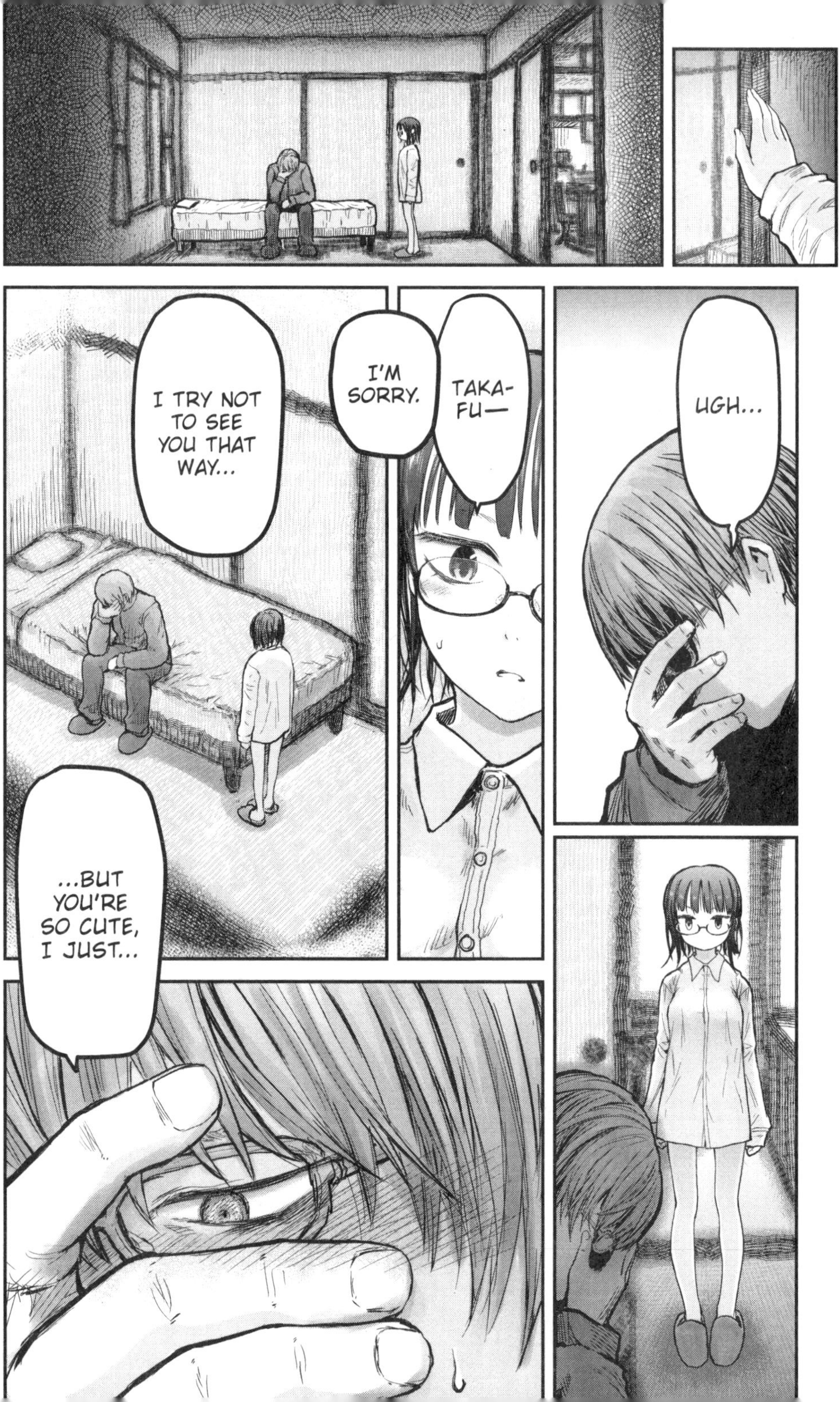
UGH...
TAKA-FU—
I'M SORRY.
I TRY NOT TO SEE YOU THAT WAY...
...BUT YOU'RE SO CUTE, I JUST...

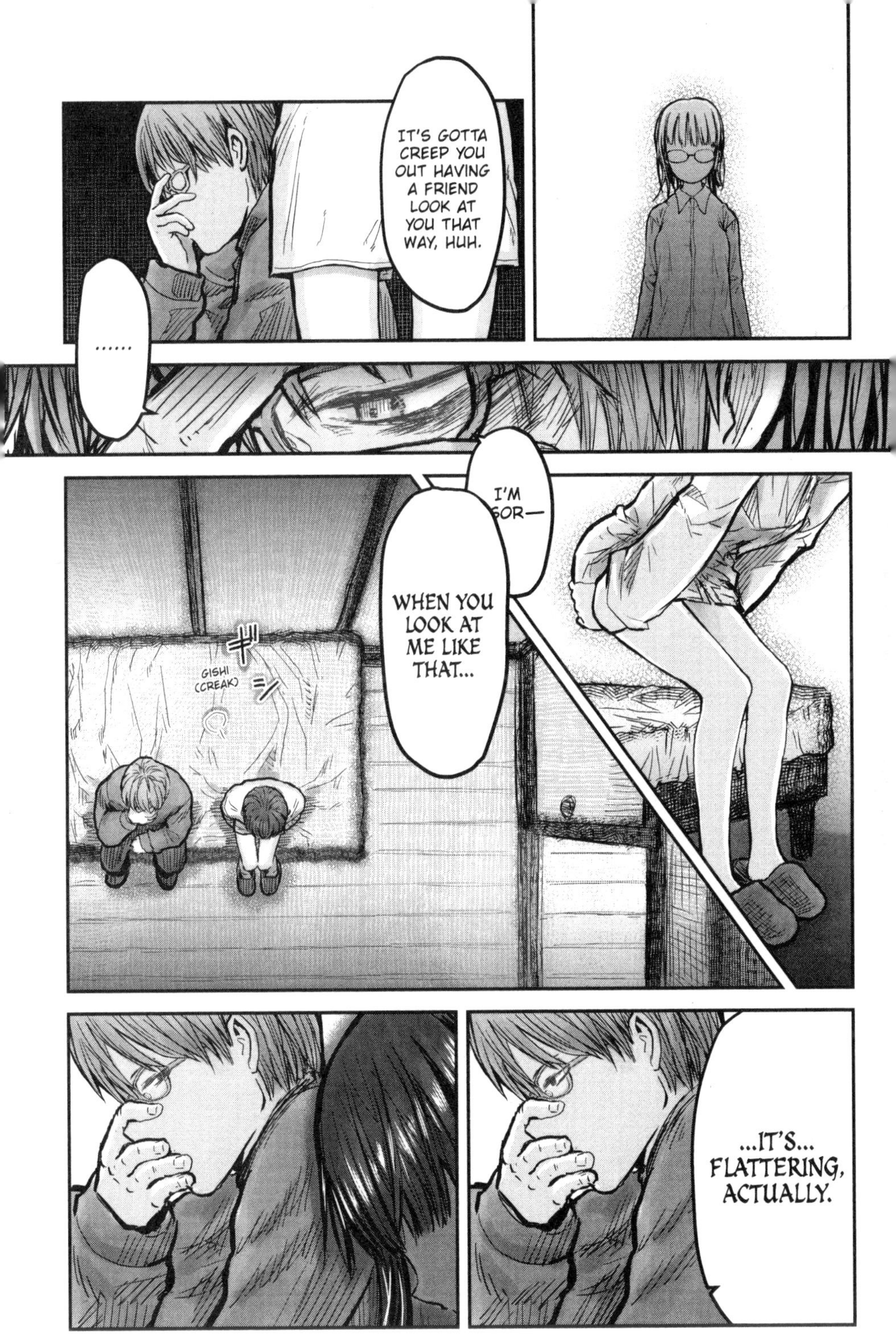
IT'S GOTTA CREEP YOU OUT HAVING A FRIEND LOOK AT YOU THAT WAY, HUH.
......
I'M SOR—
WHEN YOU LOOK AT ME LIKE THAT...
ギシ
GISHI (CREAK)
...IT'S... FLATTERING, ACTUALLY.

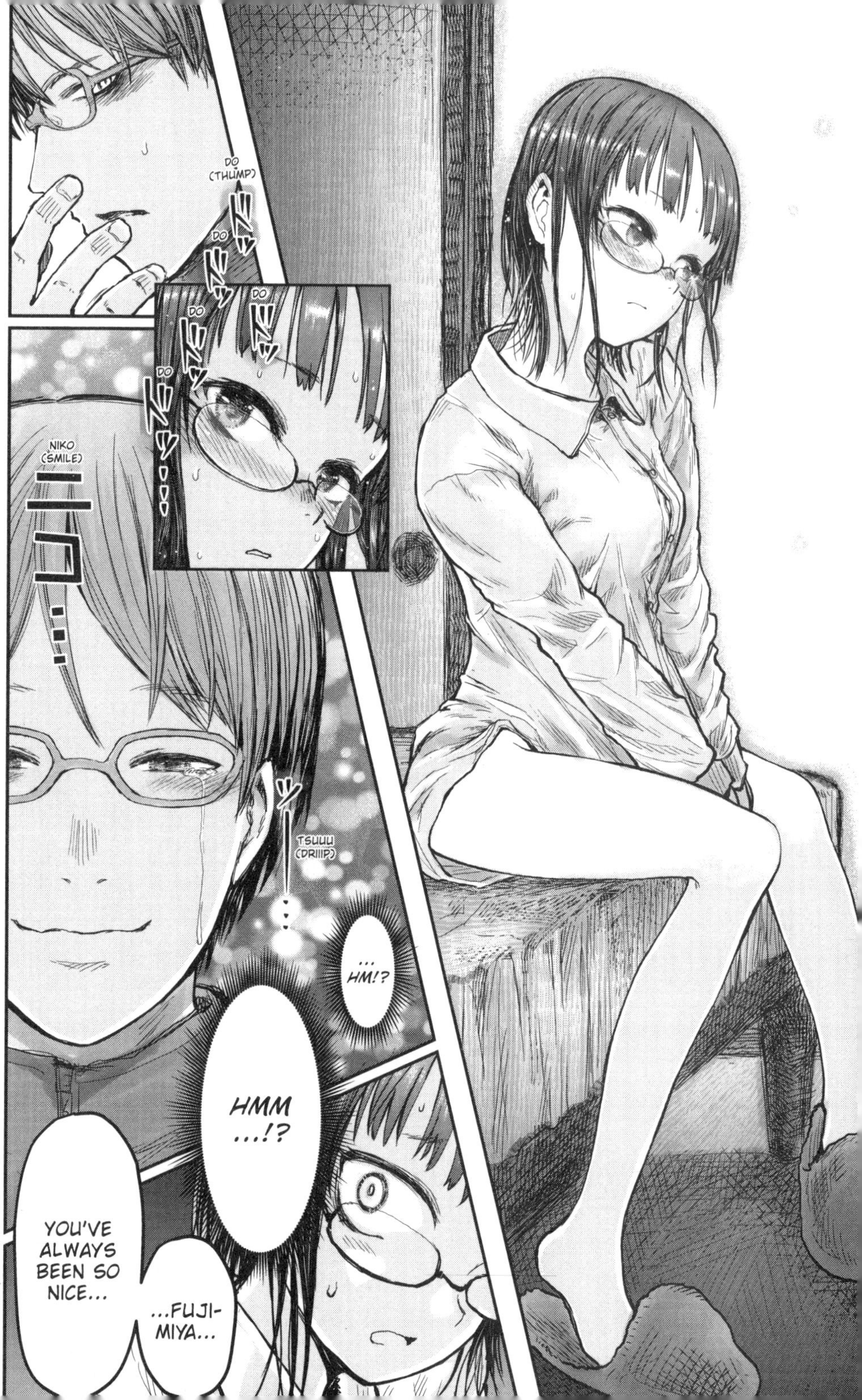
DO
(THUMP)
DO
DO
DO
DO
NIKO
(SMILE)
TSUUU
(DRIIIP)
...HM!?
HMM...!?
YOU'VE ALWAYS BEEN SO NICE...
...FUJI-MIYA...

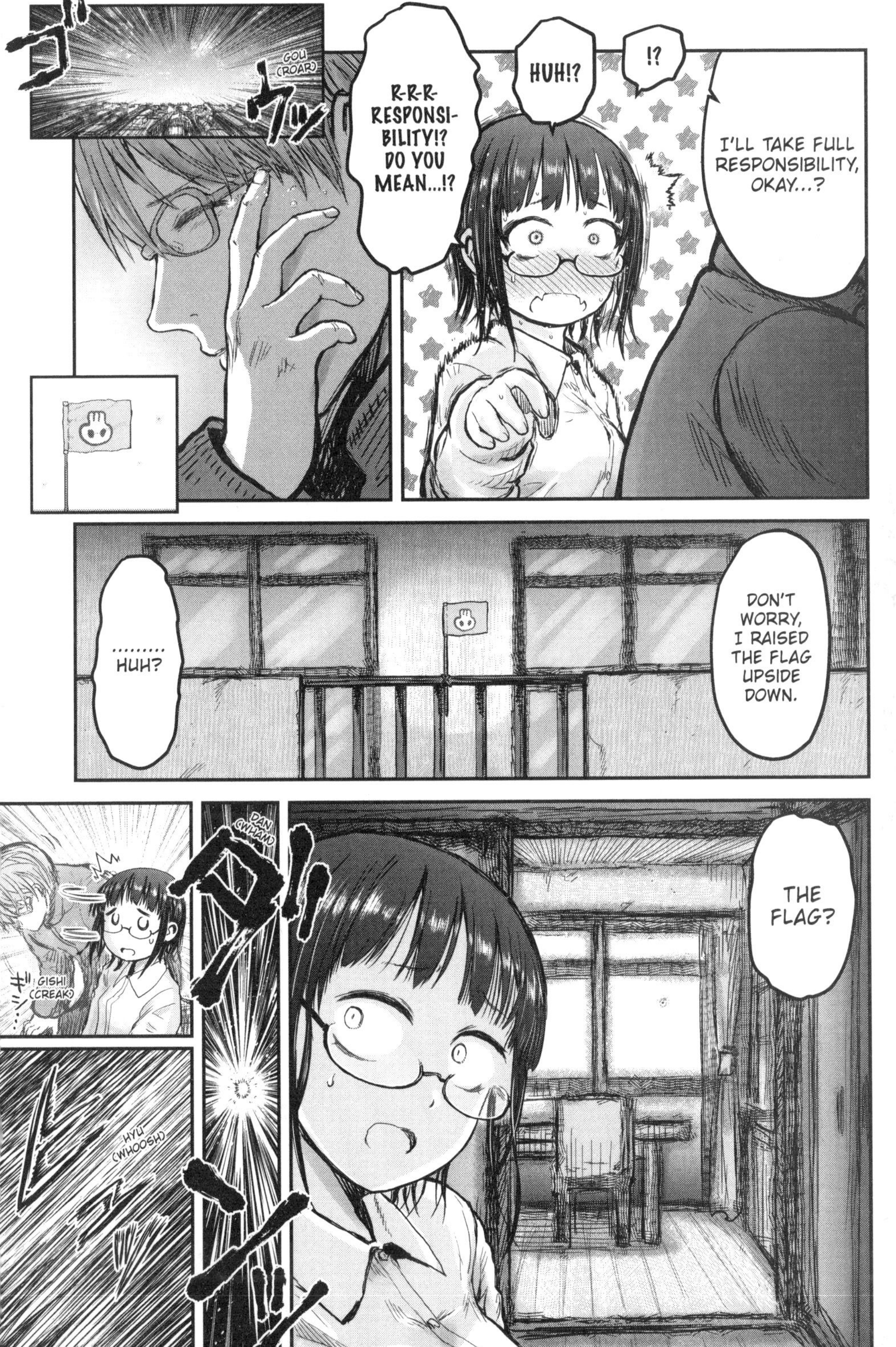
I'LL TAKE FULL RESPONSIBILITY, OKAY...?
!?
HUH!?
R-R-R-RESPONSIBILITY!? DO YOU MEAN...!?
GOU (ROAR)
DON'T WORRY, I RAISED THE FLAG UPSIDE DOWN.
.... HUH?
THE FLAG?
DAN (WHAM)
GISHI (CREAK)
HYU (WHOOSH)

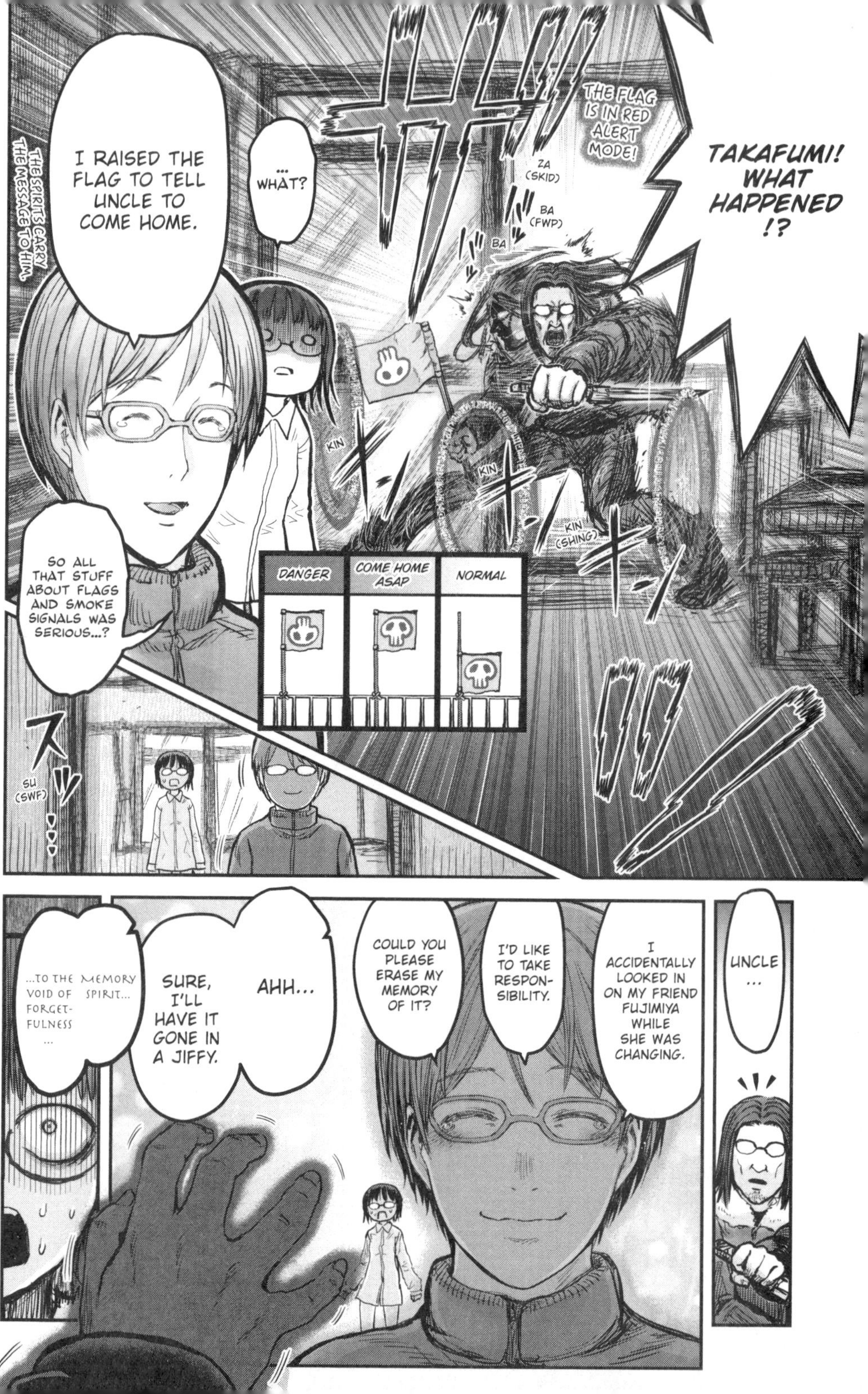
TAKAFUMI! WHAT HAPPENED!?
THE FLAG IS IN RED ALERT MODE!
ZA (SKID)
BA (FWP)
BA
KIN
KIN
KIN (SHING)
...WHAT?
I RAISED THE FLAG TO TELL UNCLE TO COME HOME.
THE SPIRITS CARRY THE MESSAGE TO HIM.
DANGER
COME HOME ASAP
NORMAL
SO ALL THAT STUFF ABOUT FLAGS AND SMOKE SIGNALS WAS SERIOUS...?
SU (SWF)
UNCLE ...
I ACCIDENTALLY LOOKED IN ON MY FRIEND FUJIMIYA WHILE SHE WAS CHANGING.
I'D LIKE TO TAKE RESPON-SIBILITY.
COULD YOU PLEASE ERASE MY MEMORY OF IT?
AHH...
SURE, I'LL HAVE IT GONE IN A JIFFY.
...TO THE MEMORY SPIRIT...
VOID OF FORGET-FULNESS ...

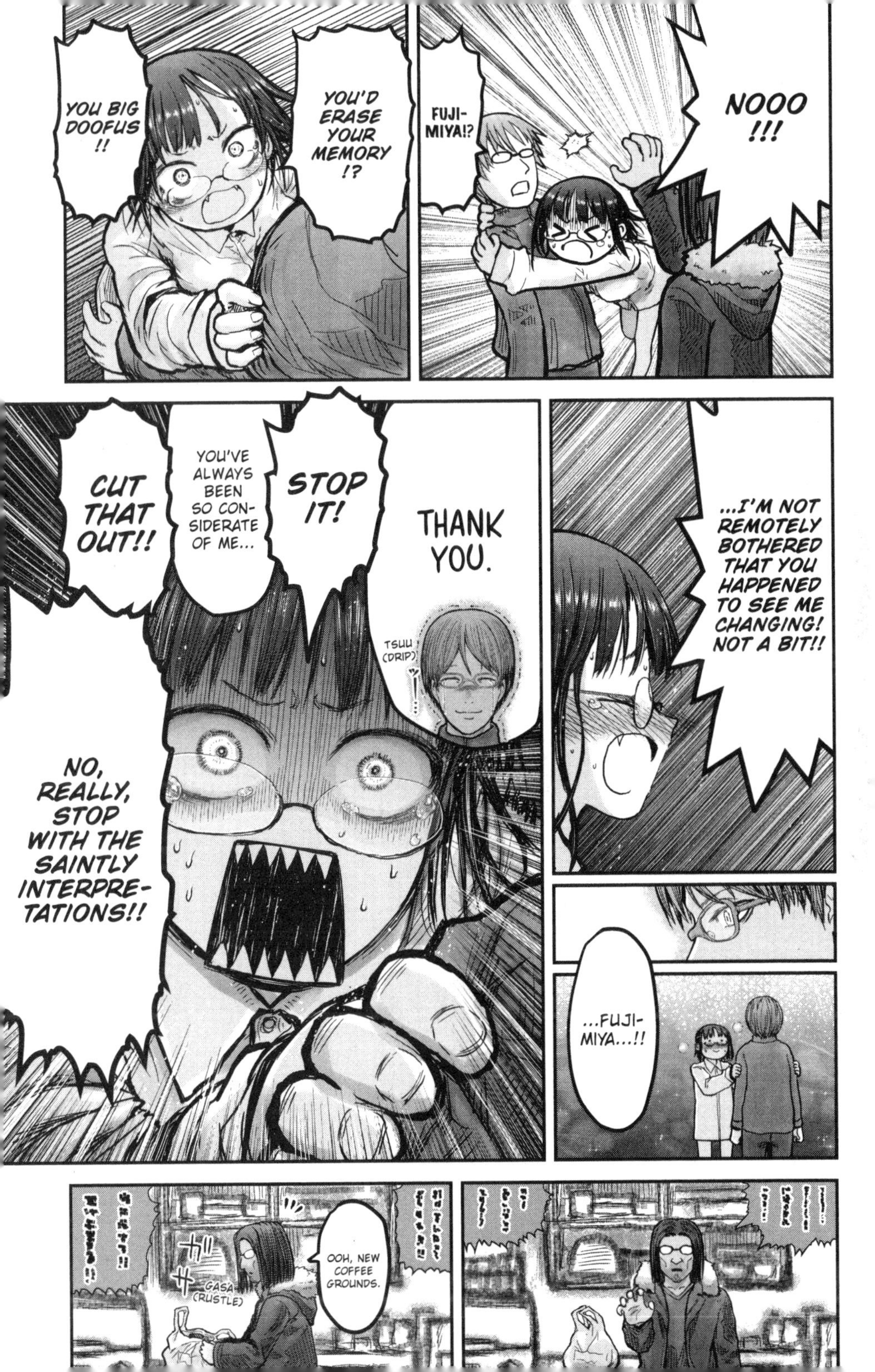
NOOO!!!
FUJI-MIYA!?
YOU'D ERASE YOUR MEMORY!?
YOU BIG DOOFUS!!
...I'M NOT REMOTELY BOTHERED THAT YOU HAPPENED TO SEE ME CHANGING! NOT A BIT!!
...FUJI-MIYA...!!
THANK YOU.
TSUU (DRIP)
STOP IT!
YOU'VE ALWAYS BEEN SO CON-SIDERATE OF ME...
CUT THAT OUT!!
NO, REALLY, STOP WITH THE SAINTLY INTERPRE-TATIONS!!
OOH, NEW COFFEE GROUNDS.
GASA (RUSTLE)

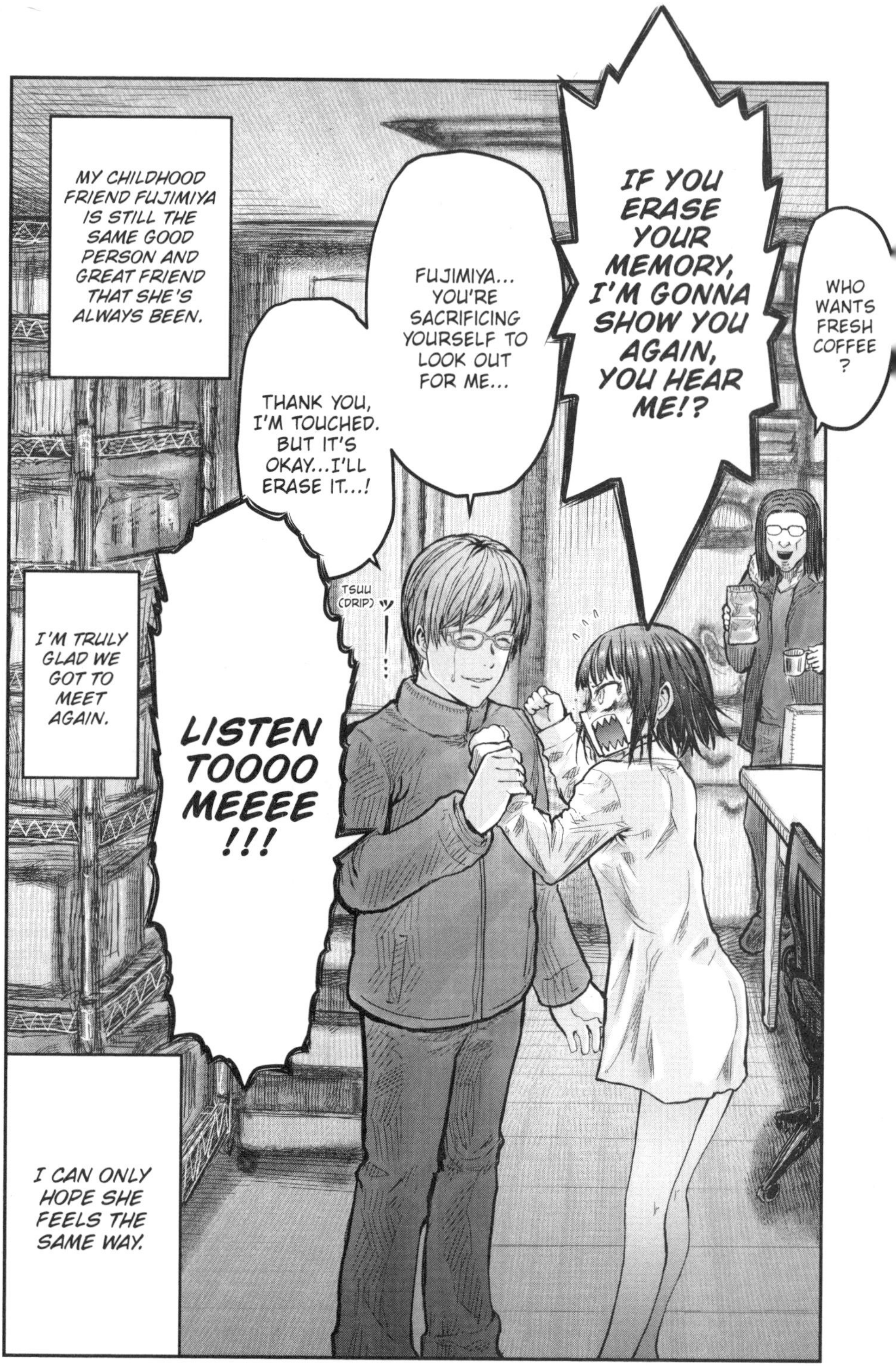
IF YOU ERASE YOUR MEMORY, I'M GONNA SHOW YOU AGAIN, YOU HEAR ME!?
WHO WANTS FRESH COFFEE?
FUJIMIYA... YOU'RE SACRIFICING YOURSELF TO LOOK OUT FOR ME...
MY CHILDHOOD FRIEND FUJIMIYA IS STILL THE SAME GOOD PERSON AND GREAT FRIEND THAT SHE'S ALWAYS BEEN.
THANK YOU, I'M TOUCHED. BUT IT'S OKAY...I'LL ERASE IT...!
TSUU (DRIP)
LISTEN TOOOO MEEEE!!!
I'M TRULY GLAD WE GOT TO MEET AGAIN.
I CAN ONLY HOPE SHE FEELS THE SAME WAY.

Childhood Friend

Someone who has been close friends with a person since a young age. Due to its use as a staple in works of fiction, this figure is often assumed to be a close friend of the opposite sex, but the original term has no gender-related connotations.

UNCLE from ANOTHER WORLD

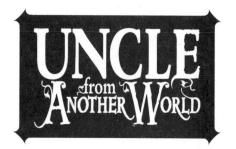

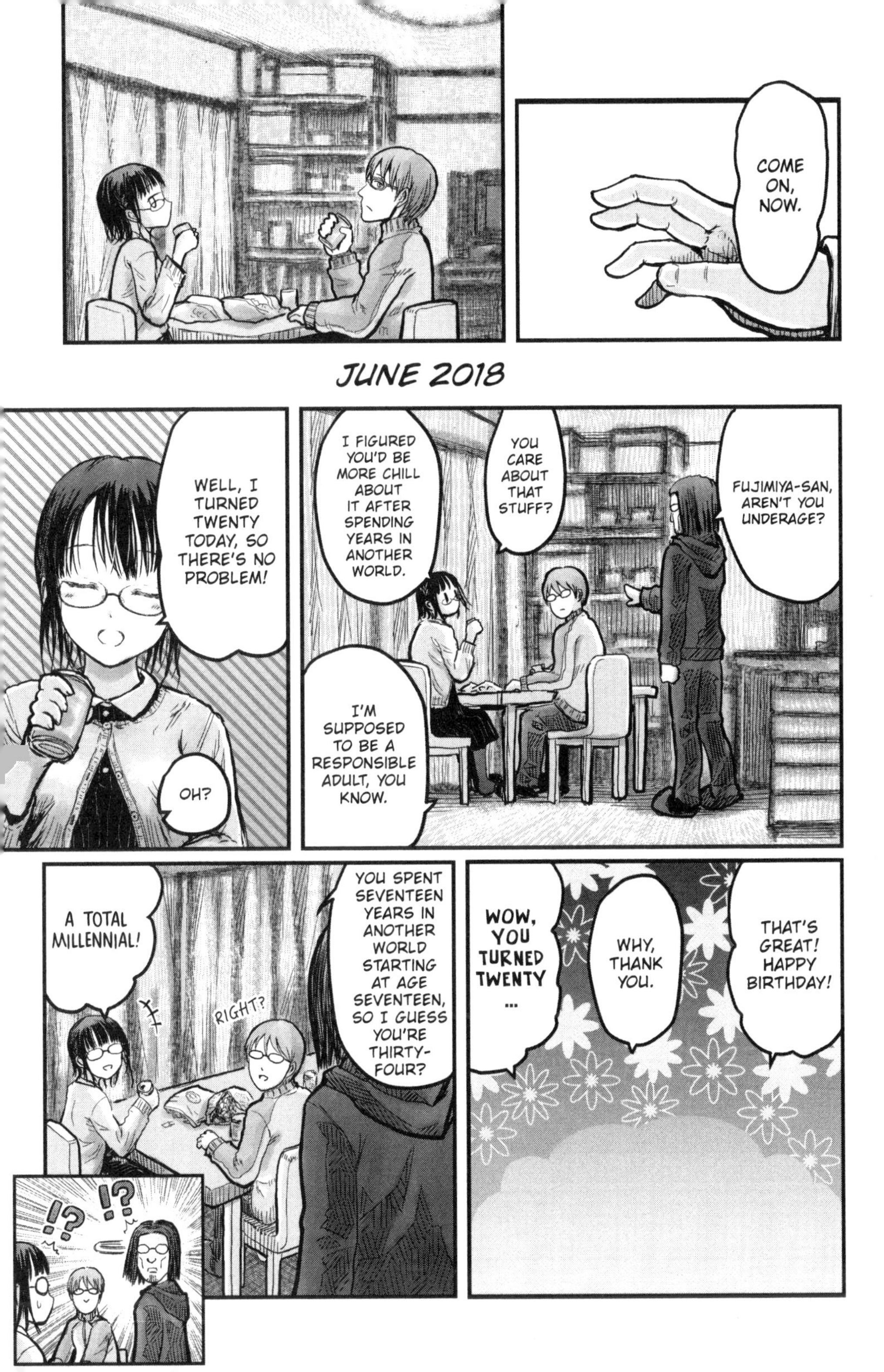
COME ON, NOW.
JUNE 2018
FUJIMIYA-SAN, AREN'T YOU UNDERAGE?
YOU CARE ABOUT THAT STUFF?
I FIGURED YOU'D BE MORE CHILL ABOUT IT AFTER SPENDING YEARS IN ANOTHER WORLD.
I'M SUPPOSED TO BE A RESPONSIBLE ADULT, YOU KNOW.
WELL, I TURNED TWENTY TODAY, SO THERE'S NO PROBLEM!
OH?
THAT'S GREAT! HAPPY BIRTHDAY!
WHY, THANK YOU.
WOW, YOU TURNED TWENTY ...
YOU SPENT SEVENTEEN YEARS IN ANOTHER WORLD STARTING AT AGE SEVENTEEN, SO I GUESS YOU'RE THIRTY-FOUR?
A TOTAL MILLENNIAL!
RIGHT?
!? !?

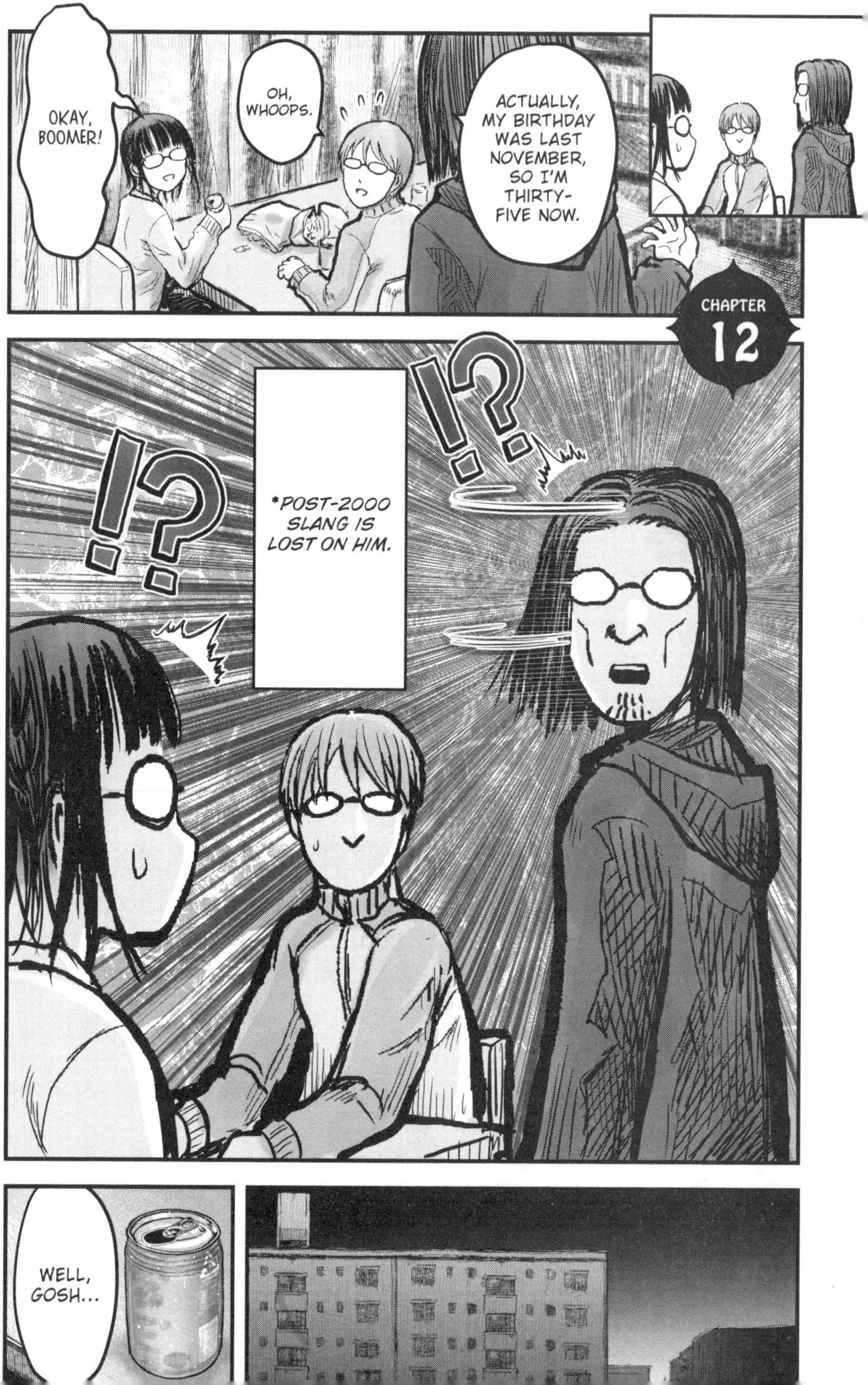
ACTUALLY, MY BIRTHDAY WAS LAST NOVEMBER, SO I'M THIRTY-FIVE NOW.
OH, WHOOPS.
OKAY, BOOMER!
CHAPTER 12
*POST-2000 SLANG IS LOST ON HIM.
WELL, GOSH...

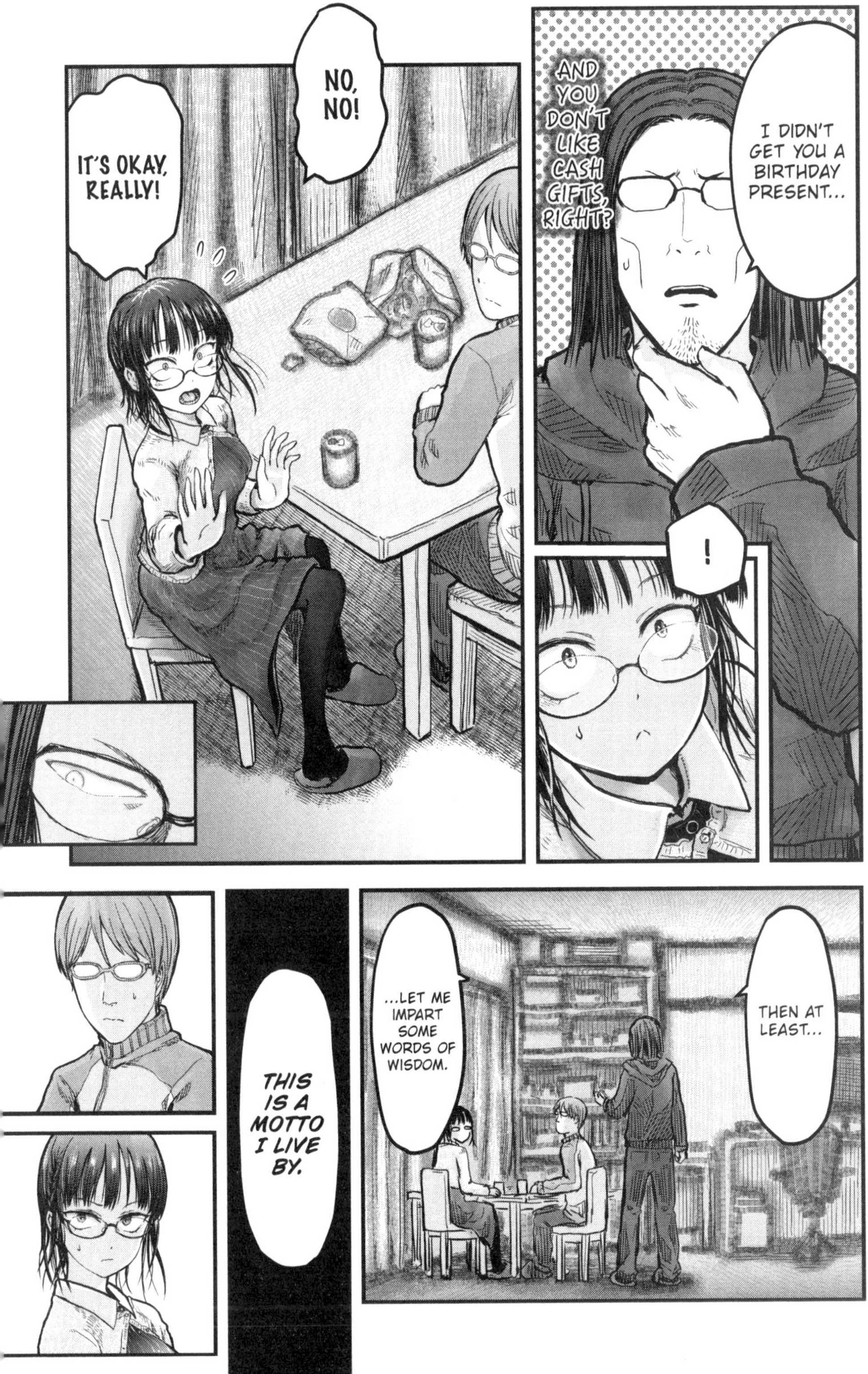
I DIDN'T GET YOU A BIRTHDAY PRESENT...
AND YOU DON'T LIKE CASH GIFTS, RIGHT?
!
NO, NO!
IT'S OKAY, REALLY!
THEN AT LEAST...
...LET ME IMPART SOME WORDS OF WISDOM.
THIS IS A MOTTO I LIVE BY.

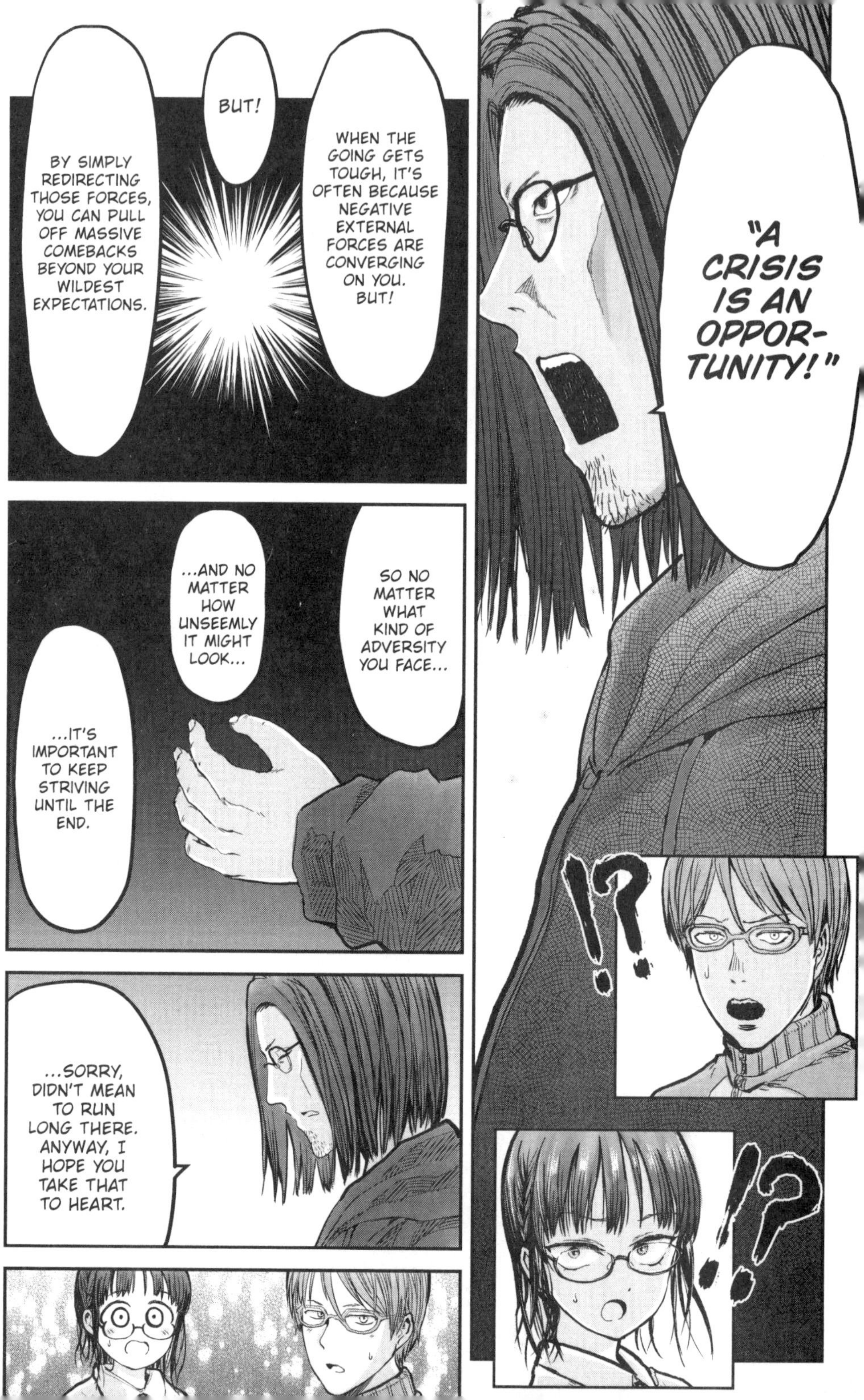
"A CRISIS IS AN OPPOR-TUNITY!"
!?
!?
WHEN THE GOING GETS TOUGH, IT'S OFTEN BECAUSE NEGATIVE EXTERNAL FORCES ARE CONVERGING ON YOU. BUT!
BUT!
BY SIMPLY REDIRECTING THOSE FORCES, YOU CAN PULL OFF MASSIVE COMEBACKS BEYOND YOUR WILDEST EXPECTATIONS.
SO NO MATTER WHAT KIND OF ADVERSITY YOU FACE...
...AND NO MATTER HOW UNSEEMLY IT MIGHT LOOK...
...IT'S IMPORTANT TO KEEP STRIVING UNTIL THE END.
...SORRY, DIDN'T MEAN TO RUN LONG THERE. ANYWAY, I HOPE YOU TAKE THAT TO HEART.

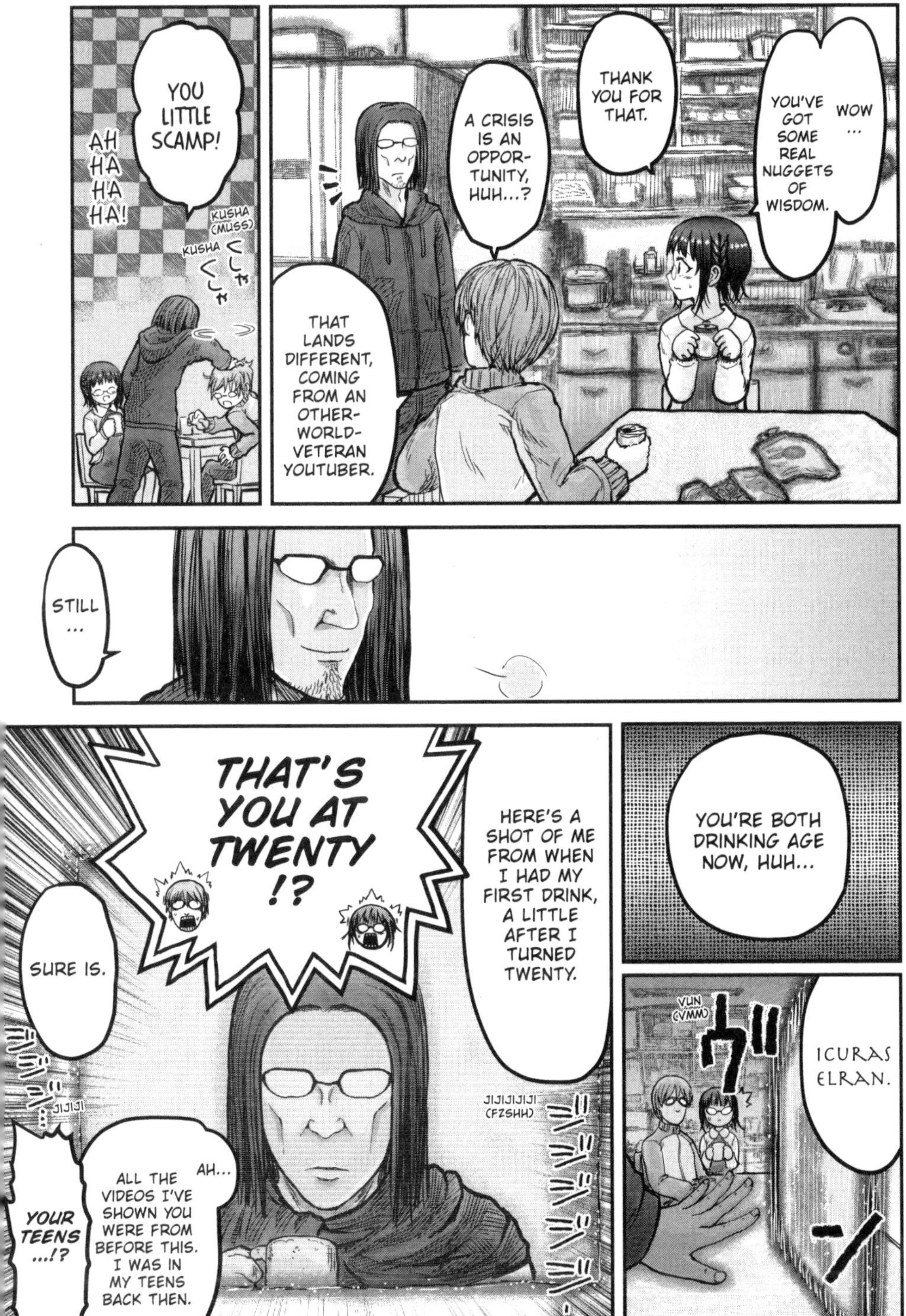
WOW...
YOU'VE GOT SOME REAL NUGGETS OF WISDOM.
THANK YOU FOR THAT.
A CRISIS IS AN OPPORTUNITY, HUH...?
THAT LANDS DIFFERENT, COMING FROM AN OTHER-WORLD-VETERAN YOUTUBER.
YOU LITTLE SCAMP!
AH HA HA HA!
KUSHA (MUSS)
KUSHA
くしゃくしゃ
STILL...
YOU'RE BOTH DRINKING AGE NOW, HUH...
VUN (VMM)
ヴー
ICURAS ELRAN.
HERE'S A SHOT OF ME FROM WHEN I HAD MY FIRST DRINK, A LITTLE AFTER I TURNED TWENTY.
THAT'S YOU AT TWENTY!?
SURE IS.
JIJIJIJIJI (FZSHH)
AH...
ALL THE VIDEOS I'VE SHOWN YOU WERE FROM BEFORE THIS. I WAS IN MY TEENS BACK THEN.
YOUR TEENS...!?
JIJIJI

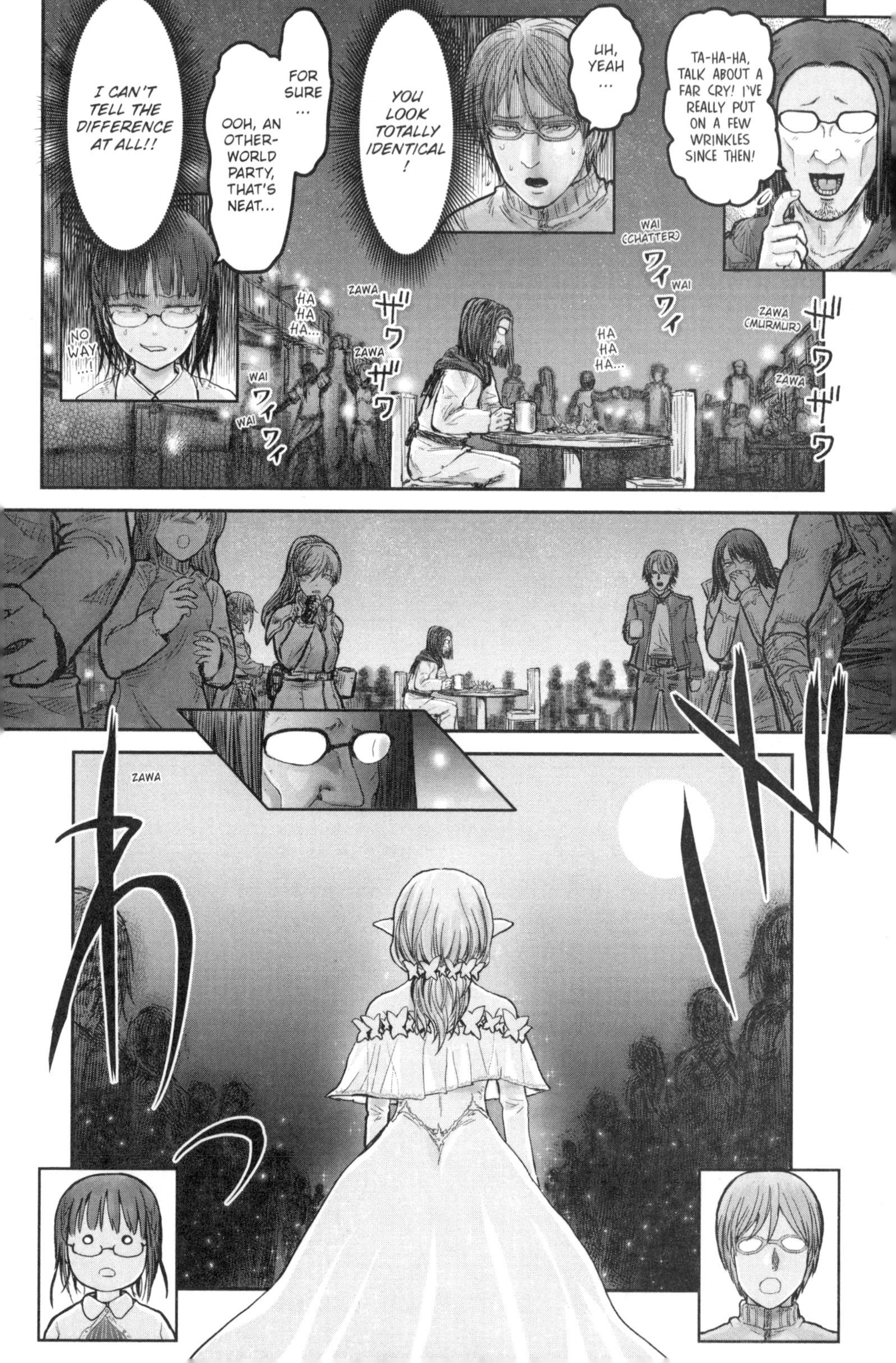
TA-HA-HA, TALK ABOUT A FAR CRY! I'VE REALLY PUT ON A FEW WRINKLES SINCE THEN!
UH, YEAH ...
YOU LOOK TOTALLY IDENTICAL !
FOR SURE ...
OOH, AN OTHER-WORLD PARTY, THAT'S NEAT...
I CAN'T TELL THE DIFFERENCE AT ALL!!
NO WAY ...!
ZAWA (MURMUR) ザワ ZAWA ザワ
WAI (CHATTER) ワイ WAI ワイ
HA HA HA...
ZAWA ザワ ZAWA ザワ
HA HA HA...
WAI ワイ WAI ワイ
ZAWA

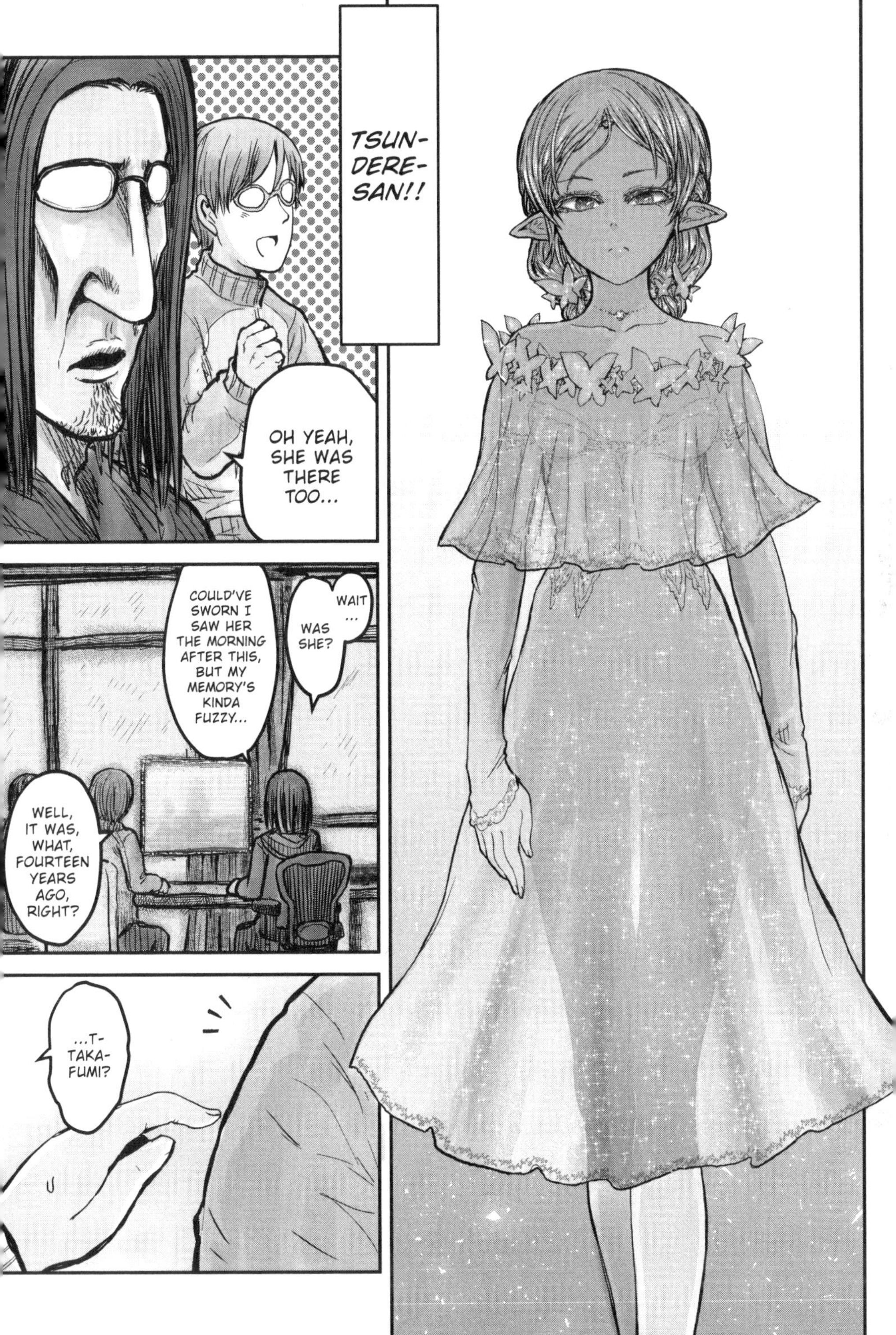
TSUN-DERE-SAN!!
OH YEAH, SHE WAS THERE TOO...
WAIT... WAS SHE?
COULD'VE SWORN I SAW HER THE MORNING AFTER THIS, BUT MY MEMORY'S KINDA FUZZY...
WELL, IT WAS, WHAT, FOURTEEN YEARS AGO, RIGHT?
...T-TAKAFUMI?

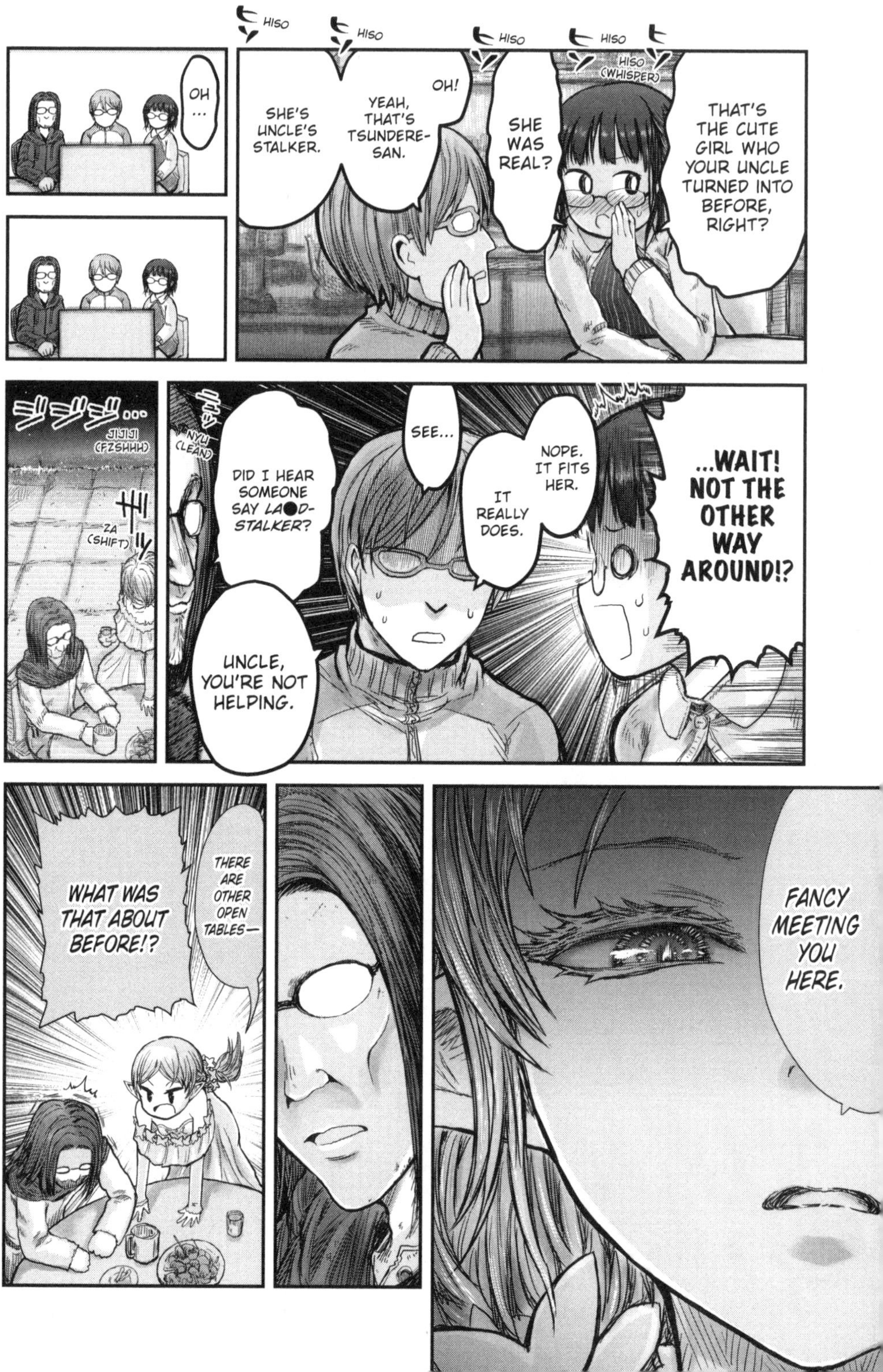
HISO
HISO
HISO
HISO
HISO (WHISPER)
THAT'S THE CUTE GIRL WHO YOUR UNCLE TURNED INTO BEFORE, RIGHT?
SHE WAS REAL?
OH!
YEAH, THAT'S TSUNDERE-SAN.
SHE'S UNCLE'S STALKER.
OH ...
...WAIT! NOT THE OTHER WAY AROUND!?
NOPE. IT FITS HER.
IT REALLY DOES.
SEE...
DID I HEAR SOMEONE SAY LA●D-STALKER?
NYU (LEAN)
UNCLE, YOU'RE NOT HELPING.
JIJIJI (FZSHHH)
ZA (SHIFT)
FANCY MEETING YOU HERE.
THERE ARE OTHER OPEN TABLES—
WHAT WAS THAT ABOUT BEFORE!?

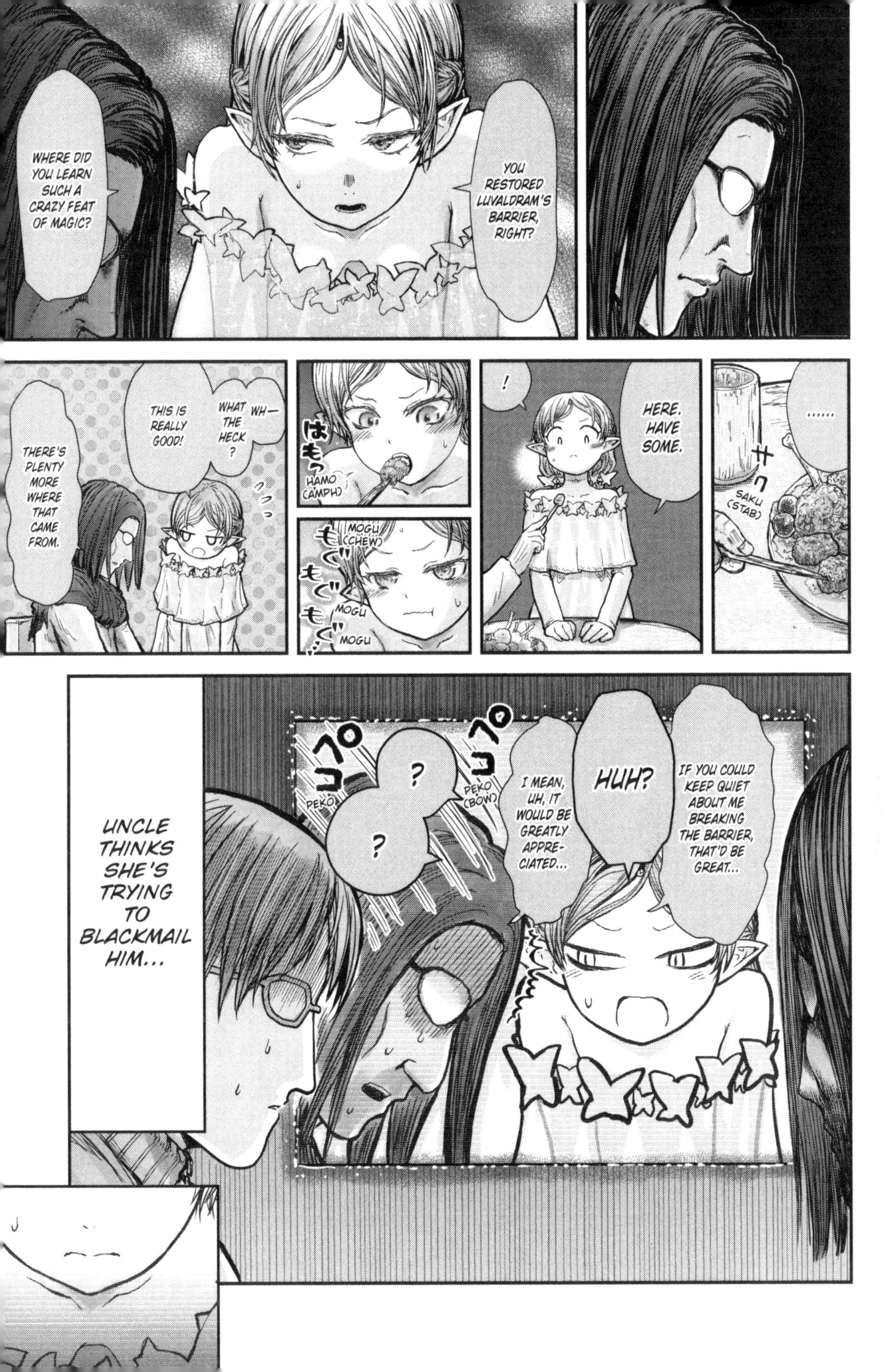
YOU RESTORED LUVALDRAM'S BARRIER, RIGHT?
WHERE DID YOU LEARN SUCH A CRAZY FEAT OF MAGIC?
......
サク
SAKU (STAB)
!
HERE. HAVE SOME.
はもっ
HAMO (CAMPH)
もぐもぐもぐ
MOGU (CHEW)
MOGU
MOGU
WH—
WHAT THE HECK?
THIS IS REALLY GOOD!
THERE'S PLENTY MORE WHERE THAT CAME FROM.
IF YOU COULD KEEP QUIET ABOUT ME BREAKING THE BARRIER, THAT'D BE GREAT...
HUH?
I MEAN, UH, IT WOULD BE GREATLY APPRE-CIATED...
ペコ
PEKO (BOW)
ペコ
PEKO
?
?
UNCLE THINKS SHE'S TRYING TO BLACKMAIL HIM...

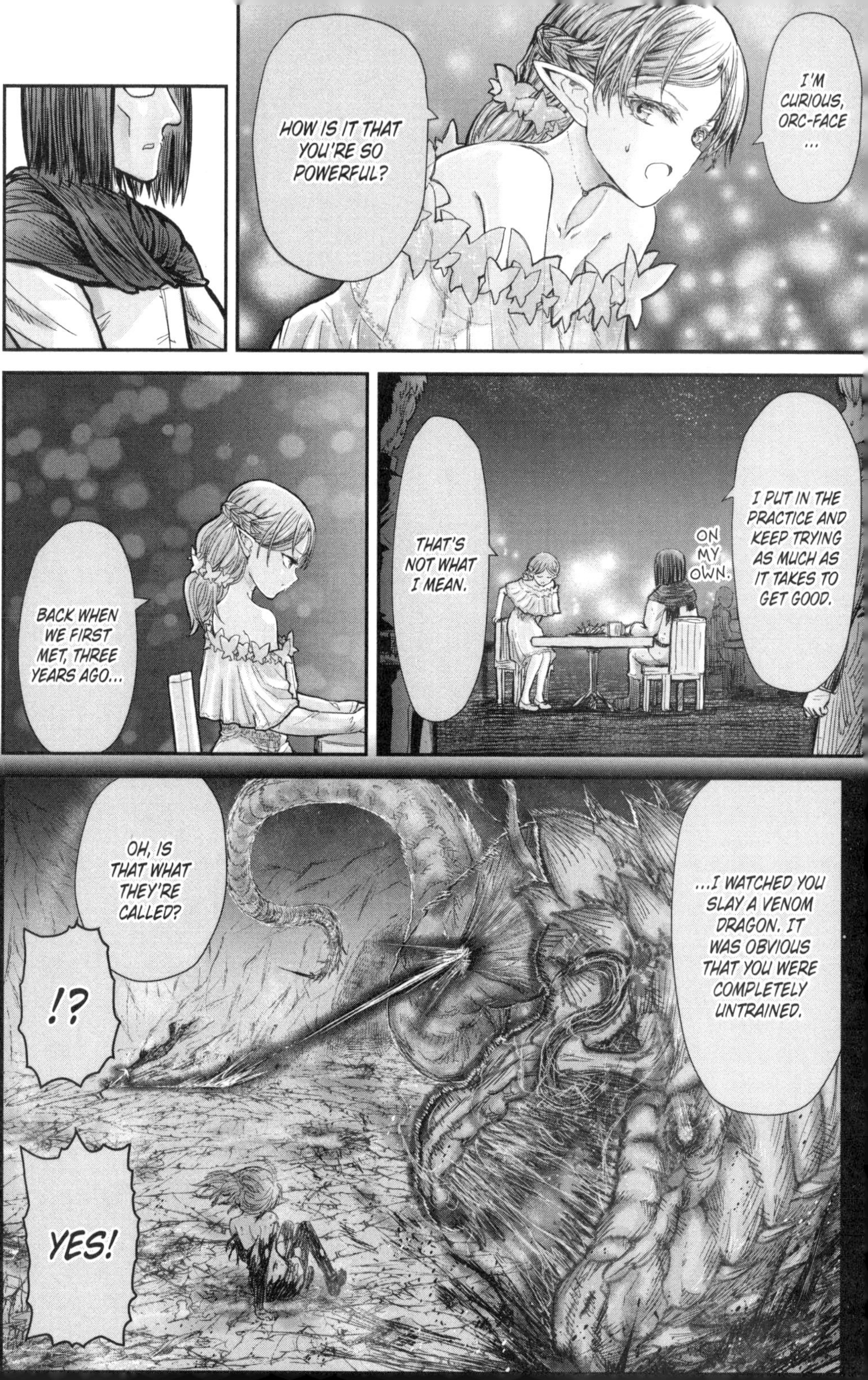

I'M CURIOUS, ORC-FACE ...
HOW IS IT THAT YOU'RE SO POWERFUL?
I PUT IN THE PRACTICE AND KEEP TRYING AS MUCH AS IT TAKES TO GET GOOD.
ON MY OWN.
THAT'S NOT WHAT I MEAN.
BACK WHEN WE FIRST MET, THREE YEARS AGO...
...I WATCHED YOU SLAY A VENOM DRAGON. IT WAS OBVIOUS THAT YOU WERE COMPLETELY UNTRAINED.
OH, IS THAT WHAT THEY'RE CALLED?
!?
YES!

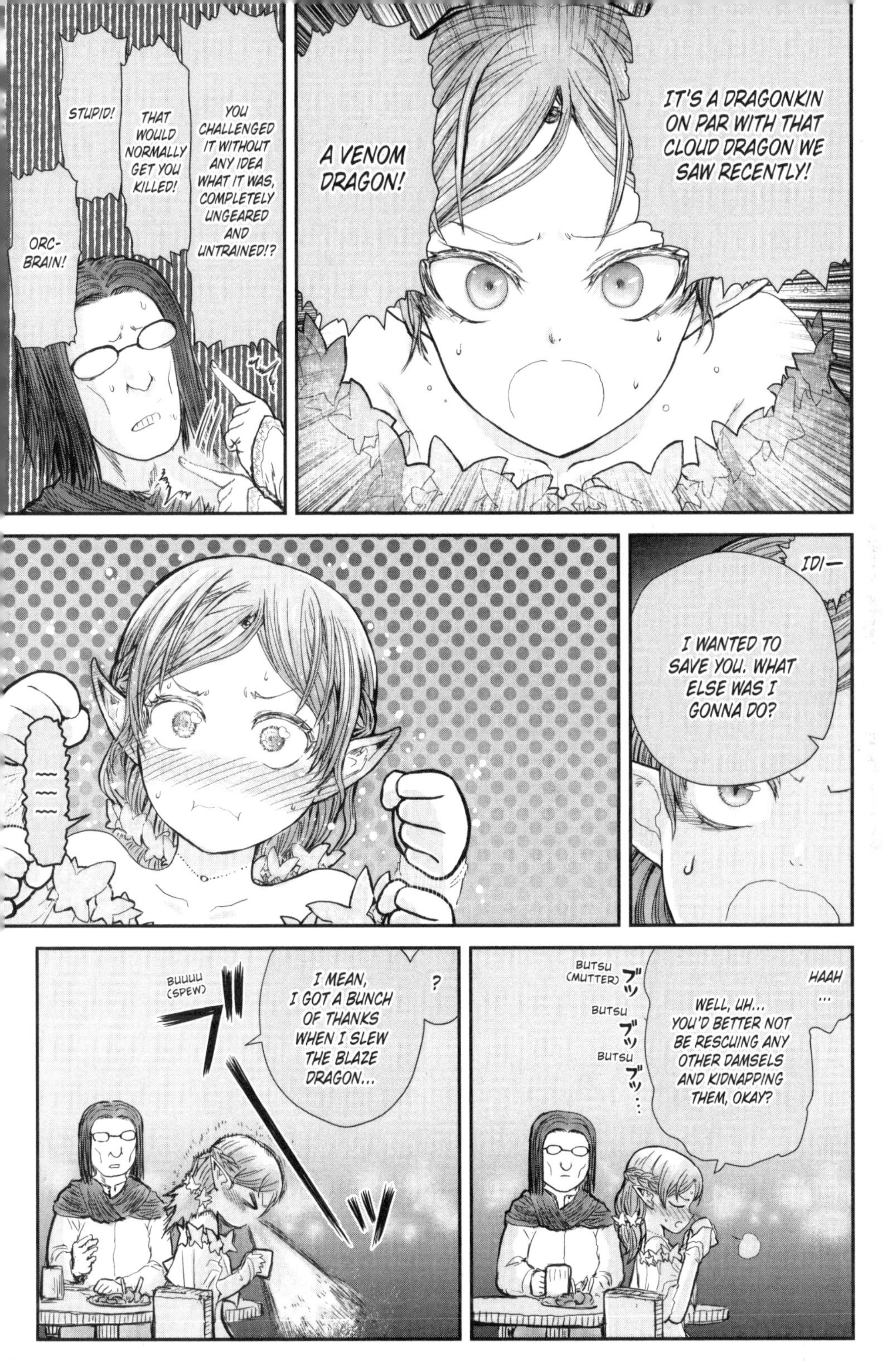
IT'S A DRAGONKIN ON PAR WITH THAT CLOUD DRAGON WE SAW RECENTLY!
A VENOM DRAGON!
YOU CHALLENGED IT WITHOUT ANY IDEA WHAT IT WAS, COMPLETELY UNGEARED AND UNTRAINED!?
THAT WOULD NORMALLY GET YOU KILLED!
STUPID!
ORC-BRAIN!
IDI—
I WANTED TO SAVE YOU. WHAT ELSE WAS I GONNA DO?
~~~
HAAH ...
WELL, UH... YOU'D BETTER NOT BE RESCUING ANY OTHER DAMSELS AND KIDNAPPING THEM, OKAY?
BUTSU (MUTTER) ブッ
BUTSU ブッ
BUTSU ブッ...
?
I MEAN, I GOT A BUNCH OF THANKS WHEN I SLEW THE BLAZE DRAGON...
BUUUU (SPEW) ブッ
~~~

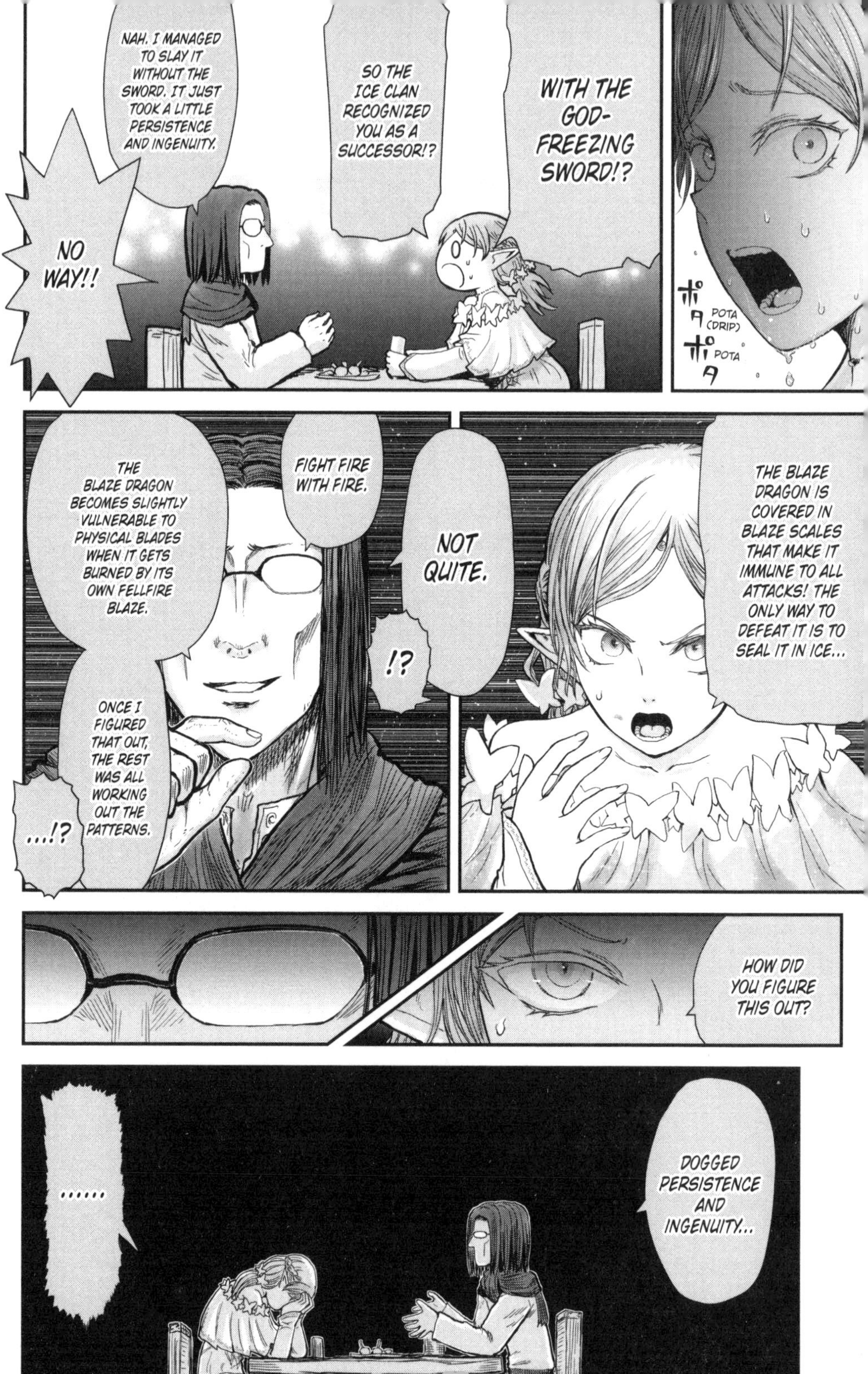
ポタ POTA (DRIP)
ポタ POTA
WITH THE GOD-FREEZING SWORD!?
SO THE ICE CLAN RECOGNIZED YOU AS A SUCCESSOR!?
NAH. I MANAGED TO SLAY IT WITHOUT THE SWORD. IT JUST TOOK A LITTLE PERSISTENCE AND INGENUITY.
NO WAY!!
THE BLAZE DRAGON IS COVERED IN BLAZE SCALES THAT MAKE IT IMMUNE TO ALL ATTACKS! THE ONLY WAY TO DEFEAT IT IS TO SEAL IT IN ICE...
NOT QUITE.
FIGHT FIRE WITH FIRE.
THE BLAZE DRAGON BECOMES SLIGHTLY VULNERABLE TO PHYSICAL BLADES WHEN IT GETS BURNED BY ITS OWN FELLFIRE BLAZE.
!?
ONCE I FIGURED THAT OUT, THE REST WAS ALL WORKING OUT THE PATTERNS.
...!?
HOW DID YOU FIGURE THIS OUT?
DOGGED PERSISTENCE AND INGENUITY...
......

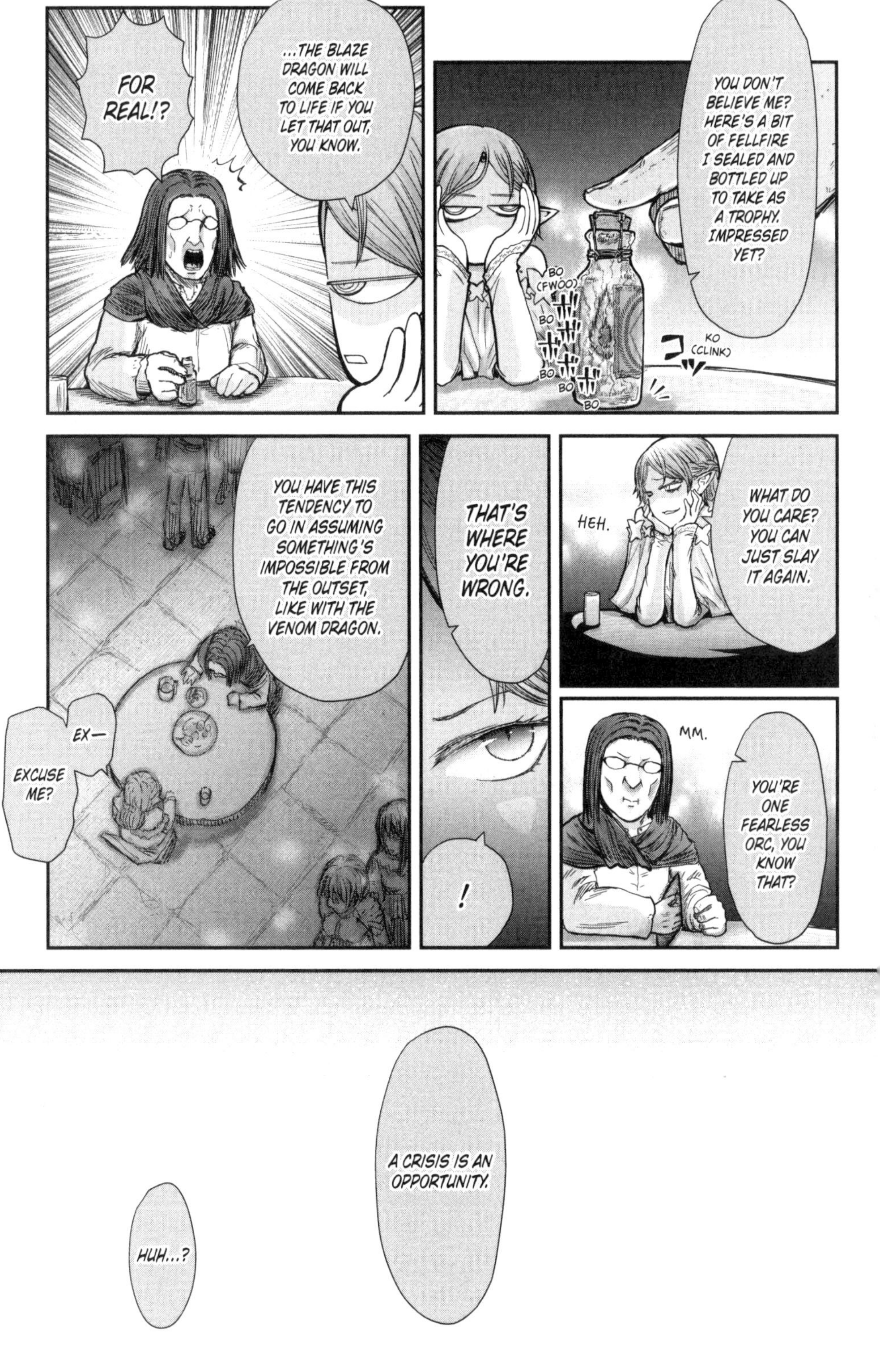
YOU DON'T BELIEVE ME? HERE'S A BIT OF FELLFIRE I SEALED AND BOTTLED UP TO TAKE AS A TROPHY. IMPRESSED YET?
KO (CLINK)
BO (FWOO)
BO
BO
BO
BO
...THE BLAZE DRAGON WILL COME BACK TO LIFE IF YOU LET THAT OUT, YOU KNOW.
FOR REAL!?
WHAT DO YOU CARE? YOU CAN JUST SLAY IT AGAIN.
HEH.
MM.
YOU'RE ONE FEARLESS ORC, YOU KNOW THAT?
THAT'S WHERE YOU'RE WRONG.
!
YOU HAVE THIS TENDENCY TO GO IN ASSUMING SOMETHING'S IMPOSSIBLE FROM THE OUTSET, LIKE WITH THE VENOM DRAGON.
EX—
EXCUSE ME?
A CRISIS IS AN OPPORTUNITY.
HUH...?

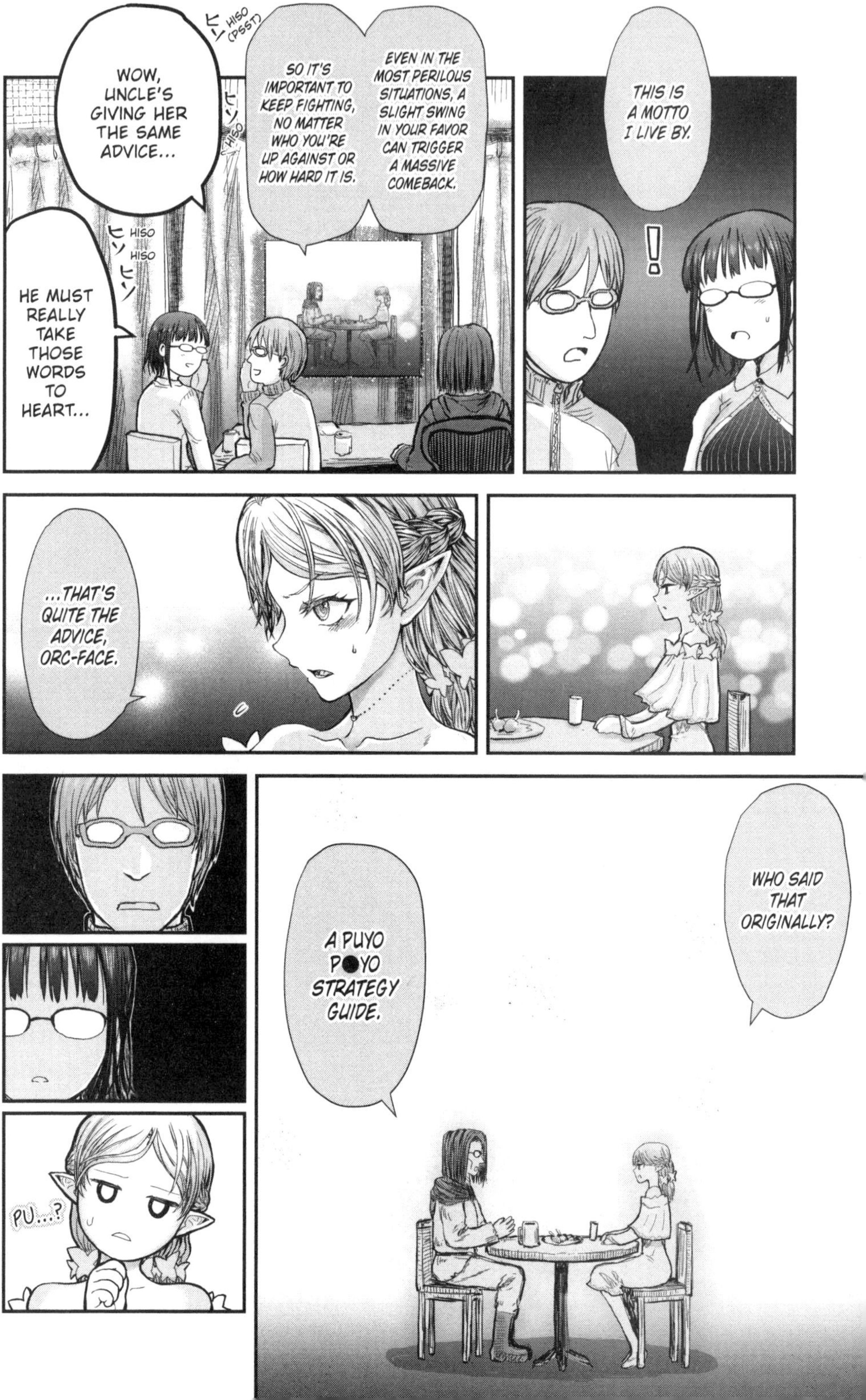
EVEN IN THE MOST PERILOUS SITUATIONS, A SLIGHT SWING IN YOUR FAVOR CAN TRIGGER A MASSIVE COMEBACK.
SO IT'S IMPORTANT TO KEEP FIGHTING, NO MATTER WHO YOU'RE UP AGAINST OR HOW HARD IT IS.
THIS IS A MOTTO I LIVE BY.
!
ヒソ HISO (PSST)
ヒソ HISO
WOW, UNCLE'S GIVING HER THE SAME ADVICE...
ヒソ HISO
ヒソ HISO
HE MUST REALLY TAKE THOSE WORDS TO HEART...
...THAT'S QUITE THE ADVICE, ORC-FACE.
WHO SAID THAT ORIGINALLY?
A PUYO P●YO STRATEGY GUIDE.
PU...?

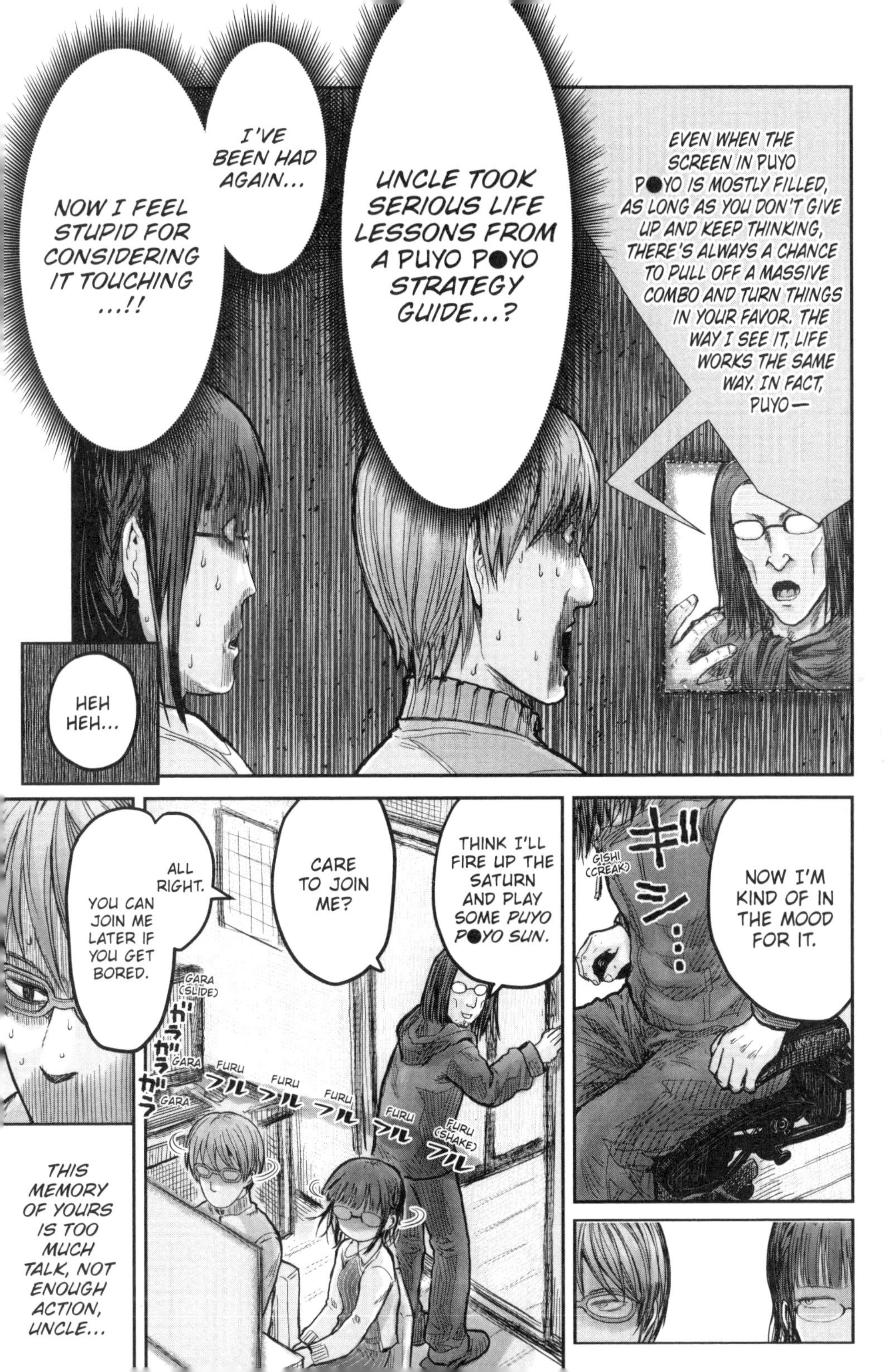

EVEN WHEN THE SCREEN IN PUYO P●YO IS MOSTLY FILLED, AS LONG AS YOU DON'T GIVE UP AND KEEP THINKING, THERE'S ALWAYS A CHANCE TO PULL OFF A MASSIVE COMBO AND TURN THINGS IN YOUR FAVOR. THE WAY I SEE IT, LIFE WORKS THE SAME WAY. IN FACT, PUYO—
UNCLE TOOK SERIOUS LIFE LESSONS FROM A PUYO P●YO STRATEGY GUIDE...?
I'VE BEEN HAD AGAIN...
NOW I FEEL STUPID FOR CONSIDERING IT TOUCHING...!!
HEH HEH...
GISHI (CREAK)
NOW I'M KIND OF IN THE MOOD FOR IT.
THINK I'LL FIRE UP THE SATURN AND PLAY SOME PUYO P●YO SUN.
CARE TO JOIN ME?
ALL RIGHT. YOU CAN JOIN ME LATER IF YOU GET BORED.
GARA (SLIDE) GARA GARA
FURU FURU FURU FURU FURU (SHAKE)
THIS MEMORY OF YOURS IS TOO MUCH TALK, NOT ENOUGH ACTION, UNCLE...

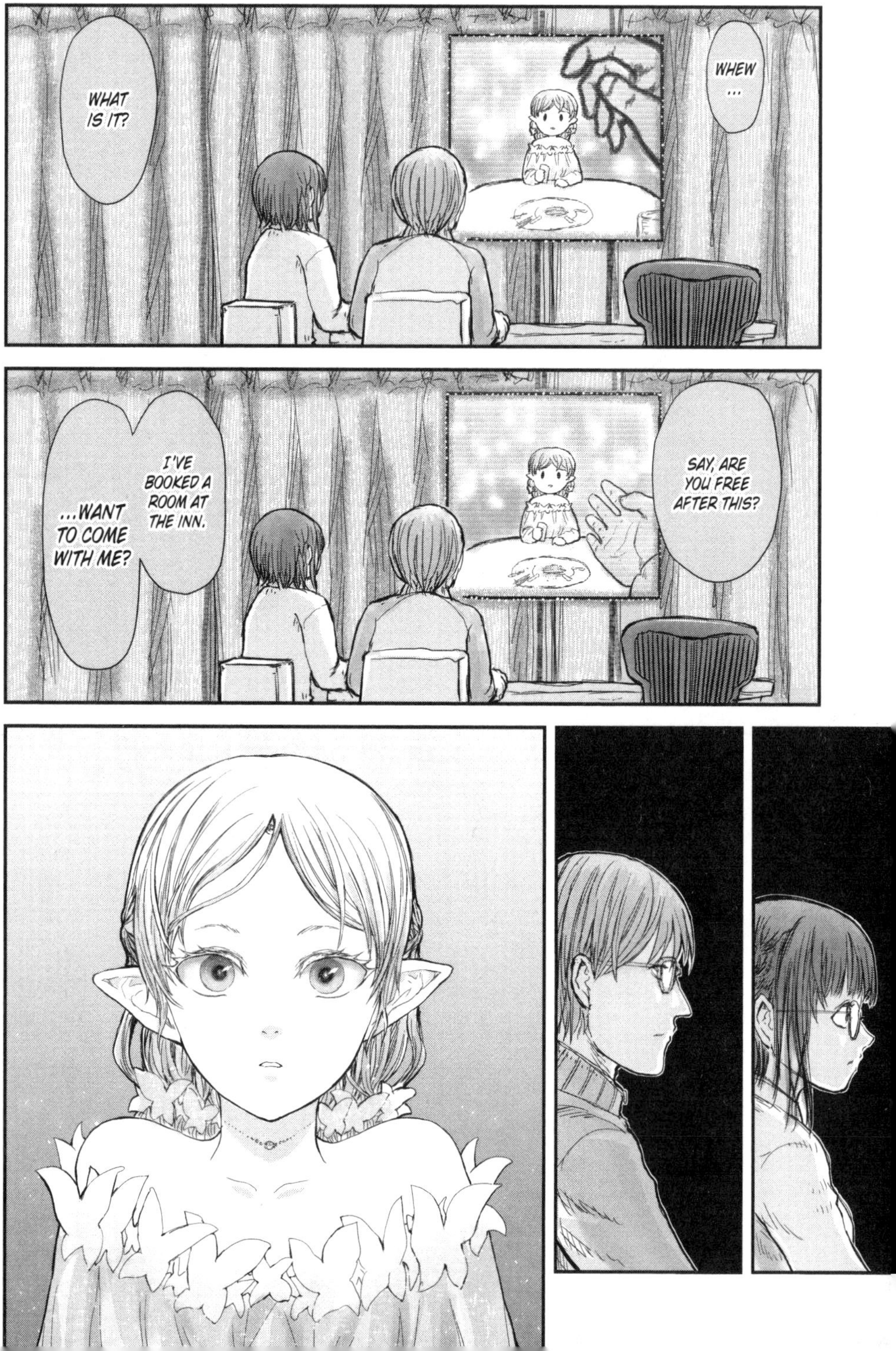
WHEW
...
WHAT IS IT?
SAY, ARE YOU FREE AFTER THIS?
I'VE BOOKED A ROOM AT THE INN.
...WANT TO COME WITH ME?

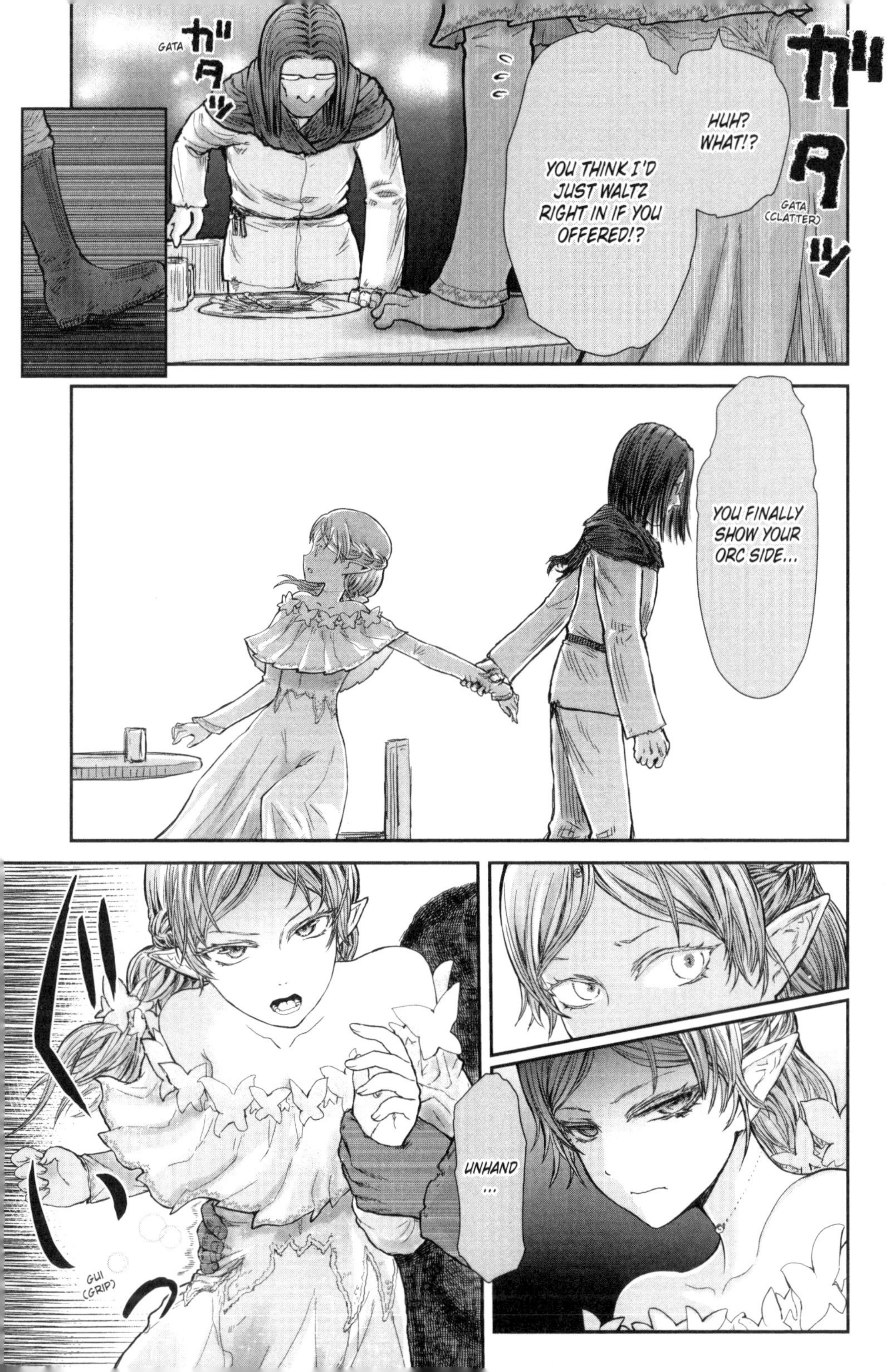
ガタッ
GATA (CLATTER)
HUH? WHAT!?
YOU THINK I'D JUST WALTZ RIGHT IN IF YOU OFFERED!?
ガタッ
GATA
YOU FINALLY SHOW YOUR ORC SIDE...
UNHAND ...
GUI (GRIP)

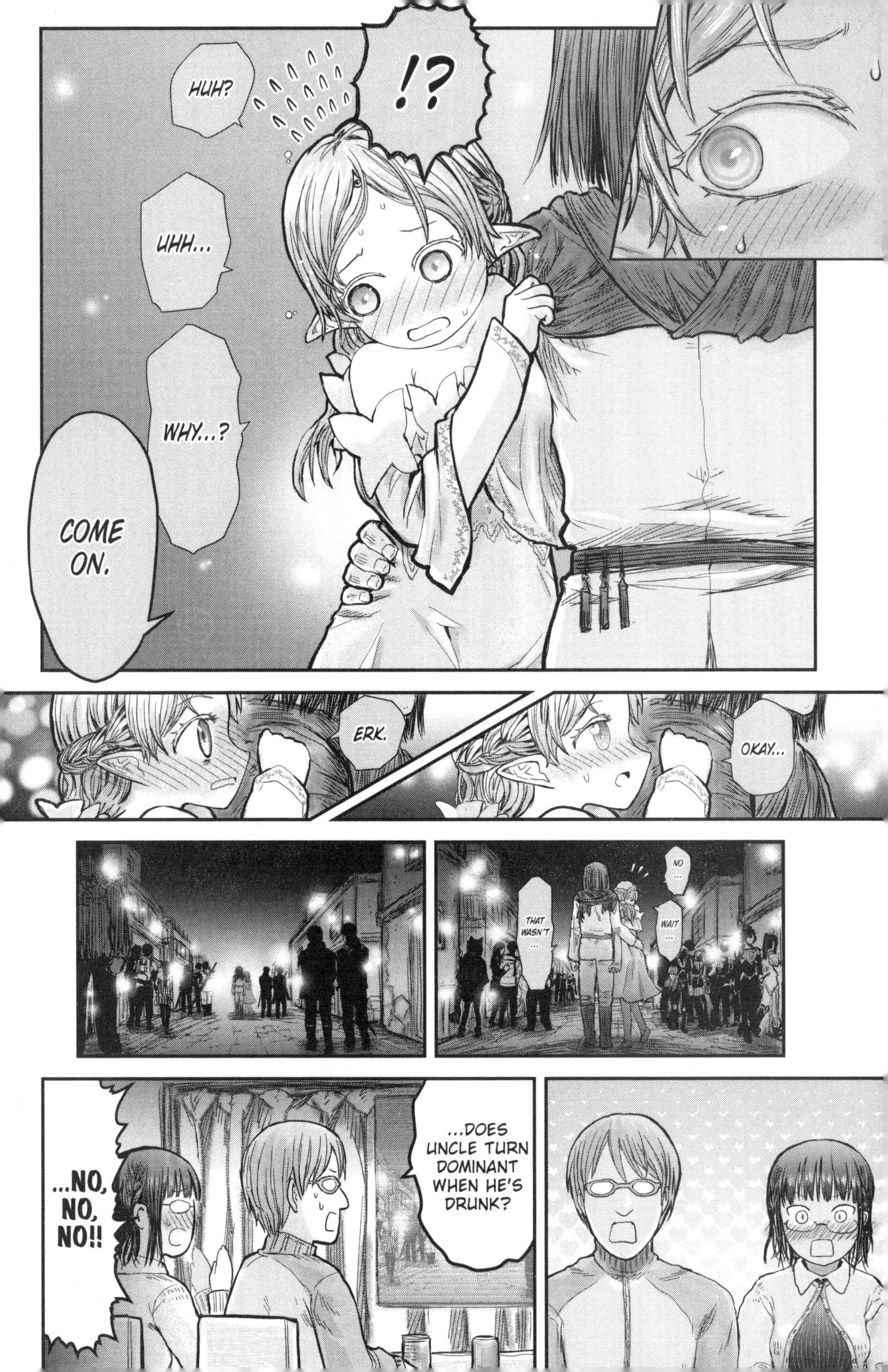
!?
HUH?
UHH...
WHY...?
COME ON.
OKAY...
ERK.
NO ...
WAIT ...
THAT WASN'T ...
...DOES UNCLE TURN DOMINANT WHEN HE'S DRUNK?
...NO, NO, NO!!

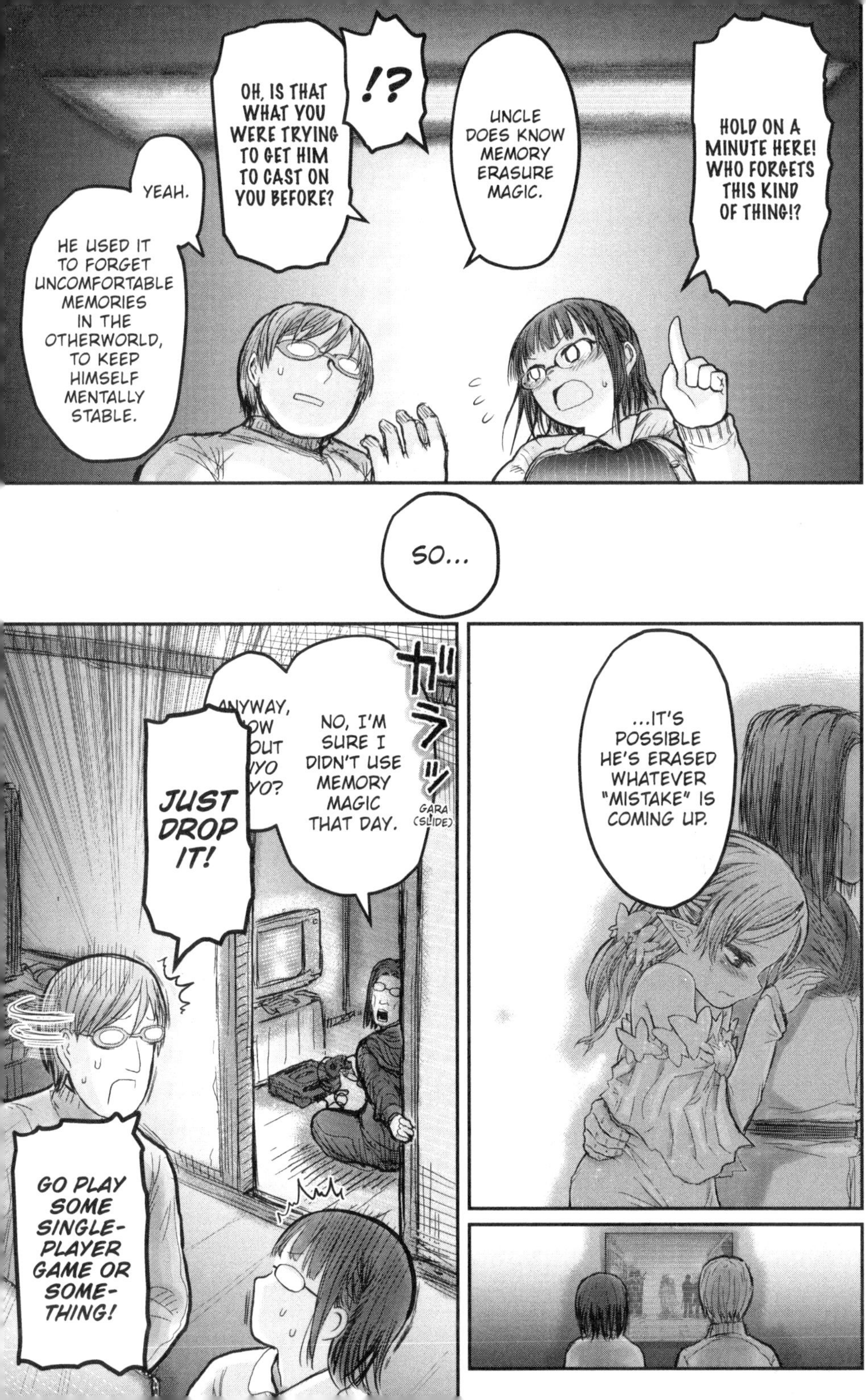
HOLD ON A MINUTE HERE! WHO FORGETS THIS KIND OF THING!?
UNCLE DOES KNOW MEMORY ERASURE MAGIC.
!?
OH, IS THAT WHAT YOU WERE TRYING TO GET HIM TO CAST ON YOU BEFORE?
YEAH.
HE USED IT TO FORGET UNCOMFORTABLE MEMORIES IN THE OTHERWORLD, TO KEEP HIMSELF MENTALLY STABLE.
SO...
...IT'S POSSIBLE HE'S ERASED WHATEVER "MISTAKE" IS COMING UP.
GARA (SLIDE)
NO, I'M SURE I DIDN'T USE MEMORY MAGIC THAT DAY.
ANYWAY,
JUST DROP IT!
GO PLAY SOME SINGLE-PLAYER GAME OR SOME-THING!

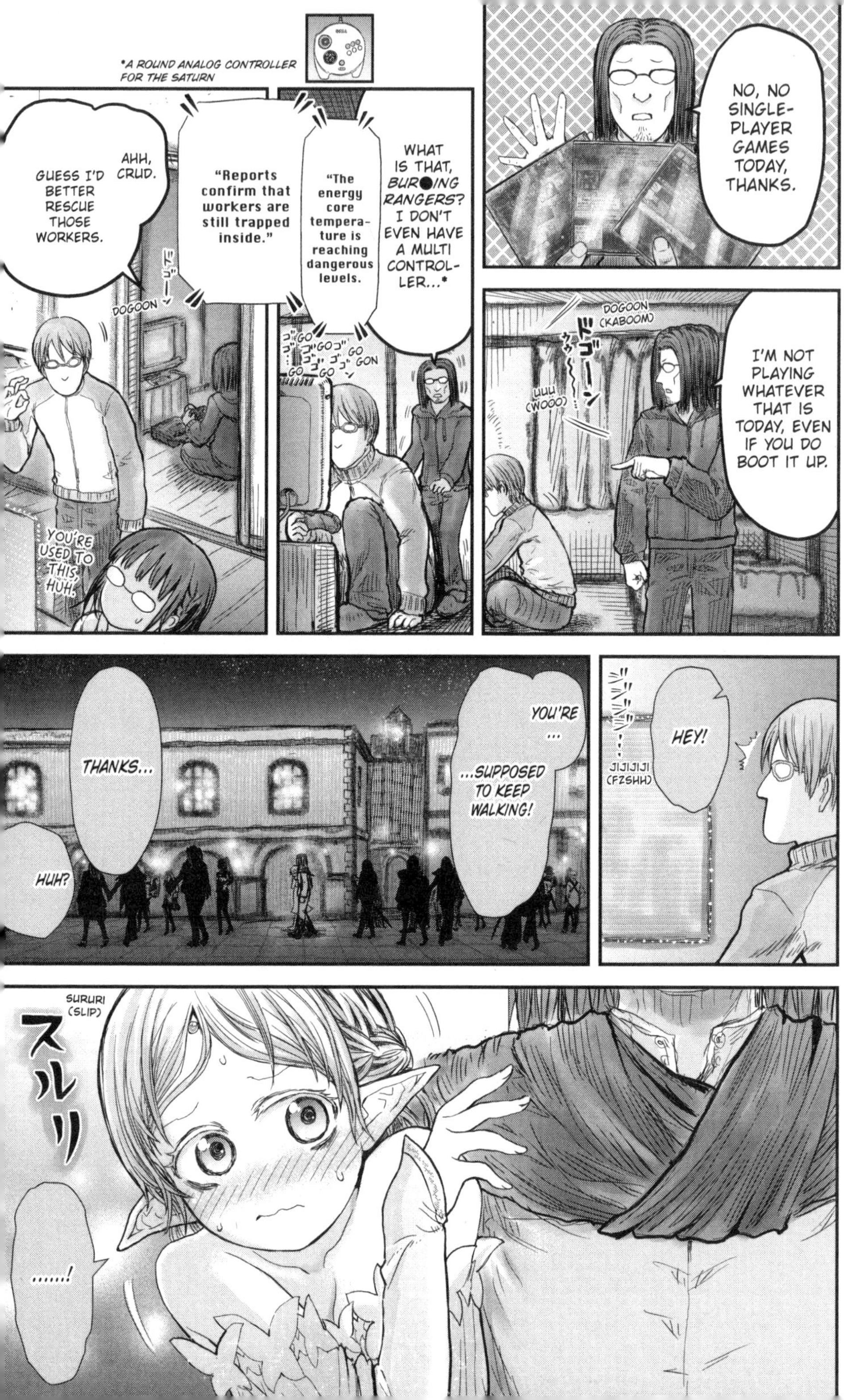

*A ROUND ANALOG CONTROLLER FOR THE SATURN
NO, NO SINGLE-PLAYER GAMES TODAY, THANKS.
DOGOON (KABOOM)
UUU (WOOO)
I'M NOT PLAYING WHATEVER THAT IS TODAY, EVEN IF YOU DO BOOT IT UP.
WHAT IS THAT, BUR●ING RANGERS? I DON'T EVEN HAVE A MULTI CONTROLLER...*
"The energy core temperature is reaching dangerous levels."
GO GO GO GO GO GO GON
"Reports confirm that workers are still trapped inside."
AHH, CRUD.
GUESS I'D BETTER RESCUE THOSE WORKERS.
DOGOON
YOU'RE USED TO THIS, HUH.
JIJIJIJI (FZSHH)
HEY!
YOU'RE ...
...SUPPOSED TO KEEP WALKING!
THANKS...
HUH?
SURURI (SLIP)
......!

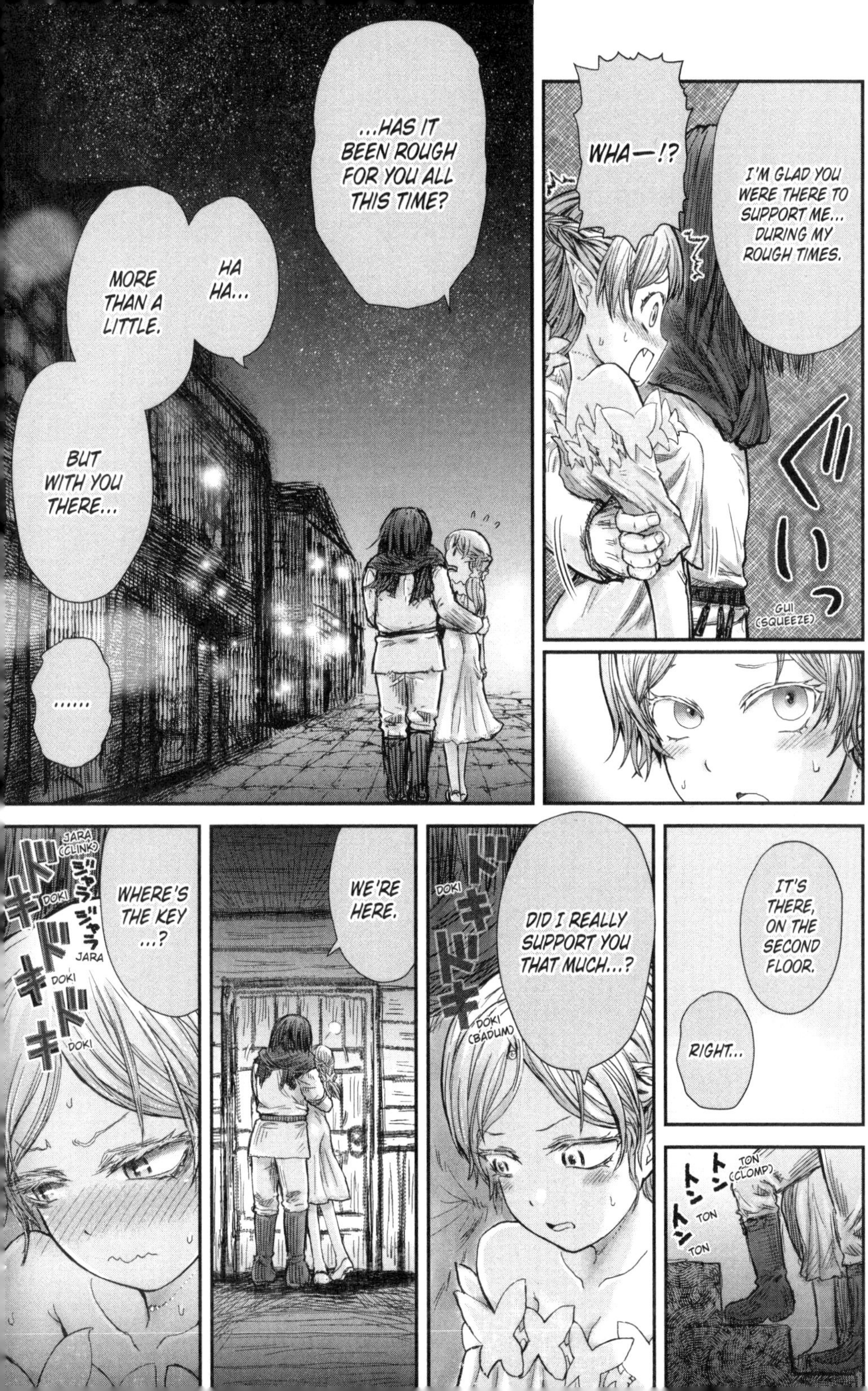
I'M GLAD YOU WERE THERE TO SUPPORT ME... DURING MY ROUGH TIMES.
WHA—!?
GUI (SQUEEZE)
...HAS IT BEEN ROUGH FOR YOU ALL THIS TIME?
HA HA...
MORE THAN A LITTLE.
BUT WITH YOU THERE...
......
IT'S THERE, ON THE SECOND FLOOR.
RIGHT...
TON (CLOMP)
TON
TON
DOKI
DID I REALLY SUPPORT YOU THAT MUCH...?
DOKI (BADUM)
WE'RE HERE.
JARA (CLINK)
JARA
WHERE'S THE KEY ...?
DOKI
DOKI
DOKI

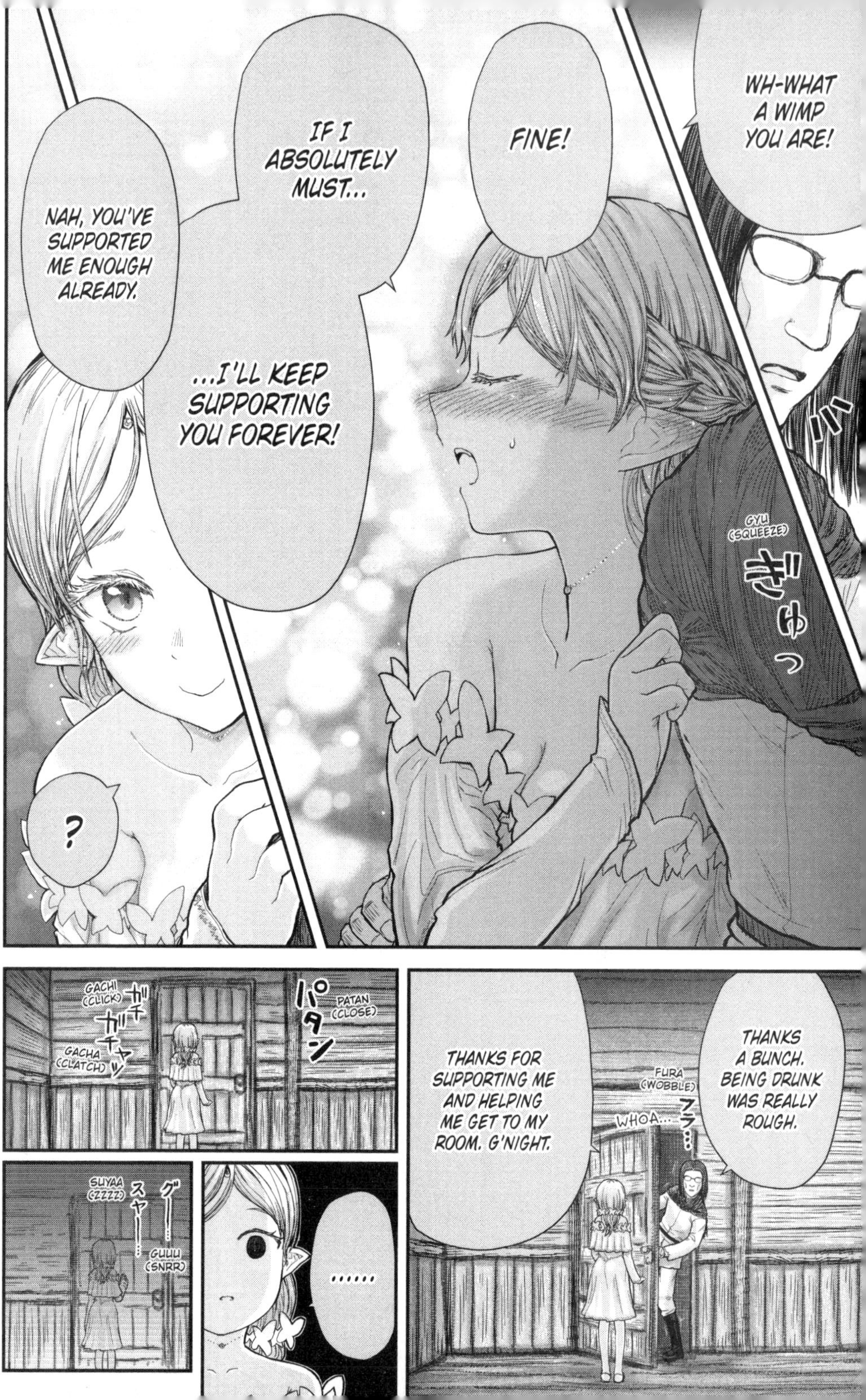
WH-WHAT A WIMP YOU ARE!
バ
GYU (SQUEEZE)
ぎゅっ
FINE!
IF I ABSOLUTELY MUST...
...I'LL KEEP SUPPORTING YOU FOREVER!
NAH, YOU'VE SUPPORTED ME ENOUGH ALREADY.
?
THANKS A BUNCH. BEING DRUNK WAS REALLY ROUGH.
FURA (WOBBLE)
フラ…
WHOA...
THANKS FOR SUPPORTING ME AND HELPING ME GET TO MY ROOM. G'NIGHT.
PATAN (CLOSE)
パタン
GACHI (CLICK)
ガチ
GACHA (CLATCH)
ガチャッ
......
GUUU (SNRR)
グー…
SUYAA (ZZZZ)
スヤー…

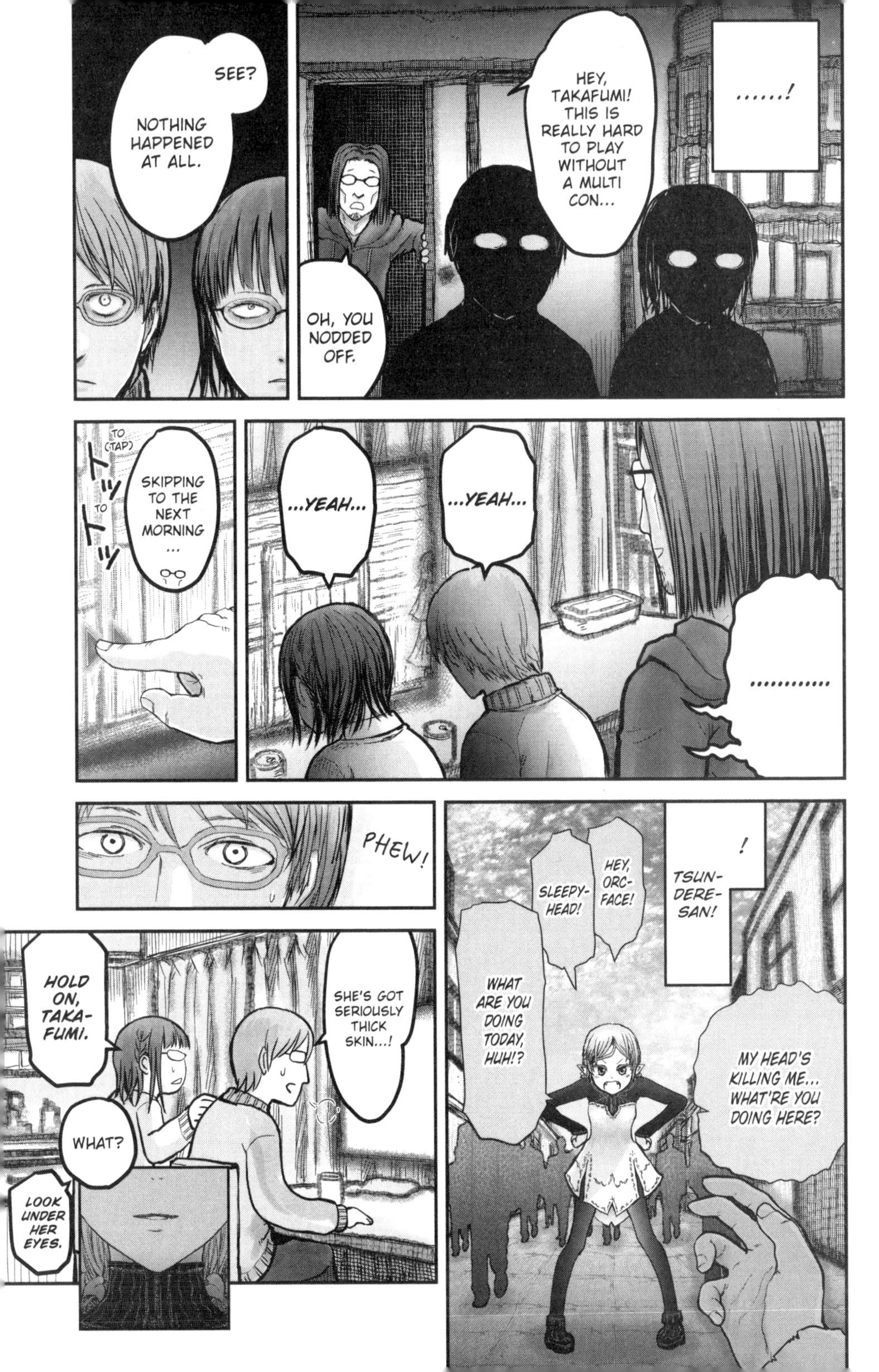
......!
HEY, TAKAFUMI! THIS IS REALLY HARD TO PLAY WITHOUT A MULTI CON...
OH, YOU NODDED OFF.
SEE?
NOTHING HAPPENED AT ALL.
....
...YEAH...
...YEAH...
TO (TAP) TO
SKIPPING TO THE NEXT MORNING ...
!
TSUNDERE-SAN!
HEY, ORC-FACE!
SLEEPY-HEAD!
WHAT ARE YOU DOING TODAY, HUH!?
MY HEAD'S KILLING ME... WHAT'RE YOU DOING HERE?
PHEW!
SHE'S GOT SERIOUSLY THICK SKIN...!
HOLD ON, TAKAFUMI.
WHAT?
LOOK UNDER HER EYES.

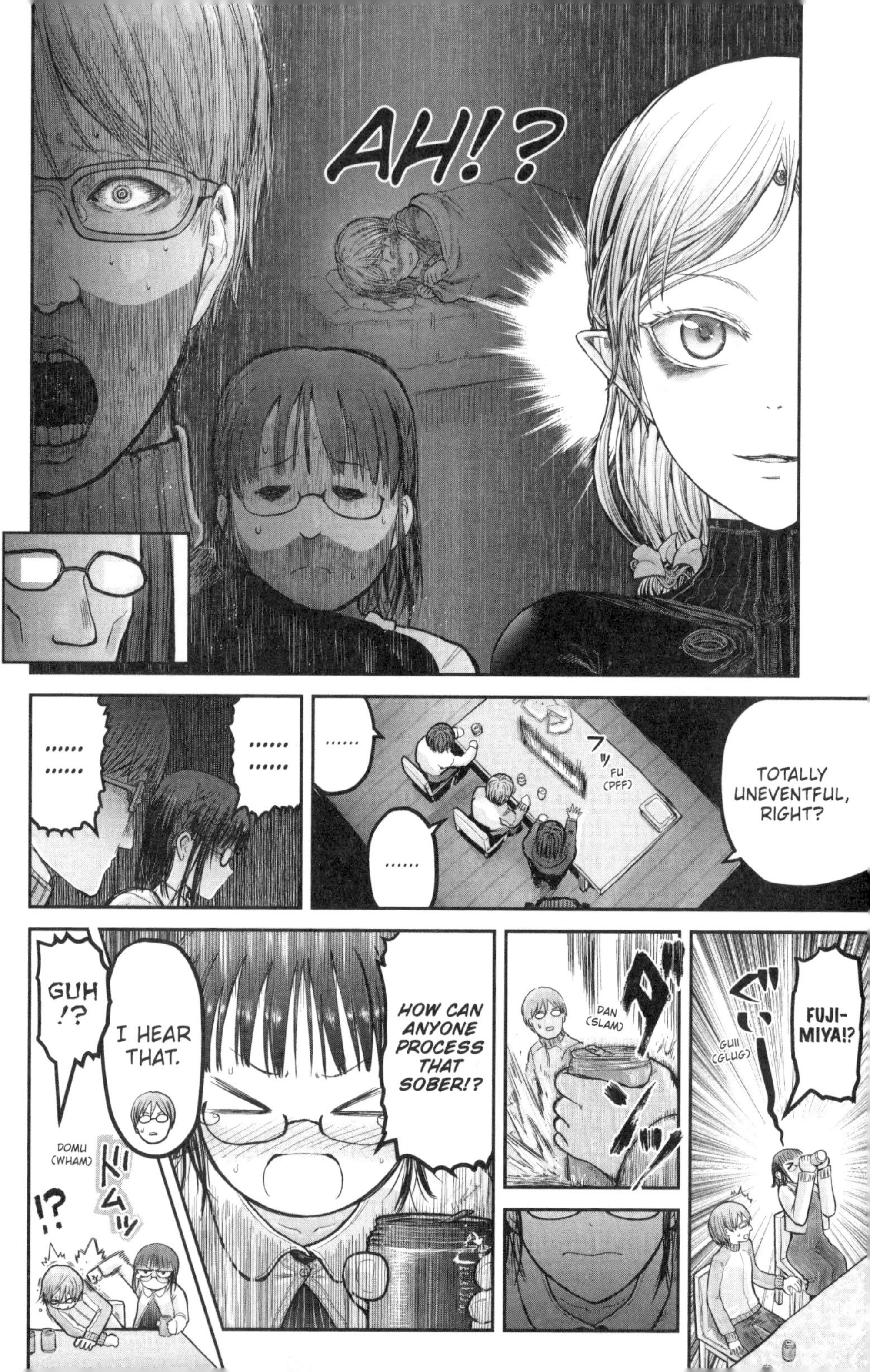
AH!?
TOTALLY UNEVENTFUL, RIGHT?
FU (PFF)
......
......
......
......
......
......
FUJI-MIYA!?
GUII (GLUG)
DAN (SLAM)
HOW CAN ANYONE PROCESS THAT SOBER!?
I HEAR THAT.
GUH!?
DOMU (WHAM)
!?

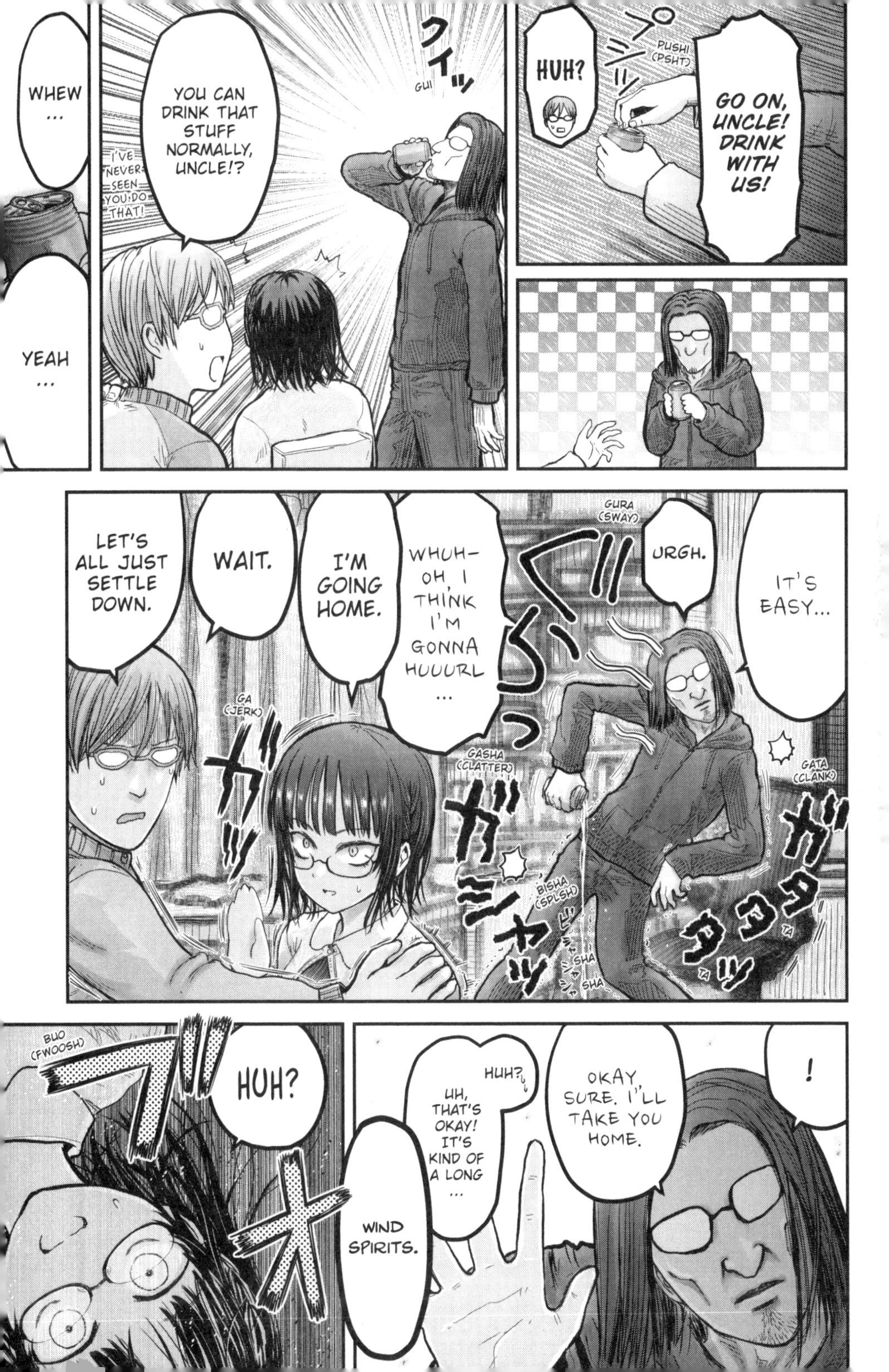
GO ON, UNCLE! DRINK WITH US!
PUSHI (PSHT)
HUH?
GUI
YOU CAN DRINK THAT STUFF NORMALLY, UNCLE!?
I'VE NEVER SEEN YOU DO THAT!
WHEW ...
YEAH ...
IT'S EASY...
URGH.
GURA (SWAY)
WHUH-OH, I THINK I'M GONNA HUUURL ...
I'M GOING HOME.
WAIT.
LET'S ALL JUST SETTLE DOWN.
GATA (CLANK)
TA
TA
GASHA (CLATTER)
BISHA (SPLSH)
SHA
SHA
SHA
GA (JERK)
!
OKAY, SURE. I'LL TAKE YOU HOME.
HUH?
UH, THAT'S OKAY! IT'S KIND OF A LONG ...
WIND SPIRITS.
HUH?
BUO (FWOOSH)

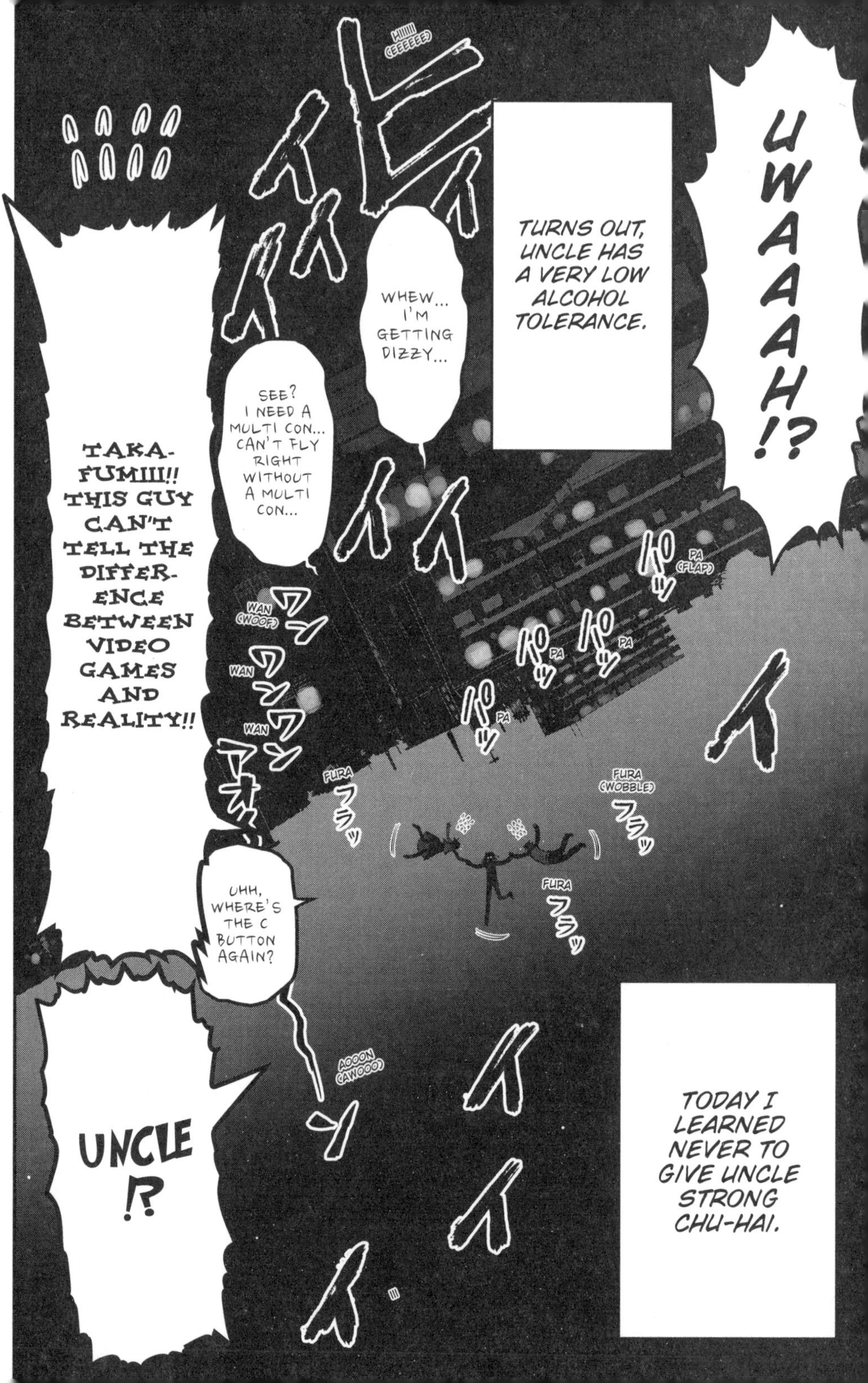

UWAAAAH!?
TURNS OUT, UNCLE HAS A VERY LOW ALCOHOL TOLERANCE.
HIIIIII (EEEEEEE)
WHEW... I'M GETTING DIZZY...
SEE? I NEED A MULTI CON... CAN'T FLY RIGHT WITHOUT A MULTI CON...
PA (FLAP)
PA
PA
PA
WAN (WOOF)
WAN
WAN
FURA (WOBBLE)
FURA
FURA
UHH, WHERE'S THE C BUTTON AGAIN?
AOOON (AWOOO)
TAKA-FUMIII!! THIS GUY CAN'T TELL THE DIFFER-ENCE BETWEEN VIDEO GAMES AND REALITY!!
UNCLE!?
TODAY I LEARNED NEVER TO GIVE UNCLE STRONG CHU-HAI.

TIPS

Birthdays

Uncle: November 30
Takafumi: May 23
Fujimiya: June 3

UNCLE from ANOTHER WORLD

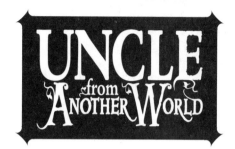

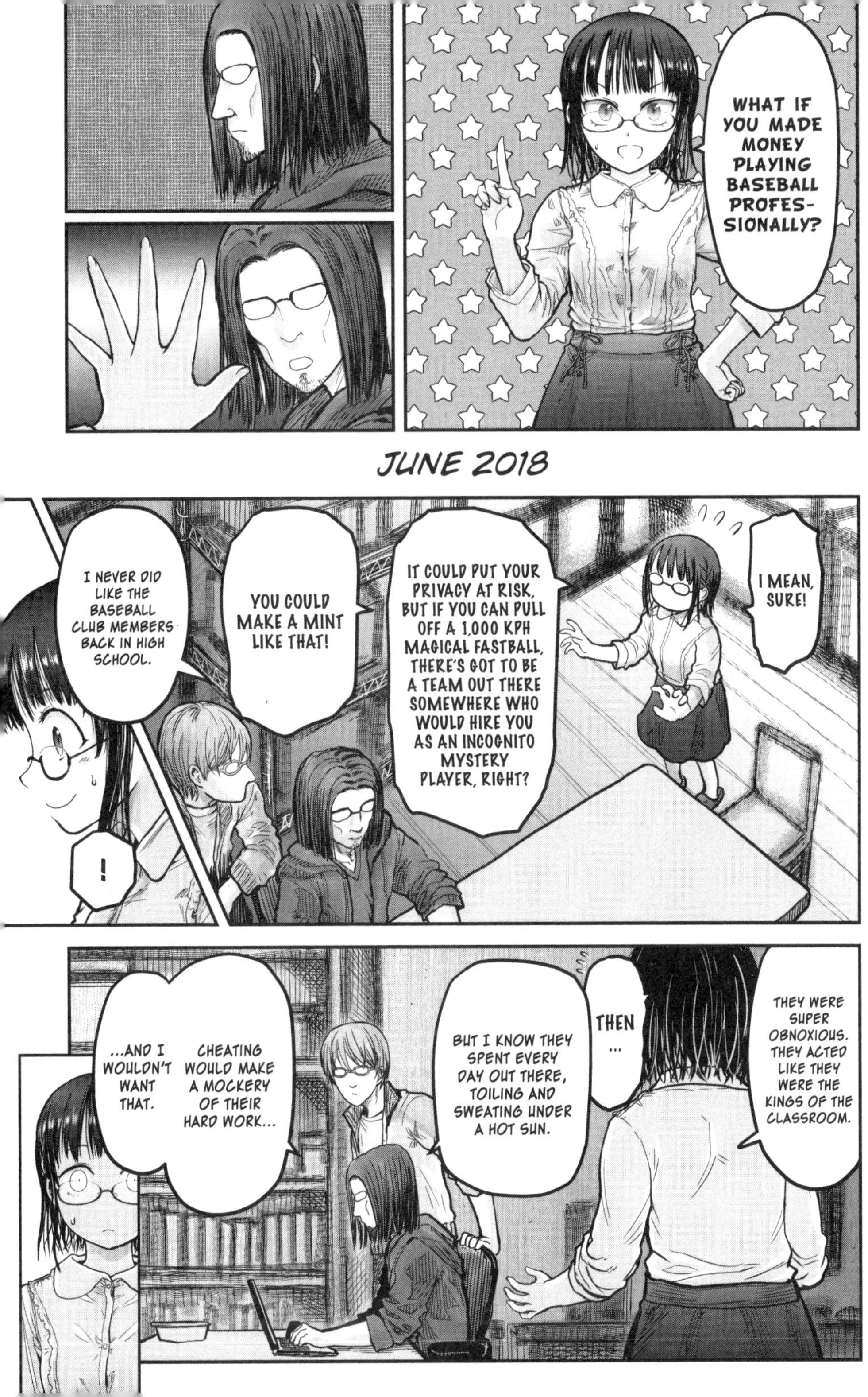
WHAT IF YOU MADE MONEY PLAYING BASEBALL PROFES-SIONALLY?
JUNE 2018
I MEAN, SURE!
IT COULD PUT YOUR PRIVACY AT RISK, BUT IF YOU CAN PULL OFF A 1,000 KPH MAGICAL FASTBALL, THERE'S GOT TO BE A TEAM OUT THERE SOMEWHERE WHO WOULD HIRE YOU AS AN INCOGNITO MYSTERY PLAYER, RIGHT?
YOU COULD MAKE A MINT LIKE THAT!
I NEVER DID LIKE THE BASEBALL CLUB MEMBERS BACK IN HIGH SCHOOL.
!
THEY WERE SUPER OBNOXIOUS. THEY ACTED LIKE THEY WERE THE KINGS OF THE CLASSROOM.
THEN...
BUT I KNOW THEY SPENT EVERY DAY OUT THERE, TOILING AND SWEATING UNDER A HOT SUN.
CHEATING WOULD MAKE A MOCKERY OF THEIR HARD WORK...
...AND I WOULDN'T WANT THAT.

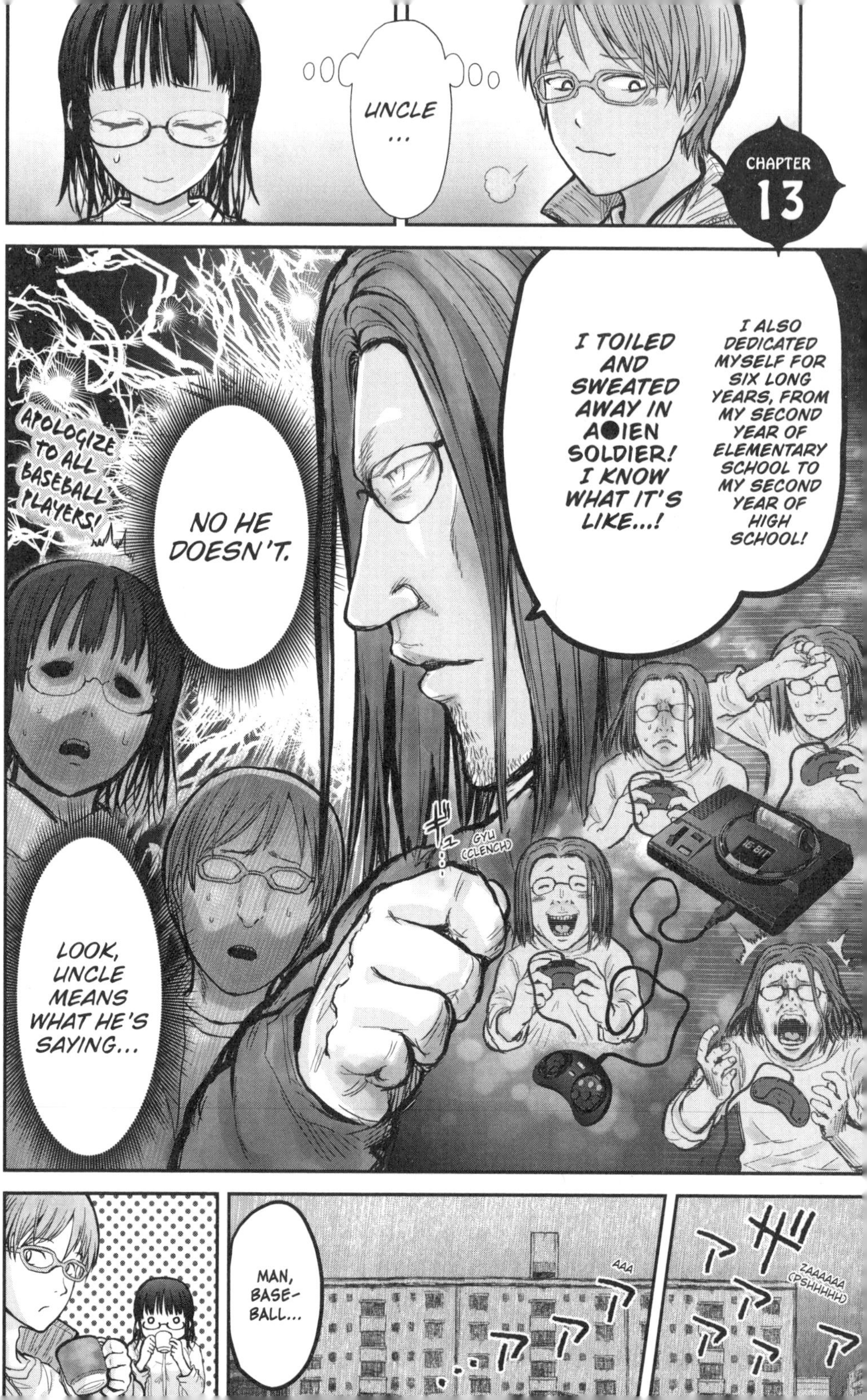
CHAPTER 13
UNCLE ...
I ALSO DEDICATED MYSELF FOR SIX LONG YEARS, FROM MY SECOND YEAR OF ELEMENTARY SCHOOL TO MY SECOND YEAR OF HIGH SCHOOL!
I TOILED AND SWEATED AWAY IN A●IEN SOLDIER! I KNOW WHAT IT'S LIKE...!
NO HE DOESN'T.
APOLOGIZE TO ALL BASEBALL PLAYERS!
GYU (CLENCH)
LOOK, UNCLE MEANS WHAT HE'S SAYING...
ZAAAAAA (PSHHHHH)
AAA
MAN, BASE-BALL...

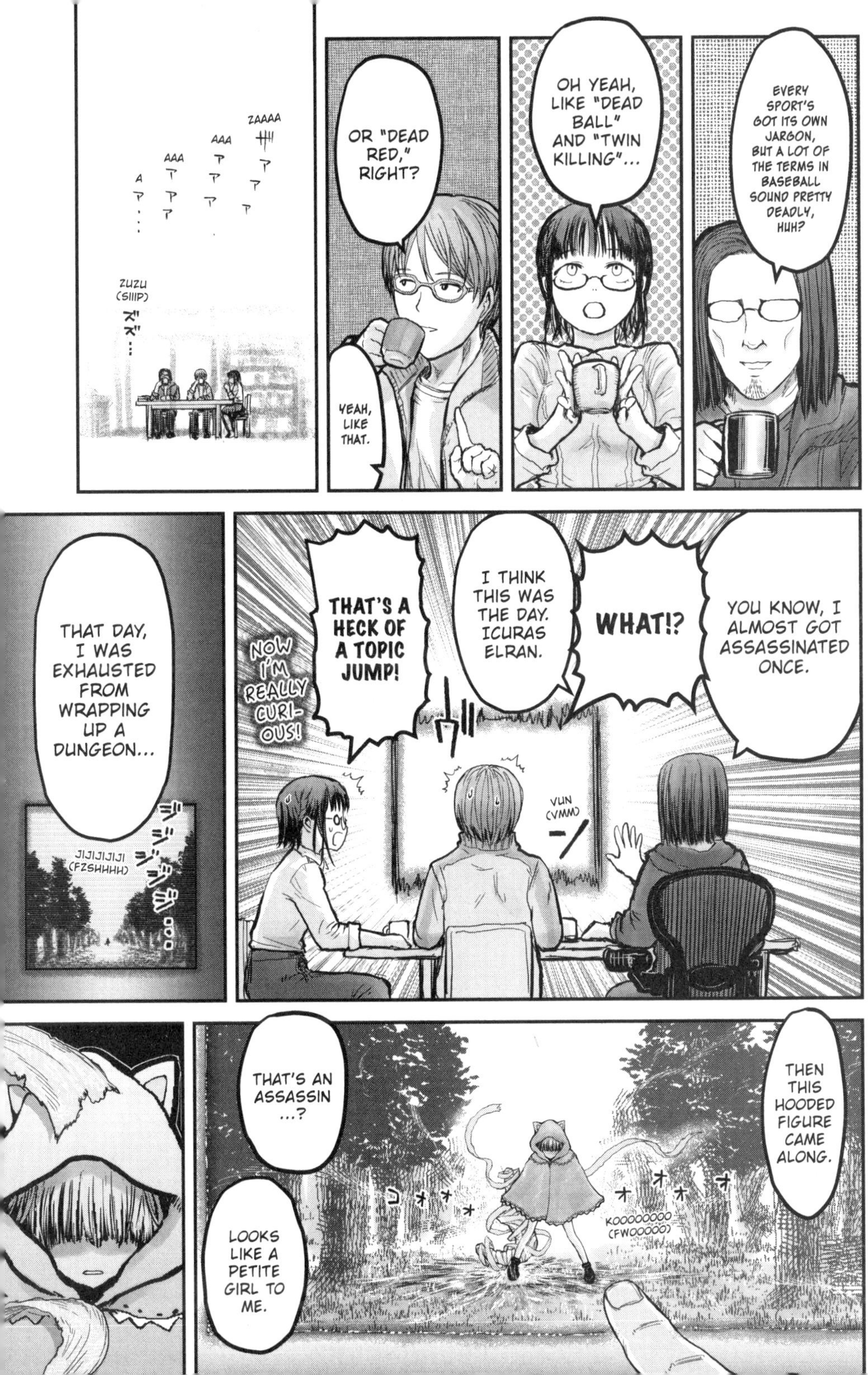
EVERY SPORT'S GOT ITS OWN JARGON, BUT A LOT OF THE TERMS IN BASEBALL SOUND PRETTY DEADLY, HUH?
OH YEAH, LIKE "DEAD BALL" AND "TWIN KILLING"...
OR "DEAD RED," RIGHT?
YEAH, LIKE THAT.
ZAAAA
AAA
AAA
A
ZUZU (SIIIP)
ズズ…
YOU KNOW, I ALMOST GOT ASSASSINATED ONCE.
WHAT!?
I THINK THIS WAS THE DAY. ICURAS ELRAN.
THAT'S A HECK OF A TOPIC JUMP!
NOW I'M REALLY CURIOUS!
VUN (VMM)
THAT DAY, I WAS EXHAUSTED FROM WRAPPING UP A DUNGEON...
JIJIJIJIJI (FZSHHHH)
THEN THIS HOODED FIGURE CAME ALONG.
KOOOOOOOO (FWOOOOO)
THAT'S AN ASSASSIN ...?
LOOKS LIKE A PETITE GIRL TO ME.

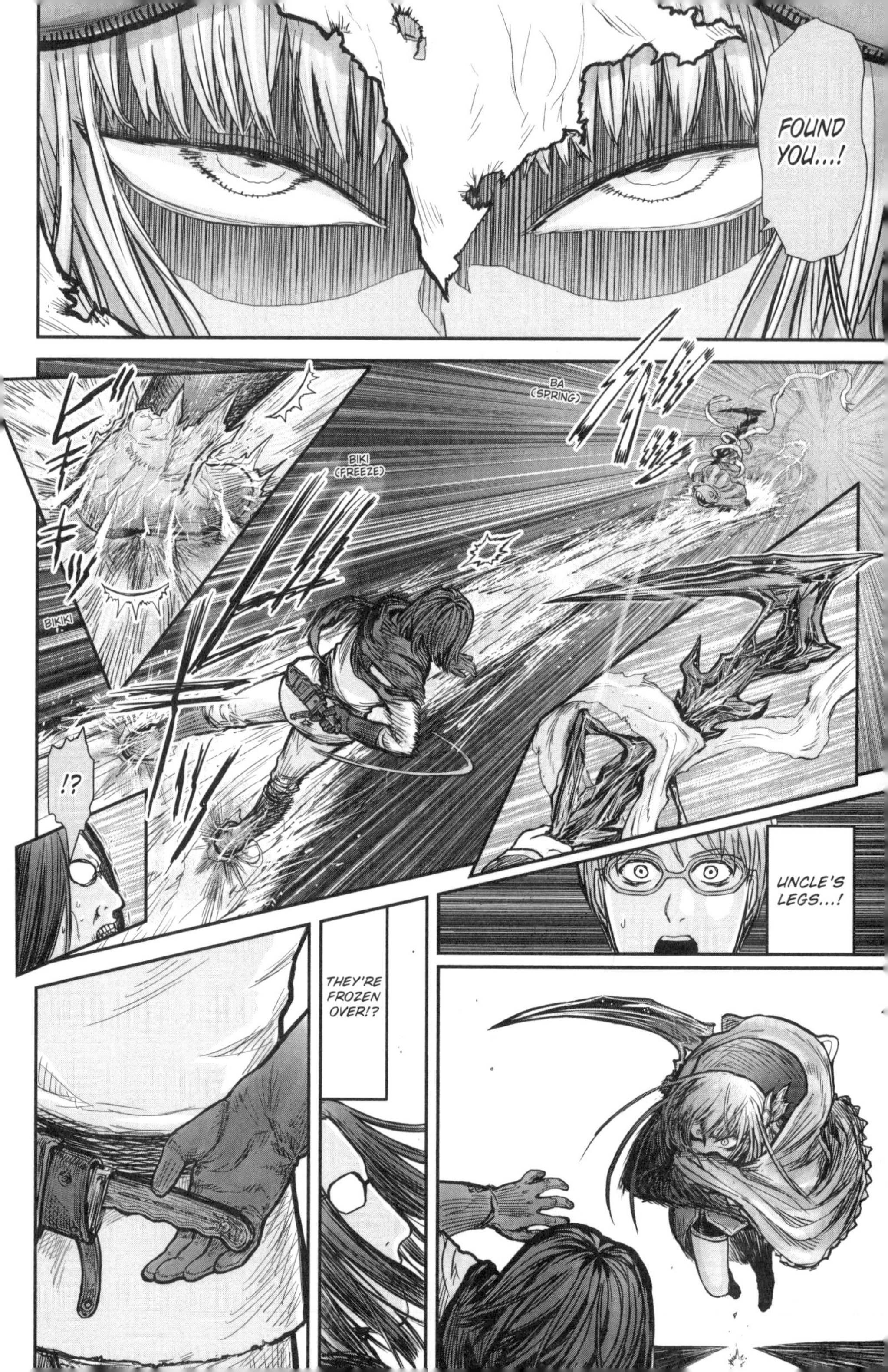
FOUND YOU...!
BA
(SPRING)
BIKI
(FREEZE)
BIKIKI
!?
UNCLE'S LEGS...!
THEY'RE FROZEN OVER!?

ZUZAZAZAZA
(CKSHHHH)

DOGAA
(WHAAM)

MABEL.

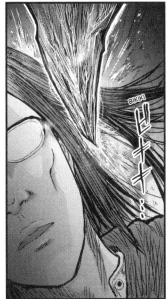

BIKKI

MABEL-
SAN!?

WHAT'S
WRONG?

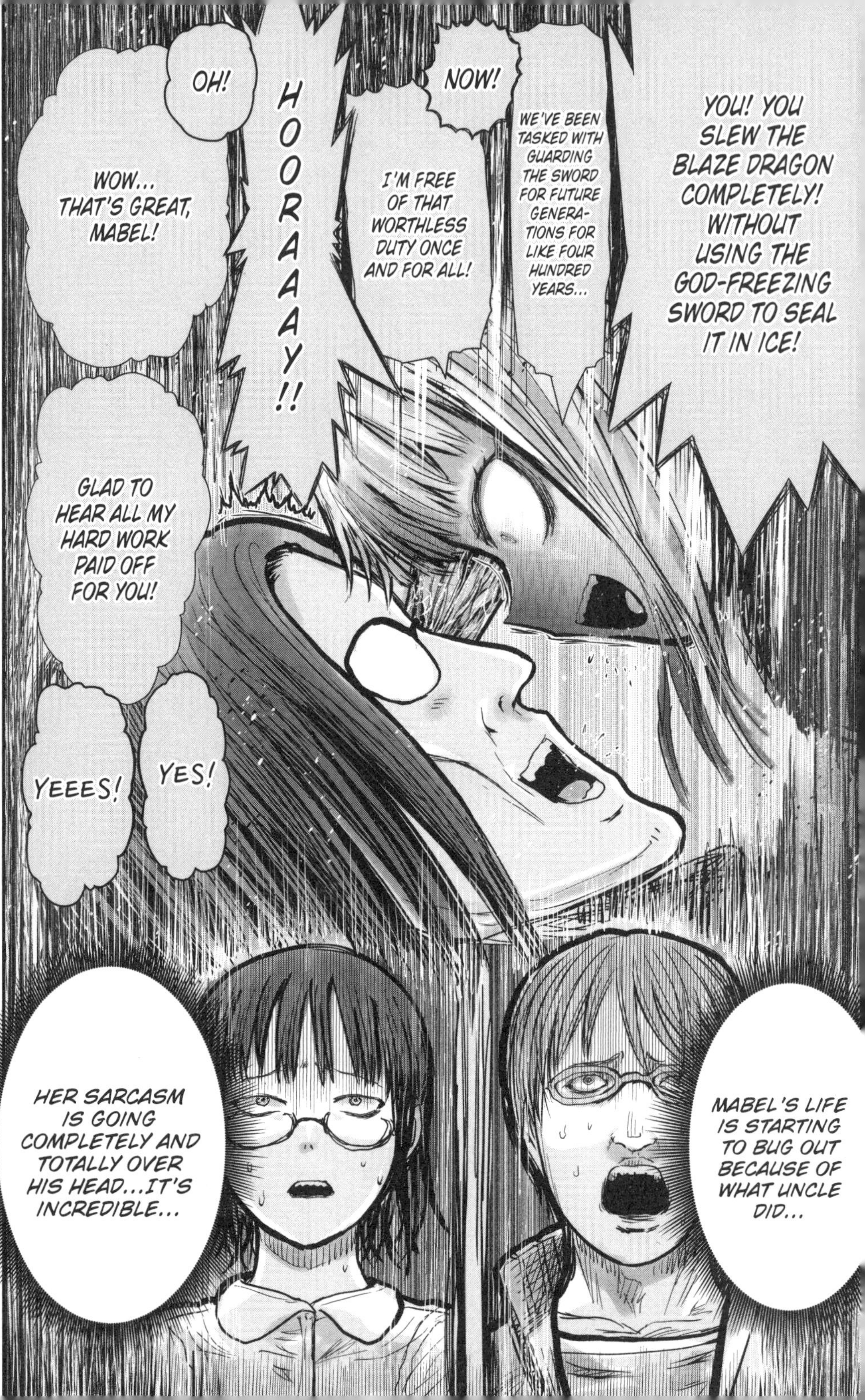
YOU! YOU SLEW THE BLAZE DRAGON COMPLETELY! WITHOUT USING THE GOD-FREEZING SWORD TO SEAL IT IN ICE!
WE'VE BEEN TASKED WITH GUARDING THE SWORD FOR FUTURE GENERATIONS FOR LIKE FOUR HUNDRED YEARS...
NOW!
I'M FREE OF THAT WORTHLESS DUTY ONCE AND FOR ALL!
HOORAAAAY!!
OH!
WOW... THAT'S GREAT, MABEL!
GLAD TO HEAR ALL MY HARD WORK PAID OFF FOR YOU!
YES!
YEEES!
MABEL'S LIFE IS STARTING TO BUG OUT BECAUSE OF WHAT UNCLE DID...
HER SARCASM IS GOING COMPLETELY AND TOTALLY OVER HIS HEAD...IT'S INCREDIBLE...

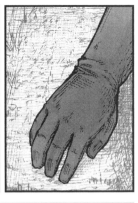

GYUKI (CLENCH)
ギュキッ
WHY DON'T YOU DRAW YOUR WEAPON?
I KNOW YOU COULD.
PLEASE. I BASICALLY LIVE IN A PSIKYO BULLET HELL. I'M CONSTANTLY BARRAGED WITH ATTACKS FROM LOCALS THAT ARE MEANT TO KILL.
YOU, THOUGH? I DON'T SENSE ANY BLOODLUST FROM YOU.
EVEN NOW.
I DON'T NEED TO DEFEND MYSELF.
ANYWAY, UH... YOU'RE NOT LOOKING TOO HOT THERE.
ARE YOU GETTING ENOUGH TO EAT?

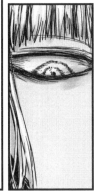

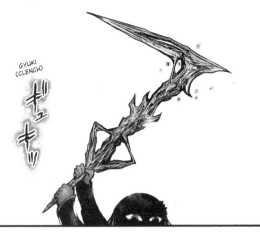

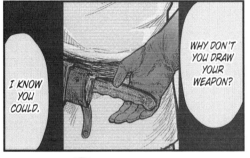

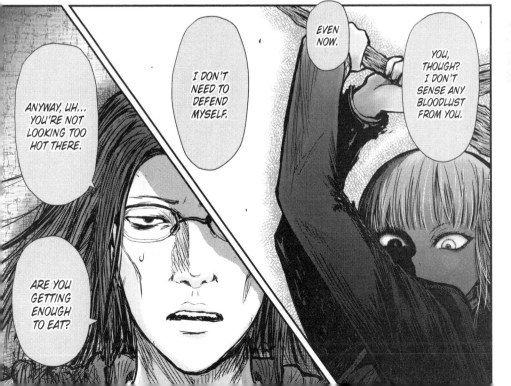

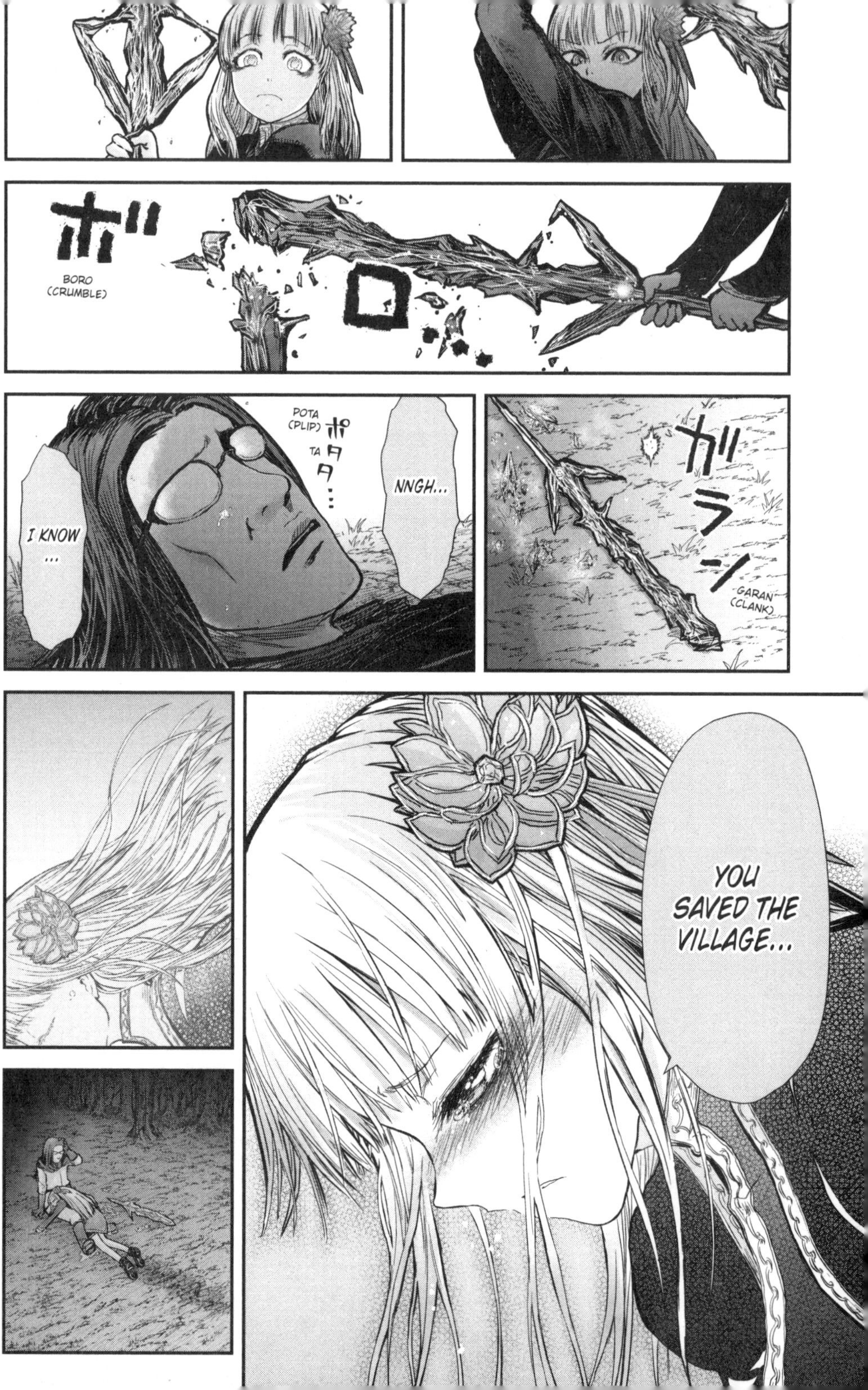
ボロ
BORO (CRUMBLE)
ガラン
GARAN (CLANK)
ポタタ…
POTA (PLIP) TA
NNGH...
I KNOW...
YOU SAVED THE VILLAGE...

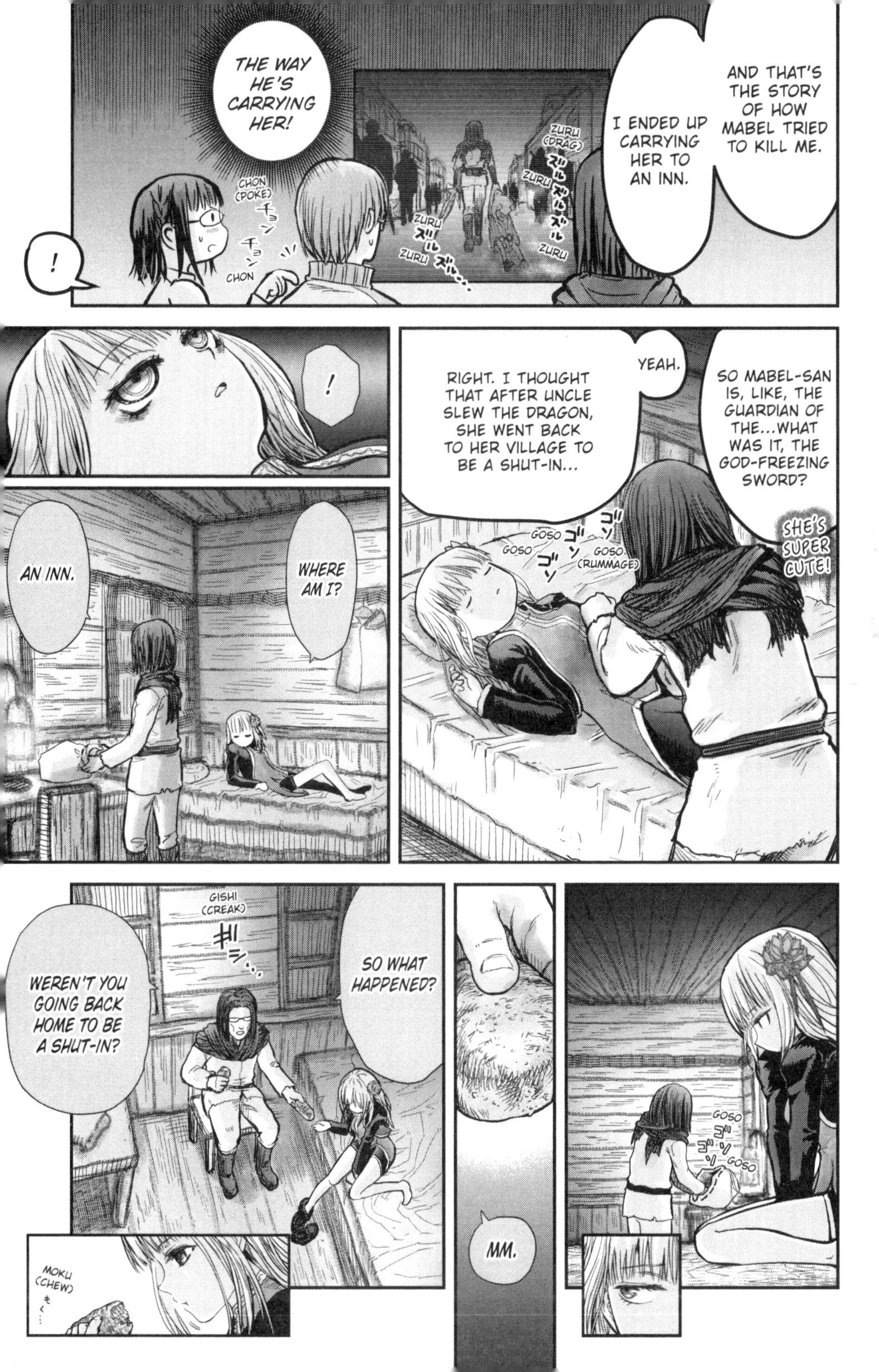
AND THAT'S THE STORY OF HOW MABEL TRIED TO KILL ME.
I ENDED UP CARRYING HER TO AN INN.
ZURU (DRAG)
ZURU
ZURU
ZURU
ZURU
THE WAY HE'S CARRYING HER!
CHON (POKE)
CHON
!
SO MABEL-SAN IS, LIKE, THE GUARDIAN OF THE...WHAT WAS IT, THE GOD-FREEZING SWORD?
YEAH.
RIGHT. I THOUGHT THAT AFTER UNCLE SLEW THE DRAGON, SHE WENT BACK TO HER VILLAGE TO BE A SHUT-IN...
GOSO
GOSO
GOSO (RUMMAGE)
SHE'S SUPER CUTE!
!
WHERE AM I?
AN INN.
GOSO
GOSO
MM.
GISHI (CREAK)
SO WHAT HAPPENED?
WEREN'T YOU GOING BACK HOME TO BE A SHUT-IN?
MOKU (CHEW)

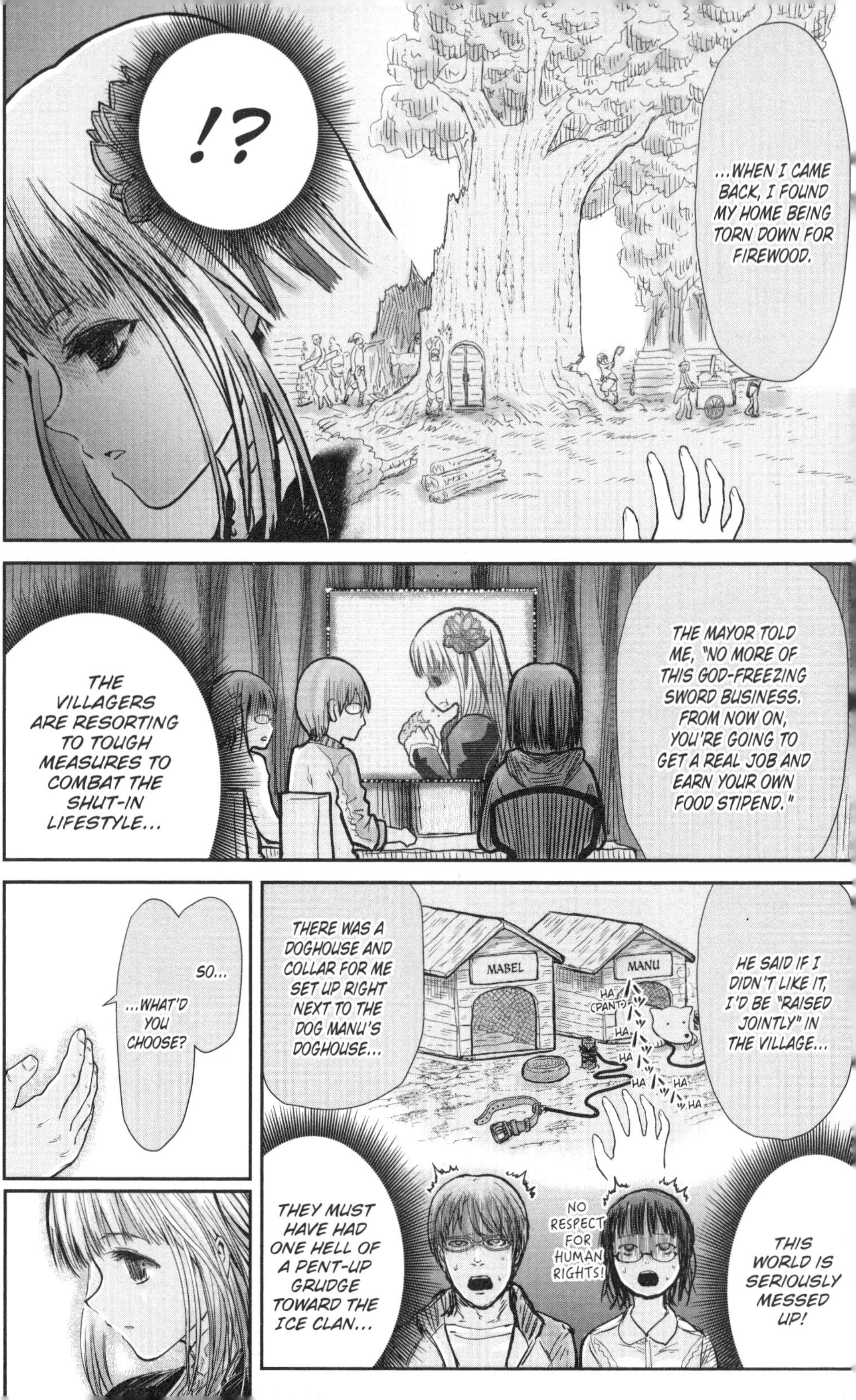
...WHEN I CAME BACK, I FOUND MY HOME BEING TORN DOWN FOR FIREWOOD.
!?
THE MAYOR TOLD ME, "NO MORE OF THIS GOD-FREEZING SWORD BUSINESS. FROM NOW ON, YOU'RE GOING TO GET A REAL JOB AND EARN YOUR OWN FOOD STIPEND."
THE VILLAGERS ARE RESORTING TO TOUGH MEASURES TO COMBAT THE SHUT-IN LIFESTYLE...
HE SAID IF I DIDN'T LIKE IT, I'D BE "RAISED JOINTLY" IN THE VILLAGE...
MANU
MABEL
HA (PANT) HA HA HA HA HA
THERE WAS A DOGHOUSE AND COLLAR FOR ME SET UP RIGHT NEXT TO THE DOG MANU'S DOGHOUSE...
THIS WORLD IS SERIOUSLY MESSED UP!
NO RESPECT FOR HUMAN RIGHTS!
THEY MUST HAVE HAD ONE HELL OF A PENT-UP GRUDGE TOWARD THE ICE CLAN...
SO...
...WHAT'D YOU CHOOSE?

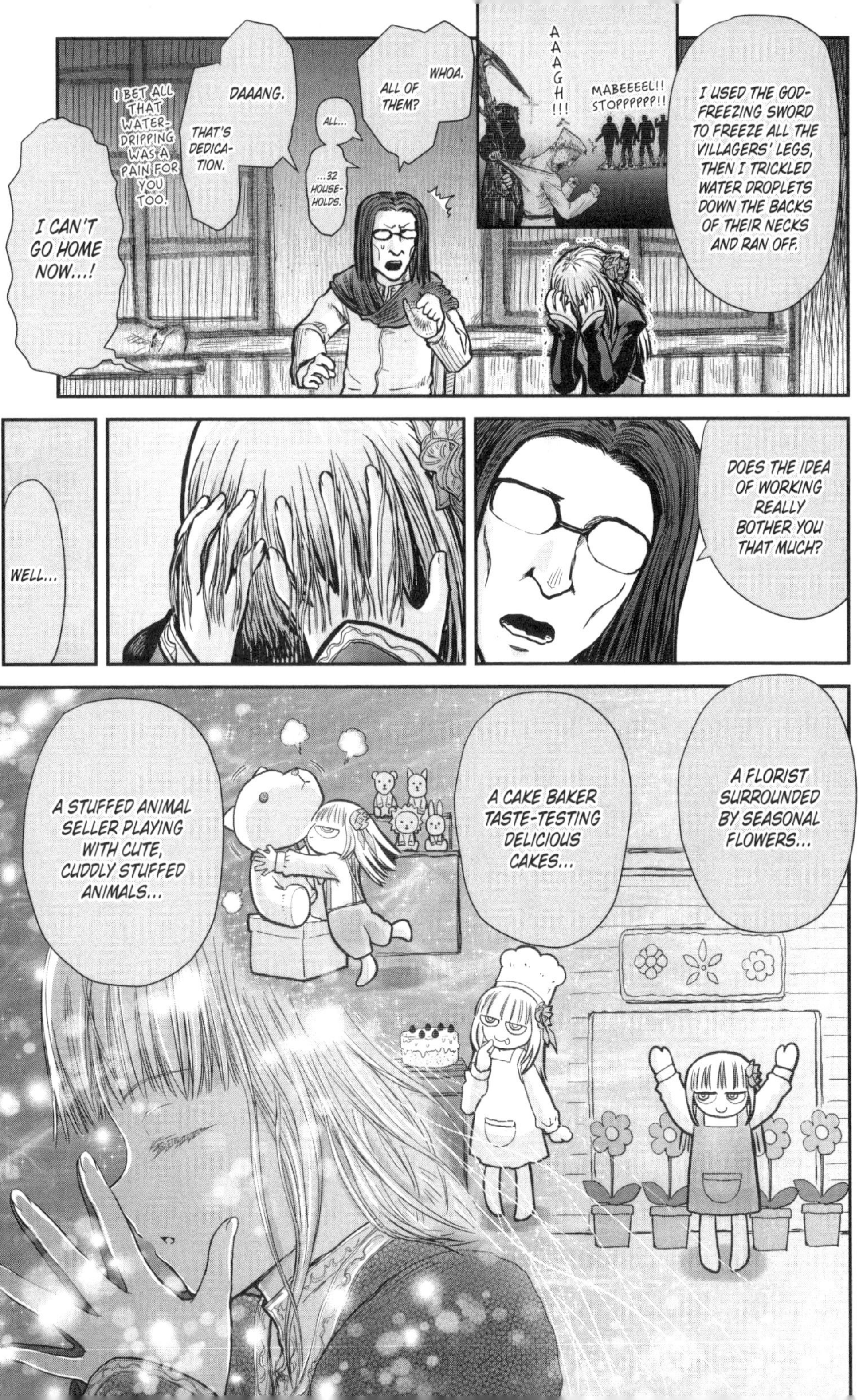
I USED THE GOD-FREEZING SWORD TO FREEZE ALL THE VILLAGERS' LEGS, THEN I TRICKLED WATER DROPLETS DOWN THE BACKS OF THEIR NECKS AND RAN OFF.
MABEEEEEL!! STOPPPPPPP!!
AAAAGH!!!
WHOA. ALL OF THEM?
ALL...
...32 HOUSE-HOLDS.
DAAANG. THAT'S DEDICA-TION.
I BET ALL THAT WATER-DRIPPING WAS A PAIN FOR YOU TOO.
I CAN'T GO HOME NOW...!
DOES THE IDEA OF WORKING REALLY BOTHER YOU THAT MUCH?
WELL...
A FLORIST SURROUNDED BY SEASONAL FLOWERS...
A CAKE BAKER TASTE-TESTING DELICIOUS CAKES...
A STUFFED ANIMAL SELLER PLAYING WITH CUTE, CUDDLY STUFFED ANIMALS...

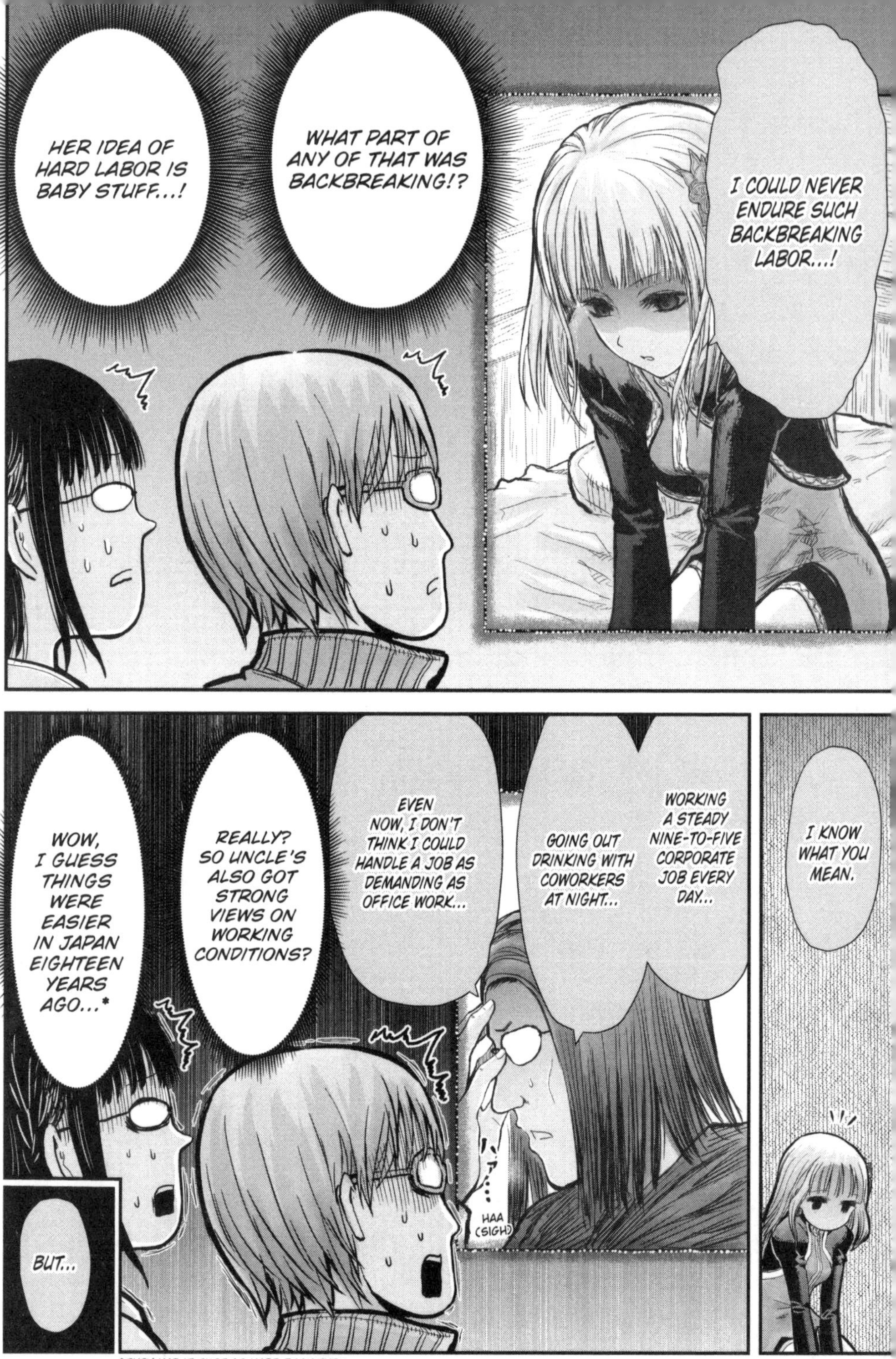
I COULD NEVER ENDURE SUCH BACKBREAKING LABOR...!
WHAT PART OF ANY OF THAT WAS BACKBREAKING!?
HER IDEA OF HARD LABOR IS BABY STUFF...!
I KNOW WHAT YOU MEAN.
WORKING A STEADY NINE-TO-FIVE CORPORATE JOB EVERY DAY...
GOING OUT DRINKING WITH COWORKERS AT NIGHT...
EVEN NOW, I DON'T THINK I COULD HANDLE A JOB AS DEMANDING AS OFFICE WORK...
HAA (SIGH)
REALLY? SO UNCLE'S ALSO GOT STRONG VIEWS ON WORKING CONDITIONS?
WOW, I GUESS THINGS WERE EASIER IN JAPAN EIGHTEEN YEARS AGO...*
BUT...

*THEY HAD IT JUST AS HARD BACK THEN.

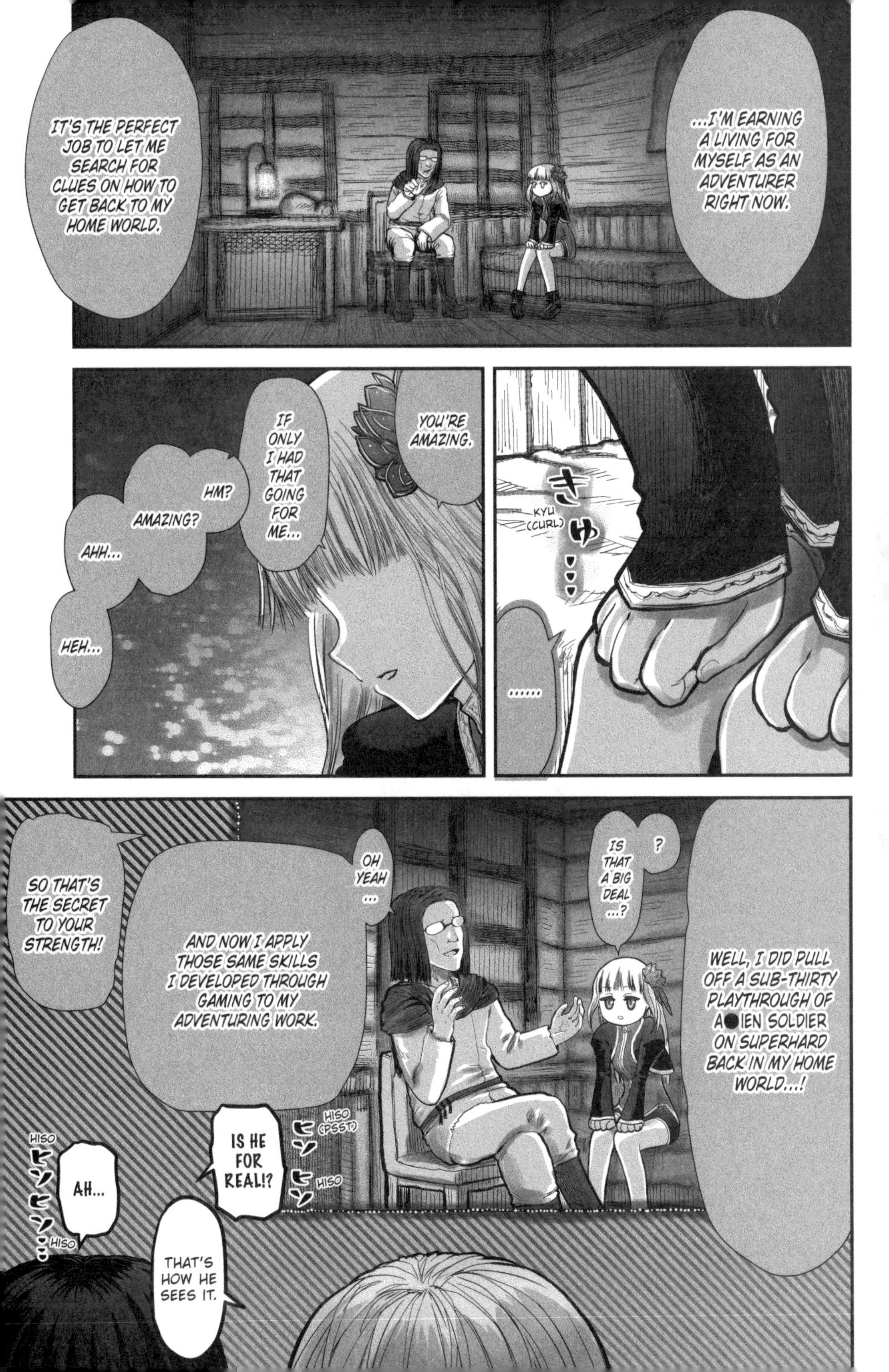

...I'M EARNING A LIVING FOR MYSELF AS AN ADVENTURER RIGHT NOW.
IT'S THE PERFECT JOB TO LET ME SEARCH FOR CLUES ON HOW TO GET BACK TO MY HOME WORLD.
きゅ…
KYU (CURL)
......
YOU'RE AMAZING.
IF ONLY I HAD THAT GOING FOR ME...
HM?
AMAZING?
AHH...
HEH...
WELL, I DID PULL OFF A SUB-THIRTY PLAYTHROUGH OF A●IEN SOLDIER ON SUPERHARD BACK IN MY HOME WORLD...!
?
IS THAT A BIG DEAL ...?
OH YEAH ...
AND NOW I APPLY THOSE SAME SKILLS I DEVELOPED THROUGH GAMING TO MY ADVENTURING WORK.
SO THAT'S THE SECRET TO YOUR STRENGTH!
ヒソ
HISO (PSST)
ヒソ
HISO
IS HE FOR REAL!?
ヒソヒソ…
HISO
HISO
AH...
THAT'S HOW HE SEES IT.

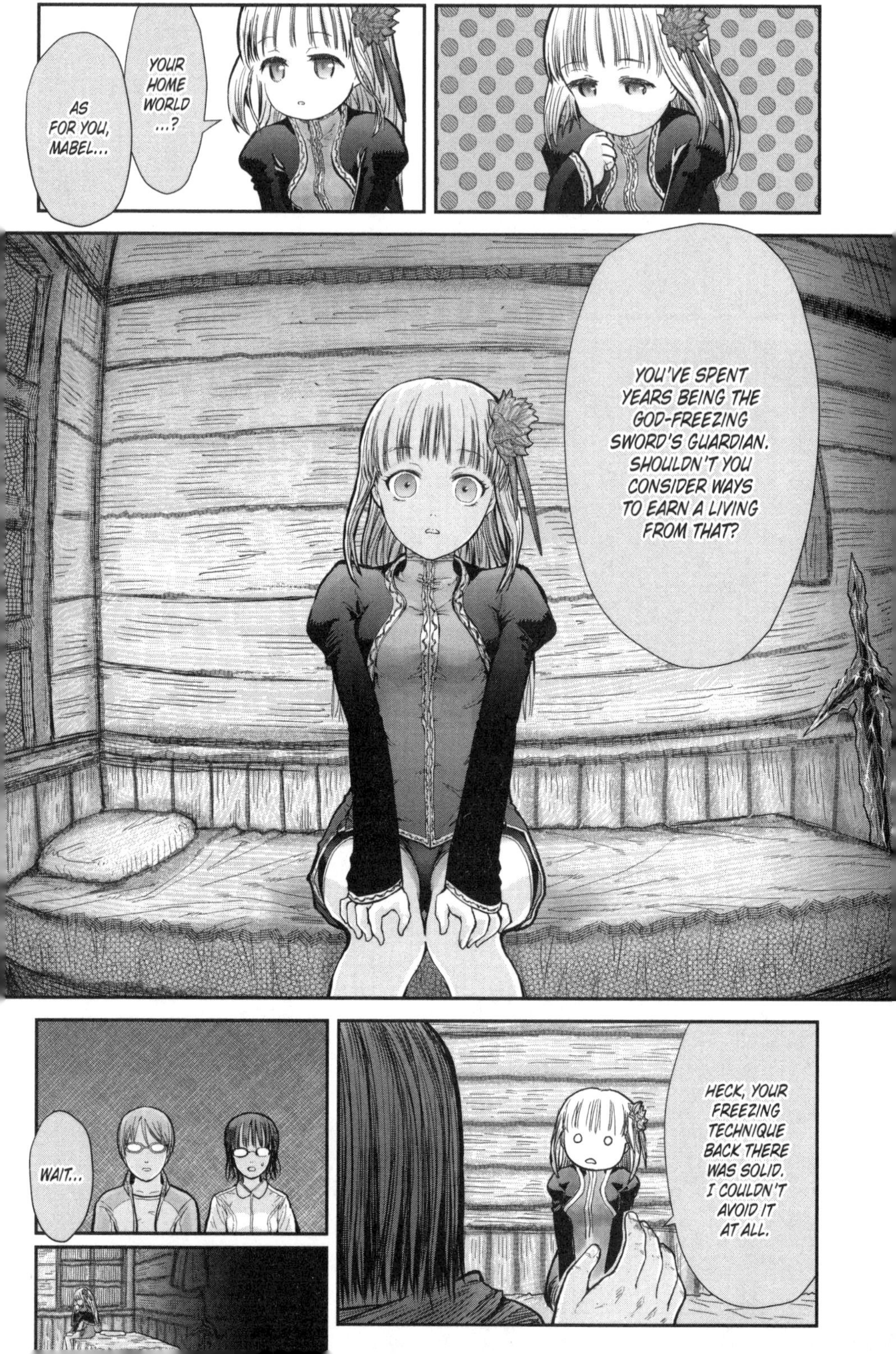
YOUR HOME WORLD ...?
AS FOR YOU, MABEL...
YOU'VE SPENT YEARS BEING THE GOD-FREEZING SWORD'S GUARDIAN. SHOULDN'T YOU CONSIDER WAYS TO EARN A LIVING FROM THAT?
HECK, YOUR FREEZING TECHNIQUE BACK THERE WAS SOLID, I COULDN'T AVOID IT AT ALL.
WAIT...

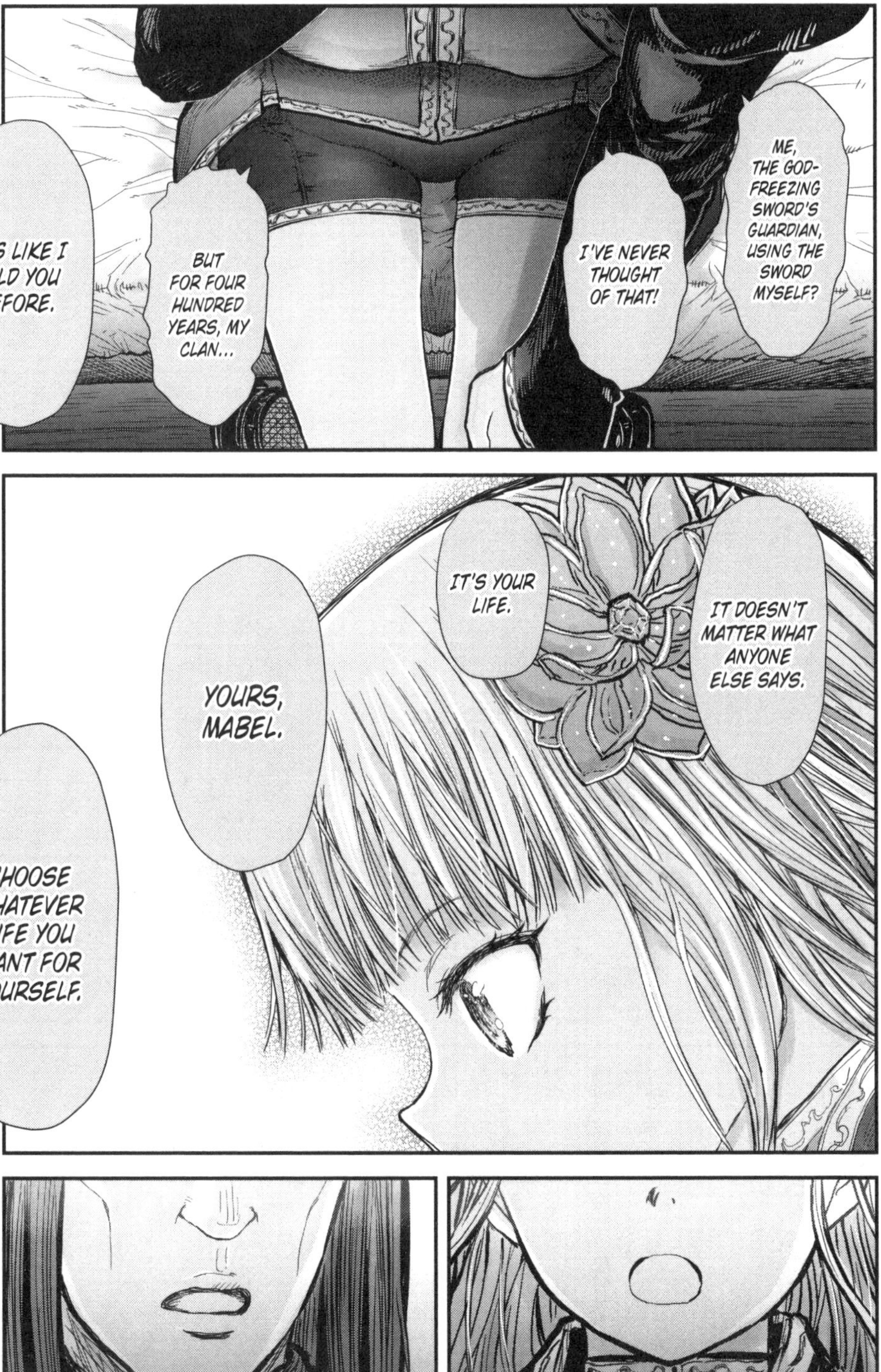
ME, THE GOD-FREEZING SWORD'S GUARDIAN, USING THE SWORD MYSELF?
I'VE NEVER THOUGHT OF THAT!
BUT FOR FOUR HUNDRED YEARS, MY CLAN...
IT'S LIKE I TOLD YOU BEFORE.
IT DOESN'T MATTER WHAT ANYONE ELSE SAYS.
IT'S YOUR LIFE.
YOURS, MABEL.
CHOOSE WHATEVER LIFE YOU WANT FOR YOURSELF.

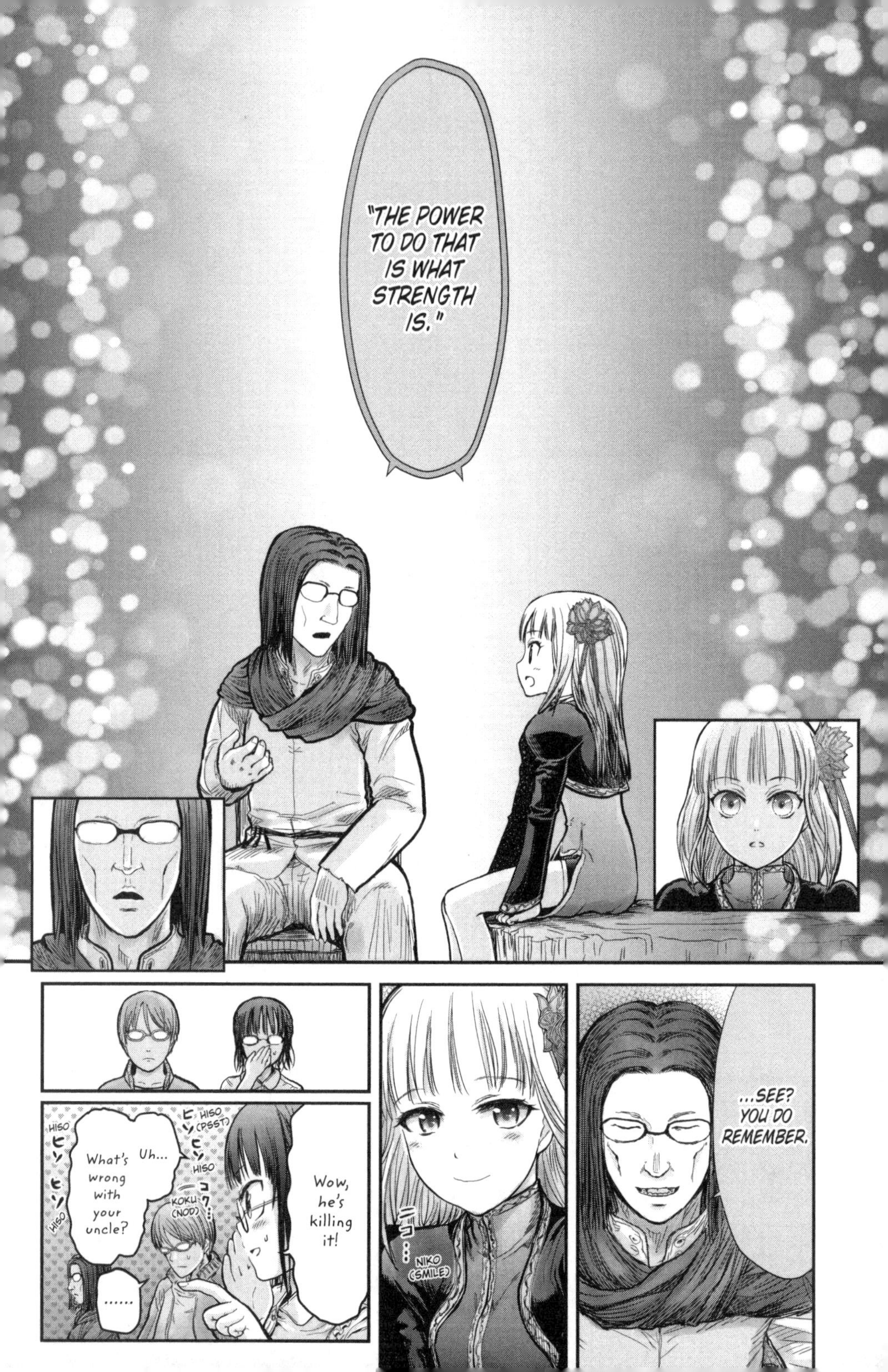
"THE POWER TO DO THAT IS WHAT STRENGTH IS."
...SEE? YOU DO REMEMBER.
ニコ…
NIKO (SMILE)
Wow, he's killing it!
ヒソ ヒソ
HISO (PSST)
HISO
Uh...
ヒソ ヒソ
HISO
HISO
What's wrong with your uncle?
コク…
KOKU (NOD)
......

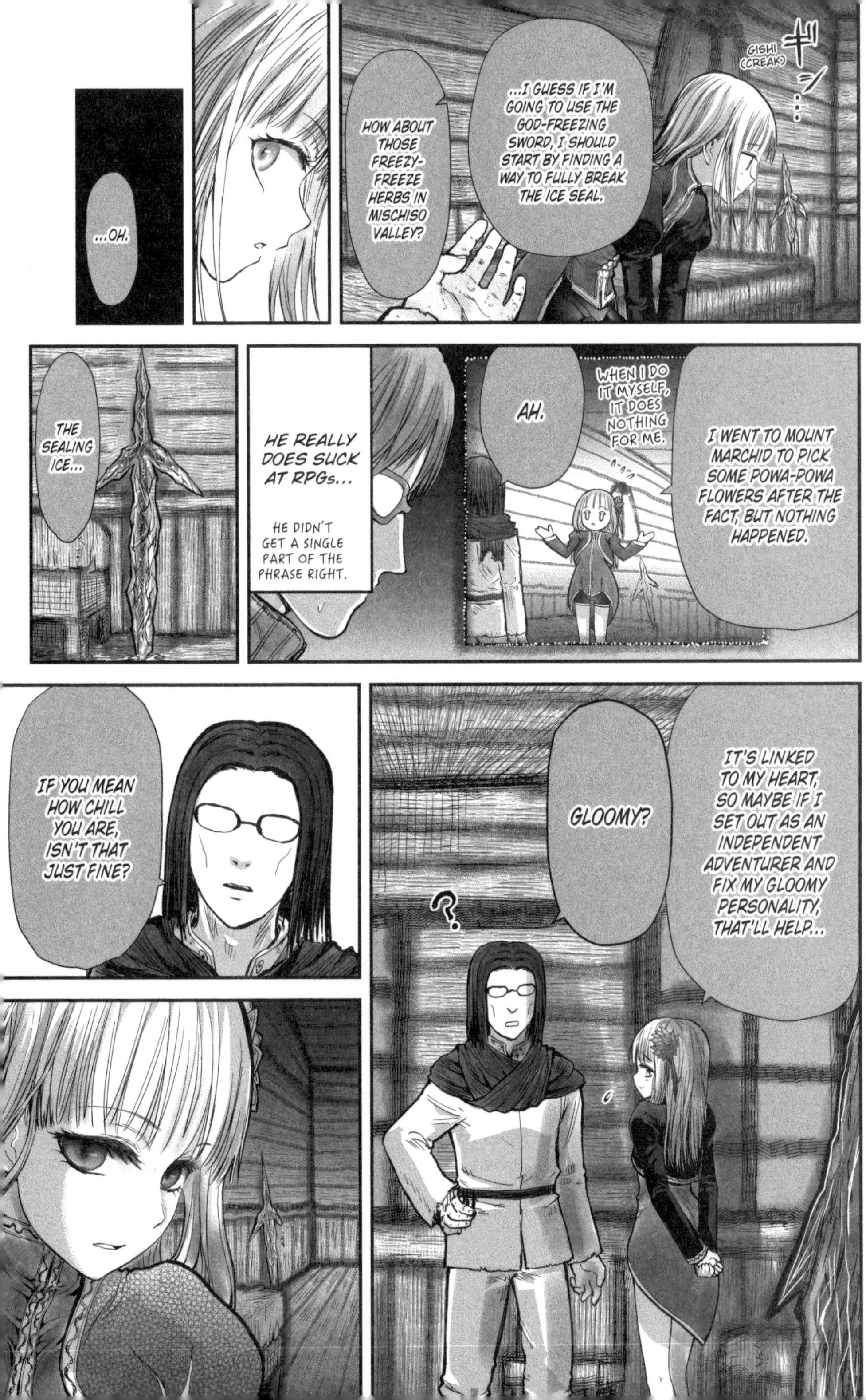
GISHI (CREAK)
...I GUESS IF I'M GOING TO USE THE GOD-FREEZING SWORD, I SHOULD START BY FINDING A WAY TO FULLY BREAK THE ICE SEAL.
HOW ABOUT THOSE FREEZY-FREEZE HERBS IN MISCHISO VALLEY?
...OH.
I WENT TO MOUNT MARCHID TO PICK SOME POWA-POWA FLOWERS AFTER THE FACT, BUT NOTHING HAPPENED.
WHEN I DO IT MYSELF, IT DOES NOTHING FOR ME.
AH.
HE REALLY DOES SUCK AT RPGs...
HE DIDN'T GET A SINGLE PART OF THE PHRASE RIGHT.
THE SEALING ICE...
IT'S LINKED TO MY HEART, SO MAYBE IF I SET OUT AS AN INDEPENDENT ADVENTURER AND FIX MY GLOOMY PERSONALITY, THAT'LL HELP...
GLOOMY?
?
IF YOU MEAN HOW CHILL YOU ARE, ISN'T THAT JUST FINE?

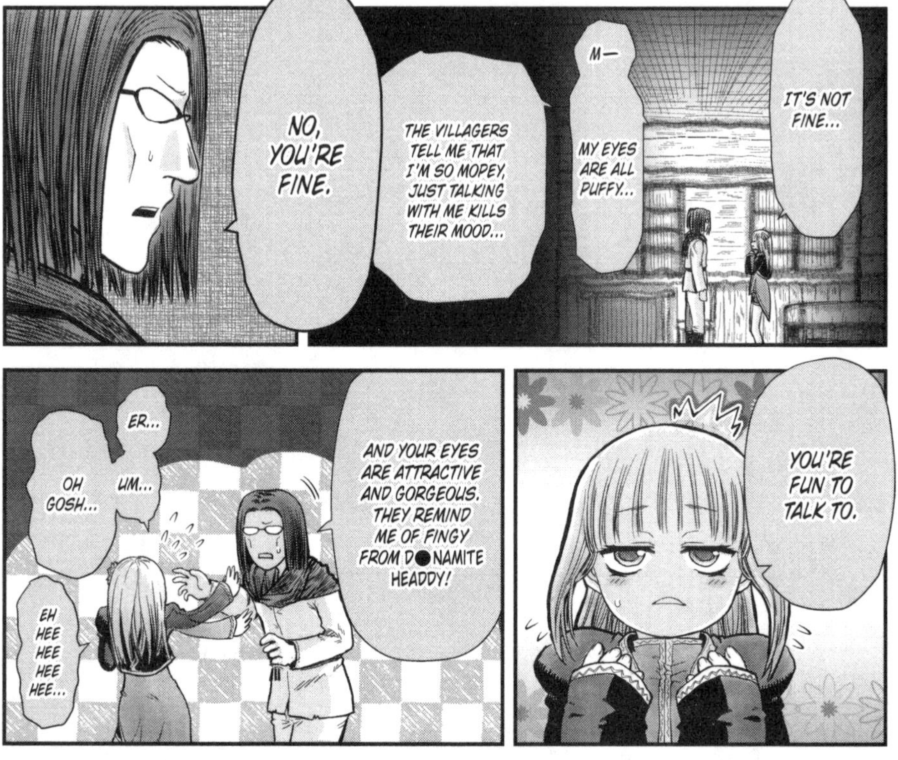
IT'S NOT FINE...
M—
MY EYES ARE ALL PUFFY...
THE VILLAGERS TELL ME THAT I'M SO MOPEY, JUST TALKING WITH ME KILLS THEIR MOOD...
NO, YOU'RE FINE.
YOU'RE FUN TO TALK TO.
AND YOUR EYES ARE ATTRACTIVE AND GORGEOUS. THEY REMIND ME OF FINGY FROM D●NAMITE HEADDY!
ER...
UM...
OH GOSH...
EH HEE HEE HEE HEE...
WAIT...
I THOUGHT UNCLE WAS SUPPOSED TO LOOK SUPER UGLY AND ORCISH TO OTHER-WORLDERS?
WHY DOES SHE SEEM TICKLED PINK BY THIS?
AND WHO'S FINGY?
WHO KNOWS?
MAYBE SHE DOESN'T CARE ABOUT PEOPLE'S APPEARANCES...
NOT THAT I KNOW MUCH ABOUT IT, BUT ISN'T SHE BASICALLY A CUTE GIRL CHARACTER IN A VIDEO GAME?

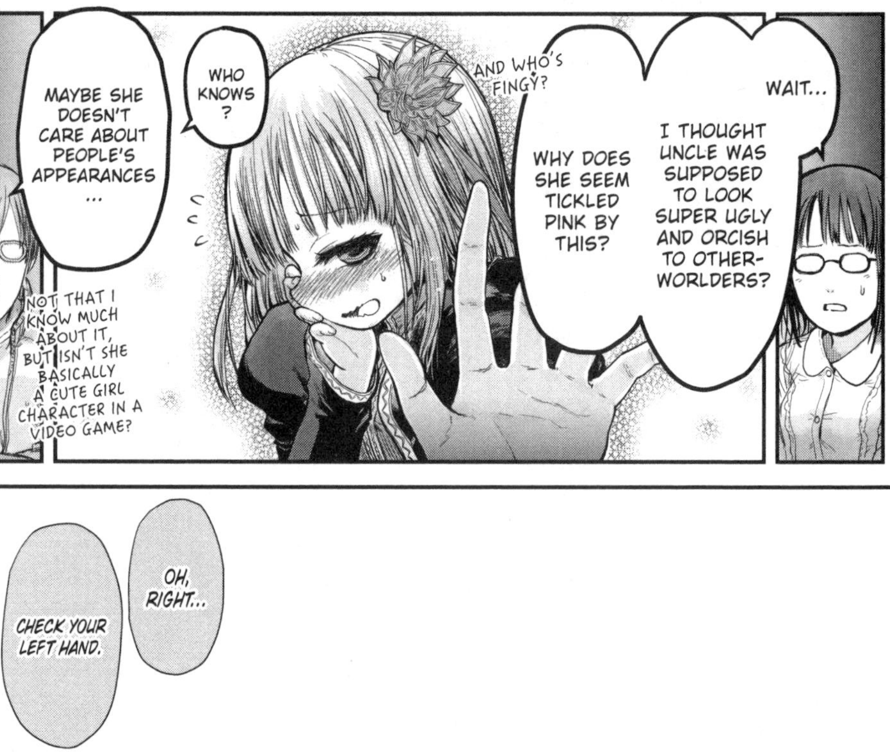
OH, RIGHT...
CHECK YOUR LEFT HAND.

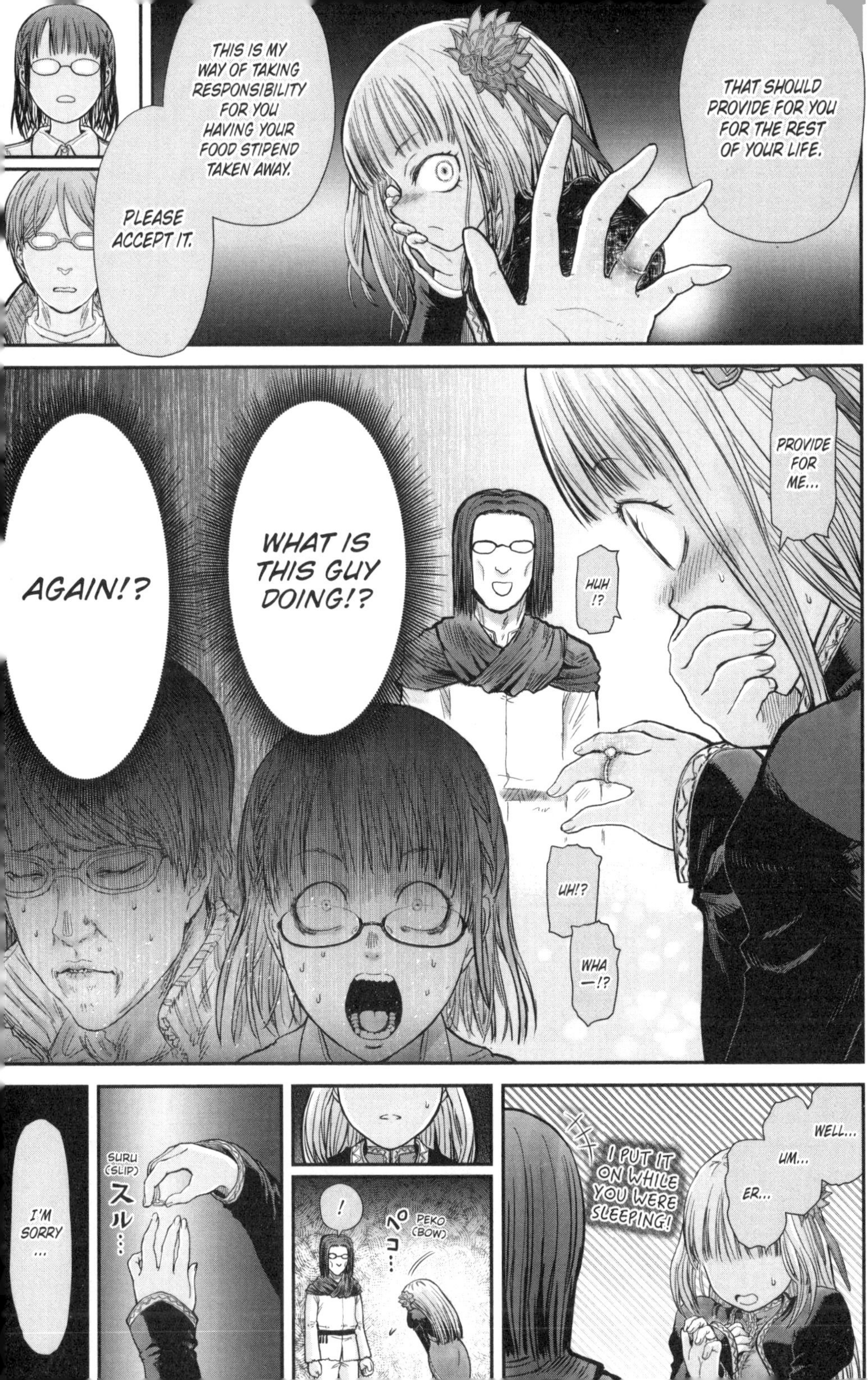
THAT SHOULD PROVIDE FOR YOU FOR THE REST OF YOUR LIFE.
THIS IS MY WAY OF TAKING RESPONSIBILITY FOR YOU HAVING YOUR FOOD STIPEND TAKEN AWAY.
PLEASE ACCEPT IT.
PROVIDE FOR ME...
HUH!?
UH!?
WHA—!?
WHAT IS THIS GUY DOING!?
AGAIN!?
WELL...
UM...
ER...
I PUT IT ON WHILE YOU WERE SLEEPING!
!
PEKO (BOW)
ペコ…
SURU (SLIP)
スル…
I'M SORRY ...

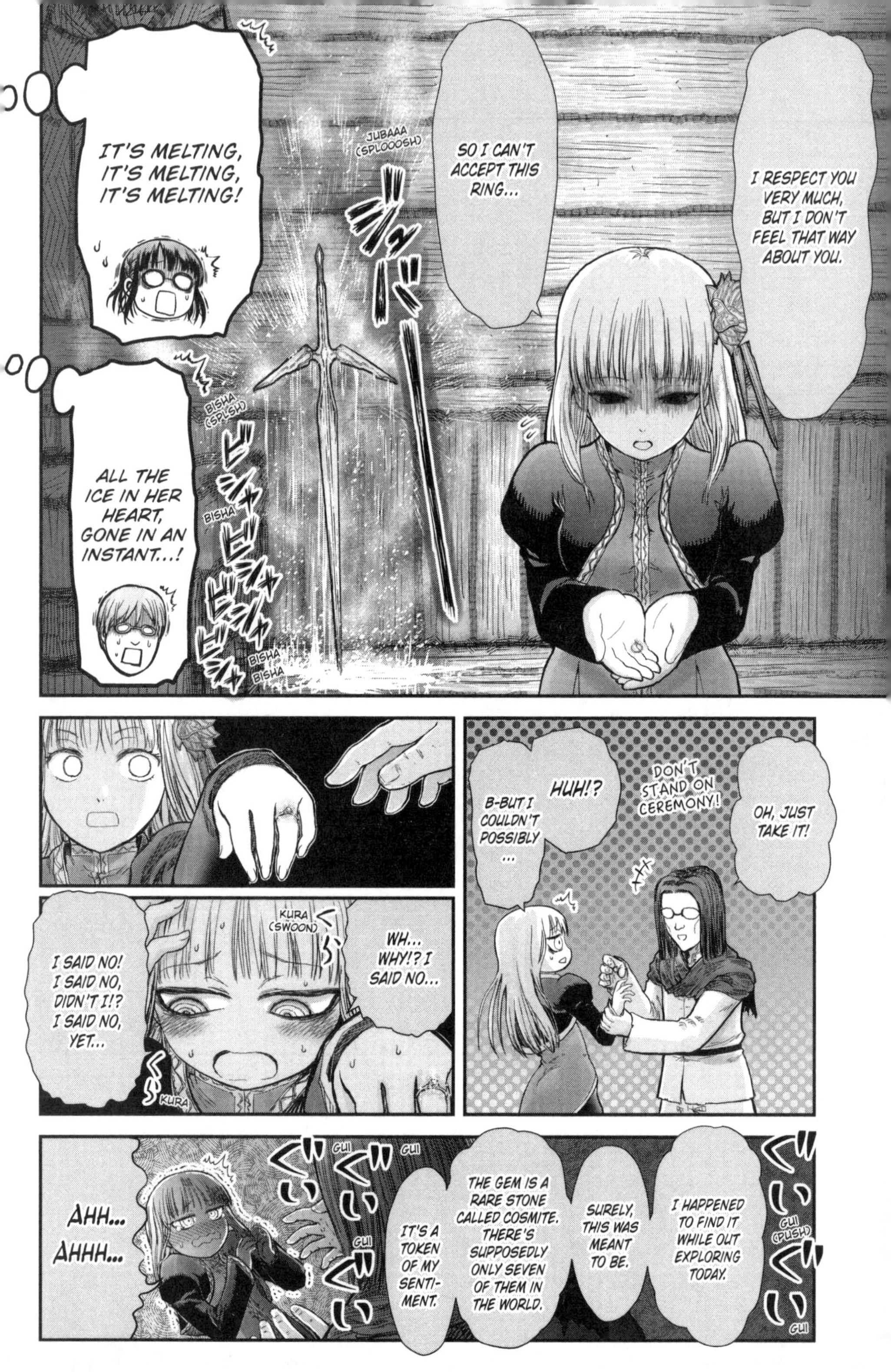

I RESPECT YOU VERY MUCH, BUT I DON'T FEEL THAT WAY ABOUT YOU.
SO I CAN'T ACCEPT THIS RING...
JUBAAA (SPLOOOSH)
IT'S MELTING, IT'S MELTING, IT'S MELTING!
BISHA (SPLSH)
BISHA
BISHA
BISHA
ALL THE ICE IN HER HEART, GONE IN AN INSTANT...!
OH, JUST TAKE IT!
DON'T STAND ON CEREMONY!
HUH!?
B-BUT I COULDN'T POSSIBLY ...
KURA (SWOON)
WH... WHY!? I SAID NO...
I SAID NO! I SAID NO, DIDN'T I!? I SAID NO, YET...
KURA
GUI (PUSH)
GUI
I HAPPENED TO FIND IT WHILE OUT EXPLORING TODAY.
SURELY, THIS WAS MEANT TO BE.
THE GEM IS A RARE STONE CALLED COSMITE. THERE'S SUPPOSEDLY ONLY SEVEN OF THEM IN THE WORLD.
IT'S A TOKEN OF MY SENTI-MENT.
GUI
GUI
GUI
AHH... AHHH...

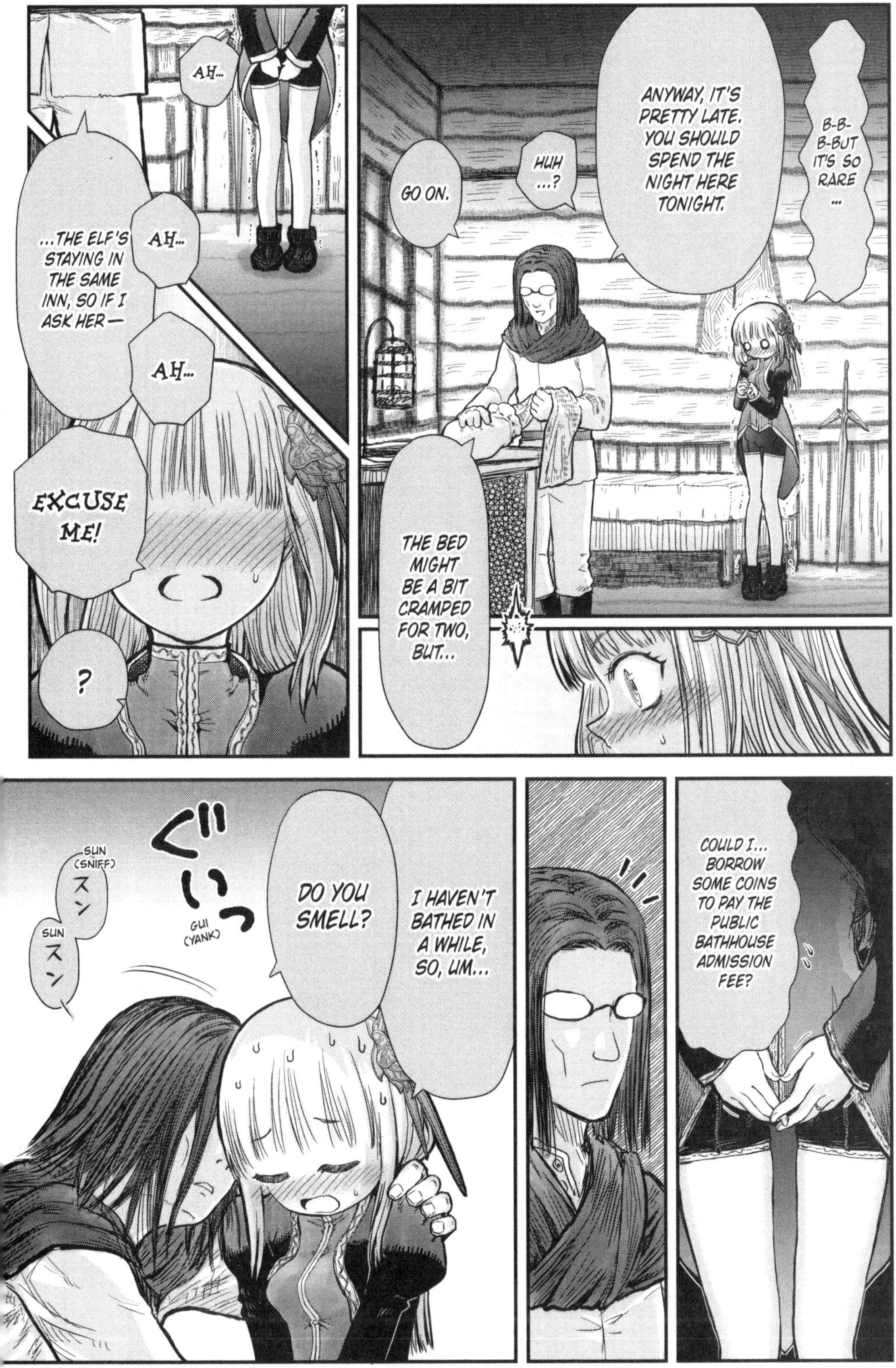
B-B-B-BUT IT'S SO RARE...
ANYWAY, IT'S PRETTY LATE. YOU SHOULD SPEND THE NIGHT HERE TONIGHT.
HUH...?
GO ON.
THE BED MIGHT BE A BIT CRAMPED FOR TWO, BUT...
AH...
AH...
...THE ELF'S STAYING IN THE SAME INN, SO IF I ASK HER—
AH...
EXCUSE ME!
?
COULD I... BORROW SOME COINS TO PAY THE PUBLIC BATHHOUSE ADMISSION FEE?
I HAVEN'T BATHED IN A WHILE, SO, UM...
DO YOU SMELL?
ぐいっ
GUI (YANK)
SUN (SNIFF)
スン
SUN
スン

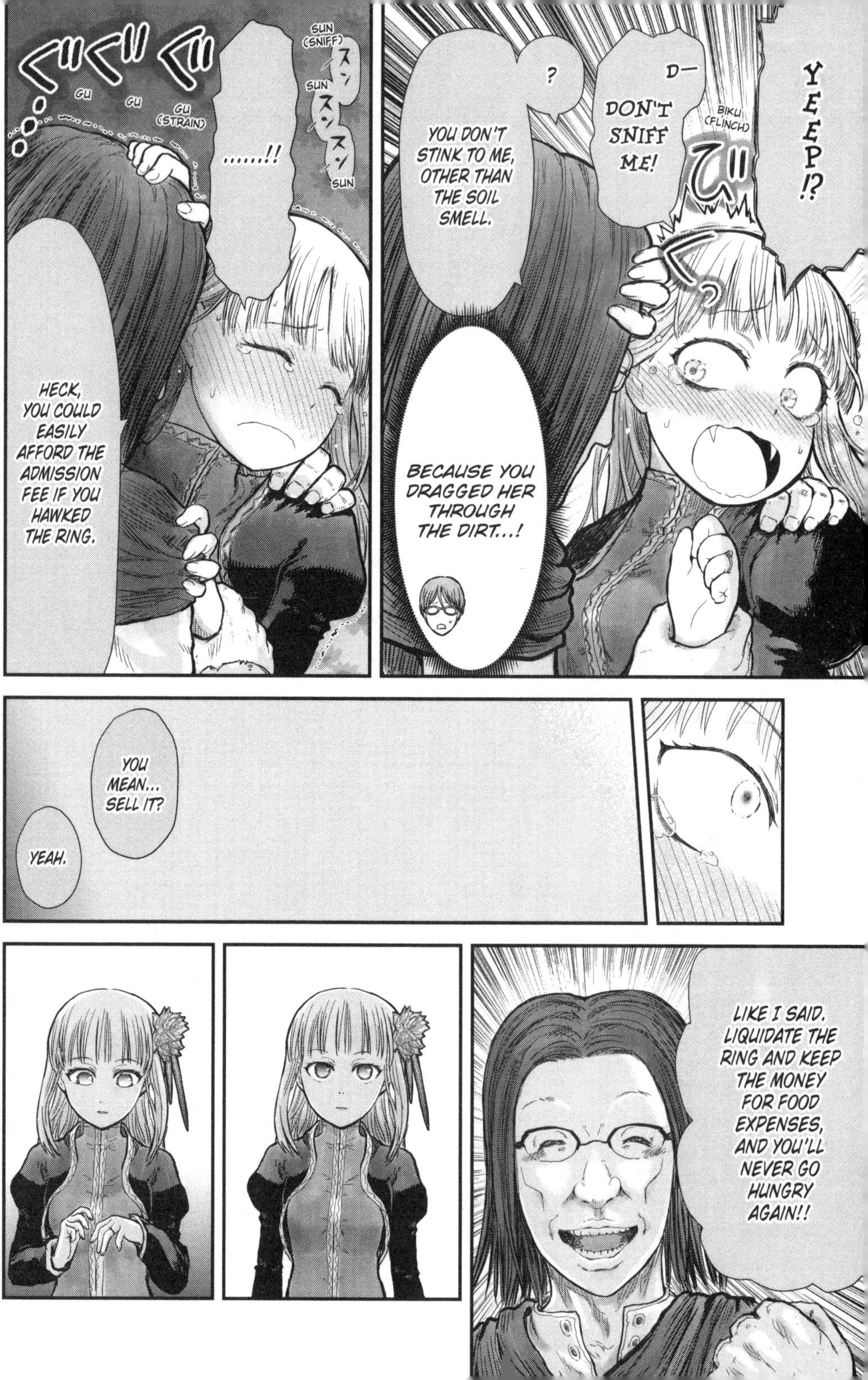
YEEP!?
BIKU (FLINCH)
D— DON'T SNIFF ME!
?
YOU DON'T STINK TO ME, OTHER THAN THE SOIL SMELL.
BECAUSE YOU DRAGGED HER THROUGH THE DIRT...!
SUN (SNIFF) スン
SUN スン
スン SUN
GU GU GU (STRAIN)
......!!
HECK, YOU COULD EASILY AFFORD THE ADMISSION FEE IF YOU HAWKED THE RING.
YOU MEAN... SELL IT?
YEAH.
LIKE I SAID. LIQUIDATE THE RING AND KEEP THE MONEY FOR FOOD EXPENSES, AND YOU'LL NEVER GO HUNGRY AGAIN!!

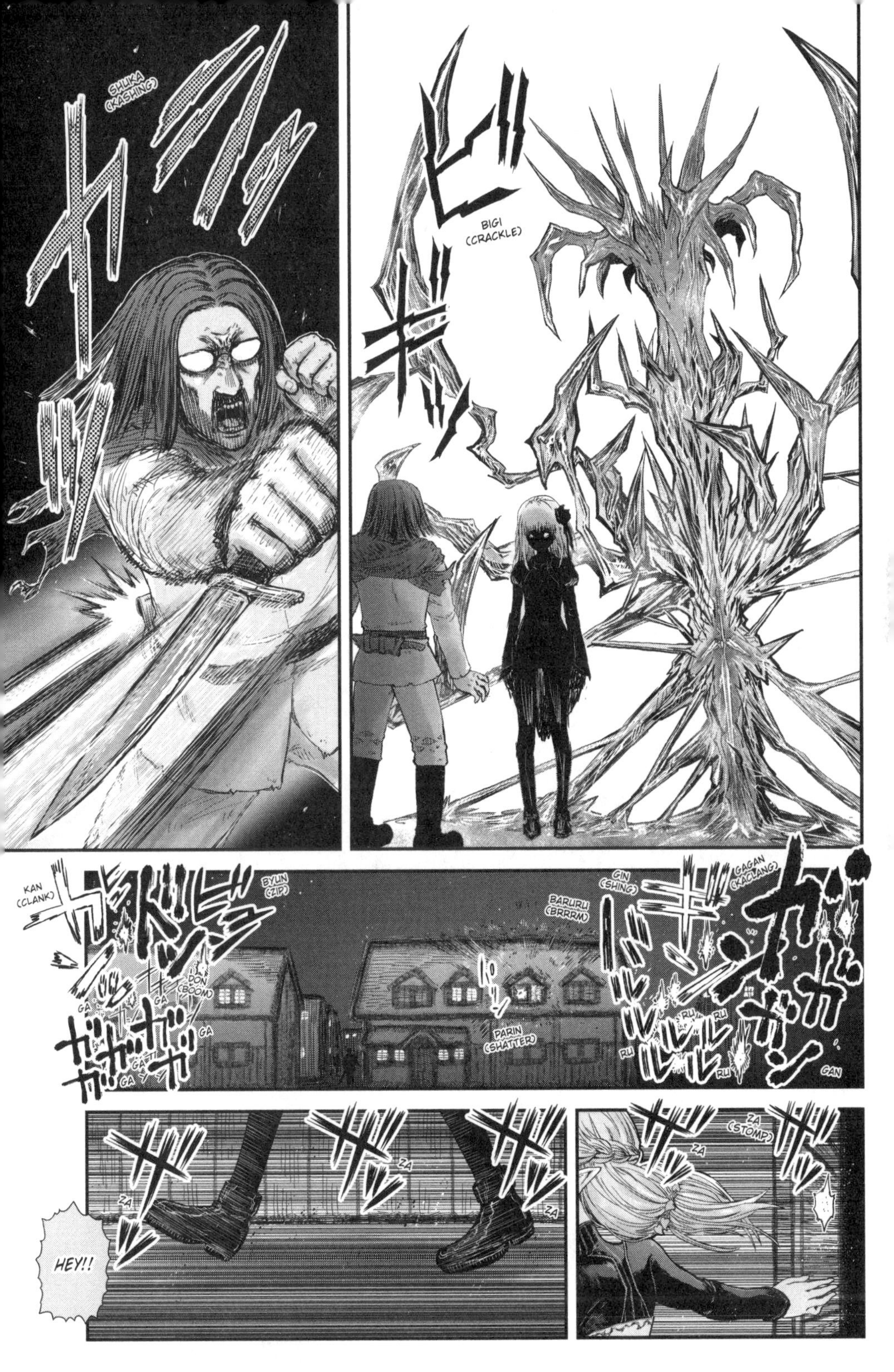
BIGI (CRACKLE)
SHUKA (KASHING)
GAGAN (KACLANG)
GIN (SHING)
RU
RU
RU
RU
GAN
BARURU (BRRRM)
PARIN (SHATTER)
BYUN (ZIP)
KAN (CLANK)
DON (BOOM)
GA
GA
GA
GA
GA
ZA (STOMP)
ZA
ZA
ZA
HEY!!

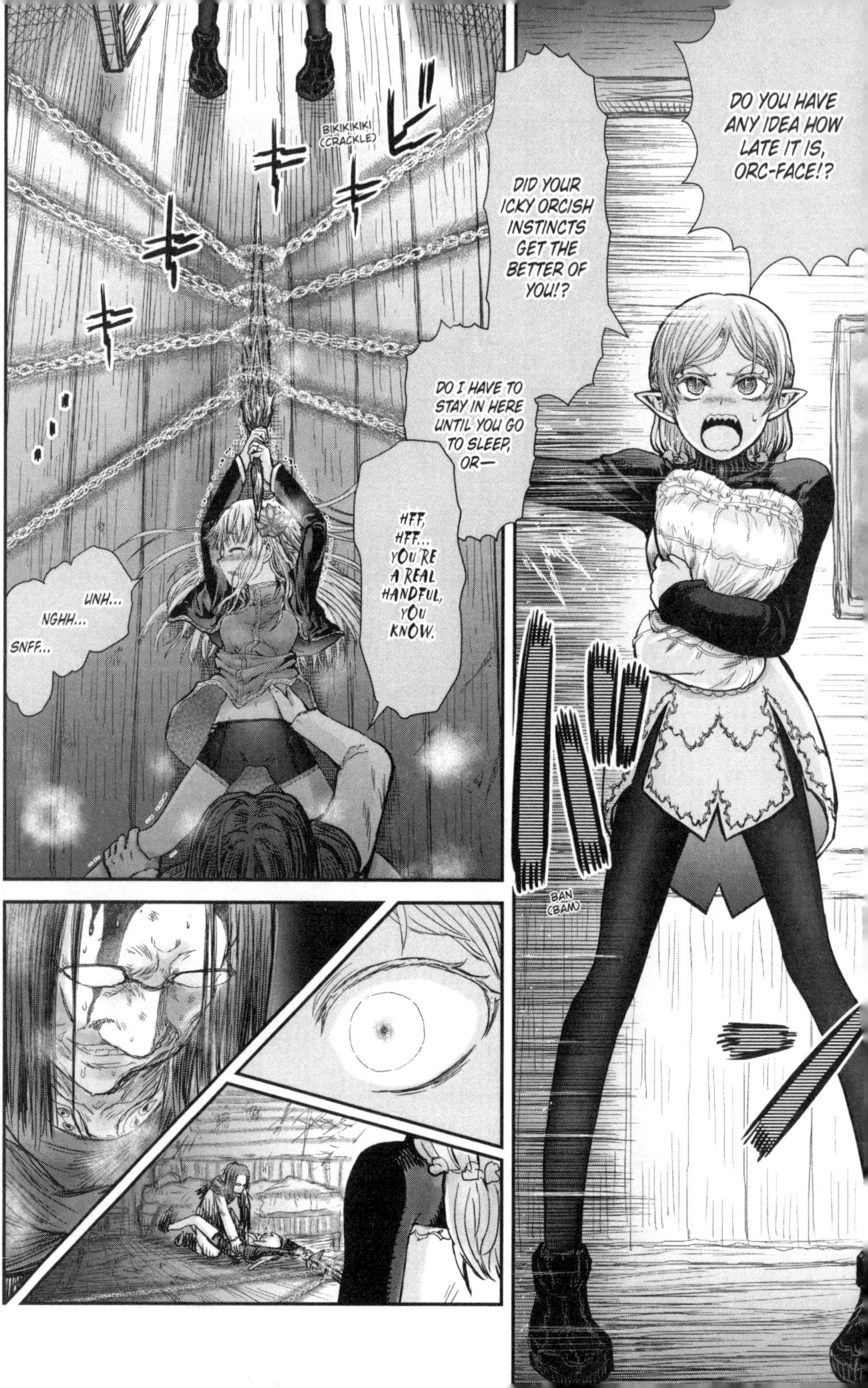
DO YOU HAVE ANY IDEA HOW LATE IT IS, ORC-FACE!?
DID YOUR ICKY ORCISH INSTINCTS GET THE BETTER OF YOU!?
DO I HAVE TO STAY IN HERE UNTIL YOU GO TO SLEEP, OR—
BAN (BAM)
BIKIKIKIKI (CRACKLE)
HFF, HFF... YOU'RE A REAL HANDFUL, YOU KNOW.
UNH...
NGHH...
SNFF...

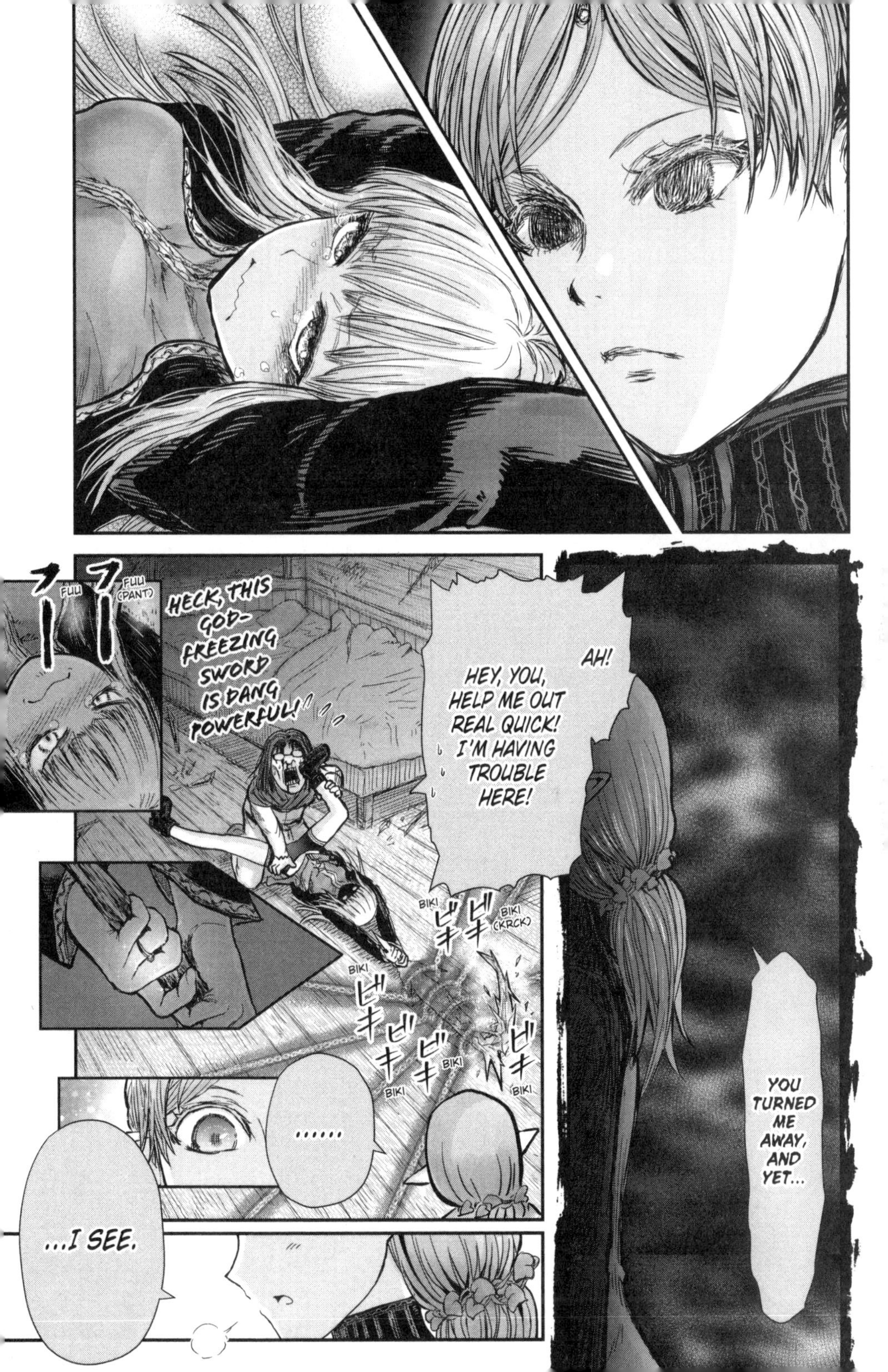
YOU TURNED ME AWAY, AND YET...
AH!
HEY, YOU, HELP ME OUT REAL QUICK! I'M HAVING TROUBLE HERE!
HECK, THIS GOD-FREEZING SWORD IS DANG POWERFUL!
FUU (PANT)
FUU
BIKI (KRCK)
BIKI
BIKI
BIKI
BIKI
......
...I SEE.

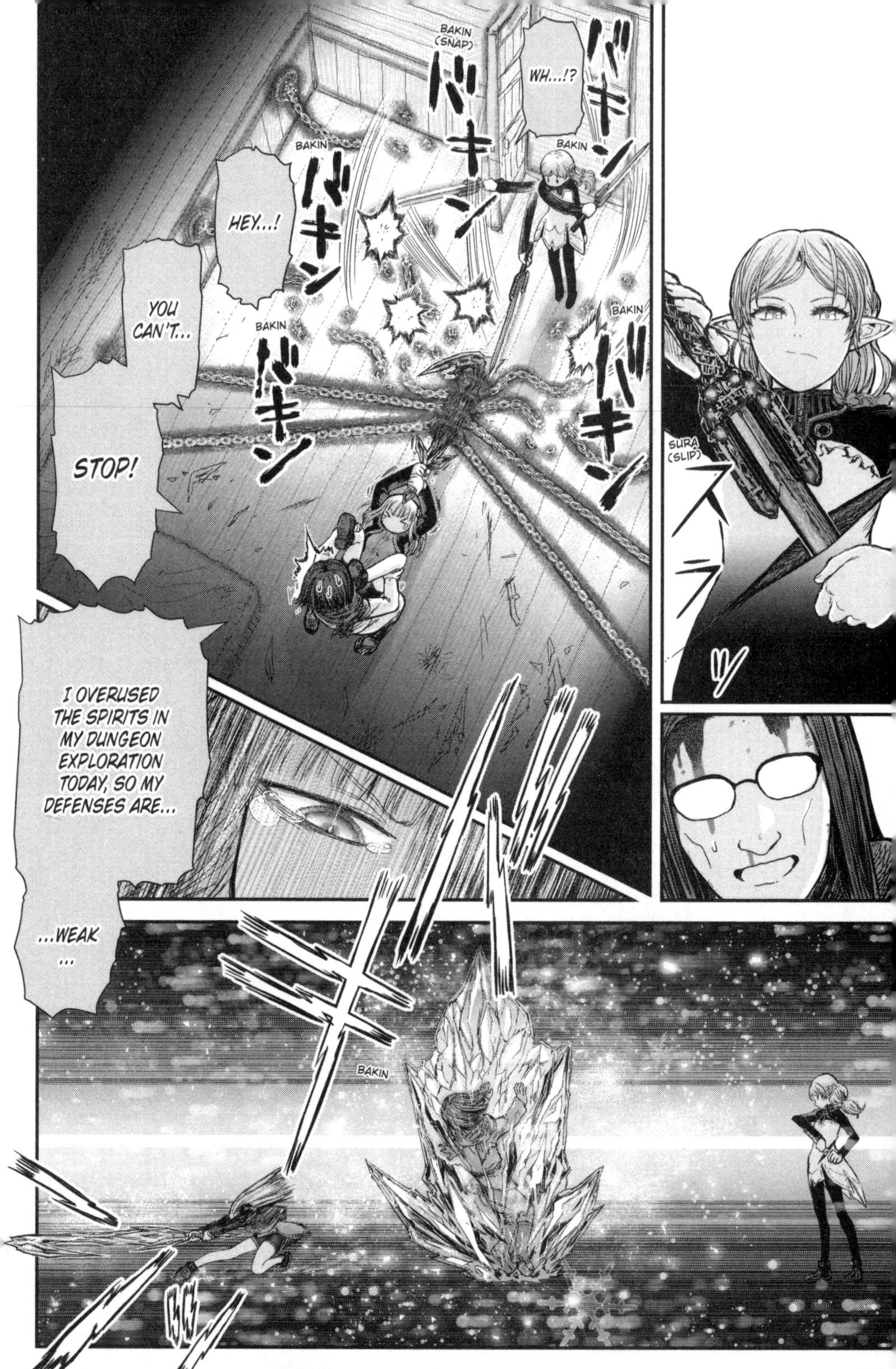
BAKIN (SNAP)
バキン
WH...!?
BAKIN
バキン
BAKIN
バキン
HEY...!
BAKIN
バキン
BAKIN
バキン
YOU CAN'T...
STOP!
SURA (SLIP)
I OVERUSED THE SPIRITS IN MY DUNGEON EXPLORATION TODAY, SO MY DEFENSES ARE...
...WEAK ...
BAKIN

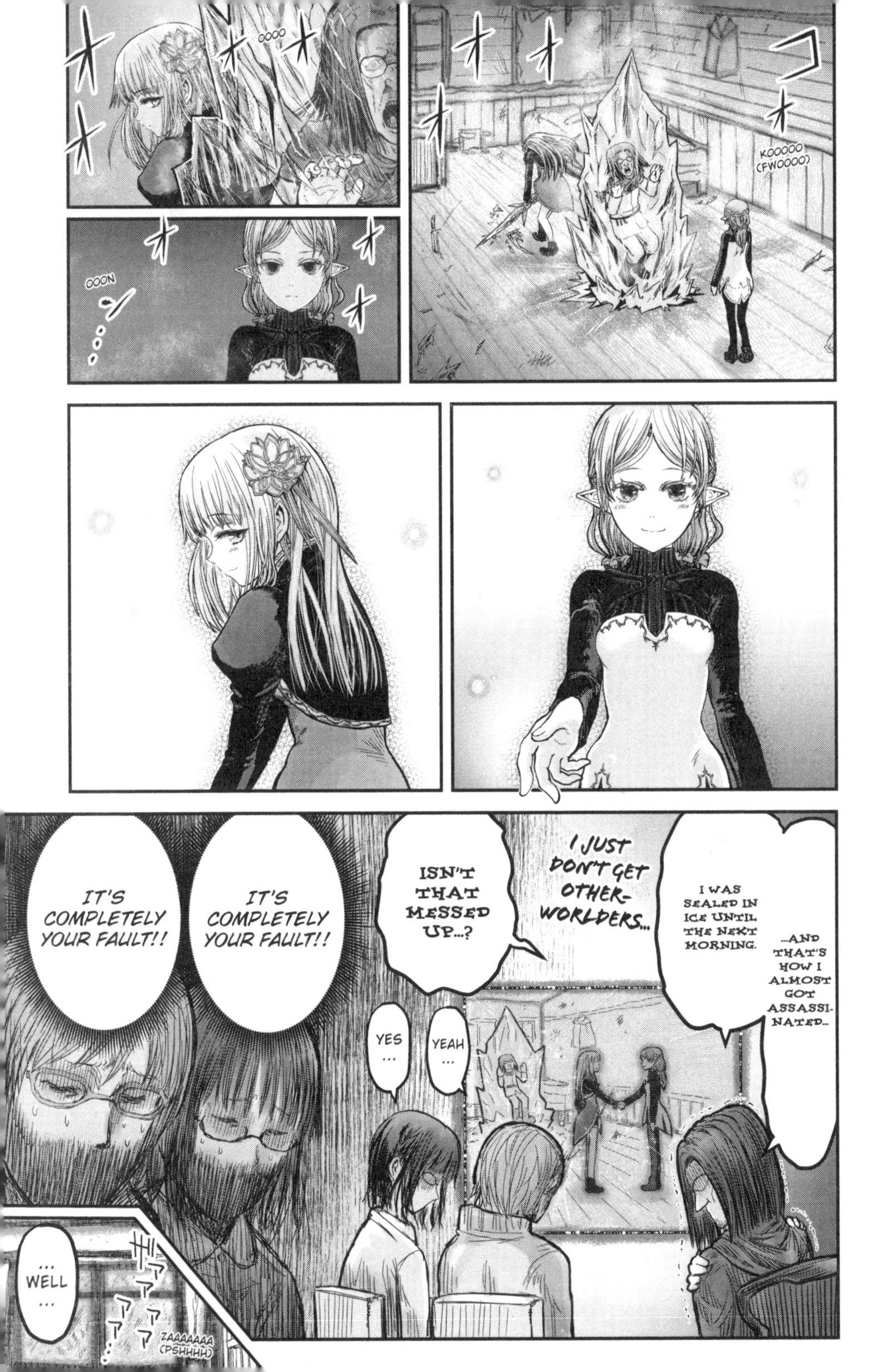
KOOOOO (FWOOOO)
OOOO
OOON
...AND THAT'S HOW I ALMOST GOT ASSASSI-NATED...
I WAS SEALED IN ICE UNTIL THE NEXT MORNING.
I JUST DON'T GET OTHER-WORLDERS...
ISN'T THAT MESSED UP...?
YEAH...
YES...
IT'S COMPLETELY YOUR FAULT!!
IT'S COMPLETELY YOUR FAULT!!
...WELL...
ZAAAAAAA (PSHHHH)

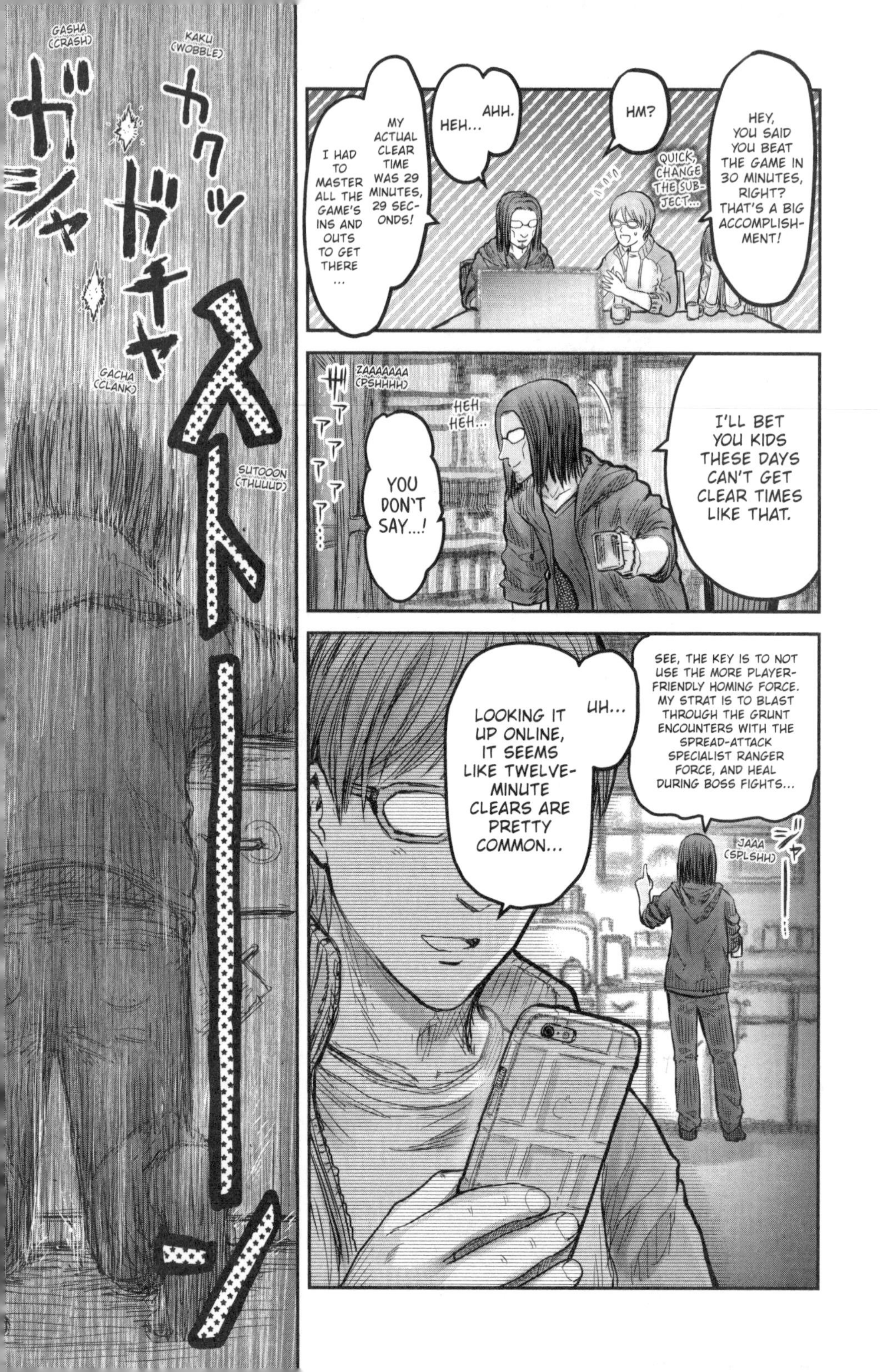
HEY, YOU SAID YOU BEAT THE GAME IN 30 MINUTES, RIGHT? THAT'S A BIG ACCOMPLISHMENT!
QUICK, CHANGE THE SUBJECT...
HM?
AHH.
HEH...
MY ACTUAL CLEAR TIME WAS 29 MINUTES, 29 SECONDS!
I HAD TO MASTER ALL THE GAME'S INS AND OUTS TO GET THERE...
I'LL BET YOU KIDS THESE DAYS CAN'T GET CLEAR TIMES LIKE THAT.
HEH HEH...
YOU DON'T SAY...!
ZAAAAAAA (PSHHHH)
SEE, THE KEY IS TO NOT USE THE MORE PLAYER-FRIENDLY HOMING FORCE. MY STRAT IS TO BLAST THROUGH THE GRUNT ENCOUNTERS WITH THE SPREAD-ATTACK SPECIALIST RANGER FORCE, AND HEAL DURING BOSS FIGHTS...
JAAA (SPLSHH)
UH...
LOOKING IT UP ONLINE, IT SEEMS LIKE TWELVE-MINUTE CLEARS ARE PRETTY COMMON...
KAKU (WOBBLE)
GASHA (CRASH)
GACHA (CLANK)
SUTOOON (THUUUD)

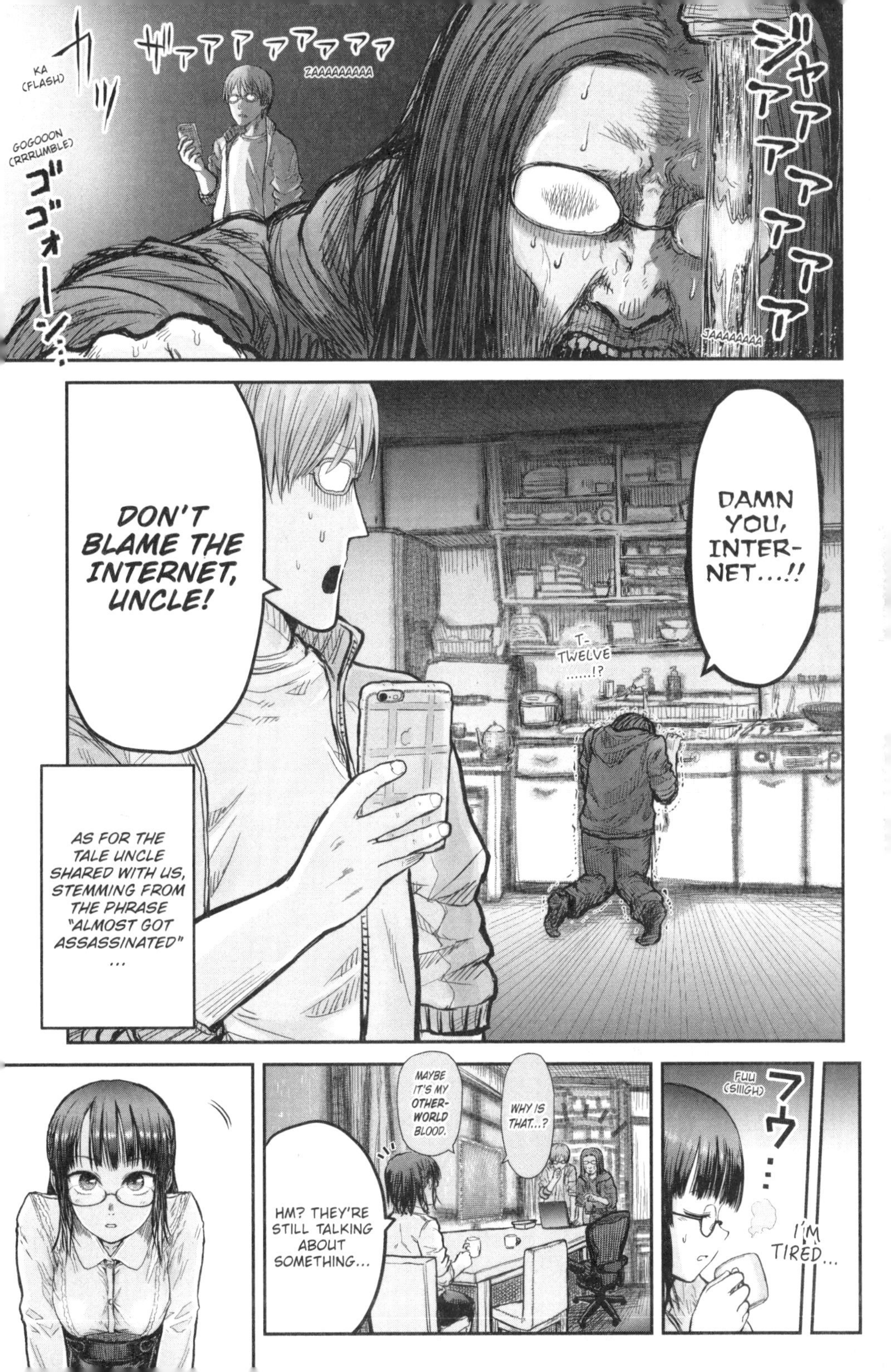
ジャアアアアアアア
JAAAAAAAA
ザァァァァァァァァ
ZAAAAAAAAA
カッ
KA (FLASH)
ゴゴォーン…
GOGOOON (RRRUMBLE)
DAMN YOU, INTERNET....!!
T-TWELVE......!?
DON'T BLAME THE INTERNET, UNCLE!
AS FOR THE TALE UNCLE SHARED WITH US, STEMMING FROM THE PHRASE "ALMOST GOT ASSASSINATED"...
フゥ…
FUU (SIIIGH)
I'M TIRED...
WHY IS THAT...?
MAYBE IT'S MY OTHER-WORLD BLOOD.
HM? THEY'RE STILL TALKING ABOUT SOMETHING...

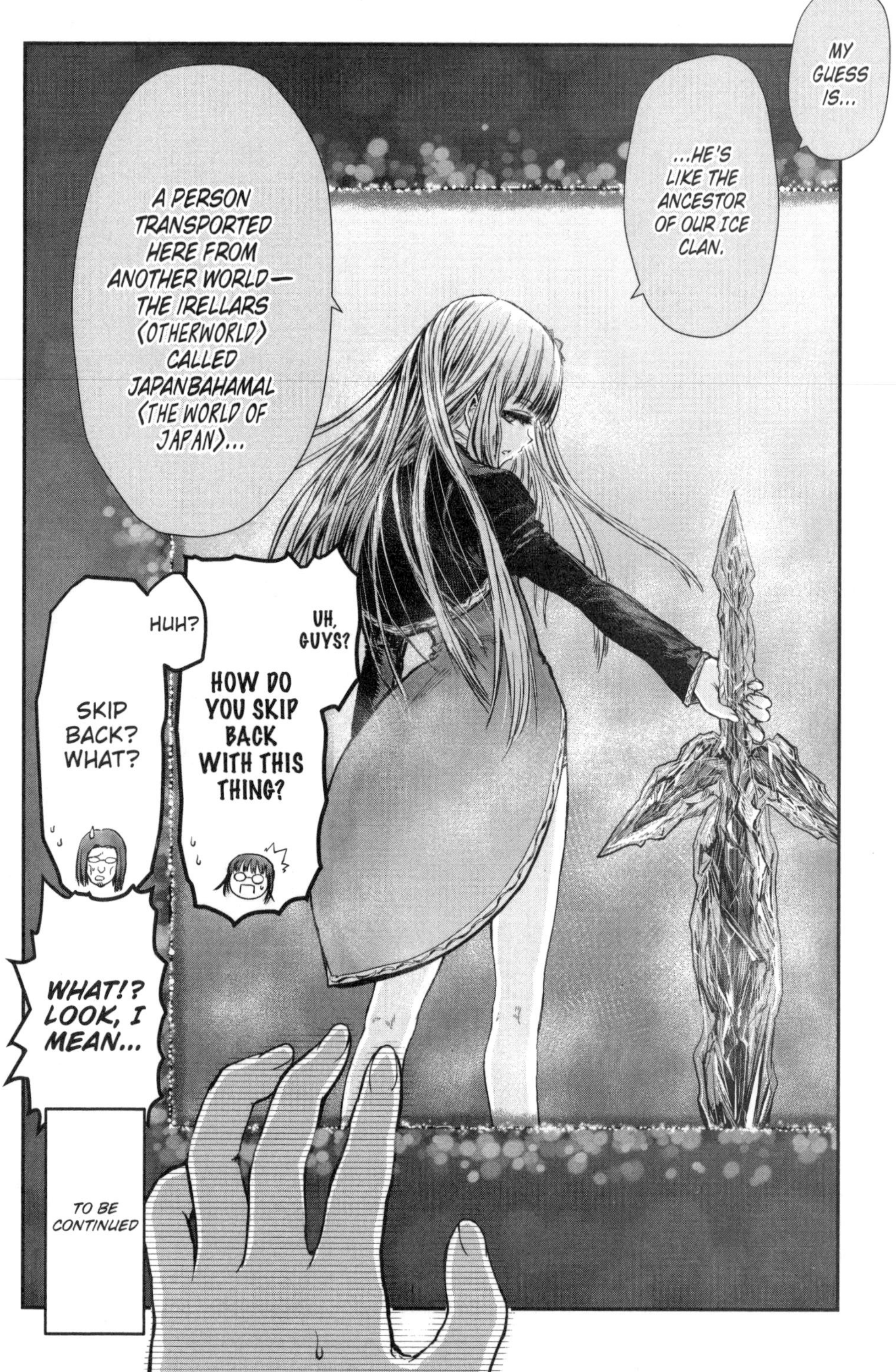
MY GUESS IS...
...HE'S LIKE THE ANCESTOR OF OUR ICE CLAN.
A PERSON TRANSPORTED HERE FROM ANOTHER WORLD—THE IRELLARS (OTHERWORLD) CALLED JAPANBAHAMAL (THE WORLD OF JAPAN)...
UH, GUYS?
HOW DO YOU SKIP BACK WITH THIS THING?
HUH?
SKIP BACK? WHAT?
WHAT!? LOOK, I MEAN...
TO BE CONTINUED

UNCLE from ANOTHER WORLD

UNCLE from ANOTHER WORLD

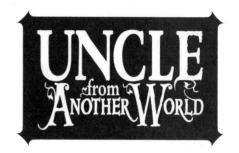

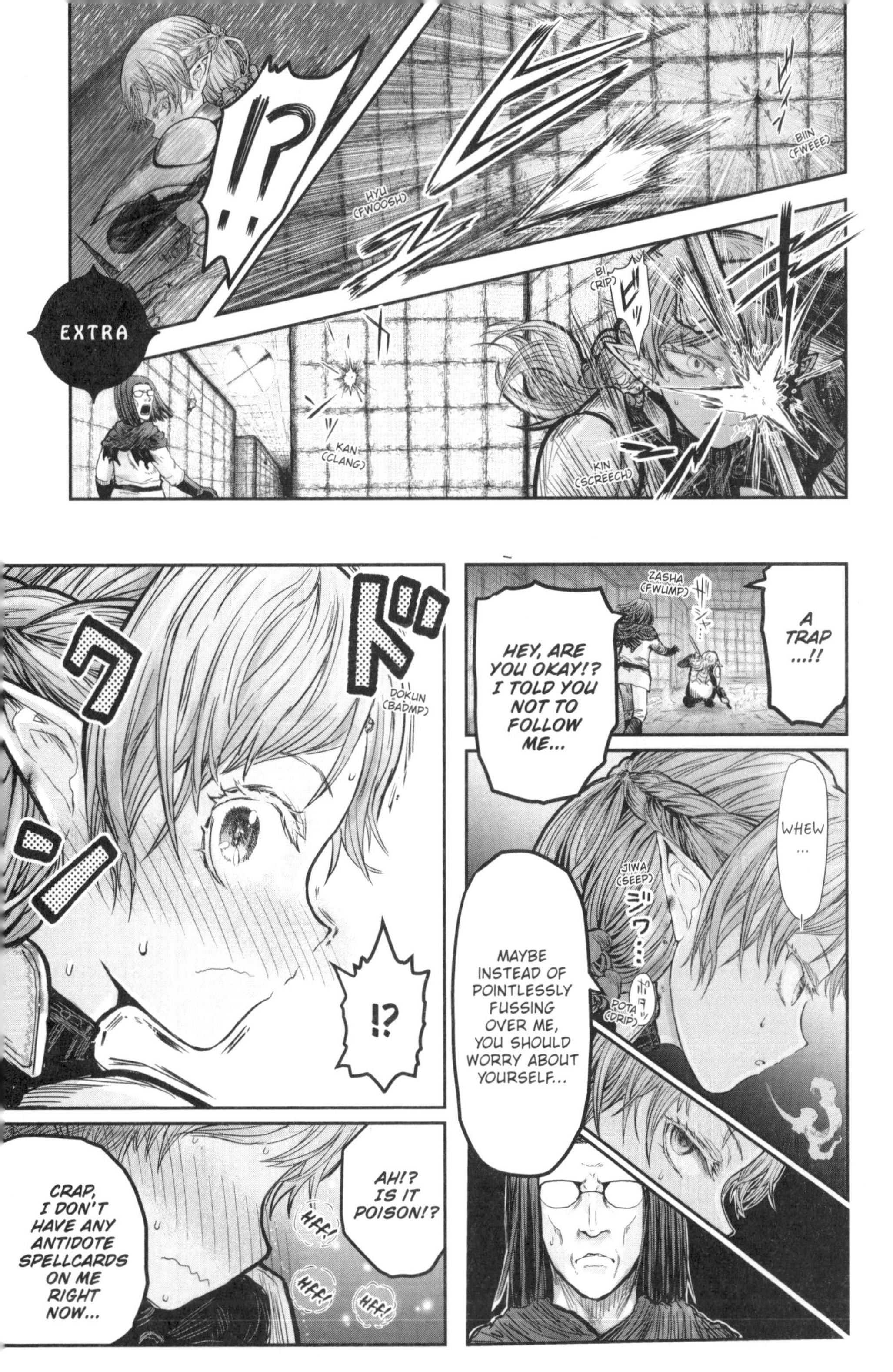
EXTRA
BIIN (FWEEE)
!?
HYU (FWOOSH)
BI (RIP)
KIN (SCREECH)
KAN (CLANG)
A TRAP ...!!
ZASHA (FWUMP)
HEY, ARE YOU OKAY!? I TOLD YOU NOT TO FOLLOW ME...
WHEW ...
JIWA (SEEP)
MAYBE INSTEAD OF POINTLESSLY FUSSING OVER ME, YOU SHOULD WORRY ABOUT YOURSELF...
POTA (DRIP)
DOKUN (BADMP)
!?
AH!? IS IT POISON!?
CRAP, I DON'T HAVE ANY ANTIDOTE SPELLCARDS ON ME RIGHT NOW...
Hff!
Hff!
Hff!

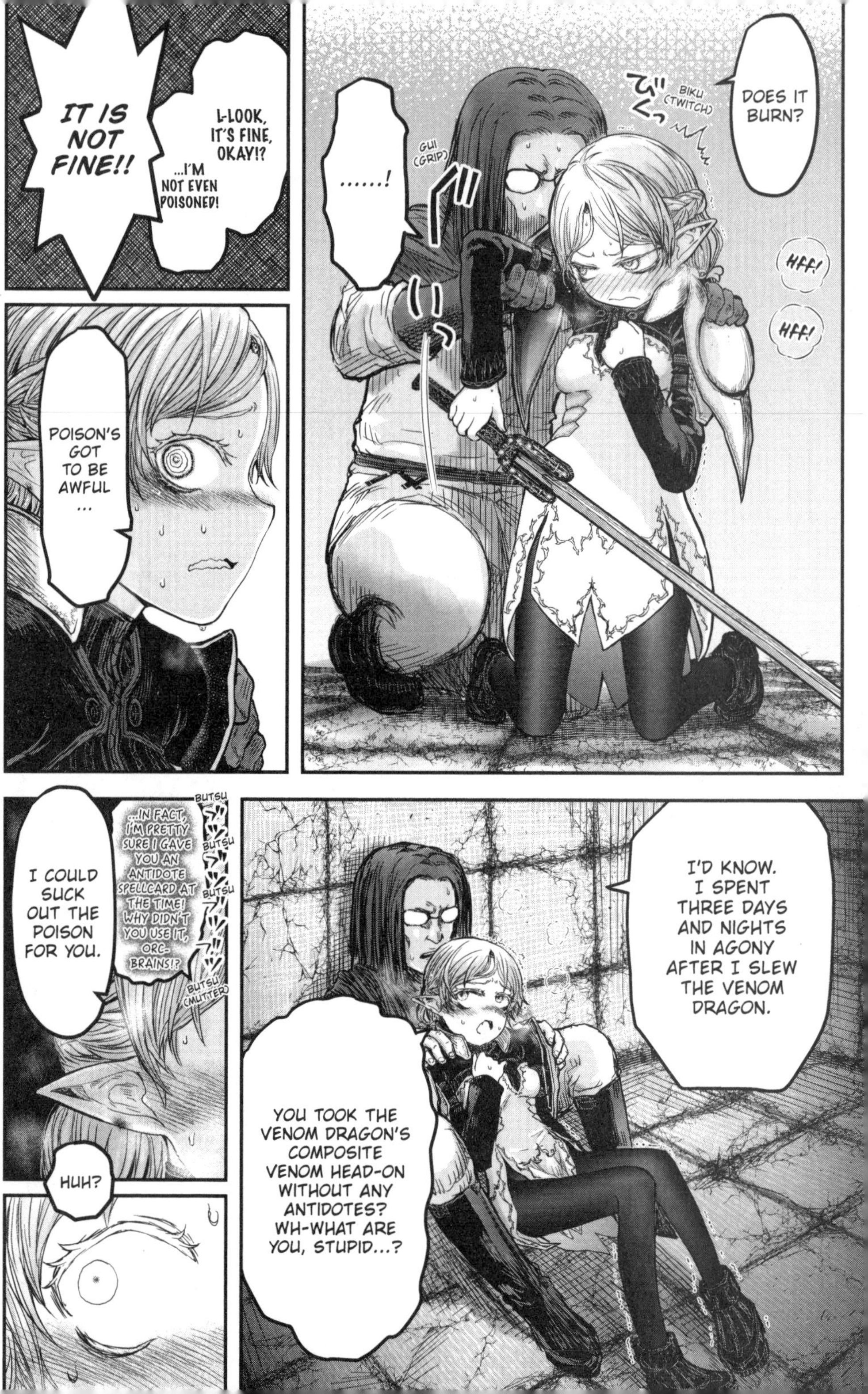
DOES IT BURN?
BIKU (TWITCH)
GUI (GRIP)
......!
HFF!
HFF!
L-LOOK, IT'S FINE, OKAY!?
...I'M NOT EVEN POISONED!
IT IS NOT FINE!!
POISON'S GOT TO BE AWFUL ...
I'D KNOW. I SPENT THREE DAYS AND NIGHTS IN AGONY AFTER I SLEW THE VENOM DRAGON.
YOU TOOK THE VENOM DRAGON'S COMPOSITE VENOM HEAD-ON WITHOUT ANY ANTIDOTES? WH-WHAT ARE YOU, STUPID...?
BUTSU BUTSU BUTSU BUTSU (MUTTER)
...IN FACT, I'M PRETTY SURE I GAVE YOU AN ANTIDOTE SPELLCARD AT THE TIME! WHY DIDN'T YOU USE IT, ORC-BRAINS!?
I COULD SUCK OUT THE POISON FOR YOU.
HUH?

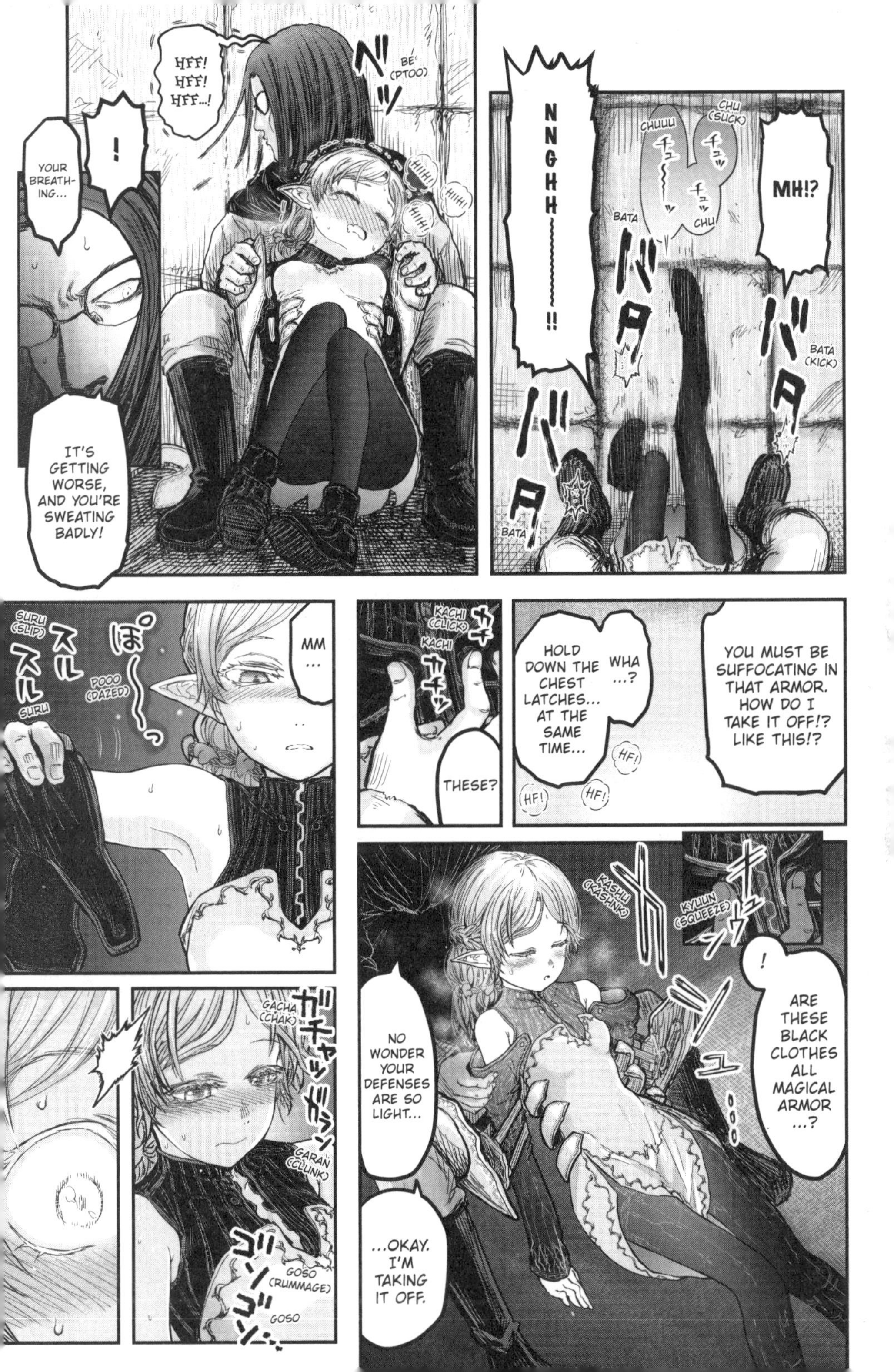

MH!?
NNGHH————!!
CHU (SUCK)
CHUUU
CHU
BATA
BATA (KICK)
BATA
HFF! HFF! HFF...!
BE (PTOO)
!
YOUR BREATHING...
IT'S GETTING WORSE, AND YOU'RE SWEATING BADLY!
YOU MUST BE SUFFOCATING IN THAT ARMOR. HOW DO I TAKE IT OFF!? LIKE THIS!?
WHA ...?
HOLD DOWN THE CHEST LATCHES... AT THE SAME TIME...
HF!
HF!
HF!
THESE?
KACHI (CLICK)
KACHI
MM ...
POOO (DAZED)
SURU (SLIP)
SURU
!
ARE THESE BLACK CLOTHES ALL MAGICAL ARMOR ...?
KYUUN (SQUEEZE)
KASHU (KASHNK)
NO WONDER YOUR DEFENSES ARE SO LIGHT...
...OKAY. I'M TAKING IT OFF.
GACHA (CHAK)
GARAN (CLUNK)
GOSO (RUMMAGE)
GOSO

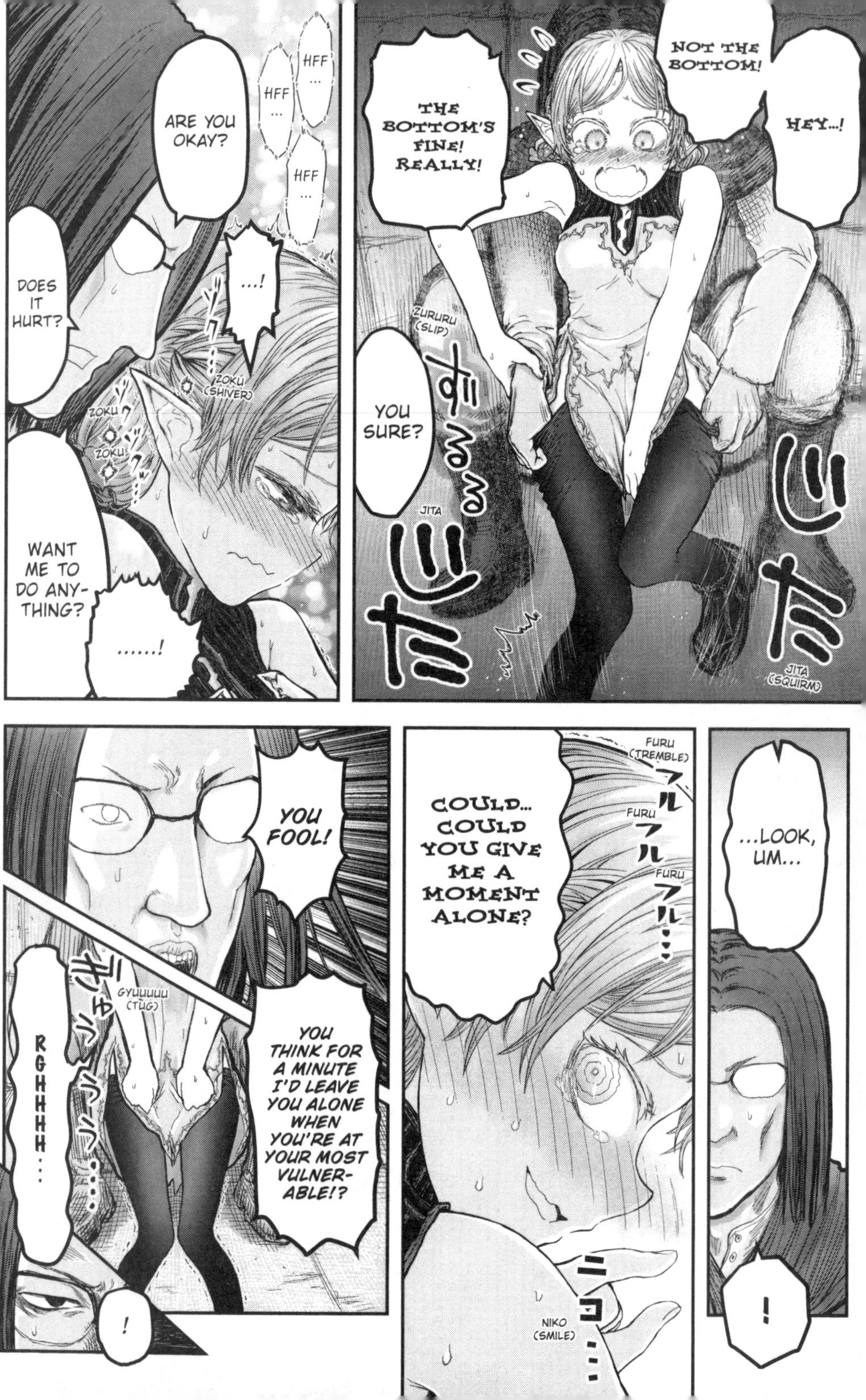
NOT THE BOTTOM!
HEY...!
THE BOTTOM'S FINE! REALLY!
ZURURU (SLIP)
YOU SURE?
JITA (SQUIRM)
JITA
HFF...
HFF...
ARE YOU OKAY?
HFF...
...!
ZOKU (SHIVER)
DOES IT HURT?
ZOKU
ZOKU
WANT ME TO DO ANY-THING?
......!
...LOOK, UM...
!
FURU (TREMBLE)
COULD... COULD YOU GIVE ME A MOMENT ALONE?
FURU
FURU
NIKO (SMILE)
YOU FOOL!
YOU THINK FOR A MINUTE I'D LEAVE YOU ALONE WHEN YOU'RE AT YOUR MOST VULNER-ABLE!?
GYUUUUU (TUG)
RGHHHH...
!

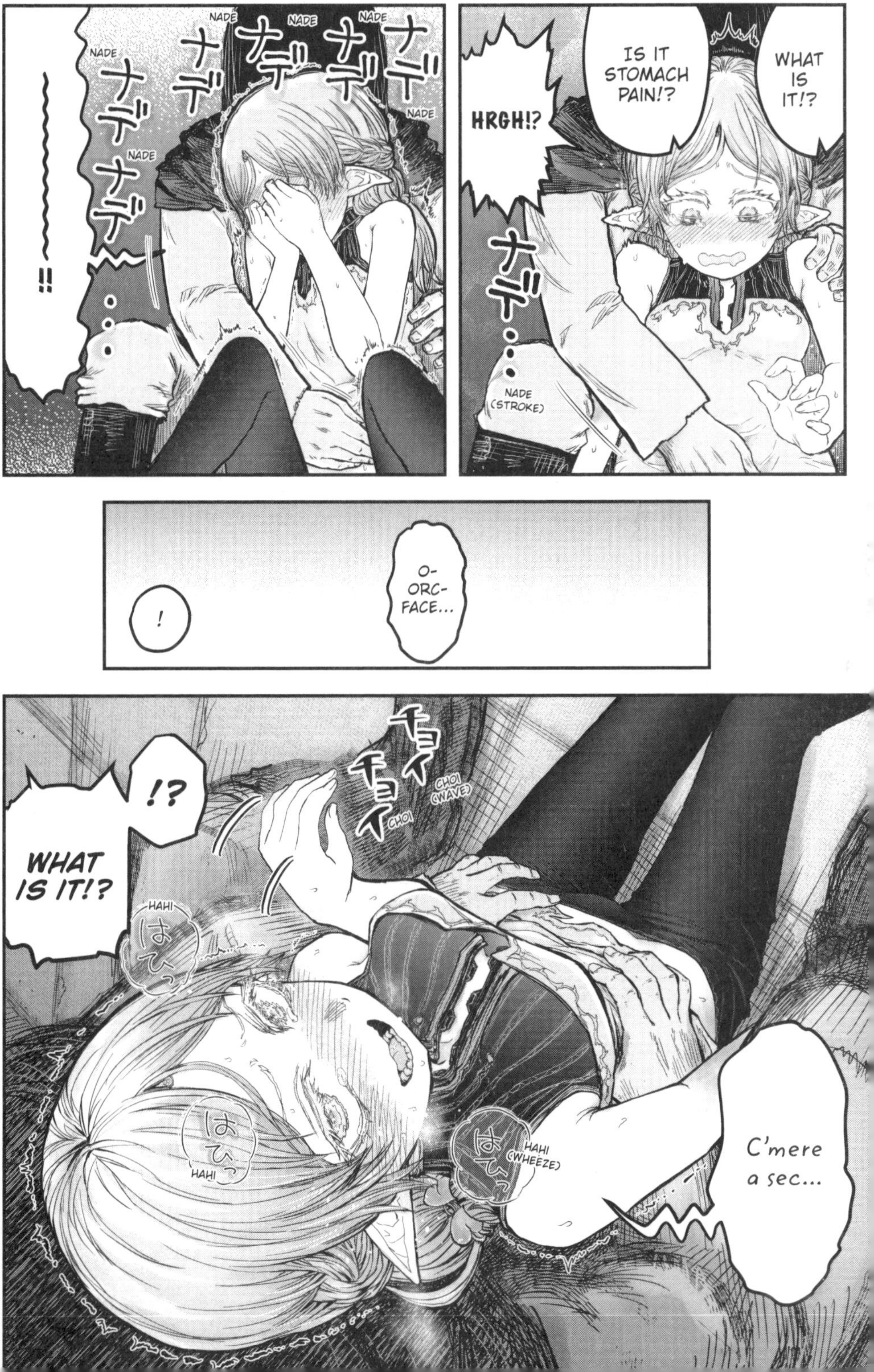
WHAT IS IT!?
IS IT STOMACH PAIN!?
HRGH!?
ナデ…
NADE (STROKE)
ナデ
NADE
ナデ
NADE
ナデ
NADE
ナデ
NADE
ナデ
NADE
ナデ…
~~~~~~~~!!
O-ORC-FACE...
!
C'mere a sec...
はひっ
HAHI (WHEEZE)
はひっ
HAHI
はひっ
HAHI
!?
WHAT IS IT!?
チョイ
CHOI (WAVE)
チョイ
CHOI
~~~~~~~~

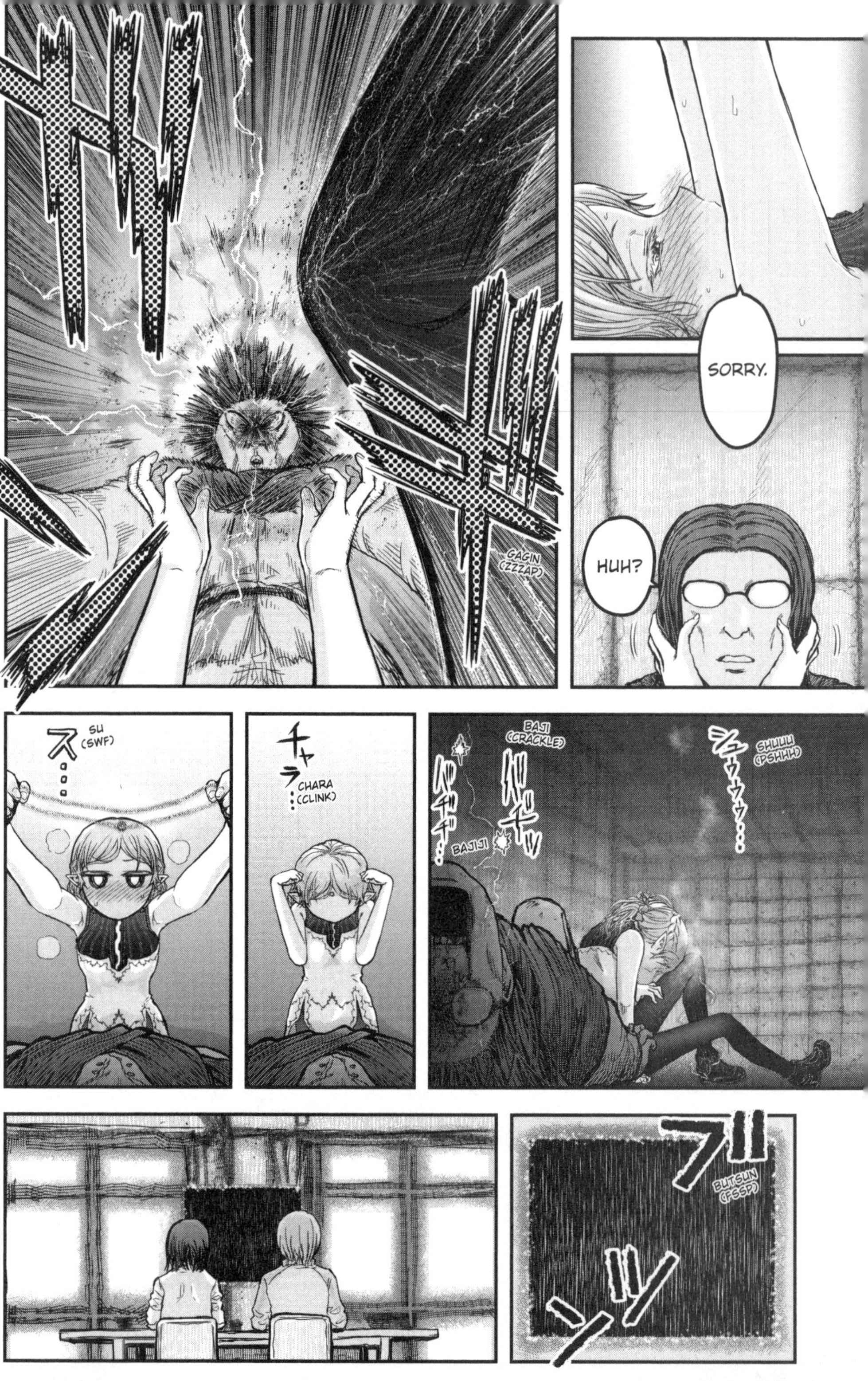
SORRY.
HUH?
GAGIN (ZZZAP)
SHUUU (PSHHH)
BAJI (CRACKLE)
BAJIJI
CHARA (CLINK)
SU (SWF)
BUTSUN (FSSP)

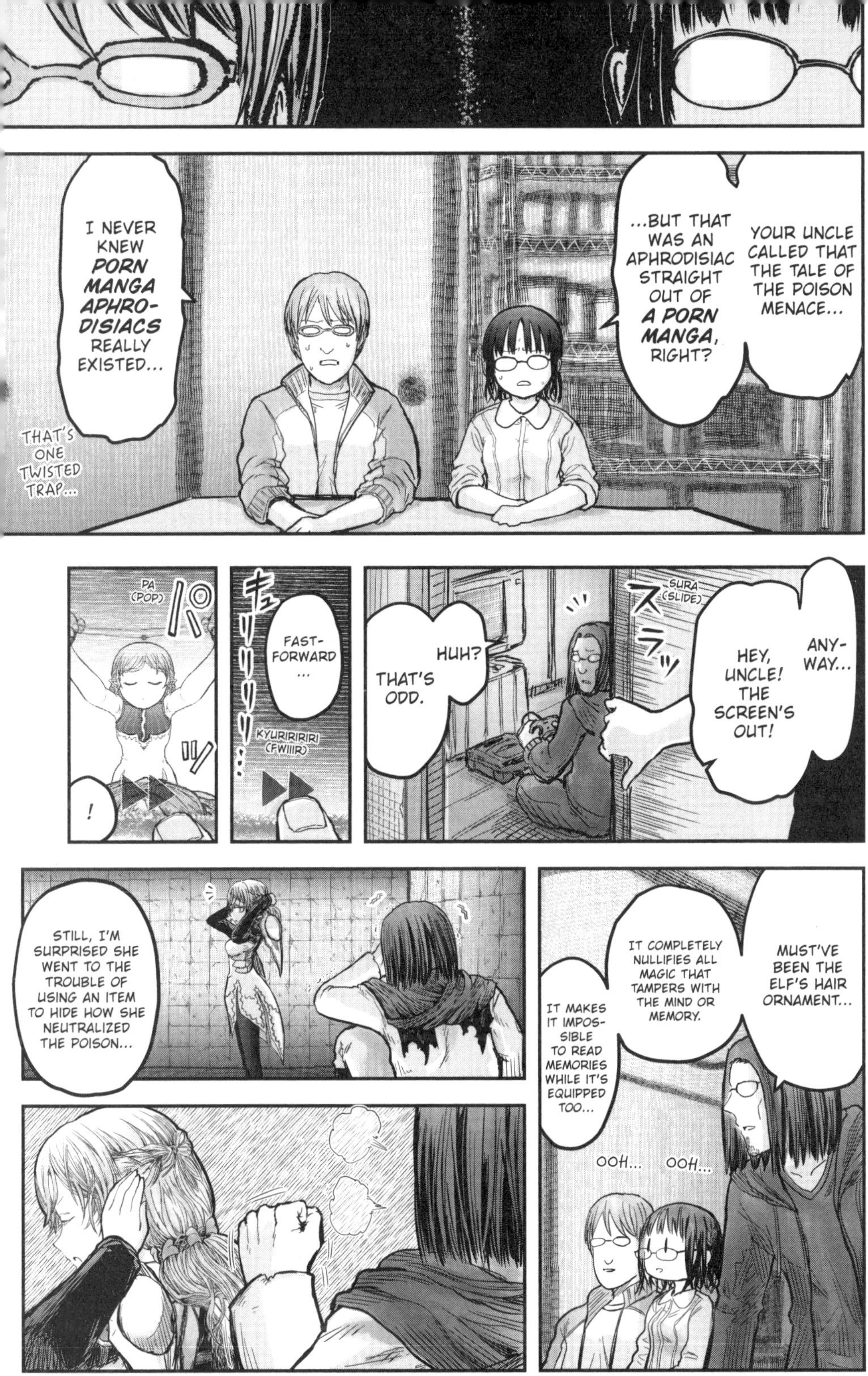
YOUR UNCLE CALLED THAT THE TALE OF THE POISON MENACE...
...BUT THAT WAS AN APHRODISIAC STRAIGHT OUT OF A PORN MANGA, RIGHT?
I NEVER KNEW PORN MANGA APHRODISIACS REALLY EXISTED...
THAT'S ONE TWISTED TRAP...
ANYWAY...
HEY, UNCLE! THE SCREEN'S OUT!
SURA (SLIDE)
HUH? THAT'S ODD.
FAST-FORWARD...
KYURIRIRIRI (FWIIIR)
PA (POP)
!
MUST'VE BEEN THE ELF'S HAIR ORNAMENT...
IT COMPLETELY NULLIFIES ALL MAGIC THAT TAMPERS WITH THE MIND OR MEMORY.
IT MAKES IT IMPOSSIBLE TO READ MEMORIES WHILE IT'S EQUIPPED TOO...
OOH... OOH...
STILL, I'M SURPRISED SHE WENT TO THE TROUBLE OF USING AN ITEM TO HIDE HOW SHE NEUTRALIZED THE POISON...

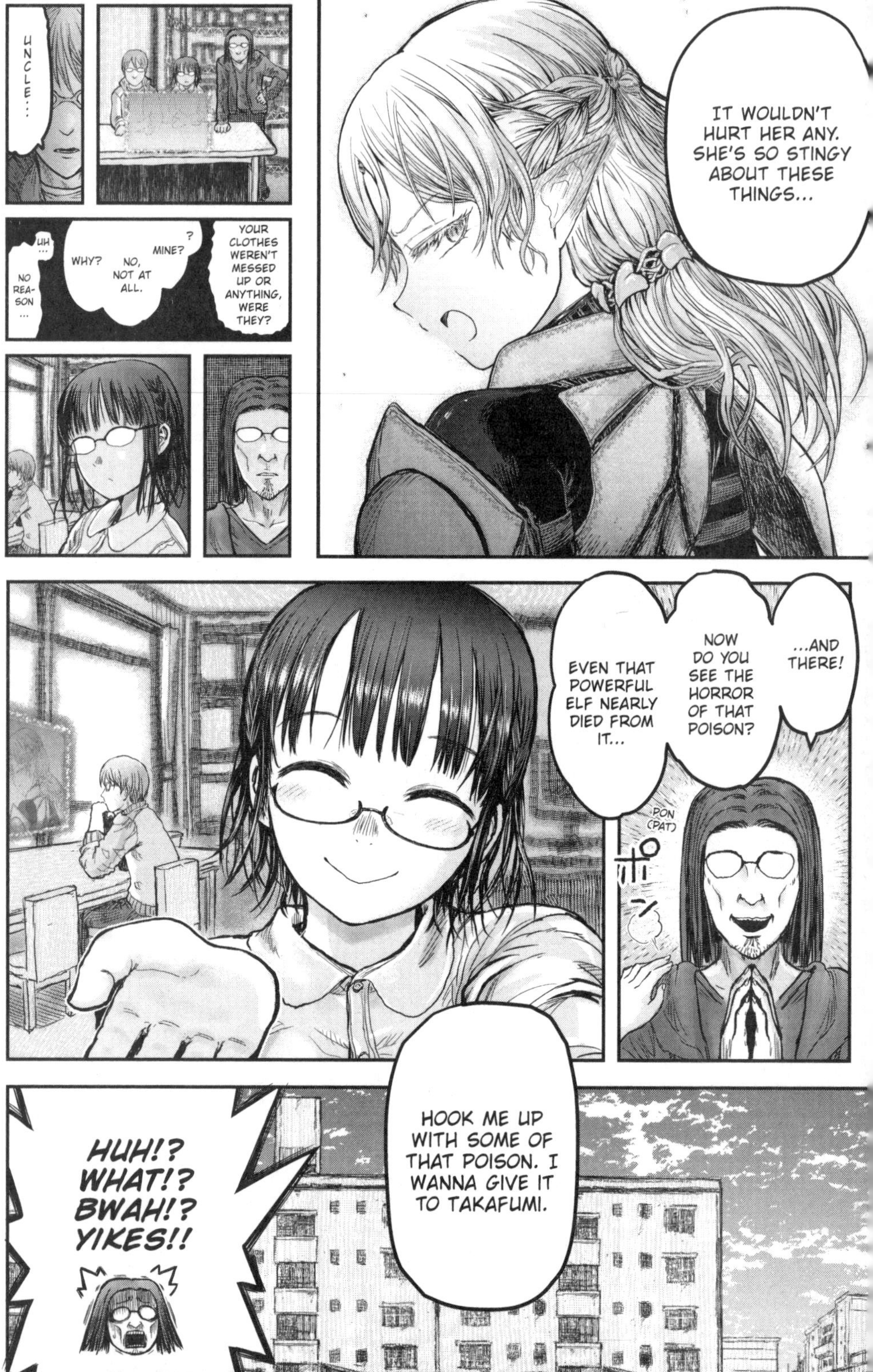
IT WOULDN'T HURT HER ANY. SHE'S SO STINGY ABOUT THESE THINGS...
UNCLE...
YOUR CLOTHES WEREN'T MESSED UP OR ANYTHING, WERE THEY?
MINE?
?
NO, NOT AT ALL.
WHY?
UH... NO REASON...
...AND THERE!
NOW DO YOU SEE THE HORROR OF THAT POISON?
EVEN THAT POWERFUL ELF NEARLY DIED FROM IT...
PON (PAT)
HOOK ME UP WITH SOME OF THAT POISON. I WANNA GIVE IT TO TAKAFUMI.
HUH!? WHAT!? BWAH!? YIKES!!

Translation Notes

COMMON HONORIFICS

no honorific: Indicates familiarity or closeness; if used without permission or reason, addressing someone in this manner would constitute an insult.

-san: The Japanese equivalent of Mr./Mrs./Miss. If a situation calls for politeness, this is the fail-safe honorific.

-sama: Conveys great respect; may also indicate that the social status of the speaker is lower than that of the addressee.

-dono: Roughly equivalent to "master" or "milord."

-kun: Used most often when referring to boys, this indicates affection or familiarity. Occasionally used by older men among their peers, but it may also be used by anyone referring to a person of lower standing.

-chan: An affectionate honorific indicating familiarity used mostly in reference to girls; also used in reference to cute persons or animals regardless of gender.

-senpai: An honorific for one's senior classmate, colleague, etc., although not as senior or respected as a *sensei* (teacher).

¥100 is approximately $1 USD.

PAGE 9
Tsundere is an archetype common to anime and manga where a character either grows from hating someone to loving someone, or acts especially prickly toward a character they have feelings for.

PAGE 25
Team Uncle is a reference to the 2012 anime *Girls und Panzer*.

PAGE 30
NEET stands for "Not in Education, Employment, or Training." Originally coined in the United Kingdom, the term gained widespread use in Japan beginning in the 2000s.

PAGE 35
Medusa Force is one of the transformations of Kaede Nanase from A●ien Soldier in her boss form, Seven Force.

PAGE 39
In the original Japanese, the mistake about **S●nic** and his buddy **Ta●ls** is that the latter's name in Japanese is pronounced with a distinct *s* sound instead of a *z*.

PAGE 44
Kuma means "bear" in Japanese.

PAGE 47
Uncle's response to the "**virtual**" in "virtual YouTubers" here is because Se●a has developed and released multiple games that begin with the word "**Virtua**."

PAGE 48
The **Se●a Saturn** was a 1994 home console. While capable of 3D graphics, its original emphasis on 2D sprite graphics put it at a disadvantage against its competitors.

Guardian H□roes is a 1996 beat-'em-up game with elements of fighting games and role-playing games. It also includes branching story paths leading to multiple different endings.

PAGE 56
The **M●ga Drive** was a 1988 16-bit home video game console released by Se●a touted for its "blast processing."

PAGE 58
The 1998 **D●amcast** was Se●a's final home console before they pulled out from that market.

PAGE 59
There are only two difficulty settings in 1995's A●ien Soldier: Supereasy and **Superhard**. Supereasy is a misnomer—as the game is notoriously tough to beat either way—but the latter is especially unforgiving because it only allows three continues and no ability to save progress.

G●lden Axe is a 1989 beat-'em-up arcade game that later saw home console releases. The game (as well as its sequels) features players fighting with both weapons and magic.

PAGE 76
Shinrei Jusatsush● Taroumaru is a 1997 Saturn side-scrolling action game in which players control psychic ninjas. Due to a very small print run, it is one of the console's rarest games.

Game G●ar is a 1990 Se●a handheld video game console that, unlike its main competition, featured color graphics.

PAGES 107–108
Millennial and "**Okay, boomer!**" in the original Japanese are *arasa* ("around thirty years old") and *arafo* ("around forty years old"). These words came into prominence around 2006.

PAGE 114
La●dstalker is a 1992 action-adventure game starring a treasure hunter named Nigel and featuring an isometric view.

PAGES 120–121
Puyo P●yo is a 1991 puzzle game featuring squishy little bean-like creatures. While it originally began as a spin-off title, it has become a popular franchise itself. **Puyo P●yo Sun** is the third game in the franchise.

PAGE 126
The **Multi Controller** (also known as the Multi Con or Mul Con for short) was released in different parts of the world as the 3D Control Pad, the Multi Pad, and the Joystick 3D.

Bur●ing Rangers is a 1998 action game about futuristic firefighters who stop blazes and rescue people. In addition to its gameplay, it's famous for its passionate opening theme song.

PAGE 132
A *chu-hai* is an alcoholic drink: a *shochu* highball. One brand markets itself as being **strong** while containing zero sugar.

PAGE 137
In Japanese, common baseball terms like "runner out," "assist," and "double play" use translations whose literal meanings sound rather deadly—"stab," "catch and kill," and "side-by-side killing," respectively. These have been adapted to make sense in English.

PAGE 141
Psikyo was a video game company known for its difficult **bullet hell** shoot-'em-ups and erotic mahjong games.

PAGE 152
D●namite Headdy is a 1994 platformer from the creators of A●ien Soldier. **Fingy** is known as Heather outside of Japan.

INSIDE COVER (FRONT)
Dyn●mite Deka is a 1996 3D beat-'em-up arcade game. Outside of Japan, it went under a different name as a tie-in to an action film franchise famous for its detective hero's resilience and his cowboy-esque, profanity-laden one-liner.

Hotondoshindeiru

TRANSLATOR: **Christina Rose**
LETTERER: **Alexis Eckerman**

ISEKAI OJISAN Vol. 2
©Hotondoshindeiru 2019
©SEGA

First published in Japan in 2019 by KADOKAWA CORPORATION, Tokyo.
English translation rights arranged with KADOKAWA CORPORATION, Tokyo through TUTTLE-MORI AGENCY, Inc.

English translation © 2021 by Yen Press, LLC

Yen Press
150 West 30th Street, 19th Floor
New York, NY 10001

Visit us at yenpress.com + facebook.com/yenpress
twitter.com/yenpress + yenpress.tumblr.com + instagram.com/yenpress

First Yen Press Edition: July 2021

Yen Press is an imprint of Yen Press, LLC.
The Yen Press name and logo are trademarks of Yen Press, LLC.

Library of Congress Control Number: 2021932161

ISBNs: 978-1-9753-2394-3 (paperback)
978-1-9753-2395-0 (ebook)

10 9 8 7 6 5 4 3 2 1

WOR

Printed in the United States of America